STRATEGIC
MARKET
MANAGEMENT

STRATEGIC MARKET MANAGEMENT

FOURTH EDITION

DAVID A. AAKER
University of California, Berkeley

JOHN WILEY & SONS, INC.

New York • Chichester • Brisbane • Toronto • Singapore

ACQUISITIONS EDITOR Tim Kent
ASSISTANT EDITOR Ellen Ford
MARKETING MANAGER Debra Riegert
SENIOR PRODUCTION EDITOR Edward Winkleman
COVER DESIGNER Dawn L. Stanley
MANUFACTURING MANAGER Susan Stetzer
SR. ILLUSTRATION COORDINATOR Gene Aiello

This book was set in Palatino by TCSystems, Inc. and printed and bound by Courier Stoughton. The cover was printed by NEBC.

Library of Congress Cataloging-in-Publication Data:
Aaker, David A.
       Strategic market management / David A. Aaker.—4th ed.

       p.   cm.
     Includes index.

     ISBN 0-471-30956-7 (pbk.)
       1. Marketing—Management.   I. Title.
     HF5415.13.A23   1995
     658.8—dc20   94-2988
                                                                        CIP

Printed in the United States of America

10 9 8 7 6 5 4 3

PREFACE

The development, evaluation, and implementation of business strategies are essential to successful management. The key is a management system that will help managers

- Provide vision to their businesses.
- Monitor and understand a dynamic environment.
- Generate strategic options that will be responsive to changes facing a business.
- Develop strategies based on sustainable competitive advantages.

FOUR THRUSTS

This book has four key thrusts. The first is a structure and methodology for analyzing the external environment. Strategic planning that represents an automatic extension of what was done last year and that is dominated by financial objectives and spreadsheets will be inadequate and may even inhibit or prevent strategic change and innovation. Rather, strategy development should look outside the business to sense changes, trends, threats, and opportunities and then create strategies that are responsive. This book describes and illustrates a structured approach to external analysis that business managers should find helpful in generating strategic options. This approach is supported by a summary flow diagram, a set of agendas to help start the process, and a set of planning forms.

The second thrust is toward sustainable competitive advantages (SCAs). Having SCAs is crucial to long-term success. Without them a business will eventually be treading water if it survives at all. SCAs need to be based on organizational assets and skills. Thus, this book presents methods and concepts that will help readers to select relevant assets and skills and to develop strategies in branding, advertising, distribution, manufacturing, and finance to exploit them.

The third thrust involves the investment decision. The need is to select investment or disinvestment levels for existing product-market business areas and to chart growth directions. Among the alternative growth directions are market penetration, product expansion, market expansion, diversification, and vertical integration. By using a variety of concepts and methods such as strategic questions, portfolio models, and scenario analysis, this book will help managers identify and evaluate numerous strategic investment alternatives.

A fourth thrust is implementation. It is important to understand how an organization's structure, systems, people, and culture contribute to strategic success. In addition, how can an organization create dynamic strategies that are responsive to changing conditions? How can alliances be used to gain strategic advantage? What are the implementation issues when markets are mature or declining or when competition is global in scope?

THE FOURTH EDITION

A popular feature of this book has been that it was compact—the fourth edition retains that quality. Although about 25 percent of the book is new, the length and structure remain intact. There are new illustrative examples in most sections of the book and new graphics in the figures. There are also new sections on economic value analysis, total quality management, the virtual corporation, competitor image and personality, exchanging assets and skills, competing in hostile markets, the borderless organization, and reengineering. A new format for the competitor strength grid has been designed. Material has been added on quality function deployment, brand extension strategies, strategic questions, strategic vision and opportunism, strategic alliances, the distinction between pioneering and preemptive strategies, and the pitfalls of planning without soul.

OBJECTIVES OF THE BOOK

This book has a number of objectives that influence its approach and style. The book attempts to

- Introduce a long-term perspective that may help a business avoid weaknesses or problems caused by the dominance of short-term goals or operational problems. The focus upon assets and skills and away from short-term financials provides one approach.

- Provide methods and structures to create entrepreneurial thrusts. In many organizations the key problem is how to support both efficiency and an entrepreneurial spirit.

- Emphasize a global perspective. Increasingly, effective strategies must consider—and be responsive to—both international competitors and markets.

- Present a proactive approach to strategic market management in which, rather than merely detecting and reacting to change, a business anticipates, or even creates it. In this approach, the strategy development process is driven by a dynamic analysis of the market and the environment. The inclusion of the term "market" into the phrase "strategic market management" emphasizes the external orientation and the proactive approach.

- Encourage "on-line" strategy development which involves gathering information, analyzing the strategic context, precipitating strategic decisions, and developing strategic implementation plans outside the annual planning cycle.

- Draw upon multiple disciplines. During the past decade many disciplines have made relevant and important contributions to strategic market management. An effort has been made to draw on and integrate developments in marketing, economics, organizational behavior, finance, accounting, management science, and the field of strategy itself.

- Incorporate several important empirical research streams that have helped strategic market management become more professional and scientific.

- Introduce concepts, models, and methods that are or have promise of being useful to the strategy development process. Among the concepts covered are strategic groups; exit, entry, and mobility barriers; industry structure; segmentation; unmet needs; positioning; strategic problems; strategic questions; strengths; weaknesses; strategic skills and assets; mission; brand equity; flexibility; sustainable competitive advantage; synergy; preemptive strategies; strategic alliances; key success factors; usage gap; corporate culture; organizational structure; the virtual corporation; strategic types; vision; strategic opportunism; strategic intent; and global strategies. The models and methods covered include researching lead customers, scenario analysis, impact analysis, total quality control, reengineering, the competitor strength grid, technological forecasting, the experience curve, value chain analysis, portfolio models, customer-based competitor identification, and shareholder value analysis.

AN OVERVIEW

The book is divided into five parts. The first part structures the book by introducing concepts, methods, and strategy alternatives and by providing an overview of strategic market management based on a comprehensive flow model. The second part, drawing heavily from marketing and economics, covers external analysis, which includes analysis of the customer, competitors, market, and environment.

The third part considers internal analysis, including performance analysis, the analysis of strategically important organizational characteristics, and portfolio analysis. The fourth part discusses and illustrates the SCA concept, differentiation strategies, strategies based upon low cost, focus, or a preemptive move, alternative growth strategies, global competition, and competition in mature and declining industries. The final part contains a chapter on how organizational components interact with strategy, a chapter on developing a formal planning system, and an appendix that includes a set of sample planning forms.

THE AUDIENCE

This book is suitable for any management or business school course that focuses on the management of strategies. It is especially appropriate for

- Marketing strategy courses, such as strategic market management, strategic market planning, strategic marketing, or marketing strategy.
- Policy or entrepreneurship courses such as strategic management, strategic planning, business policy, entrepreneurship, or policy administration.

The book is also designed to be used by managers who need to develop strategies—especially those who have recently moved into a general management position or who run a small business and want to improve their strategy development and planning processes. Another intended audience consists of those general managers, top executives, and planning specialists who would like an overview of recent issues and methods in strategic market management.

ACKNOWLEDGMENTS

This book could not have been created without help from my friends and colleagues. This fourth edition benefited from the helpful comments of many students who attended my course in strategic market management, the work of some able research assistants—Steve Markey, Beth Ulman, Vincent Weller, Scott Poland, Bob Herbst, and Kirsten Mundschau—and an excellent editor, Carol Chapman.

Among the people who read large portions of earlier editions were Lois Brown, Ziv Carmon, John Coppett, Dan Dias, Ken Hardy, Peter Kaminski, Stephen McDaniel, Reed Moyer, Carol Penskar, Alan Shocker, Robert Shoemaker, Norm Smothers, Gloria Thomas, John Wagle, Bart Weitz and, again, MBA students in my strategy course and executive programs. The current edition benefited from the help of Gregory Gundlach, Robert Headen, Chauncey Burke, Tom Gilpatrick, Frank Acito, George Jackson, Sid Dudley, R. Vishwanathan, Andrew Forman, Patricia Hopkins, and Bruce McNab. In addition, I imposed on a host of specialists to help with individual segments including Gene Laczniak, Don Leemon, Baruch Lev, Ray Miles, Steve Penman, Charles O'Reilly, and David Teece. I owe a large debt to all of these people.

I am pleased to be associated with Wiley, a "class" organization, and three superb editors—Rich Esposito and John Woods, who guided the book through the first three editions, and Tim Kent, the capable current editor who is a pleasure to know and work with. I am also grateful for the patient guidance provided by Edward Winkleman, the senior production editor for this edition. It is reassuring to be supported by competent professionals.

This book is dedicated to the women in my life, my mother, Ida, my wife, Kay, and my children, Jennifer, Jan, and Jolyn. They all have contributed understanding, support and, sometimes, patience.

David A. Aaker
May 1994

CONTENTS

PART ONE

INTRODUCTION AND OVERVIEW

1

BUSINESS STRATEGY:
The Concept and Trends
in Its Management

Plans are nothing, planning is everything.

Dwight D. Eisenhower

Where absolute superiority is not attainable, you must produce a relative one at the decisive point by making skillful use of what you have.

Karl von Clausewitz, On War, 1832

In the period from 1962 to 1972, the W. T. Grant Company nearly doubled its size in square footage and increased its profits from $9 million to $37 million. Four years later, the company went into bankruptcy and its assets were liquidated. In the 1930s, Sears and Montgomery Ward were approximately equal in sales, profits, capability, and potential. Two decades later, Sears was roughly three times bigger than Ward. In 1991, Wal-Mart, an upstart that began as a discounter to small towns in the rural South, surpassed Sears and Kmart to become the largest U.S. retailer. Clearly, some strategy choices caused these outcomes. Although these examples are dramatic, nearly every organization is affected by strategic decisions or, sometimes, nondecisions.

This book is concerned with helping managers identify, select, and implement strategies. The intent is to provide decision makers with concepts, methods, and procedures by which they can improve the quality of their strategic decision making.

This and the following chapter have several functions. First, they identify the approach toward strategy and its management that is taken in this book. Second, they introduce and position most of the concepts and methods that will be covered in the book. Third, they position and structure the other parts and chapters. Fourth, they provide a general overview and summary. Thus, the reader can productively reread these two chapters as a way to review.

The chapter begins by defining the concept of a business strategy. It then describes five strategic thrusts, discusses the key concept of a strategic business unit, provides a historical perspective to strategy, and, finally, presents some characteristics, trends, and rationales of strategic market management.

WHAT IS A BUSINESS STRATEGY?

Before discussing the process of developing sound business strategies, it is fair to ask what a business strategy is in the first place. A business strategy, sometimes termed competitive strategy or simply strategy, is here defined by six elements or dimensions. The first four apply to any business, even if it exists by itself. The remaining two are introduced when the business exists in an organization with other business units. A business strategy specification includes a determination of

1. *The product market in which the business is to compete.* The scope of a business is defined by the products it offers and chooses not to offer, by the markets it seeks to serve and not serve, by the competitors it chooses to compete with and to avoid, and by its level of vertical integration. Sometimes the most important business scope decision is

what products or segments to avoid because such a decision, if followed by discipline, can conserve resources needed to compete successfully elsewhere.

2. *The level of investment.* Although there are obvious variations and refinements, it is useful to conceptualize the alternatives in terms of

   - Invest to grow (or enter the product market).
   - Invest only to maintain the existing position.
   - Milk the business by minimizing investment.
   - Recover as much of the assets as possible by liquidating or divesting the business.

3. *The functional area strategies needed to compete in the selected product market.* The specific way to compete will usually be characterized by one or more functional area strategies such as a

   - Product line strategy.
   - Positioning strategy.
   - Pricing strategy.
   - Distribution strategy.
   - Manufacturing strategy.
   - Information technology strategy.
   - Segmentation strategy.
   - Global strategy.

4. *The strategic assets or skills that underlie the strategy and provide the sustainable competitive advantage (SCA).* A strategic skill or, simply, skill, is something a business unit does exceptionally well, such as manufacturing or promotion, which has strategic importance to that business. A strategic asset or, simply, asset, is a resource, such as a brand name or installed customer base, that is strong relative to competitors. Strategy formulation must consider the cost and feasibility of generating or maintaining assets or skills that will provide the basis for a sustainable competitive advantage.

Multiple Businesses.   Except for the rare focused enterprise, most modern business units share an organizational framework with other business units. At the highest level, it may mean a group of diverse divisions, each involving many businesses. At the lowest level, it may mean a single product being delivered to a sharply segmented set of markets, or a set of product variations being delivered to a common market. In either situation, the concept of a business strategy for a group of business units is introduced, and two additional components of strategy are needed:

FIGURE 1.1 A Business Strategy

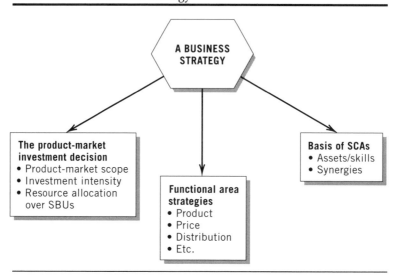

5. *The allocation of resources over the business units.* Financial resources, generated either internally or externally, plus nonfinancial resources such as plant, equipment, and people, all need to be allocated. Even for a small organization, the allocation decision is key to strategy.

6. *The development of synergistic effects across the businesses—the creation of value by having business units that support and complement each other.* It is only logical that multiple business organizations that can achieve synergistic effects will have an advantage over those that ignore or fail to achieve synergy.

All six elements of the strategy concept can be capsuled into three core elements as shown in Figure 1.1:

- The product-market investment decision that encompasses the product-market scope of the business strategy, its investment intensity, and the resource allocation over multiple businesses.
- The functional area strategies—what you do.
- The basis of a sustainable competitive advantage to compete in those markets. This core concept encompasses assets, skills, and/or synergies matched with functional area strategies.

STRATEGIC THRUSTS—THE SEARCH FOR SCAs

In any context, there is an infinite variety of potential strategies and many routes to achieving SCAs. It is useful to identify types of strategies that have similar strategic thrusts. Two stand out as particularly encompassing: differentiation and low cost. Harvard's Michael Porter, an economist and influential strategy researcher, has suggested that low cost and differentiation represent the two basic strategies available to firms, and that all successful strategies will involve one or both of these thrusts.[1]

Differentiation Versus Low-Cost Strategies

A differentiation strategy is one in which the product offering is differentiated from the competition by providing value to the customer, perhaps by enhancing the performance, quality, prestige, features, service backup, reliability, or convenience of the product. A successful differentiation strategy such as that of Nordstrom, Lexus, Marriott, or Maytag can make price less critical to the customer, thereby leading to a price premium. However, a differentiation strategy such as that of Domino's Pizza or Blockbuster Video can also result in increased customer loyalty at a parity rather than a premium price.

In contrast, a low-cost strategy is one based on achieving a sustainable cost advantage in some important element of the product or service. The overall cost leadership position can be achieved through a high market share or through other advantages such as favorable access to raw materials or state-of-the-art manufacturing equipment. However, a low-cost player usually develops a low-cost culture and strategy involving an attack on costs across the board. A low-cost strategy need not always be associated with low prices, because lower cost could lead to enhanced profits or increased advertising or promotion instead of reduced prices.

In some industries, a focus on either low cost or differentiation leaves a business vulnerable to competitors. Caterpillar is an example of a company that gained a dominant position in the earth-moving equipment industry by differentiating with respect to parts and service and using its volume to achieve low costs. In the 1970s, Komatsu challenged Caterpillar by building upon its low-cost labor advantage with product differentiation in niche markets. Procter & Gamble, with its everyday low pricing (EDLP) strategy, recognized that even with strong brands, it needed to reduce the cost advantage of private label and price brands by removing inefficiencies from the channel.

Focus, Preemptive Moves, and Synergy

Although most strategies will involve either or both differentiation and low cost, many other strategic thrusts (or strategy types) such as innovativeness, global thinking, entrepreneurial style, or the ability to exploit information technology can be identified. We will consider three that are frequently strategically important and are not easily covered by the umbrella of differentiation and low cost—namely, focus, preemptive moves, and synergy.

The Focus Strategy.　A focus strategy, which involves focusing the business on either a relatively small buyer group or a restricted portion of the product line, is also explicitly discussed by Michael Porter. Focus can be central to the creation of an SCA and therefore is the driving force, even if differentiation or low cost are also associated with the strategy. Thus, a retailer could focus on smaller women with hard-to-fit sizes or on a relatively narrow line such as fashion accessories.

A Preemptive Move.　A preemptive strategic move is the pioneering implementation of a strategy into a business area that, because it is first, generates an asset or skill which forms the basis of an SCA. For a first strategy implementation to create "first mover advantages," competitors must be inhibited or prevented from duplicating or countering it. Coca-Cola achieved an SCA in Japan by securing the best distributors in each area. Pepsi and other competitors were at a substantial disadvantage because they had been preempted.

Synergy.　Synergy occurs when a business has an advantage because it is linked to another business within the same firm or division. The two businesses, for example, may be able to share a sales force, office, or warehouse, and thus reduce costs or investment. They may be able to jointly offer a customer a combination of coordinated products, such as tennis shoes and tennis apparel. The combination thus creates a value that would not exist if the two businesses were distinct. Synergy is introduced in Chapter 9 where the concept of a sustainable competitive advantage is discussed in more depth. Differentiation strategies are discussed in Chapter 10. In Chapter 11, low cost, focus, and preemptive moves are detailed.

A STRATEGIC BUSINESS UNIT

A strategic business unit or SBU is any organizational unit that has (or should have) a defined business strategy and has a manager with sales and profit responsibility. The concept was formulated by firms such as General Electric as a way to help develop an entrepreneurial thrust in a diversified firm by creating business units that were more autonomous and by making strategy development less centralized.

A selection of the most appropriate level of aggregation for an SBU will involve some judgment. An SBU could be formed at the brand level—

for instance, Tide, Drift, Ivory, and others, or at the category level—for example, laundry products. In fact, there is a sharp movement toward managing and developing strategies at a broader level than brands, that is, at the level of product categories or brand families. The driving force is the power of the retailer. To deal with that force, manufacturers need to manage with a perspective that involves more scope. Retailers want to think in terms of the Minute Maid line and not just in terms of Minute Maid frozen orange juice.

The level of aggregation will largely depend upon two factors, commonality and size. If two businesses have a high degree of commonality in areas such as manufacturing, distribution, or customers, for example, it could be strategically important to avoid inconsistencies. Grouping them into one SBU will insure that the strategies and their implementation are coordinated. Size is the second consideration; an SBU needs to have sufficient size to support its own organization. Of course, two SBUs can share some elements of the operations such as a sales force or a facility to gain economies, but separate SBUs imply a meaningful degree of autonomy.

Often the conceptualization of a strategy is best done at an SBU level—the Sony Walkman, for example. However, a given SBU may well contain different product lines and be involved in very different markets. It may be useful to develop strategies or at least strategy refinements for subunits of an SBU based on the specific product markets involved—for instance, the European market for the Sony Walkman.

STRATEGIC MARKET MANAGEMENT: A HISTORICAL PERSPECTIVE

The process of developing and implementing strategies has been described over the years by various terms, including budgeting and control, long-range planning, strategic planning, strategic management, and strategic market management. All these terms have similar meanings and are often used interchangeably. However, when they are placed in a historical perspective, some useful distinctions emerge.[2]

Budgeting/Control

The development of budgeting/control management systems can be roughly associated with the early 1900s. The emphasis is on controlling deviations and managing complexity. An annual budget is set for various departments, and deviations from that budget are carefully scrutinized to find explanations and determine whether remedial action is appropriate. The basic assumption is that the past will repeat itself. Figure 1.2 summarizes this approach.

Long-Range Planning

The second management system shown in Figure 1.2 is long-range planning, the development of which Igor Ansoff, long a leading strategy theorist, has associated with the 1950s. Its focus is on anticipating growth and managing complexity. The basic assumption is that past trends will continue into the future. The planning process typically involves projecting sales, costs, technology, and so on into the future using data and experience from the past. The planning task is then to develop human resources and facilities to accommodate the anticipated growth or contraction. The time frame is not necessarily as limited as in the budgeting/control system and can anticipate two, five, or ten years, depending on the context.

Included under long-range planning is gap analysis. A gap occurs if the projected sales and profits do not meet the organizational goals. Changes in operations such as increasing the sales forces and/or plant capacity are then considered to remove the gap.

Strategic Planning

Strategic planning, the emergence of which might be associated with the 1960s and 1970s, is concerned with changing strategic thrusts and capabilities. The basic assumption is that past extrapolations are inadequate. There will be discontinuities from past projections and new trends, both of which will require strategic adjustments. An adjustment in strategic thrust or direction could involve moving into a new product market. The enhancement of research and development competence could represent an adjustment in strategic capability.

Strategic planning, also termed strategic market planning, focuses on the market environment facing the firm. Thus, the emphasis is not only on projections but also on an in-depth understanding of the market environment, particularly the competitors and customers. The hope is not only to gain insight into current conditions, but also to be able to anticipate changes that have strategic implications.

One characteristic that strategic planning shares with budgeting/control and long-range planning management systems is that it is largely based on a periodic planning system, usually an annual system. Typically, an organization will develop a strategic plan in the spring and summer and then, during the fall, will use that plan as a base for developing the annual operating plans and budgets for the next year. The periodic

FIGURE 1.2 Evolution of Management Systems

	Budgeting/ Control	Long-Range Planning	Strategic Planning	Strategic Market Management
Management Emphasis	Control deviations and manage complexity	Anticipate growth and manage complexity	Change strategic thrust and capability	Cope with strategic surprises and fast-developing threats / opportunities
Assumptions	The past repeats	Past trends will continue	New trends and discontinuities are predictable	Planning cycles inadequate to deal with rapid changes
Process	← Periodic →			Real time
Time Period Associated With System	From 1900s	From 1950s	From 1960s	From mid–1980s

planning cycle does provide a time in which managers must address strategic questions. Without such a device, artificial though it may be, even managers who realize the importance of strategic thinking might find their time absorbed by day-to-day operations and crises.

The difficulty with the periodic planning process is that the need for strategic analysis and decision making does not always occur on an annual basis. The environment and technology may change so rapidly and environmental shocks occur so unexpectedly that being tied to a planning cycle can be disadvantageous or even disastrous. If the planning process is allowed to suppress strategic response outside the planning cycle, performance can suffer, particularly in dynamic industries.

A study of managers making strategy decisions in a simulated business focused on the impact of planning. The study found that when the environment was made more turbulent (by reducing product life cycles and increasing product change), those businesses that were asked to plan formally (by projecting performance using planning forms) had performances inferior to those that did not plan.[3] Planning enhanced those in a less turbulent environment, however.

Strategic Market Management

Strategic market management or, simply, strategic management is motivated by the assumption that the planning cycle is inadequate to deal with the rapid rate of change that can occur in a firm's external environment. To cope with strategic surprises and fast-developing threats and opportunities, strategic decisions need to be precipitated and made outside the planning cycle.

Recognition of the demands of a rapidly changing environment has stimulated the development or increased use of methods, systems, and options that are responsive. In particular, it suggests a need for continuous, real-time information systems rather than, or in addition to, periodic analysis. More sensitive environmental scanning, the identification and continuous monitoring of information-need areas, efforts to develop strategic flexibility, and the enhancement of the entrepreneurial thrust of the organization may be helpful. An information-need area is an area of uncertainty that will affect strategy, such as an emerging consumer interest area. Strategic flexibility involves strategic options that allow quick and appropriate responses to sudden changes in the environment.

Another characteristic of strategic market management is that it doesn't necessarily accept the environment as given, with the strategic role confined to adaptation and reaction. Rather, the possibility exists for strategy to be proactive, affecting environmental change. Thus, governmental policies, customer needs, and technological developments can be influenced—and perhaps even controlled—by creative, active strategies.

The evolving systems shown in Figure 1.2 build on, rather than replace, earlier systems. In that spirit, strategic market management actually includes all four management systems: the budgeting/control system, the projection-based approach of long-range planning, the elements of strategic planning, and the refinements needed to adapt strategic decision making to real time. In strategic market management, there is normally a periodic planning process supplemented by techniques to allow the organization to be strategically responsive outside the planning process.

The inclusion of the term "market" into the phrase "strategic management" emphasizes that strategy development needs to be driven by the market and its environment rather than being internally oriented. It also points out that the process should be proactive rather than reactive, and that the task should be to try to influence the environment in addition to responding to it.

STRATEGIC MARKET MANAGEMENT: CHARACTERISTICS AND TRENDS

Several distinct characteristics and trends have emerged in the strategy field, some of which have already been mentioned. A review of these thrusts or trends will provide additional insight into strategic market management and into the perspective and orientation of the balance of the book.

External, Market Orientation

As already noted, organizations need to be oriented externally—toward customers, competitors, the market, and the market's environment. In sharp contrast to the projection-based, internally oriented, long-range planning systems, the goal is to develop market-driven strategies that are sensitive to the customer.

Proactive Strategies

A proactive strategy attempts to influence events in the environment rather than simply reacting to environmental forces as they occur. A proactive strategy is important for at least two reasons. First, one way to be sure of detecting and quickly reacting to major environmental changes is to participate in their creation. Second, such environmental changes can be so significant that it is important to influence them when possible.

For example, an insurance firm may need to be involved in tort reform strategy.

Importance of the Information System

An external orientation puts demands on the supporting information system. The determination of what information is needed, how it can be obtained efficiently and effectively, and how it should best be analyzed, processed, and stored can be the key to making the strategy development process effective.

On-Line Analysis and Decision Making

There is also a trend away from using only the annual planning cycle and toward more of a continuous, "on-line" system of information gathering, analysis, and strategic decision making. The design of such a system is demanding and requires new methods and concepts. The system must be structured enough to provide assistance in an inherently complex decision context, sensitive enough to detect the need to precipitate a strategic choice, and flexible enough to be applied in a variety of situations.

Entrepreneurial Thrust

The importance of developing and maintaining an entrepreneurial thrust is increasingly being recognized. There is a need for the development of organizational forms and strategic market management support systems that allow the firm to be responsive to opportunities. The entrepreneurial skill is particularly important to the large, diversified firm and to the firm involved in extremely fast-moving industries. Consider the high-tech firms or "hit industries" like video games, CDs, or movies. The strategy in such contexts must include providing an environment where entrepreneurs can function and flourish.

Implementation

There is a growing recognition that implementation of strategy is critical. There needs to be concern about whether the strategy fits the organization—its structure, systems, people, and culture—or whether the organization can be changed to make the strategy fit. Links also need to be made to the functional area policies and the operating plan. Chapter 16 is devoted to implementation issues.

Global Realities

Increasingly, the global dimension is affecting strategy. Global markets are extremely relevant to many businesses, from Boeing to McDonald's. Conversely, it is a rare firm that is not affected by competitors either based in or with operations in other countries. The global element represents both direct and indirect opportunities and threats. The financial difficulty of a major country or a worldwide shortage of some raw material may have a dramatic impact on an organization's strategy. Chapter 15 focuses on global strategies.

Longer Time Horizon

A major problem for many businesses is the development of effective long-term objectives and strategies. Many observers have suggested that the visible success of Japanese firms is due, in part, to their ability to operate strategically with long time horizons. Furthermore, some of the competitive problems of industries such as automobile, consumer electronics, and steel have been attributed by management theorists to a short-term orientation. Managing with respect to a longer time horizon is more difficult and places heavier demands on the strategic decision-making process. As a result, there is an increased need for better constructs and methods that reflect a long-term perspective.

Empirical Research

Historically, the field of strategy has been dominated by conceptual contributions based on personal experience and insights, as the writings of Alfred Sloan, the architect of General Motors, and Peter Drucker, the author of the classic book, *The Practice of Management*, illustrate.[4] More recently, an empirical research tradition has begun to materialize. The qualitative case-study approach has provided useful hypotheses and insights. In addition, a host of quantitative research streams exists in which the performance and characteristics of samples of business units are compared and studied through time. These research streams can now be found in most of the basic disciplines and in the field of strategy itself. They are an important indication that the strategy field is finally reaching a maturity in which theories can be, and are being, subjected to scientific testing.

Interdisciplinary Developments

One purpose of this book is to draw on and integrate a variety of disciplines now making important conceptual and methodological contributions to strategic market management. Among these disciplines, which have been remarkably isolated from strategic market management and each other, are the following:

Marketing. Marketing is by its very nature concerned with the interaction between the firm and the marketplace. During the last decade, strategic decisions have received increasing attention. Tools and concepts such as product positioning, the product life cycle, brand equity, brand loyalty, and customer-need analysis all have the potential to improve strategic decision making.

Organizational Behavior. Organizational behavior theorists have built on the classic works of the early 1960s on strategy and organizational structure. They have also considered the link between strategy and other elements of the organization, such as systems and the management of people. Of particular relevance is the concept of corporate culture and its impact on strategy.

Finance and Accounting. One major contribution of the finance and accounting disciplines to strategy is shareholder value analysis (covered in Chapter 7)—the concept that strategists should be concerned with the impact of strategy on the value of the firm. Another is a rich research tradition relating to diversification efforts, acquisitions, and mergers. Finance has, of course, also contributed to an understanding of the concept of risk and its management.

Economics. The industrial organization theory subarea of economics has been applied to strategy using concepts and methods such as industry structure, exit barriers, entry barriers, and strategic groups. Furthermore, the concept of transaction costs has been developed and applied to the issue of vertical integration. Finally, economists have contributed to the experience curve concept, which has considerable strategic implications.

Strategy. The discipline of strategy is not only increasingly overlapping with other disciplines, but is itself maturing. One sign of this maturity is the quantitative research streams that are emerging. Another is the maturity of some of the tools and techniques. Still another is the fact that the premier strategy journal, *Strategic Management Journal*, has given exposure for more than a decade to the top academic efforts which provide theoretical and empirical insights into strategy.

WHY STRATEGIC MARKET MANAGEMENT?

Strategic market management is often frustrating because the environment is so difficult to understand and predict. Communication and choices within the organization are required that can create strains and internal resistance. The most valuable organization resource, management time, is absorbed. The alternative of simply waiting for and reacting to the exceptional opportunities often seems efficient and adequate.

Despite these costs and problems, however, strategic market management has the potential to

- *Precipitate the consideration of strategic choices.* What is happening externally that is creating opportunities and threats to which a timely and appropriate reaction should be generated? What strategic issues face the firm? What strategic options should be considered? The alternative to strategic market management usually is to drift strategically, becoming absorbed in day-to-day problems. Nothing is more tragic than an organization that fails because a strategic decision was not even addressed until it was too late.

- *Force a long-range view.* The pressures to manage with a short-term focus are strong and frequently lead to strategic errors.

- *Make visible the resource allocation decision.* Allowing resource allocation to be dictated by the accounting system, political strengths, or inertia (the same as last year) is only too easy. One result is that the small but promising business with "no problems" or the unborn business may suffer from a lack of resources, whereas the larger business areas with "problems" absorb an excessive amount.

- *Provide methods to help strategic analysis and decision making.* Concepts, models, and methodologies are now available to help a business collect and analyze information and address difficult strategic decisions.

- *Provide a strategic management and control system.* The focus on assets and skills and the development of objectives and programs associated with strategic thrusts will provide the basis for managing a business strategically.

- *Provide a communication and coordination system both horizontally and vertically.* Strategic market management provides a way to communicate problems and proposed strategies within an organization. In particular, the vocabulary adds precision.

- *Help a business cope with change.* If a particular environment is extremely stable and the sales patterns are satisfactory, there may be little need for meaningful strategic change—either in direction or intensity. In that case, strategic market management is much less crucial. However, most organizations now exist in rapidly changing and increasingly unpredictable environments and therefore need approaches for coping strategically.

George Yip studied strategy development in 13 firms and concluded that strategic market management approaches have particular value for businesses that[5]

- Need multifunctional strategies; one marketing-oriented firm used them to provide a strategic role for functions other than marketing.
- Need to achieve synergy among multiple markets.
- Need to coordinate the strategies of multiple brands.
- Are involved in complex markets where multiple or layered channels, regional variations, or multiple elements of the marketing mix are involved.

Summary

A business strategy includes the determination of the product-market scope, the intensity of the business investment, the functional area strategy, and the assets or skills to be employed. When multiple businesses are involved, the strategy includes the allocation of resources over the business units and the creation of synergy. Strategies that have similar strategic thrusts share characteristics that drive the strategy and are linked to the SCAs. Most strategies have either a differentiation or low-cost strategic thrust, or both. Other strategic thrusts that are isolated in this book are focus, preemptive moves, and synergy.

A budgeting/control management system focuses on an annual budget and deviations from it. Long-range planning relies on projections of past trends. Strategic planning involves the prediction and detection of discontinuities from past projections. Strategic market management breaks away from the annual planning cycle, recognizing the need for on-line decision making in a rapidly changing environment. It also includes the concept of proactive as opposed to reactive strategy development.

Among the thrusts in strategic market management is the development of strategies that are externally oriented, proactive, timely, entrepreneurial, global, implementable, and appropriate for a long time horizon. Strategic market management provides an approach to raising and addressing strategic choices and to managing complex organizations in a context of changing external pressures and threats.

FOOTNOTES

[1] Michael E. Porter, *Competitive Strategy*, New York: The Free Press, 1980, Chapter 2.

[2] This section and Figure 1.2 draw on the work of H. Igor Ansoff. Typical examples are his articles: "Strategic Issue Management," *Strategic Management Journal*, April–June 1980, pp. 131–148, and "The State of Practice in Planning Systems," *Sloan Management Review*, Winter 1977, pp. 61–69.

[3] Rashi Glazer and Alan Weiss, "Planning in a Turbulent Environment," Working Paper, University of California at Berkeley, April 1991.

[4] Alfred P. Sloan, Jr., *My Years with General Motors*, New York: Doubleday, 1963, and Peter F. Drucker, *The Practice of Management*, New York: Harper & Row, 1954.

[5] George S. Yip, "Who Needs Strategic Planning?" *The Journal of Business Strategy*, Vol. 6, Fall 1985, pp. 30–41.

2

STRATEGIC MARKET MANAGEMENT:
An Overview

Chance favors the prepared mind.

Louis Pasteur

Far better an approximate answer to the
right question, which is often vague, than an
exact answer to the wrong question, which
can always be made precise.

John Tukey, Statistician

If you don't know where you're going, you
might end up somewhere else.

Casey Stengel

Strategic market management is a system designed to help management both precipitate and make strategic decisions, as well as create strategic visions. A strategic decision involves the creation, change, or retention of a strategy. In contrast to a tactical decision, a strategic decision is usually costly in terms of the resources and time required to reverse or change it. Sometimes a wrong decision is so costly to alter that it can threaten the very existence of an organization. Normally, a strategic decision will have a time frame greater than one year; sometimes decades are involved.

A strategic vision is a vision of a future strategy or sets of strategies. The realization of an optimal strategy for a firm may involve a delay because the firm is not ready or the emerging conditions are not yet in place. A vision will provide direction and purpose for interim strategies and strategic activities.

An important role of the system is to precipitate as well as make strategic decisions. In fact, the identification of the need for a strategic response is frequently a critical step. Strategic blunders have often occurred because a strategic decision process was never activated, not because an incorrect decision was made. Furthermore, the role of strategic market management is not limited to selecting among decision alternatives, but includes the identification of alternatives as well. Much of the analysis will therefore be concerned with identifying alternatives.

Figure 2.1 shows an overview of the external analysis and self-analysis that provide the input to strategy development and the set of strategic decisions that is the ultimate output. It provides a structure for strategic market management and for this book. A brief overview of its three principal elements and an introduction to the key concepts will be provided in this chapter.

EXTERNAL ANALYSIS

External analysis involves an examination of the relevant elements external to an organization. The analysis should be purposeful, focusing on the identification of threats, opportunities, strategic questions, and strategic choices. The danger of being excessively descriptive is always present. Because there is literally no limit to the scope of a descriptive study, the result can be a considerable expenditure of resources with little impact on strategy.

One output of external analysis is an identification and understanding of opportunities and threats facing the organization, both present and potential. An opportunity is a trend or event that could lead to a significant upward change in sales and profit patterns—given the appropriate strategic response. A threat is a trend or event that will result, in the absence

FIGURE 2.1   Overview of Strategic Market Management

EXTERNAL ANALYSIS

- Customer analysis:
  Segments, motivations, unmet needs.
- Competitor analysis:
  Identity, strategic groups, performance, image, objectives, strategies, culture, cost structure, strengths, weaknesses.
- Market analysis:
  Size, projected growth, profitability, entry barriers, cost structure, distribution system, trends, key success factors.
- Environmental analysis:
  Technological, governmental, economic, cultural, demographic, scenarios, information need areas.

Opportunities, threats, trends, and strategic questions

SELF-ANALYSIS

- Performance analysis:
  Profitability, sales, shareholder value analysis, customer satisfaction, product quality, brand associations, relative cost, new products, employee attitude and performance, product portfolio analysis.
- Determinants of strategic options:
  Past and current strategies, strategic problems, organizational capabilities and constraints, financial resources and constraints, strengths, weaknesses.

Strategic strengths, weaknesses, problems, constraints, and questions

STRATEGY IDENTIFICATION AND SELECTION

- Review mission alternatives.
- Identify strategic alternatives.
  - Product market investment strategies.
  - Functional area strategies.
  - Assets, skills, and synergies.
- Select strategy.
- Implement the operating plan.
- Review strategies.

of a strategic response, in a significant downward departure from current sales and profit patterns. For example, consumers' concern with calories and cholesterol represents a threat to the dairy industry.

Another output is the identification of strategic questions regarding an area of uncertainty about a business or its environment that has the potential to affect strategy. If the area is important and urgent, an in-depth analysis leading to a strategy decision may be needed; otherwise, an information-gathering effort will usually be appropriate.

The frame of reference for an external analysis is usually a defined SBU. However, it is useful to conduct the external analysis at several levels. External analyses of submarkets provide insight sometimes critical to developing strategy. Thus, an external analysis of the mature beer industry might contain analyses of the import and nonalcoholic beer submarkets, which are growing and have important differences. It is also possible to conduct external analyses for groups of SBUs, such as divisions, when there is sufficient commonality with respect to such characteristics as the segments served, the competitors faced, and environmental trends.

External analysis, discussed at the outset of Chapter 3, is divided into four sections or components: customer analysis, competitor analysis, market analysis, and environmental analysis.

Customer Analysis

Customer analysis, the first step of external analysis and the subject of Chapter 3, involves identifying the organization's customer segments and each segment's motivations and unmet needs. Segment identification defines alternative product markets and thus structures the strategic investment decision (what investment levels to assign to each market). The analysis of customer motivations provides information needed to decide whether the firm can and should attempt to gain or maintain a sustainable competitive advantage. An unmet need, a need not currently being met by existing products, can be strategically important because it may represent a way that entrenched competitors can be dislodged.

For example, consider the luxury hotel industry. One segmentation scheme distinguishes between tourists, convention attendees, and business travelers. Each has a very different set of motivations. The tourist is more concerned with price, the conventioneer with convention facilities, and the business traveler with comfort. An unmet need for the tourist could be obtaining tickets for events such as plays or concerts.

Frozen-novelty industry products include individually packaged, single servings of a frozen snack or dessert such as chocolate-covered ice cream, Popsicles, juice bars, pudding bars, and ice cream-cookie combinations. One way to segment this industry is to distinguish between retail purchases and the food service segment; food service includes schools, hospitals, and recreational facilities that could be attracted by the ease of storing and serving the product. The market might also be segmented by motivation. Groups can be identified according to whether they are primarily concerned with calories, fat, taste, refreshment, price, or convenience. An unmet need for a nutritious snack in this industry in the early 1980s provided an opening for the frozen fruit bar.

Competitor Analysis

Competitor analysis, covered in Chapter 4, starts with the identification of competitors, current and potential. Some competitors will compete more intensely than others. Jell-O's pudding pop competes more vigorously with yogurt bars and juice bars than with ice cream, frozen cakes, cake mixes, and packaged cookies. Although the intense competitors should be examined in more detail, all competitors are usually relevant to strategy development.

Especially when there are many competitors, it is helpful to divide them into strategic groups, groups that have similar characteristics (e.g., size and resources), strengths (e.g., brand name, distribution), and strategies (e.g., high quality). The luxury hotel industry might be grouped into those hotels that offer businessperson-oriented amenities and those that are ultraplush and prestigious. These two groups might be further divided into those that are members of chains with reservation systems and those that are autonomous. Regional dairies with strong ice cream brands are one strategic group in the frozen-novelty industry, a group that is declining in the face of competitors with national advertising and promotion support.

To develop a strategy, it is important to understand the competitor's

- *Performance.* Sales, sales growth, and profitability signal how healthy and formidable a competitor is.
- *Image and personality.* How is the competitor positioned and perceived?
- *Objectives.* Is this competitor committed to the business and aiming for high growth?
- *Current and past strategy.* What are the implications for future strategic moves?
- *Culture.* What is most important to the organization—cost control, entrepreneurship, or the customer?
- *Cost structure.* Does the competitor have a cost advantage?
- *Strengths and weaknesses.* Is a brand name, distribution, or R&D a strength or a weakness?

Of special interest are the competitor's strengths and weaknesses. Strategy development often focuses on exploiting a competitor's weakness, or neutralizing or bypassing a competitor's strength.

Market Analysis

Market analysis, the subject of Chapter 5, has two primary objectives. The first is to determine the attractiveness of the market and submarkets. Will competitors, on the average, earn attractive profits or will they lose money? If the market is so difficult that everyone is losing money, it is not a place in which to invest. The second objective is to understand the dynamics of the market so that threats and opportunities can be detected and strategies adapted. The analysis should include an examination of the market size, growth, profitability, cost structure, channels, trends, and key success factors.

Size. A basic characteristic of a market (or a submarket) is its size. Of interest, in addition to current sales, is its potential, the additional sales that could be obtained if new users were attracted, new uses were found, or existing buyers were enticed to use the product or service more frequently.

Growth Prospects. An assessment of the growth trend and product life-cycle stage for the industry and its submarkets needs to be made. An investment in a declining industry is not always unwise, but it would be if the erroneous impression were held that it was, in fact, a growth situation. Conversely, it is important to recognize growth contexts even though they will not always be attractive investments for a given firm.

Market Profitability. The competitive intensity of the market depends on five factors—the number and vigor of existing competitors, the threat of new competitors, the threat of substitute products, the profit impact of powerful suppliers, and the power of customers to force price concessions. For example, a luxury hotel could be faced with convention organizers who have the power to negotiate low rates and thus affect the profitability of the market. Important structural components are the barriers to entry that must be overcome by potential competitors entering the industry. A barrier to entry for the luxury hotel business in Chicago is the availability of desirable sites.

Cost Structures. One issue is what value-added stage represents the most important cost component. In the parcel delivery system, there is local pickup and delivery versus the sorting and combining function versus between-city transportation versus the customer service function. Achieving a cost advantage in an important value-added stage can be crucial. Another cost issue is whether the industry is appropriate for a low-cost strategy based on the experience curve model, discussed in Chapter 11.

Distribution Channels.   An understanding of the alternative distribution channels and trends can be of strategic value. Growth in the importance of self-service retail gasoline stations and companion growth in the convenience store industry have strategic significance to oil companies and distributors as well as food retailing firms, as the ARCO chain of AM/PM stores illustrates.

A significant factor in the frozen-novelty business is the distribution squeeze caused by product proliferation. There are more than 2,000 products and space for only 100 of them in the frozen-food area of a grocery store. Clearly, the products without substantial backing and the ability to generate sales will be in trouble. Being a comfortable number three in a category will be risky.

Market Trends.   Trends within the market can affect current or future strategies and assessments of market profitability. For example, an important trend in luxury hotels is toward businessperson suites that include a host of amenities, such as a living room/den with a library of books and VCR movies, a stereo system, a well-stocked refrigerator, and elegant furnishings. Several chains are aggressively building and promoting all-suite hotels. Particularly popular among businesswomen, the occupancy rate of such hotels is 70 percent, about 6 percent higher than that of all hotels.

Trends in the frozen-novelty industry include the demand for "healthy" snacks, the exploitation of strong brand names such as Dole and Jell-O, the consolidation of competitors, product proliferation, and increased promotion and advertising.

Key Success Factors.   A key success factor is a competitive skill or asset that is needed to compete successfully. Successful firms are usually strong in several key success factors and are not weak in any. In the luxury hotel business, key success factors might be those characteristics that contribute to image, such as ambience or quality of service. A hotel cannot compete successfully in the business traveler, luxury hotel business without creating the "right" atmosphere.

Strategy development, however, needs to be based on difficult judgments about what the key success factors will be in the future.[1] Popsicle Industries, makers of Popsicles, Fudgsicles, and Creamsicles, recognized that control over product quality and the ability to engage in national advertising and promotion were emerging key success factors. Thus, it changed from a system using local dairies to one in which production was centralized in 25 manufacturers under tight supervision, with distribution and marketing still controlled by Popsicle.

In the catalog business, a key success factor of the future will be the ability to deal with automated mailing lists. Employees of Williams-Sonoma, for example, track up to 150 different pieces of information per customer.[2] They know what a person has bought from each of their five catalogs and use this information to refine mailing lists and even to locate retail stores. As a result of this technology, a new Williams-Sonoma catalog, *The Chambers*, featuring bed and bath products, turned a profit on its first mailing.

Environmental Analysis

Important forces outside an organization and its immediate markets and competitors will shape its operation and thrust. Environmental analysis, the subject of Chapter 6, is the process of identifying and understanding emerging opportunities and threats created by these forces. It is important to limit environmental analysis to the manageable and relevant, because it can easily get bogged down by excessive scope and volume. It is helpful to divide environmental analysis into five components: technological, governmental, economic, cultural, and demographic.

A technological development can dramatically change an industry and create difficult decisions for those who are committed to profitable "old" technologies. For example, digital watches, transistors, and nylon all revolutionized industries. Technology can also make less dramatic but strategically important changes. Information technology has created a significant advantage for those hotels able to develop and exploit systems that allow them to serve customers more efficiently and with a personalized touch. Many important new products in the frozen-novelty industry are based on recently developed technologies such as the ability to quickly process, package, and transport food—for example, frozen-fruit bars.

The governmental environment can be especially important to multinationals that operate in politically sensitive countries. A luxury hotel chain may be interested in building codes and restrictions that might affect new hotels it is planning.

Strategic judgments in many contexts are affected by the cultural environment. For example, the key success factor for many clothing industries is the capability to be "right" with respect to fashion. Understanding the reasons behind the public's interest in nutrition and health is important to strategists in the frozen-novelty business.

Understanding the economic environment facing a country or an industry helps in projecting that industry's sales over time and in identifying special risks or threats. The hotel industry, for example, can see a link between the overall health of the economy in general and its primary customer segments in particular.

Demographic trends are important to many firms. Age patterns are crucial to those whose customers are in certain age groups, such as infants, students, baby boomers, or retirees. The frozen-novelty industry was fighting a losing demographic battle until it developed products that appealed to adults as well as children. Geographic patterns can affect the investment decisions of such service firms as hotels.

One way to understand a complex and changing environment is to create two or three future scenarios, relatively comprehensive views of the future environment. One scenario might be optimistic, another pessimistic, and a third in between. For example, a pessimistic scenario for the frozen-novelty business in five years might depict a high level of competition in terms of the number and intensity of competitors. Each scenario should have strategic implications.

A strategic question stimulated by any external analysis component can generate an information-need area, a strategically important area for which there is likely to be a continuing need for information. Special studies and ongoing information gathering might be justified.

SELF-ANALYSIS

Self-analysis, presented in Chapter 7 and summarized in Figure 2.1, aims to provide a detailed understanding of those aspects of the organization that are of strategic importance. In particular, it covers performance analysis and an examination of the key determinants of strategy such as strengths, weaknesses, and strategic problems. Self-analysis, like external analysis, usually has an SBU as a frame of reference but can also be productive at the level of aggregations of SBUs, such as divisions or firms.

Performance Analysis

Profitability and sales provide an evaluation of past strategies and an indication of the current market viability of a product line. Return on assets (ROA), the most commonly used measure of profitability, needs to be compared to the cost of capital in order to determine if the business is adding value for the shareholder. ROA can be distorted by the limitations of accounting measures—in particular, it ignores intangible assets such as brand equity. Sales is another performance measure that can reflect changes in the customer base that have long-term implications.

Shareholder value analysis is based on generating a discounted present value of the cash flow associated with a strategy. It is theoretically sound and appropriately forward-looking (as opposed to current financials that measure the results of past strategies). However, it focuses attention on financial measures rather than other indicators of strategic performance. Developing the needed estimates is most difficult and subject to a variety of biases.

Other, nonfinancial performance measures are available that often provide better measures of long-term business health:

- Customer satisfaction/brand loyalty—How are we doing relative to our competitors at attracting customers and building loyalty?
- Product/service quality—Is our product delivering value to the customer and is it performing as intended?
- Brand/firm associations—What do our customers associate with our business in terms of perceived quality, innovativeness, product class expertise, customer orientation, and so on?
- Relative cost—Are we at a cost disadvantage with respect to materials, assembly, product design, or wages?
- New product activity—Do we have a stream of new products or product improvements that have made an impact?
- Manager/employee capability and performance—Have we created the type, quantity, and depth of personnel that is needed to support projected strategies?

Product Portfolio Analysis.   This analysis considers the performance/ strength of each business area, together with the attractiveness of the business area in which it competes. One goal is to generate a business mix with an appropriate balance between new and mature products. An organization that lacks a flow of new products faces stagnation or decline. A balance must also exist between products generating cash and those using cash. Product portfolio analysis is covered in detail in Chapter 8.

Determinants of Strategic Options

Self-analysis should also review characteristics of the business that will influence strategy choice. Five areas are noted in Figure 2.1: past and current strategy, strategic problems, organizational capabilities and constraints, financial resources and constraints, and organizational strengths and weaknesses.

Strategy Review.   The past and current strategy provides an important reference point and should be understood. Has the strategy been one of milking, maintenance, or growth? Has it involved differentiation or low cost? What are its target segments? What is the sustainable competitive advantage?

Strategic Problems.   A strategic problem is one that, if uncorrected, could have damaging strategic implications. An airline faces a strategic problem if it needs to finance new equipment; an instrument firm may have a quality problem. A weakness, on the other hand, is more of an inherent characteristic, such as a bad hotel location, with which the organization may have to live. Of course, any weakness can be corrected. A hotel's location can be changed. In general, however, problems are corrected and weaknesses are neutralized by a strategy or compensated by strengths.

Organizational Capabilities and Constraints.   Self-analysis includes an examination of the internal organization, its structure, systems, people, and culture. The internal organization can be important strategically when it is a source of

- A strength—The culture in some firms can be so strong and positive that it provides the basis for a sustainable competitive advantage.
- A weakness—A firm may lack the marketing personnel to compete in a business in which a key success factor is marketing.
- A constraint—A proposed strategy must "fit" the internal organization. A realistic appraisal of an organization may preclude some strategies.

Financial Resources and Constraints.   An analysis of the financial resources available for investment, either from planned cash flow or from debt financing, helps determine how much net investment should be considered. One result could be a financial constraint such as having only $20 million per year available for investment during the next few years.

Strengths and Weaknesses.   Future strategies are often developed by building on strengths and neutralizing weaknesses. Strengths are based on assets, such as a brand name, or skills, such as advertising or manufacturing.

THE ROLE OF THE BUSINESS MISSION

A business mission, which can take several forms, may be used to address some basic questions about a business. What business are we in? What type of an organization are we? What is our strategic vision?

A business mission can be a very general statement about the strategy of a business. It thus could include a specification of

---

Pudding Pops: A Case Study

General Foods' Jell-O line of packaged dessert products was declining in the 1970s, in part due to the changing environment.[3] The number of households with children was declining, fewer traditional meals were being eaten, people were snacking more, money was available to buy more exotic gourmet products, and there was a greater concern about diet and health. The Jell-O line was inconvenient, unexciting, and linked to the declining dessert occasion and child population.

Jell-O did have substantial strengths: the Jell-O name; the wholesomeness and taste of the pudding; and its already established national marketing, manufacturing, and distribution system. The question was how to exploit these strengths to provide a new growth direction. An analysis of potential growth markets focused on the huge snack area. Snacks, perceived as good-tasting, convenient, and fun, but lacking nutrition, seemed like an ideal target for a new Jell-O product.

Initial efforts to make the existing Jell-O product seem more convenient were not enough, because the product was still linked to the dessert category. The development thrust then turned to the idea of a frozen pudding on a stick. Consumer tests of the basic concept were positive, with a 24-percent "definitely buy" score. When the concept was refined with a taste plus nutrition positioning, however, the score climbed to 36 percent.

The final product was distributed to stores with two other General Foods brands, Cool Whip frozen topping and Bird's Eye frozen vegetable products. The advertising stressed Jell-O's pudding heritage, the creamy taste and natural wholesomeness that it had brought to the snack market. A phenomenal success, the product has been followed with Jell-O Gelatin Pops and Jell-O Fruit Bars.

- **The business scope**—the product markets in which the business does and does not want to compete.
- **The growth direction**—the product markets and technologies of the future.
- **The essence of the functional area strategies.**
- The key assets and skills on which the business is based.

The development of a business mission statement can provide a vehicle for generating and screening a wide variety of strategic options. The analysis and screening of these options would not involve the same detailed appraisal of a strategy alternative as is needed when a final strategy choice has to be made. Thus, the widest possible range of strategy alternatives can be considered. For example, it is often useful to consider generic customer needs (see insert that follows) such as gaining information, rather than products such as managing databases.

A variety of dimensions and concepts can provide the basis for a strategy-defining mission statement, including product definition, market

---

Generic Customer Need

In his classic article, "Marketing Myopia," Theodore Levitt suggested that firms that myopically define their business in product terms can stagnate even though the basic customer need that they are serving is enjoying healthy growth.[4] Because of a myopic product focus, others gain the benefits of growth. Thus, if firms regard themselves as being in the transportation rather than the railroad business, the energy instead of petroleum business, or the communication rather than the telephone business, they are more likely to exploit opportunities.

The concept is simple. Define the business in terms of the basic customer need rather than the product. Xerox changed its focus from copiers to the "document" company. Visa has defined itself as being in the business of enabling a customer to exchange value—to exchange any asset including cash on deposit, the cash value of life insurance, the equity in a home—for virtually anything, anywhere in the world. As the business is redefined, both the set of competitors and the range of opportunities are often radically expanded. After redefining its business, Visa estimated that it had reached only 5 percent of its potential given the new definition.

Defining a business in terms of generic need can be extremely useful for fostering creativity in generating strategic options and avoiding an internally oriented, product/production focus.

---

definition, technology, levels of production/distribution, and asset or skill. Although it is useful to consider each, the selection of which combination will be the most helpful depends on the context. Any effort to specify rigid formulas to the desired form of a mission statement will be constraining and counterproductive.

Another role of the mission statement is to provide employees, customers, and other organization stakeholders with a business definition that captures the essence of the strategic vision of the business in order to establish a sense of purpose, identity, and commitment. In that spirit, it can be helpful to develop a metaphor or an elegant, positive phrase like "desktop publishing." A focus on competitors can also provide such a definition. For example, Komatsu motivated its organization with an "encircle (beat) CAT" competitor focus.

A business mission can also be a vehicle for the values that are associated with an organization. For example, policies toward the environment, employees, and the community can help provide a direction for an organization that will influence strategy and provide stakeholders with a positive sense of identity.

STRATEGY IDENTIFICATION AND SELECTION

The purpose of external analysis and self-analysis is twofold: to help generate strategic alternatives and to provide criteria to select among them. The consideration of mission, just discussed, often provides a first cut at strategy development. The operating plan provides the implementation details and controls. Finally, it is necessary to monitor the strategies to detect the need for review and change.

Figure 2.2 highlights the three dimensions of strategic alternatives. The first is the selection of the product markets in which the firm will operate and how much investment should be allocated to each. The second is the development of the functional area strategies and the third is the determination of the bases of sustainable competitive advantages in those product markets.

Product-Market Investment Strategies

Product Definition. As a practical matter, many strategic decisions involve products: which product lines to continue, which to add, and which to delete. Mother's Cookies is in the cookie business, but not in

---

FIGURE 2.2 Selecting Strategic Alternatives

IDENTIFICATION OF STRATEGIC ALTERNATIVES

- Product-market investment strategies.
  - Product-market scope.
  - Growth directions.
  - Investment strategies.
- Functional area strategies.
- Bases of competitive advantage—assets, skills, synergies.

CRITERIA FOR STRATEGY SELECTION

- Consider scenarios suggested by strategic questions and environmental opportunities/threats.
- Pursue a sustainable competitive advantage.
  - Exploit organizational strengths or competitor weaknesses.
  - Neutralize organizational weaknesses or competitor strengths.
- Be consistent with organizational vision/mission/objectives.
  - Achieve a long-term return on investment.
  - Be compatible with vision/mission/objectives.
- Be feasible.
  - Need only available resources.
  - Be compatible with the internal organization.
- Consider the relationship to other strategies within the firm.
  - Foster product portfolio balance.
  - Consider flexibility.
  - Exploit synergy.

the cracker or bakery business. Several firms have found it useful to reduce the scope of their product lines. In the early 1980s, Transamerica decided to return to the concept of being a financial services company. It sold United Artists, its film subsidiary, and used the proceeds to buy Fred S. James, the nation's fifth largest insurance broker.

Product position is sometimes so critical that it becomes much more than a tactical marketing effort—it represents the essence of a business. A product (or service) position involves a set of associations. Thus, Dior is positioned as a French designer and Neiman-Marcus as a prestige retailer with expensive, unusual items.

Market Definition. Markets need to be selected in which a competitive advantage will exist. A small California savings and loan firm defined its business as serving individual savers who lived near its office. Dean Witter has focused on individual investors, and moved away from mortgage banking. Gerber Products used age, defining its market as infants and young children. ServiceMaster has defined its business as servicing the maintenance needs of hospitals and other healthcare facilities. Such statements of focus can drive the operations of a firm.

Vertical Integration. A strategic option not covered by product-market scope is vertical integration. Some publishing companies have integrated backward into paper and wood products. General Motors makes batteries, spark plugs, and a host of other components. Other firms, such as Xerox and IBM, have the option of integrating forward into retailing. The question is, at what vertical levels should the business operate? The trade-offs between increased control and potential return from vertical integration on the one hand, and increased risk and loss of flexibility caused by the associated investment on the other, are discussed in detail in Chapter 12.

Growth Directions. It is crucial in strategy development to have a dynamic rather than static focus. The concept of a product-market matrix shown in Figure 2.3 is helpful for identifying options and encouraging a dynamic perspective.

In the product-market matrix, four growth vectors are shown. The first is to penetrate the existing product market. A firm may attempt to attract customers from competitors or increase usage by existing customers. A second growth vector involves product expansion while remaining in the current market. Thus, a firm offering cleaning services to healthcare facilities might expand into supervision of other healthcare functions such as purchasing and building maintenance. A third growth vector is to apply the same products in new markets. The cleaning firm could alternatively expand its cleaning services into other industries. These first three growth

FIGURE 2.3 Product-Market Structured
Growth Directions

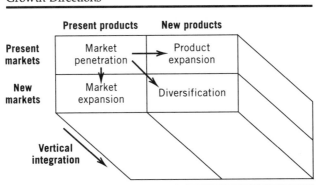

directions are explored in more detail in Chapter 12. The fourth growth
vector, to diversify into new product markets, is discussed in detail in
Chapter 13.

Figure 2.3 adds a third dimension to the product-market matrix. It
represents a growth vector based on vertical integration. Nike opening
large Nike retail stores is one example of forward integration. Safeway
supermarkets starting in-store bakeries and fresh fish operations is an
example of backward integration.

Investment Strategies. For each product market, four investment
options are possible. The firm could reduce or control the investment in
a business area by either a milk or a hold strategy. Alternatively, it could
withdraw completely if prospects become extremely unattractive or if the
business area becomes incompatible with the overall thrust of the firm.
Finally, it could invest to enter or grow.

Functional Area Strategies

The development of a business strategy involves the specification of the
strategies in functional areas such as sales, brand management, R&D,
manufacturing, and finance. The coordination of various functional area
strategies so that they don't work at cross-purposes can be difficult. The
role of strategic objectives is to help in that task.

Five strategic thrusts representing different routes to achieving sustainable competitive advantages were introduced in Chapter 1 and are
elaborated in Chapters 10 and 11. All can be achieved in a variety of ways.
Differentiation, for example, can be based on product quality, product
features, innovation, service, distribution, or a strong brand name. Low-

cost strategies can be based on an "experience curve," which links cost reduction to cumulative production volume. However, it also can be based on other factors such as "no-frills" products or automated production processes.

The remaining strategic thrusts introduced in Chapter 1—focus, preemptive moves, and synergy—are characteristics of strategies that can accompany a differentiation or low-cost approach. A firm employing a focus strategy will direct its efforts toward a narrow part of either the product line or the market. A preemptive move attempts to generate a "first mover" advantage. For example, in the frozen-novelty industry, the first firm to introduce a new novelty into a market and establish an identity usually has a substantial SCA. A strategy based on synergy will capitalize on links to other businesses in a firm. The ability to share the facilities of an R&D staff can reduce costs and improve effectiveness, for example.

Bases of Sustainable Competitive Advantage

A strategy, if it is to be effective over time, needs to involve assets and skills or synergies based on unique combinations of businesses. Thus, identifying which assets, skills, and synergies to develop or maintain becomes a key decision. Approaches to identifying candidate assets and skills are presented in Chapter 4.

SELECTING AMONG STRATEGIC ALTERNATIVES

Figure 2.2 provides a list of some of the criteria useful for selecting alternatives. These are grouped into five general criteria:

- *Consider scenarios.* A future scenario can be stimulated by strategic questions or environmental opportunities or threats. Thus, the strategic question, "Will a breakthrough in storage batteries make a general-use electric automobile feasible?" could lead to both "yes" and "no" scenarios. The threat of extreme pollution laws could also generate scenarios relevant to the strategies of automobile and energy firms. It is useful and prudent to evaluate strategic options in the context of any major scenarios identified.

- *Pursue a sustainable competitive advantage.* A useful operational criterion is whether a sustainable competitive advantage exists as part of the strategy. Unless the business unit has or can develop a real competitive advantage that is sustainable over time in the face of competitor reaction, an attractive long-term return will be unlikely. To achieve a sustainable competitive advantage, a strategy should exploit organizational assets and skills and neutralize weaknesses.

- *Be consistent with organizational vision and objectives.* A primary purpose of a vision—what a future strategy should be—and objectives is to help make strategic decisions. Thus, it is appropriate to look toward them for guidance. They can be changed, of course, if circumstances warrant. An explicit decision to change a strategy is very different from ignoring it in the face of a tempting alternative.

- *Be feasible.* A practical criterion is that the strategy be feasible. It should be within the resources of the organization. It also should be internally consistent with other organizational characteristics such as structure, systems, people, and culture. These organizational considerations will be covered in Chapter 16.

- *Consider the relationship to other firm strategies.* A strategy can relate to other business units by

  - *Balancing the sources and uses of cash flow.* Some business units should generate cash and others should provide attractive places to invest that cash. Chapter 8 elaborates on this.

  - *Enhancing flexibility.* Flexibility, in general, is reduced when heavy commitments are made in the form of fixed investment, long-term contracts, and vertical integration.

  - *Exploiting synergy.* A firm that does not exploit potential synergy may be missing an opportunity.

Implementation

The implementation stage involves converting strategic alternatives into an operating plan. If a new product market is to be entered, then a systematic program is required to develop or acquire products as an entry vehicle. If a strong R&D group is to be assembled, a program to hire people, organize them, and obtain facilities will be needed. The operating plan may span more than one year. It might be useful to provide a detailed plan for the upcoming year that contains specific short-term objectives.

Strategy Review

One of the key questions in a strategic market management system is to determine when a strategy requires review and change. It is usually necessary to monitor a limited number of key measures of strategy performance and the environment. Thus, sales, market share, margins, profit, and ROA may be regularly reported and analyzed. Externally, the process is more difficult, requiring an effective information-scanning system. The heart of such a system will be an identified set of strategic questions or issues that needs to be continuously considered.

THE PROCESS

Figure 2.1 implies a logical, sequential process. After external analysis and self-analysis are completed, the mission and strategic options are then detailed and the optimal ones selected. Finally, the operating plan and strategy review program are implemented. Later, perhaps in the next annual planning cycle, the process is repeated and the plan updated.

Although Figure 2.1 provides a useful structure, the process should be more iterative and circular than sequential. The identification and selection of strategies should occur during external analysis and self-analysis. Furthermore, the process of evaluating strategies often suggests the need for additional external analysis, thus making it necessary to cycle through the process several times. As suggested earlier, strategies and indicators of the need to change them should be continually monitored to avoid being tied to an annual planning cycle. The process supporting the development of business strategies is covered in detail in Chapter 17.

SUMMARY

External analysis includes analyses of customers, competitors, markets, and the environment. The components of each are summarized in Figure 2.1. The role of these analyses is to identify existing or emerging opportunities, threats, trends, strategic questions, and, ultimately, strategic options.

Self-analysis begins with an appraisal of performance, which should include not only financial performance but also indicators of long-term health such as customer satisfaction and delivered and perceived product quality. It should also include an examination of determinants of strategic options such as strategic problems and organizational capabilities and constraints. One role of self-analysis is to identify organizational strengths, weaknesses, problems, and constraints. Successful strategies often build on organizational strengths or competitor weaknesses.

The mission statement can play several roles, one of which is to provide a way to consider different strategy options without becoming immersed in detailed analysis. Identification of strategic options involves considering the product-market scope and degree of vertical integration. The concept of a product-market matrix and its associated growth directions can be useful for providing a dynamic perspective to strategy. A strategy choice includes specification of the investment decision with alternatives such as withdraw, milk, hold, or enter/grow. In addition, a strategy will involve functional area strategies and the development or maintenance of assets and skills to serve as the bases of SCAs.

Strategies should be selected that are responsive to the external environment as indicated by strategic questions, reflect threats and opportunities, include an SCA, are consistent with vision/objectives, are feasible, and fit with the other firm strategies. The process should be more iterative than sequential.

FOOTNOTES

[1] Richard W. Stevenson, "The Popsicle's Rejuvenation," *The New York Times,* July 18, 1986, p. D1.

[2] Fleming Meeks, "Preserving the Magic," *Forbes,* February 18, 1991, pp. 60–62.

[3] Drawn from John Small, "Pudding Pops: The Story Behind Their Success," *Prepared Foods,* April 1985, pp. 130–133.

[4] Theodore Levitt, "Marketing Myopia," *Harvard Business Review,* July–August 1960, pp. 45–56.

PART TWO

EXTERNAL ANALYSIS

3

CUSTOMER ANALYSIS

The purpose of an enterprise is to create and keep a customer.

Theodore Levitt

Consumers are statistics. Customers are People.

Stanley Marcus

Strategy development or review logically starts with external analysis, an analysis of the factors external to a business that can affect strategy. The four chapters of Part Two present concepts and methods useful in conducting an external analysis.

EXTERNAL ANALYSIS

A successful external analysis needs to be directed and purposeful. There is always the danger that it will become an endless process resulting in an excessively descriptive report. In any business there is no end to the material that appears potentially relevant which could be assembled. Without discipline and direction, volumes of useless descriptive material can easily be generated.

Affecting Strategic Decisions

The external analysis process should not be an end in itself. Rather, it should be motivated throughout by a desire to affect strategy, to generate or evaluate strategic options. As Figure 3.1 shows, it can impact strategy directly by suggesting strategic decision alternatives or influencing a choice among them. More specifically, it should contribute to the investment decision, the selection of functional area strategies, and the development of a sustainable competitive advantage.

The investment decision—where to compete—involves questions like

- Should existing business areas be liquidated, milked, maintained, or invested for growth?
- What growth directions should receive investment?

FIGURE 3.1 The Role of External Analysis

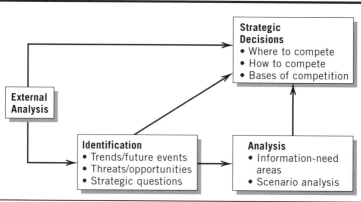

- Should there be market penetration, product expansion, or market expansion?
- Should new business areas be entered?

The selection of functional area strategies—how to compete—suggests questions like

- What functional area strategies should be implemented?
- What should be the positioning strategy, segmentation strategy, distribution strategy, manufacturing strategy, and so on?

The development of sustainable competitive advantages (SCAs)—the bases of competition—includes questions like

- What are the key success factors?
- What skills and assets should be created, enhanced, or maintained?

Additional Analysis Objectives

Figure 3.1 also suggests that an external analysis can contribute to strategy indirectly by identifying

- Significant trends and future events.
- Threats and opportunities.
- Strategic questions, key areas of uncertainty that could affect strategy outcomes.

A significant trend or event, such as concern with saturated fat or the emergence of a new competitor, can dramatically affect the evaluation of strategy options. A new technology can represent both a threat to an established firm and an opportunity to a prospective competitor.

Strategic Questions

A strategic question, a particularly useful concept in conducting an external analysis, involves an area of uncertainty that has the potential to affect strategy. If you could know the answer to one question prior to making a strategic commitment, what would that question be? Important strategic questions for Dreyer's Ice Cream, a strong West Coast premium ice cream firm, as it considers options with respect to the superpremium market might include

- What are Pillsbury's plans for Häagen-Dazs in the West?
- What will consumer response be to Dreyer's expansion into the superpremium category?

Strategic Questions	
Strategic Questions	**Strategic Decisions**
• Will a major firm enter?	• Investment in a product market
• Will a tofu-based dessert product be accepted?	• Investment in a tofu-based product
• Will a technology be replaced?	• Investment in a technology
• Will the dollar strengthen against an off-shore currency?	• Commitment to off-shore manufacturing
• Will computer-based operations be feasible with current technology?	• Investment in a new system
• How sensitive is the market to price?	• A strategy of maintaining price parity

A strategic question is different from a strategic decision in that it focuses on uncertainties that will affect outcomes of strategic decisions. "Should Dreyer's extend its brand to the superpremium category?" is a strategic decision. "What will the consumer response be to Dreyer's expansion?" is a strategic question. Most strategic decisions will be driven by a set of strategic questions. Above are some examples of strategic questions and the strategic decisions to which they might relate.

Strategic questions often suggest subquestions. One common strategic question is, "What will be the future demand for a product?" such as ultrasound diagnostic equipment, for example. Asking "On what does that depend?" will usually generate useful subquestions. One subquestion might address uncertainty about technological improvements, whereas another might consider the technological development and cost/benefit levels achieved by competitive technologies. Still another might look into the financial capacity of the healthcare industry to continue capital improvements. Each of these subquestions can, in turn, generate still another level of sub-subquestions.

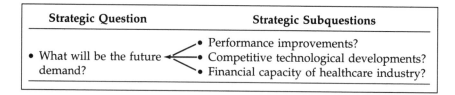

Strategic Question	Strategic Subquestions
• What will be the future demand?	• Performance improvements? • Competitive technological developments? • Financial capacity of healthcare industry?

Analysis

There is usually substantial uncertainty surrounding events/trends and threats/opportunities as well as strategic questions. There are three ways of handling that uncertainty as suggested by Figure 3.1. First, a strategic decision can be precipitated because the logic for a decision is compelling and/or because a delay would be costly or risky. Second, it is worthwhile to attempt to reduce the uncertainty by information acquisition and analysis of an "information need area." The effort could range from a high-priority task force to a low-key monitoring effort. The level of resources expended will depend upon the potential impact on strategy and its immediacy. Third, the uncertainty could be modeled by a scenario analysis.

A scenario is an alternative view of the future environment that is usually prompted by an alternative possible answer to a strategic question or by a prospective future event or trend. Is the New Age beverage a fad like wine coolers were or is it a solid growth area? Such a question could be the basis for a positive and a negative scenario. Each could be associated with very different environmental profiles and strategy recommendations. In Chapter 6, the last chapter in the external analysis section, information-need areas and scenario analysis will be covered in more detail.

A host of concepts and methods are introduced in this and the following three chapters. It would, of course, be unusual to employ all of them in any given context, and the strategist should resist any compulsion to do so. Rather, those that are most relevant to the situation at hand should be selected. Furthermore, some areas of analysis will be more fruitful than others and will merit more effort.

External Analysis as a Creative Exercise

In part, external analysis is an exercise in creative thinking. In fact, there is often too little effort devoted to developing new strategic options and too much effort directed to solving operational problems of the day. The essence of creative thinking is to consider different perspectives. That is exactly what an external analysis does. The strategist is challenged to look at strategy from the perspectives of customer, competitor, market, and environmental analysis. Within each there are several subdimensions. In Figure 2.1 two dozen are identified. The hope is that by examining strategy from different viewpoints, options will be generated that would otherwise be missed.

The Level of Analysis—Defining the Market

An external analysis of what? To conduct an external analysis the market or submarket boundaries need to be specified. The scope of external analysis can involve an industry such as

Sporting goods or
Ski clothing and equipment or
Skis and snowboards or
Downhill skis or
Fat Boys (extra wide skis designed for powder snow)

The level of analysis will depend on the organizational unit and strategic decisions that are involved. A sporting goods company such as Wilson will be making resource decisions across sports and thus needs to be concerned with the whole industry. A ski equipment manufacturer may only be concerned with elements of sporting goods relating to skis, boots, and clothing. The maker of Fat Boys might be interested in only a subsegment of the ski industry. One approach to defining the market is to specify the business scope. The scope can be identified in terms of the product market and in terms of the competitors. Relevant, of course, are the future product market and competitors as well as the present.

There is always a trade-off to be made. A narrow scope specification will inhibit a business from identifying trends and opportunities that could lead to some attractive options and directions. Thus, a maker of downhill skis may want to include snowboards and cross-country skis because they represent business options or because they will impact the ski equipment business. On the other hand, depth of analysis might be sacrificed when the scope is excessively broad. A more focused analysis may generate more insight.

The analysis usually needs to be conducted at several levels. The downhill ski and snowboard industry might be the major focus of the analysis. However, an analysis of sporting goods might suggest and shed light on some substitute product pressures and market trends. Also, an analysis may be needed at the segment level (e.g., Fat Boys) because entry, investment, and strategy decisions are often made at that level. Furthermore, the key success factors could differ for different product markets within a market or industry. One approach is a layered analysis, with the primary level obtaining the most depth of analysis. Another approach could be multiple analyses, perhaps consecutively conducted. The first analysis might stimulate an opportunity that would justify a second analysis.

When Should an External Analysis Be Conducted?

There is often a tendency to relegate the external analysis to an annual exercise. Each year, of course, it may not require the same depth as the initial effort. It may be more productive to focus on a part of the analysis in the years immediately following major effort.

The annual planning cycle can provide a healthy stimulus to review and change strategies. However, a substantial risk exists in maintaining external analysis as an annual event. The need for strategic review and change is often continuous. Information sensing and analysis therefore also need to be continuous. The framework and concepts of external analysis can still play a key role in providing structure even when the analysis is on-line and addresses only a portion of the whole.

Kathleen Eisenhardt studied 12 microcomputer firms in depth, focusing on the pace of strategic decision making.[1] One finding revealed that firms that make fast decisions tend to obtain internal and external information on a real-time basis. The implications of significant new information are discussed at regular meetings and multiple strategic options are developed so that alternative fallback plans are usually in place. Of course, such firms are operating in a hyperactive industry, but still the lesson that on-line strategy development leads to faster decision making is instructive.

External analysis deliberately commences with customer and competitor analyses because they can serve in many contexts to define the relevant industry or industries. An industry can be defined in terms of the needs of a specific group of customers—those buying fresh cookies on the West Coast, for instance. Such an industry definition then forms the basis for the identification of competitors and the balance of external analysis. An industry such as the cookie industry can also be defined in terms of all its competitors: Mrs. Fields, Otis Spunkmeyer, David's, and others.

Because customers have such a direct relationship to a firm's operation, they are usually a rich source of relevant operational opportunities, threats, and questions.

THE SCOPE OF CUSTOMER ANALYSIS

In most strategic market-planning contexts, the first logical step is to analyze the customers. Customer analysis consists of addressing the three sets of strategic questions that are shown in Figure 3.2.

SEGMENTATION

Segmentation is often the key to developing a sustainable competitive advantage based on differentiation, low cost, or a focus strategy. Kenichi Ohmae, the longtime head of McKinsey in Japan, tells of a forklift firm that obtained an SCA in part by focusing on the retailing and construction industries. The firm left the more demanding segments in the heavy-duty harbor and logging applications to its competitors.[2] The focused product line developed a 20 percent cost advantage and still served the needs of

FIGURE 3.2 Customer Analysis

SEGMENTATION

- Who are the biggest customers? The most profitable? The most attractive potential customers? Do the customers fall into any logical groups based on needs, motivations, or characteristics?
- How should the market be segmented into groups that would require a unique business strategy? Consider variables such as
  - Benefits sought
  - Usage level
  - Application
  - Organization type
  - Geographic location
  - Customer loyalty
  - Price sensitivity

CUSTOMER MOTIVATION

- What elements of the product/service do customers value most?
- What are the customers' objectives? What are they really buying?
- How do segments differ in their motivation priorities?
- What changes are occurring in customer motivation?

UNMET NEEDS

- Why are some customers dissatisfied? Why are some changing brands or suppliers?
- What are the severity and incidence of consumer problems?
- What are unmet needs that customers can identify? Are there some of which consumers are unaware?
- Do these unmet needs represent leverage points for competitors?

---

more than 80 percent of the forklift truck market. The lower-priced, value-engineered product line soon swept to a dominant position.

In a strategic context, segmentation means the identification of customer groups that respond differently than other customer groups to competitive strategies. A segmentation strategy couples the identified segments with a program to deliver a competitive offering to those segments. Thus, the development of a successful segmentation strategy requires the conceptualization, development, and evaluation of a competitive offering.

How Should Segments Be Defined?

The task of identifying segments is difficult, in part, because in any given context there are literally millions of ways to divide up the market. Typically, the analysis will consider five, ten, or more segmentation variables. To avoid missing a useful way of defining segments, it is important to consider a wide range of variables. These variables need to be evaluated on the basis of their ability to identify segments for which different strategies are (or should be) pursued.

A segment justifying a unique strategy needs to be of worthwhile size to support a business strategy. Furthermore, that business strategy needs to be effective with respect to the target segment in order to be cost-effective. In general, it is costly to develop a strategy for a segment. The question usually is whether or not the effectiveness of the strategy will compensate for this added cost.

The selection of the most useful segment-defining variables is rarely obvious. Among the variables frequently used are those shown in Figure 3.3.

FIGURE 3.3   Examples of Approaches to Defining Segments

CUSTOMER CHARACTERISTICS

• Geographic	• Small Southern communities as markets for discount stores
• Type of organization	• Computer needs of restaurants versus manufacturing firms versus banks versus retailers
• Size of firm	• Large hospital versus medium versus small
• Lifestyle	• Jaguar buyers tend to be more adventurous, less conservative than buyers of Mercedes-Benz and BMW
• Sex	• The Virginia Slims cigarettes for women
• Age	• Cereals for children versus adults
• Occupation	• The paper copier needs of lawyers versus bankers versus dentists

PRODUCT-RELATED APPROACHES

• User type	• Appliance buyer—home builder, remodeler, homeowner
• Usage	• The heavy potato user—the fast-food outlets
• Benefits sought	• Dessert eaters—those who are calorie-conscious versus those who are more concerned with convenience
• Price sensitivity	• Price-sensitive Honda Civic buyer versus the luxury Mercedes-Benz buyer
• Competitor	• Those computer users now committed to IBM
• Application	• Professional users of chain saws versus the homeowner
• Brand loyalty	• Those committed to IBM versus others

The first set of variables shown describes segments in terms of general characteristics unrelated to the product involved. Thus, a bakery might be concerned with geographic segments, focusing on one or more regions or even neighborhoods. It might also divide its market into organizational types such as at-home customers, restaurants, dining operations in schools, hospitals, and so on. Demographics can define segments representing strategic opportunities such as single parents, professional women, and the elderly.

Marriott, for example, embarked on a $1 billion, 10-year strategy to build 200 nursing and "life-care" retirement communities for the elderly.[3] They capitalized on their proven skill in running hotels, restaurants, and a food service business as well as dramatic growth in the target segments. The number of people over 65, which stood at 32 million in 1990, will become 50 million in 2020, when more than 5 million will be 85 or older.

The second category of segment variables includes those that are related to the product. One of the most frequently employed is usage. A bakery may employ a very different strategy in serving restaurants that are heavy users of bakery products than restaurants that use fewer bakery products. Zenith has made a niche for itself in the very competitive personal computer industry by focusing on the government, the largest computer user.

Segmenting by competitor is also useful because it frequently leads to a well-defined strategy and a strong positioning statement. Thus, a target customer group for the Toyota Cressida consists of buyers of high-performance European cars such as the BMW. The Cressida is positioned against the BMW as the car that has a performance comparable to that of the BMW, but at substantially less cost. Four other useful segment variables are benefits, price sensitivity, loyalty, and applications.

Benefit Segmentation

If there is a "most useful" segmentation variable, it would be benefits sought from a product, because the selection of benefits can determine a total business strategy. In gourmet frozen dinners/entrées, for example, the market can be divided into buyers who are calorie-conscious, those who focus on nutrition and health, those interested in taste, and the price-conscious buyers. Each segment implies a very different strategy.

Price Sensitivity

The benefit dimension representing the trade-off between low price and high quality is so useful and pervasive that it is appropriate to consider it separately. In many product classes, there is a well-defined breakdown between those customers concerned first about price and others who are willing to pay extra for higher quality and features. General merchandise stores, for example, form a well-defined hierarchy from the discounters to the prestige department stores. Automobiles span the spectrum from the Honda Civic to the Lexus to the Rolls Royce. Airline service is partitioned into first class, business class, and economy class. In each case the segment dictates the strategy.

Loyalty

Brand loyalty, an important consideration in allocating resources, can be structured using a loyalty matrix as shown in Figure 3.4.[4] Each cell represents a very different strategic priority and can justify a very different program. Generally it is too easy to take the loyal customer for granted. However, a perspective of total profits over the life of a customer makes the value of an increase in loyalty more vivid. A study by Bain shows that a 5 percent increase in loyalty can nearly double the lifetime profits generated by customers in several industries such as banking, insurance, automobile service, publishing, and credit cards.[5] The loyalty matrix suggests that the brand fence sitters, including those of competitors, should also have high priority. Using the matrix involves estimating the size of each of the six cells, identifying the customers in each group, and designing programs that will influence their brand choice and loyalty level.

Application Segmentation

Some products and services, particularly industrial products, can best be segmented by use or application. A portable computer may be needed by some for use while traveling, whereas others may need a computer at the office that can be conveniently stored when not in use. One segment may use a computer for word processing and another may be more interested in data processing. Some might use a four-wheel drive for light industrial hauling and others may be buying primarily for recreation.

FIGURE 3.4   The Loyalty Matrix: Priorities

	Switchers	Fence sitters	Loyal
Customer	Medium	High	Highest
Noncustomer	Low to Medium	High	Low

The athletic shoe industry segments into the serious athletes, small in number but influential, the weekend warriors, and the casual wearers using athletic shoes for streetwear. Recognizing that the casual-wearer segment is 80 percent of the market and does not really need performance, several shoe firms such as L.A. Gear have employed a style-focused strategy as an alternative to the performance strategy adopted by firms such as Nike.

Multiple Segments Versus a Focus Strategy

Two distinct segmentation strategies are possible. The first focuses on a single segment, which can be much smaller than the market as a whole. Wal-Mart, now the largest U.S. retailer, started by concentrating on cities with populations under 25,000 in 11 South Central states, a segment totally neglected by its competition, the large discount chains. This rural geographic focus strategy was directly responsible for several significant SCAs, including an efficient and responsive warehouse supply system, a low-cost, motivated work force, relatively inexpensive retail space, and a "lean and mean," hands-on management style. Union Bank, California's eighth largest bank, makes no effort to serve individuals and thus provides a service operation tailored to business accounts that is more committed and comprehensive than those of its competitors.

An alternative to a focusing strategy is to involve multiple segments. General Motors provides the classic example. In the 1920s the firm positioned the Chevrolet for price-conscious buyers, the Cadillac for the high end, and the Oldsmobile, Pontiac, and Buick for well-defined segments in between. A granulated potato company has developed different strategies for reaching fast-food chains, hospitals and nursing homes, and schools and colleges.

In many industries aggressive firms are moving toward multiple-segment strategies. Campbell Soup, for example, makes its nacho cheese soup spicier for Texas and California customers and offers a Creole soup for Southern markets and a red-bean soup for Hispanic areas. In New York, Campbell uses promotions linking Swanson frozen dinners with the New York Giants football team, and in the Sierra mountains, skiers are treated to hot soup samples. Developing multiple strategies is costly and often must be justified by an enhanced aggregate impact.

There can be important synergies between segment offerings. For example, in the alpine ski industry, the image developed by high-performance skis is important to sales at the recreational-ski end of the business. Thus, a manufacturer that is weak at the high end will have difficulty at the low end. Conversely, a successful high-end firm will want to exploit that success by having entries in the other segments. A key success factor in the general aviation industry is to have a broad product line from fixed-gear, single-engine piston aircraft to turboprop planes, because customers tend to trade up and will switch to a different firm if the product line has major gaps.

CUSTOMER MOTIVATIONS

After identifying customer segments, the next step is to consider their motivations: What lies behind their purchase decisions? And how does that differ by segment? It is helpful to list the segments and the motivation priority of each, as shown in Figure 3.5 for air travelers.

Some motivations will help to define strategy. A truck, for example, might be designed and positioned with respect to power. Before making such a strategic commitment it is crucial to know where power fits in the motivation set. Other motivations may not define a strategy or differentiate a business, but represent a dimension for which adequate performance must be obtained or the battle will be lost. If the prime motivation for buyers of gourmet frozen-food dinners is taste, a viable firm must be able to deliver at least acceptable taste.

As Figure 3.6 suggests, consumer motivation analysis starts with the task of identifying motivations for a given segment. Although a group of managers can identify motivations, a more valid list is usually obtained by getting customers to discuss the product or service in a systematic way. Why is it being used? What is the objective? What is associated with a good or bad use experience? For a motivation like car safety, respondents might be asked why safety is important. Such probes might result in the identification of more basic motives like feeling calm and secure rather than anxious.

Customers can be accessed with group or individual interviews. Griffin and Hauser of the MIT Quality Function Deployment (QFD) program compared the two approaches in a study of food-carrying devices.[6] They found that individual interviews were more cost-effective, and that the group processes did not generate enough extra information to warrant the added expense. They also explored the number of interviews needed

FIGURE 3.5   Customer Motivation Grid: Air Travelers

Segment	Motivation
Business	Reliable service, convenient schedules, easy-to-use airports, frequent-flyer programs, and comfortable service
Vacationers	Price, feasible schedules

The Campbell Soup "Hot Button" List

Campbell Soup has identified a set of consumer motivations or "hot buttons," which they use to understand market dynamics and guide strategy development.[7] These "hot buttons" include

- Flavor. An interest in both strong, perhaps ethnic, tastes and light, delicate tastes have led to more spices, wines, and other flavorings and less salt, MSG, and bland sauces or gravies.
- Freshness and naturalness. A national love affair with salad and the more natural taste of refrigerated foods has resulted in growth in salad bars, the produce section, and the refrigerated case.
- Healthfulness. As a result of concern about additives, salt, sugar, and fat, a host of "low-sodium" and "reduced-fat" products have emerged.
- Variety. The willingness of consumers to pay for "gourmet," interesting cuisines has led to the introduction of exotic foods into the supermarket.
- Convenience. The desire of increasingly busy and affluent consumers to minimize preparation and cleanup has led to growth in take-out and home delivery.
- Portion control. Single serving packaging is responsive to demands from singles who wish to avoid wasting both food and money.

---

to gain a complete list of motivations and concluded that 20 to 30 will recover 90 to 95 percent of the motivations.

The list of motivations can be in the hundreds, so the next task is to cluster them into groups and subgroups. Affinity charts developed by a managerial team are commonly used. Each team member is given a set of motives on cards. One member puts a motive on the table or pins it to a wall and the others add "similar" cards to the pile, discussing the decision to do so. The process continues until there is a consensus that the piles represent reasonable groupings. Each pile is then structured into a hierarchy with the more general, strategic, and "effect" motives at the top and the more specific, tactical, and "causal" at the bottom.

An alternative is to use customers or groups of customers to sort the motives into piles. The customers are then asked to select one card from

FIGURE 3.6   Customer Motivation Analysis

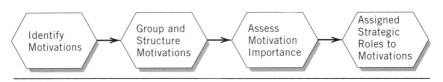

Whirlpool Listens to Customers

Each year Whirlpool mails a survey to 180,000 households asking them to rate all their appliances on dozens of attributes.[8] When a competitor gets a higher rating on an attribute, the Whirlpool engineers make sure they find out why. The answer often suggests improvements in the Whirlpool brand.

Sometimes the consumers' judgments from the annual survey and other studies need decoding. For example, when consumers said they wanted clean refrigerators, they were not really talking about being easy to clean. Rather, they wanted refrigerators that looked clean. In response, Whirlpool introduced models with stucco-like fronts and sides that hid fingerprints. Consumers said they wanted an easy-to-clean range, but prior efforts to replace dials with electronic push pads like those on microwaves had faced considerable consumer resistance. The key was to design a range with the guidance of a panel of consumers that tried out each iteration. The result was a truly user-friendly set of touch-pad controls.

---

each pile that best represents their motives. When a set of customers or groups go through the exercise, the judgments can be combined using cluster analysis statistical programs. Although managers gain "buy-in" and learning by going through the process themselves, Griffin and Hauser report that in the 20 applications at one firm, the managers considered customer-based approaches to be better representations than their own.

Another task of customer-motivation analysis is to determine the relative importance of the motivations. Again, the management team can address the issue. Alternatively, customers can be asked to assess the importance of the motivations directly or perhaps use trade-off questions. If an engineer has to sacrifice either response time or accuracy in his or her oscilloscope, which would it be? Or how would an airline passenger trade off convenient departure time with price? The trade-off question asks customers to make difficult judgments about attributes. Another approach is to see which judgments are associated with actual purchase decisions. Such an approach revealed that mothers often selected snack food based on what "the child likes" and what was "juicy" instead of qualities they had said were important (nourishing and easy to eat).

A fourth task is to identify the motivations that will play a role in defining the strategy of the business. The selection of motivation that will be central to strategy will depend not only on customer motivations, but other factors as well. It will depend in part on competitors' strategies, which will emerge in the competitor analysis. Another factor is how feasible and practical the resulting strategy is for the business. Self-analysis will be involved in making that determination, as will an analysis of the strategy's implementation.

Stop N Go Looks to the Customer

In the mature convenience store industry, Stop N Go developed a spurt of growth by looking toward the changing customer.[9] Whereas the typical convenience store is a small, cramped store featuring cigarettes, beer, soft drinks, fast food, and junk food, roomy new Stop N Go stores feature bright lights, decorative shelving, and trendy products such as fresh pasta, frozen yogurt, and deli items—a customer with an interest in health and nutrition will not be repelled. Stop N Go also has segmented the market into mainstream, upscale, and Hispanic components. Hispanic stores include a Mayan welcome sign as a logo and a host of Mexican-made products. A black-oriented segment was not developed when it was found that preferences simply did not differ significantly from those of mainstream white customers.

UNMET NEEDS

An unmet need is a customer need that is not being met by the existing product offerings. For example, ski areas have a need for snowmaking equipment that can access steep, advanced trails. Buyers of chocolate could use a healthy candy category and also more variety. Sales of small portable computers were held back for years because the industry lacked flat displays with adequate quality and reasonable cost. An unmet need for used personal computers was filled by firms now doing a large business matching sellers and buyers. Users of baby food have a need for packages that are unbreakable, microwavable, and environmentally sound. A major extension of the temporary-services industry has been created by firms responding to an unmet need for temporary lawyers, high-tech specialists, and doctors.

Unmet needs are strategically important because they represent opportunities for firms to increase their market share or break into a market. They can also represent threats to established firms in that they can be a lever for competitors to disrupt an established position.

Sometimes customers may not even be aware of their unmet needs because they are so accustomed to the implicit limitations of existing equipment. The farmer of the 1890s would have longed for a horse that worked harder and ate less, but would not have mentioned a tractor in his or her wish list. The same computer user who now views a hard disk as indispensable might not have viewed file storage as an unmet need prior to the availability of hard disks. The unmet needs that are not obvious may be more difficult to identify, but they can also represent a greater opportunity for an aggressive business, because there will be little pressure on established firms to be responsive. The key is to stretch the technology or apply new technologies in order to expose unmet needs.

User-Developed Products

For an internal application, IBM designed and built the first printed circuit card insertion machine of a particular type to be used in commercial production.[10] After building and testing the design in-house, IBM sent engineering drawings of its design to a local machine builder, along with an order for eight units. The machine builder completed this and subsequent orders and applied to IBM for permission to build essentially the same machine for sale on the open market. IBM agreed, and as a result, the machine builder became a major force in the component insertion equipment business.

In the early 1970s store owners and sales personnel in Southern California began to notice that youngsters were fixing up their bicycles to look like motorcycles, complete with imitation tailpipes and "chopper-type" handlebars. Sporting crash helmets and Honda motorcycle T-shirts, the youngsters raced fancy 20-inchers on dirt tracks. Obviously onto a good thing, the manufacturers came out with a whole new line of "motocross" models. California users refined this concept into the mountain bike. Manufacturers were guided by the California customers to develop new refinements, including the 21-speed gear shift that eliminates removing one's hand from the bars. Mountain bike firms are enjoying booming growth, and are still watching their West Coast customers.

Using Customers to Identify Unmet Needs

Customers are a prime source of unmet needs. The trick is to access them, to get customers to detect and communicate unmet needs. The first step is to conduct market research using individual or group interviews. The research usually starts with a discussion of an actual product use experience. What problems have emerged? What is frustrating about it? How does it compare with other product experiences? With expectations? Are there problems with the total-use system in which the product is embedded? How can the product be improved? This kind of research helped Dow come up with Spiffits, a line of premoistened, disposable cleaning towels that addressed the need for a towel that was already moistened with a cleaning compound.

A panel of customers can provide more in-depth insights. Black & Decker developed their line of Quantum midpriced tools by forming a panel of 50 Do-It-Yourselfers (DIYs) who owned more than six power tools.[11] Executives of Black & Decker hung out with panelists in their homes and saw firsthand how the tools were used and the problems and frustrations that were experienced. One of the problems observed was that cordless drills ran out of power before the job was done. The solution was a drill with a detachable battery pack that recharged in an hour. Sawdust problems prompted a saw and sander with a bag that acted as a mini-vacuum. To address safety issues an auto braking system (ABS) was built into the saws.

Customer surveys can play an important role as can the monitoring of customer complaints. USAA, the successful Texas financial services company, mails 500,000 questionnaires to customers every year and includes some open-ended questions about problems and new product ideas. As a result the firm has launched several mutual funds. At Hewlett-Packard each customer complaint is assigned to an employee who becomes its "owner" and not only makes sure that the customer receives a response but determines if a new product or service is suggested by the problem.

A structured approach, termed *problem research*, develops a list of potential problems with the product.[12] The problems are then prioritized by asking a group of 100 to 200 respondents to rate each problem as to whether (1) the problem is important, (2) the problem occurs frequently, and (3) a problem solution exists. A problem score is obtained by combining these ratings. A dog-food problem research study found that buyers felt dog food smelled bad, cost too much, and was not available in different sizes for different dogs. Subsequently, products responsive to these criticisms emerged. Another study led an airline to modify its cabins to provide more legroom.

From Unmet Needs to New Products.   One reaction to the identification of an unmet need is for a firm to develop a product or product modification that will be responsive. Sometimes customers will not only have identified problems but will have even developed products to solve them. MIT professor Eric von Hippel has conducted studies to determine the source of new products, and he has concluded that in some industries most new products are actually developed by customers.[13] For example, users developed 80 percent of new scientific instruments studied by von Hippel and more than 60 percent of semiconductor manufacturing equipment innovations. It might be worthwhile to identify those users that are so motivated and capable of developing useful products.

Von Hippel also notes that some firms solicit customer-based new products. The Pillsbury Bake-Off Contest has contributed one of Pillsbury's cake products and several other product improvements. IBM has long had a department that acquires user-developed programs designed to run on its computers.

Using Lead Users

Von Hippel suggests that "lead users" provide a particularly good source of unmet needs and new product concepts. Lead users are users that[14]

- Face needs that will be general in the marketplace, but face them months or years before the bulk of the marketplace. A person who is very "into" health foods and nutrition would be a lead user with respect to health foods, if we assume that there is a trend toward health foods.

- Are positioned to benefit significantly by obtaining a solution to those needs. Lead users of office automation would be firms that today would benefit significantly from technological advancement.

In addition, von Hippel suggests that lead users can be used to evaluate novel product concepts, as well as help identify them. Other potential users may find a novel concept too foreign to evaluate. Consider products such as minivans, microwave ovens, instant coffee, the personal computer, home-rental movies, a photocopying machine, an office automation system, or a completely new food product before they were introduced. Lead users are often better suited to visualize the new product, its application, and its benefits.

The challenge is to identify lead users. In a computer-aided design (CAD) application, the search for lead users involved identifying engineers who were considered experts in the use of existing CAD systems, who had developed and built their own CAD system, and who had devised applications involving the design of multiple layered boards with a high density of chips (which would thus benefit from CAD improvements).

SUMMARY

The goal of external analysis is to influence strategy by identifying opportunities, threats, trends, and strategic questions. Its ultimate goal is to improve strategic choices—decisions as to where and how to compete.

Customer analysis involves an examination of customer segmentation, motivations, and unmet needs. Segmentation means the identification of customer groups that can support different competitive strategies. Segmentation approaches include benefits sought, the price/quality dimension, customer loyalty, and application. A business can focus on a single segment or attempt to serve multiple segments, perhaps obtaining across-segment synergies.

A knowledge of motivation—what is important to customers and why they buy certain products and brands—can provide insights into what assets and skills are needed to compete and can form the bases of SCAs. Motivations can be identified through marketing research approaches such as asking attribute importance or trade-off questions.

An unmet need, a customer need that is not being met by the existing product offerings, can be strategically important because it may represent opportunities for those attempting to gain position and may pose threats to those attempting to maintain position. Customers can be used to identify unmet needs. "Lead users," users that face needs that will become more prevalent in the future and are thus positioned to benefit significantly, are particularly good sources of unmet needs and new product concepts.

FOOTNOTES

[1] Kathleen M. Eisenhardt, "Speed and Strategic Choice: How Managers Accelerate Decision Making," *California Management Review*, Spring 1990, pp. 39–54.

[2] Kenichi Ohmae, *The Mind of the Strategist*, New York: Penguin Books, 1982, pp. 43–46.

[3] Paul Farhi, "Marriott Corp. Gambles $1 Billion on Communities for Elderly," *Adweek's Marketing Week*, March 6, 1989, pp. 28–31.

[4] International Data Group, "How to Target, A Profit-Based Segmentation of the PC Industry," November 1993.

[5] Patricia Sellers, "Keeping the Buyers You Already Have," *Fortune*, Autumn/Winter 1993, pp. 56–58.

[6] Abbie Griffin and John R. Hauser, "The Voice of the Customer," *Marketing Science*, Winter 1993, pp. 1–27.

[7] Gordon McGovern, "The Consumer Revolution in the Supermarket," *The Journal of Business Strategy* Vol. 5, Fall 1984, pp. 93–95.

[8] "How to Listen to Consumers," *Fortune*, January 11, 1993, p. 77.

[9] Kevin Helliker, "Stop N Go's Van Horn Wants to Reinvent the Convenience Store," *The Wall Street Journal*, February 6, 1991.

[10] Eric von Hippel, "Leads Users: A Source of Novel Product Concepts," *Management Science*, July 1986, p. 802.

[11] Susan Caminti, "A Star is Born," *Fortune*, Autumn/Winter 1993, pp. 45–47.

[12] E. E. Norris, "Seek Out the Consumer's Problem," *Advertising Age*, March 17, 1975, pp. 43–44.

[13] Glen L. Urban and Eric von Hippel, "Lead User Analyses for the Development of New Industrial Products," *Management Science*, May 1988, pp. 569–582; Eric von Hippel, "Get New Products from Customers," *Harvard Business Review*, March–April 1982, pp. 117–122.

[14] Eric von Hippel, "Leads Users: A Source of Novel Product Concepts," *Management Science*, July 1986, p. 802.

4

COMPETITOR ANALYSIS

Induce your competitors not to invest in those products, markets and services where you expect to invest the most . . . that is the fundamental rule of strategy.

Bruce Henderson, Founder of BCG

There is nothing more exhilarating than to be shot at without result.

Winston Churchill

There are numerous well-documented reasons why the Japanese automobile firms were able to penetrate the U.S. market successfully, especially during the 1970s. One important reason, however, is that they were much better at doing competitor analysis than U.S. firms.[1]

Halberstam, in his account of the automobile industry, graphically described the Japanese efforts at competitor analysis in the 1960s. "They came in groups. . . . They measured, they photographed, they sketched, and they tape-recorded everything they could. Their questions were precise. They were surprised how open the Americans were."[2] The Japanese similarly studied European manufacturers, especially their design approaches. In contrast, according to Halberstam, the Americans were late in even recognizing the competitive threat from Japan and never did well at analyzing the competitive environment they represented.

Competitive analysis is the second phase of external analysis. Again, the goal should be on insights that will influence the product-market investment decision or the effort to obtain or maintain an SCA. The analysis should focus on the identification of threats, opportunities, or strategic questions created by emerging or potential competitor moves, weaknesses, or strengths.

Competitor analysis starts with identifying current and potential competitors. There are two very different ways of identifying current competitors. The first examines the perspective of the customer who must make choices among competitors. The result is grouping competitors according to the degree they compete for a buyer's choice. The second type of identification approach attempts to place competitors into strategic groups on the basis of their competitive strategy.

After competitors are identified, the focus shifts to attempting to understand them and their strategies. Of particular interest is an analysis of the strengths and weaknesses of each competitor or strategic group of competitors. Figure 4.1 summarizes a set of questions that can provide a structure for competitor analysis.

IDENTIFYING COMPETITORS— CUSTOMER-BASED APPROACHES

In most instances, primary competitors are quite visible and easily identified. Thus, Calistoga competes with other sparkling mineral waters such as Perrier. However, it is usually worthwhile to look more closely at competitor identification. For example, Calistoga could also define its competitors by alternative criteria such as

- Carbonated water drinks including Canada Dry soda.
- Bottled water including Evian and Arrowhead.

FIGURE 4.1 Questions to Structure Competitor Analysis

WHO ARE THE COMPETITORS?

- Against whom do we usually compete? Who are our most intense competitors? Less intense but still serious competitors? Makers of substitute products?
- Can these competitors be grouped into strategic groups on the basis of their assets, skills, and/or strategies?
- Who are the potential competitive entrants? What are their barriers to entry? Is there anything that can be done to discourage them?

EVALUATING THE COMPETITORS

- What are their objectives and strategies? Their level of commitment? Their exit barriers?
- What is their cost structure? Do they have a cost advantage or disadvantage?
- What is their image and positioning strategy?
- Which are the most successful/unsuccessful competitors over time? Why?
- What are the strengths and weaknesses of each competitor or strategic group?
- What leverage points (our strategic weaknesses or customer problems/unmet needs) could competitors exploit to enter the market or become more serious competitors?
- Evaluate the competitors with respect to their assets and skills. Generate a competitor strength grid.

- Carbonated low-calorie drinks including Diet 7UP.
- Carbonated nonalcoholic drinks.
- All nonalcoholic product substitutes such as fruit drinks, canned fruit drinks, frozen fruit drinks, packaged drinks (e.g., Kool-Aid), milk, coffee, and tea.
- All purchased beverages including product substitutes like beer and wine.

Note that substitute products such as fruit drinks can be relevant competitors.

Similarly, the makers of granulated potato buds used by institutions and restaurants for making mashed potatoes could usefully distinguish among the following types of competitors:

- Granulated potato buds.
- Other dehydrated potato products.
- Whole potatoes used to make mashed potatoes.

- Substitute potato products such as french fries, hash browns, boiled potatoes, potatoes au gratin, and so on.
- Substitute starch dishes such as rice and pasta.
- Substitute side dishes such as vegetables.

Actually, substitute potato products may be more intense competitors to granulated potato buds in the short run than whole potatoes, because institutions may not be set up to process whole potatoes. Further, an institution may well substitute starch dishes if the price of mashed potatoes should increase. In fact, mashed potatoes have lost a share of side dishes over time to rice, pasta and even vegetables, because of changing attitudes toward health and nutrition.

These examples illustrate three principles:

- In most industries, competitors can be usefully portrayed in terms of how intensely they compete with the business that is motivating the analysis. There are usually several very direct competitors, others that compete less intensely, and still others that compete indirectly but are still relevant. A knowledge of this pattern can lead to a deeper understanding of the market structure. The groups that compete most intensely may merit the most in-depth study, but other groups may still require analysis.
- The definition of the most competitive groups will depend on a few key variables, and it may be strategically important to know the relative importance of these variables. Thus, with respect to cola drinks, the most important variable could be either cola/noncola, diet/nondiet, or caffeine/noncaffeine. If noncaffeine is the most important attribute for a segment, the appropriate strategy will be different than if nondiet is the most important factor.
- Substitute products can be extremely relevant. For example, rice and pastas are very real competitors to granulated potato buds and have affected their sales level and price structure over time.

Customer Choices

A knowledge of how to identify such groupings will be of conceptual as well as practical value. One approach is to focus on customer choice. A Pepsi buyer could be asked what brand would have been purchased if Pepsi had been out of stock. A buyer for a nursing home meal service could be asked what would be substituted for granulated potato buds if they increased in price. A sample of sports car buyers could be asked what other cars they considered and perhaps what other showrooms they actually visited.

Product-Use Associations

Another approach that provides additional insights is the association of products with specific use contexts or applications.[3] Perhaps 20 or 30 product users could be asked to identify a list of use situations or applications. For each use context they would then be asked to name all the products that are appropriate. For each product so identified, appropriate use contexts would be identified so that the list of use contexts would be more complete. Another group of respondents would then be asked to make judgments about how appropriate each product would be for each use context. Then products would be clustered, based on the similarity of their appropriate use contexts. Thus, if Pepsi was regarded as appropriate for snack occasions, it would compete primarily with products similarly perceived. The same approach will work with an industrial product that might be used in several distinct applications.

These two approaches suggest a conceptual basis for identifying competitors that can be employed by managers even when marketing research is not available. The concept of alternatives from which customers choose and the concept of appropriateness to a use context can be powerful tools in helping to understand the competitive environment.

IDENTIFYING COMPETITORS—STRATEGIC GROUPS

The concept of a strategic group provides a very different approach toward understanding the competitive structure of an industry. A strategic group is a group of firms that

- Over time pursue similar competitive strategies (e.g., the use of the same distribution channel and heavy advertising).
- Have similar characteristics (e.g., size, aggressiveness).
- Have similar assets and skills (e.g., quality image).

For example, in pet food, one strategic group consists of very large, diversified, branded consumer and food product companies. All distribute through supermarkets, have strong established brands, use advertising and promotions effectively, and enjoy economies of scale.[4] Ralston Purina, with a broad product line and a 27 percent share, is the volume and price leader, while Nestlé is in second place with particular strength in cat food. Heinz has a 9 percent share of the cat market with 9-Lives and Amore. Mars, through Pedigree and Whiskas, has an 11 percent share and a worldwide presence. Quaker is a weaker player focusing on dog food. A second strategic group of highly focused, ultra-premium, specialty producers like Hills Pet Products (Science Diet and Prescription Diet) and the Iams Company (Eukanuba and Iams) sell product through veterinary offices and specialty pet stores. They use referral networks to reach pet owners concerned with health. The third strategic group is private-label producers led by Doanne Products. Ralston also paticipates in this group.

A set of strategic groups includes a set of mobility barriers that inhibit or prevent businesses from moving from one strategic group to another.[5] For example, each of the pet food strategic groups is protected from entry by barriers. The second group has the brand reputation, product, and manufacturing knowledge for the "health segment," access to the influentials, and a local customer base. The private-label manufacturers have low-cost production, low overhead, and close relationships with customers. It is possible to bypass or overcome the barriers, of course. Ralston also makes some private-label products, drawing upon its private-label contacts in cereal and other categories. It is also targeting an entry into the second strategic group. The barriers are real, however, and a firm competing across strategic groups is usually at a disadvantage.

A member of a strategic group can have exit as well as entry barriers. For example, assets such as plant investment or a specialized labor force can represent a meaningful exit barrier.

The mobility barrier concept is crucial because one way to develop a sustainable competitive advantage is to pursue a strategy that is protected from competition by assets and skills that represent barriers to competitors. The existence of mobility barriers between strategic groups is supported by economic theory and by empirical studies. For example, Sharon Oster of Yale, in a study of 19 consumer products industries, defined strategic groups by the intensity of their advertising.[6] Mobility between groups over an eight-year period was found to be generally low—especially for industries in which high levels of advertising had likely created product differentiation barriers; industries like soap, drugs, and soft drinks as opposed to carpets, paint, and furniture. A study of the oil-well drilling industry in the 1970s classified 33 firms into three groups and found that only two movements occurred out of 109 possible opportunities.[7]

The strategy differences defining groups will depend on context, but could involve any of the elements of a business strategy introduced in Chapter 1. In particular, strategic groups could be defined by the following: the extent to which firms are engaged in milking versus growth strategies, which distribution channels they use, their position on the price/quality dimension, or the technology on which they rely. In any case, firms in different groups will have different bases on which they compete and different competitive advantages. They could also differ with respect to characteristics possibly having strategic importance such as firm size, diversification, and multinational presence.

Using the Strategic Group Concept

The conceptualization of strategic groups can make the process of competitor analysis more manageable. Numerous industries contain many more competitors than can be analyzed individually. Often it is simply not feasible to consider 30 competitors, to say nothing of hundreds. Reducing this set to a small number of strategic groups makes the analysis compact, feasible, and more usable. For example, in the wine industry, competitor analysis by an upscale wine maker such as Beringer or BV would probably consider the popular premium wine firms such as Gallo, Sebastiani, Sutter Home, and Glen Ellen as a strategic group because their strengths and strategies are similar. Furthermore, little strategic content and insight will be lost in most cases, because firms in a strategic group will be affected by and react to industry developments in similar ways. Thus, in projecting future strategies of competitors, the concept of strategic groups can be helpful.

Strategic groupings can refine the strategic investment decision. Instead of determining in which industries to invest, the decision can focus on what strategic group a firm should invest in. Thus, it will be necessary to determine the current profitability and future potential profitability of each strategic group. One strategic objective is to invest in attractive strategic groups in which assets and skills can be employed to create strategic advantage.

Ultimately the selection of a strategy and its supporting assets and skills will often mean selecting or creating a strategic group. Thus, a knowledge of the strategic group structure can be extremely useful.

Projecting Strategic Groups

The concept of strategic groups can also be helpful in projecting competitive strategies into the future. A McKinsey study of the effects of deregulation on five deregulated industries (summarized in Figure 4.2) forecasts with remarkable accuracy that successful firms will move toward one of three strategic groups.[8]

The evolution of the first group involves three phases. During the first phase, the medium and small firms attempt—usually unsuccessfully—to gain enough of a market share by merging to compete with the large firms. In the second phase, strong firms make acquisitions to fill in product lines or market gaps. During this phase, which occurs about three to five years following deregulation, the major firms try to develop broad product lines and distribution coverage. In the third phase, interindustry mergers occur. Strong firms merge with others outside their industry.

FIGURE 4.2 Strategic Groups Emerging from Deregulation

Group	Industry	Examples
1. National distribution company with full line of differentiated products and emphasis on attractive service/price trade-offs	Brokerage Airlines Trucking Railroads Business terminals	Merrill Lynch Delta Consolidated Freightways Burlington Northern Western Electric
2. Low-cost producer— often a new entrant following deregulation	Brokerage Airlines Trucking Railroads Business terminals	Charles Schwab Midway Air Overnite Transportation Oki
3. Specialty firm with strong customer loyalty and specialized service targeted toward an attractive customer group	Brokerage Airlines Trucking Railroads Business terminals	Goldman Sachs Air Wisconsin Ryder Systems Sante Fe Northern Telecom

The second strategic group consists of low-cost producers entering the industry after deregulation by providing simple product lines with minimal service to the price-sensitive segment. The third group includes those pursuing a focus strategy, with a specialized service targeted toward a specific customer group.

POTENTIAL COMPETITORS

In addition to current competitors, it is important to consider potential market entrants such as firms that might engage in

1. **Market expansion.** Perhaps the most obvious source of potential competitors is firms operating in other geographic regions or in other countries. A cookie company may want to keep a close eye on a competing firm in an adjacent state, for example.

2. **Product expansion.** The leading ski firm, Rossignol, has expanded into ski clothing, thus exploiting a common market, and has moved to tennis equipment, which takes advantage of technological and distribution overlap.

3. **Backward integration.** Customers are another potential source of competition. General Motors bought dozens of manufacturers of components during its formative years. Major can users such as Campbell Soup have integrated backward, making their own containers.

4. *Forward integration.* Suppliers are also potential competitors. AST, a major computer manufacturer, started out as a maker of add-on boards for IBM computers. Suppliers, believing they have the critical ingredients to succeed in a market, may be attracted by the margins and control that come with integrating forward.

5. *The export of assets or skills.* A current small competitor with critical strategic weaknesses can turn into a major entrant if it is purchased by a firm that can reduce or eliminate those weaknesses. Predicting such moves can be difficult, but sometimes an analysis of competitor strengths and weaknesses will suggest some possible synergistic mergers to watch for. A competitor in an above-average growth industry that does not have the financial or managerial resources for the long haul might be a particularly attractive candidate for merger.

6. *Retaliatory or defensive strategies.* Firms that are threatened by a potential or actual move into their market might retaliate. Thus, Microsoft moved into networking when Novell, the networking leader, made a major move into word processing, graphics, and spreadsheets by buying WordPerfect.

COMPETITOR ANALYSIS— UNDERSTANDING COMPETITORS

Understanding competitors and their activities can provide several benefits. First, an understanding of the current strategy strengths and weaknesses of a competitor can suggest opportunities and threats that will merit a response. Second, insights into future competitor strategies may allow the prediction of emerging threats and opportunities. Third, a decision about strategic alternatives might easily hinge on the ability to forecast the likely reaction of key competitors. Finally, competitor analysis may result in the identification of some strategic questions, questions that will be worth monitoring closely over time. A strategic question, for example, might be, "Will Competitor A decide to move into the western U.S. market?"

As Figure 4.3 indicates, competitor actions are influenced by eight elements. The first of these reflects financial performance, as measured by size, growth, and profitability.

Size, Growth, and Profitability

The level and growth of sales and market share provide indicators of the vitality of a business strategy. The maintenance of a strong market position or the achievement of rapid growth usually reflects a strong competitor

FIGURE 4.3 Understanding the Competitors

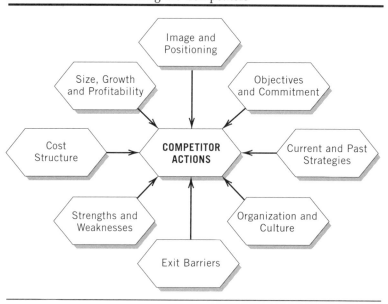

(or strategic group) and a successful strategy. In contrast, a deteriorating market position can signal financial or organizational strains that might affect the interest and ability of the business to pursue certain strategies.

After size and growth comes profitability. A profitable business will generally have access to capital for investment unless it has been designated by the parent to be milked. A business that has lost money over an extended time period or has experienced a recent sharp decrease in profitability may find it difficult to gain access to capital either externally or internally.

Image and Positioning Strategy

A cornerstone of a business strategy can be an association such as being the strongest truck, the most durable car, the smallest consumer electronics equipment, or the most effective cleaner. More often, it is useful to move beyond class-related product attributes to intangibles that span product class such as quality, innovation, or sensitivity to the environment. Thus, the global strategy for Gillette is driven by "the best a man can get." Faralon is a firm that connects computers using innovative technology. Innovation is a key element to their strategy and being perceived as innovative is an integral part of it. Another tack is to focus on personality and relationships. For example, WordPerfect is seen as concerned, caring, and "there for you" in contrast to Microsoft, which is perceived as dominating and arrogant.

In order to develop positioning alternatives, it is helpful to determine the image and brand personality of the major competitors. Weaknesses of competitors on relevant attributes or personality traits can represent an opportunity to differentiate and develop advantage. Strengths of competitors on important dimensions may represent challenges to exceed them or to outflank them. In any case it is important to know the competitive profiles before proceeding.

Competitor image and positioning information can in part be deduced by studying a firm's products, advertising, packaging, and actions, but often customer research is helpful to ensure that an accurate current portrayal is obtained. The conventional approach is to start with qualitative customer research to find out what a business and its brands mean to customers. What are the associations? What if the business were a person? What kind of person? What visual imagery, books, animals, trees, or activities are associated with the business? What is its essence?

Competitor's Objectives and Commitment

A knowledge of competitor objectives provides the potential to predict whether or not a competitor's present performance is satisfactory or strategic changes are likely. The financial objectives of the business unit can indicate the competitor's willingness to invest in that business even if the payout is relatively long-term. In particular, what are the competitor's objectives with respect to market share, sales growth, and profitability? Nonfinancial objectives are also helpful. Does the competitor want to be a technological leader? Or to develop a service organization? Or to expand distribution? Such objectives provide a good indication of the competitor's possible future strategy.

The objectives of the competitor's parent company (if one exists) are also relevant. What are the current performance levels and financial objectives of the parent? If the business unit is not performing as well as the parent, pressure might be exerted either to improve or withdraw its investment. Of critical importance is the role attached to the business unit. Is it central to the parent's long-term plans, or is it peripheral? Is it seen as a growth area, or is it expected to supply cash to fund other areas? Does the business create synergy with other operations? Does the parent have an emotional attachment to the business unit for any reason?

Current and Past Strategies of Competitors

The competitor's current and past strategies should be reviewed. In particular, past strategies that have failed should be noted, because such experiences can inhibit the competitor from trying similar strategies again. Also, a knowledge of a competitor's pattern of new product or new market moves can help one anticipate its future growth directions. If a differentiation strategy is detected, to what extent does it rely on product-line breadth, product quality, service, distribution type, or brand identification? If a low-cost strategy is employed, is it based on economies of scale, the experience curve, manufacturing facilities and equipment, or access to raw material? What is its cost structure? If a focus strategy is evident, describe the business scope.

Competitor's Organization and Culture

Knowledge about the background and experience of the competitor's top management can provide insight into future actions. Are the managers drawn from marketing, engineering, or manufacturing? Are they largely from another industry or company? Clorox, for example, has a very heavy Procter & Gamble influence in its management, lingering from the years that Procter & Gamble operated Clorox before the courts ordered divestiture.

An organization's culture, supported by its structure, systems, and people, often has a pervasive influence on strategy. A cost-oriented, highly structured organization that relies on tight controls to achieve objectives and motivate employees may have difficulty innovating or shifting into an aggressive, marketing-oriented strategy. A loose, flat organization that emphasizes innovation and risk taking may similarly have difficulty pursuing a disciplined product-refinement and cost-reduction program. In general, as Chapter 16 will make clearer, organizational elements such as culture, structure, systems, and people limit the range of strategies that should be considered.

Cost Structure

Knowledge of a competitor's cost structure, especially when the competitor is relying on a low-cost strategy, can provide an indication of its likely future pricing strategy and its staying power. The goal should be to obtain a feel for both direct costs and fixed costs, which will determine break-even levels. The following information can usually be obtained and can provide insights into cost structures:

- The number of employees and a rough breakdown of direct labor (variable labor cost) and overhead (which will be part of fixed cost).
- The relative costs of raw materials and purchased components.
- The investment in inventory, plant, and equipment (also fixed cost).

- Sales levels and number of plants (on which the allocation of fixed costs is based).

Exit Barriers

Exit barriers can be crucial to a firm's ability to exercise an exit alternative, and thus are indicators of commitment. They include[9]

- Specialized assets—plant, equipment, or other assets that are costly to transform to another application and that therefore have little salvage value.
- Fixed costs such as labor agreements, leases, and a need to maintain parts for existing equipment.
- Relationships to other business units in the firm due to the firm's image or to shared facilities, distribution channels, or sales force.
- Government and social barriers—for example, governments may regulate whether a railroad can exit from a passenger service responsibility; firms may feel a sense of loyalty to workers, thereby inhibiting strategic moves.
- Managerial pride or an emotional attachment to a business or its employees that affects economic decisions.

Assessing Strengths and Weaknesses

Knowledge of a competitor's strengths and weaknesses provides insight that is key to the firm's ability to pursue various strategies. It also offers important input into the process of identifying and selecting strategic alternatives. One approach is to attempt to exploit a competitor's weakness in an area where the firm has an existing or developing strength. The desired pattern is to develop a strategy that will pit "our" strength against a competitor's weakness. Conversely, a knowledge of "their" strength is important so it can be bypassed or neutralized.

An example of a firm that developed a strategy to neutralize a competitor's strength was a small software firm that lacked a retail distribution capability or the resources to engage in retail advertising. It directed its efforts to value-added software systems firms, firms that sell total software and sometimes hardware systems to industries such as investment firms or hospitals. These value-added systems firms could understand and exploit the power of the product, integrate it into their systems, and use it in quantity. Their superior access to a distribution channel or resources to support an advertising effort was thus neutralized.

The assessment of a competitor's strengths and weaknesses starts with an identification of relevant assets and skills for the industry and then evaluates the competitor on the basis of those assets and skills. We now turn to these topics.

COMPETITOR STRENGTHS AND WEAKNESSES

What Are the Relevant Assets and Skills?

Competitor strengths and weaknesses are based on the existence or absence of assets or skills. Thus, an asset such as a well-known name or a prime location could represent a strength, as could a skill such as the ability to develop a strong promotional program. Conversely, the absence of an asset or skill can represent a weakness.

To analyze competitor strengths and weaknesses, it is thus necessary to identify the assets and skills that are relevant to the industry. As Figure 4.4 summarizes, five sets of questions can be helpful.

1. What businesses have been successful over time? What assets or skills have contributed to their success? What businesses have had chronically low performance? Why? What assets or skills do they lack?

By definition, assets and skills that provide SCAs should affect performance over time. Thus, businesses that differ with respect to performance over time should also differ with respect to their skills and assets. Analysis of the causes of the performance usually suggests sets of relevant skills and assets. Typically, the superior performers have developed and maintained key assets and skills that have been the basis for their performance. Conversely, weakness in several assets and skills relevant to the industry and its strategy should visibly contribute to the inferior performance of the weak competitors over time.

For example, in the CT scanner industry the best performer, General Electric, has superior product technology and R&D, an established systems capability, a strong sales and service organization due, in part, to its X-ray product line, and an installed base. The largest competitor,

FIGURE 4.4   Identifying Relevant Assets and Skills

1. Why are successful businesses successful?
   Why are unsuccessful businesses unsuccessful?
2. What are the key customer motivations?
3. What are the large cost components?
4. What are the industry mobility barriers?
5. Which components of the value chain can create competitive advantage?

Johnson & Johnson, which has a CT scanner business that has been a chronic money loser for a decade, lacks the synergistic combination of businesses, the product technology and R&D, and the sales and service organization.

2. *What are the key customer motivations? What is really important to the customer?*

Customer motivations usually drive buying decisions and thus can dictate what assets or skills potentially create meaningful advantages. In the heavy-equipment industry, customers value service and parts backup. Caterpillar's promise of "24-hour parts service anywhere in the world" has been a key asset because it is important to customers. Sometimes needs exist that are unmet by current offerings. As noted in the previous chapter, unmet needs represent opportunities for the "outs" and threats for the "ins." For example, the successful Macintosh computer was developed in response to an unmet need for a user-friendly system. The technology surrounding the Macintosh has provided an enormus asset in an industry of IBM clones.

An analysis of customer motivations can also identify assets and skills that a business will need to deliver unless a strategy can be devised that will make them unimportant. If the prime buying criterion for a snack is freshness, a brand will have to develop the skills to deliver that attribute. A business that lacks competence in an area important to the customer segment can experience problems even if it has other substantial SCAs.

3. *What are the large value-added parts of the product or service? What are the large cost components?*

An analysis of the cost structure of an industry can reveal which value-added stage represents the largest percentage of total cost. Obtaining a cost advantage in a key value-added stage can represent a significant SCA whether that advantage is used to support a low price or a differentiation strategy. Cost advantages in lower value-added stages have less leverage. Thus in the metal can business, transportation costs are relatively high and a competitor that can locate plants near customers or on a customer's premises will have a significant cost advantage.

4. *What are the mobility barriers in the industry?*

The cost and difficulty of creating the assets and skills needed to support an SCA result in the mobility barriers in an industry. Mobility barriers include both entry barriers and barriers to the movement from one strategic group or competitive arena to another. For example, in the oil-well drilling industry of the 1970s and early 1980s, barriers prevented firms from moving from shallow on-shore drilling to deep on-shore drilling to off-shore to foreign drilling. Foreign, off-shore drilling requires specialized assets and skills in establishing and operating off-shore equipment, in dealing with foreign governments and firms, and in operating in different countries. The assets and skills that prevent entry into an industry or strategic group should be among those that are relevant to that industry.

5. *Consider the components of the value chain. Do any provide the potential to generate competitive advantage?*

Michael Porter conceptualized the value chain of competitors as one way to expose differences that determine competitive advantage.[10] A business's value chain (see Figure 4.5) consists of two types of value-creating activities:

Primary Value Activities

• Inbound logistics—material handling and warehousing.
• Operations—transforming inputs into the final product.
• Outbound logistics—order processing and distribution.
• Marketing and sales—communication, pricing, and channel management.
• Service—installation, repair, and parts.

Secondary Value Activities

• Procurement—procedures and information systems.
• Technology development—improving the product and processes/systems.

FIGURE 4.5 The Value Chain

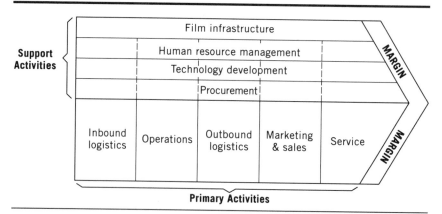

SOURCE: Reprinted with permission of The Free Press, a Division of Macmillan, Inc., from *Competitive Advantage: Creating and Sustaining Superior Performance* by Michael E. Porter. Copyright © 1985 by Michael E. Porter.

- Human resource management—hiring, training, and compensation.
- Firm infrastructure—general management, finance, accounting, government relations, and quality management.

Each of the activities in the value chain is a potential source of competitive advantage and thus should be considered in assessing a competitor.

A Checklist of Assets and Skills

Figure 4.6 provides an overview checklist of the areas in which a competitor can have strengths and weaknesses. The first category is innovation. One of the strengths of Kao Corporation is its ability to develop innovative products in soaps, detergents, skin care, and even floppy disks. Its new products usually have a distinct technological advantage. In a highly technical industry the percentage spent on R&D and the emphasis along the basic/applied continuum can be indicators of the cumulative ability to innovate. The outputs of the process in terms of product characteristics and performance capabilities, new products, product modifications, and patents provide more definitive measures of the company's ability to innovate.

The second area of competitor strengths and weaknesses is manufacturing. Perhaps the major area of strength of Texas Instruments' semiconductor and related businesses has been manufacturing. One of the key potential strength areas in manufacturing involves sources of sustainable cost advantages. Is there anything about the nature of the plant or equipment, the raw material access, the level of vertical integration, or the type of work force that would support a sustainable cost advantage? Excess capacity can increase fixed costs, but it can also be a source of strength if the market is volatile or growing.

The third area is finance, the ability to generate or acquire funds in both the short and long run. Companies with "deep pockets" (financial resources) have a decisive advantage because they can pursue strategies not available to smaller firms. Compare General Motors with Chrysler, for example, or Miller and Budweiser with some of the smaller regional breweries. Operations provide one major source of funds. What is the nature of cash flow that is being generated and will be generated given the known uses for funds? Cash or other liquid assets provide other sources, as does a parent firm. The key is the ability of the business to justify the use of debt or equity and the will to access this source.

Management is the fourth area. Controlling and motivating a set of highly disparate business operations are strengths for HP and other firms

FIGURE 4.6 Analysis of Strengths and Weaknesses

INNOVATION

- Technical product or service superiority
- New product capability
- R&D
- Technologies
- Patents

MANUFACTURING

- Cost structure
- Flexible production operations
- Equipment
- Access to raw material
- Vertical integration
- Work-force attitude and motivation
- Capacity

FINANCE—ACCESS TO CAPITAL

- From operations
- From net short-term assets
- Ability to use debt and equity financing
- Parent's willingness to finance

MANAGEMENT

- Quality of top and middle management
- Knowledge of business
- Culture
- Strategic goals and plans
- Entrepreneurial thrust
- Planning/operation system
- Loyalty—turnover
- Quality of strategic decision making

MARKETING

- Product quality reputation
- Product characteristics/ differentiation
- Brand name recognition
- Breadth of the product line— systems capability
- Customer orientation
- Segmentation/focus
- Distribution
- Retailer relationship
- Advertising/promotion skills
- Sales force
- Customer service/product support

CUSTOMER BASE

- Size and loyalty
- Market share
- Growth of segments served

that have successfully diversified. The quality, depth, and loyalty (as measured by turnover) of top and middle management provide an important asset for others. Still another is the culture. The values and norms that permeate an organization can energize some strategies and inhibit others. In particular, some organizations such as 3M possess both an entrepreneurial culture that allows them to initiate new directions and an organizational skill to nurture them. Strategic goals and plans can represent significant skills. To what extent does the business have a vision and the will and competence to pursue it?

The fifth area is marketing. Often the most important marketing strength, particularly in the high-tech fields, involves the product line, its quality reputation, the product-line breadth, and the features that serve to differentiate it from other products. Del Monte's brand name and its distribution were two areas of strength valued by Reynolds when it acquired Del Monte. The ability to develop a true customer orientation can be an important strength. Another strength can also be based on the ability and willingness to advertise effectively. The success of Perdue chickens was due, in part, to Perdue's ability to generate superior advertising. Other elements of the marketing mix such as sales force and service operation can also be sources of sustainable competitive advantage. One of Caterpillar's strengths is the quality of its dealer network. Still another possible strength, particularly in the high-tech field, is a competitor's ability to stay close to its customers.

The final area of interest is the customer base. How substantial is the customer base and how loyal is it? How are the competitor's offerings evaluated by its customers? What are the costs that customers will have to absorb if they switch to another supplier? Extremely loyal and happy customers are going to be difficult to dislodge. What are the size and growth potentials of the segments served?

The Competitive Strength Grid

With the relevant assets and skills identified, the next step is to scale your own firm and the major competitor or strategic groups of competitors on the relevant assets and skills. The result is termed a competitive strength grid and serves to summarize the position of the competitors with respect to assets and skills.

A sustainable competitive advantage is almost always based on having a position superior to that of the target competitors in one or more assets or skill areas that are relevant both to the industry and to the strategy employed. Thus, information about each competitor's position with respect to relevant assets and skills is central to strategy development and evaluation.

If a superior position does not exist with respect to assets and skills important to the strategy, it probably will have to be created or the strategy may have to be modified or abandoned. Sometimes there simply is no point of difference with respect to the firms regarded as competitors. A skill that all competitors have will not be the basis for an SCA. For example, flight safety is important among airline passengers, but if airlines are perceived to be equal with respect to pilot quality and plane maintenance, it cannot be the basis for an SCA. Of course, if some airlines can convince passengers that they are superior with respect to antiterrorist security, then an SCA could indeed emerge.

The Luxury Car Market.   A competitor strength grid is illustrated in Figure 4.7 for the luxury car market. The relevant assets and skills are listed on the left, grouped as to whether they are considered keys to success or are of secondary importance. The principal competitors are shown as column headings across the top. Each cell is coded as to whether the brand is strong, above average, average, below average, or weak in that asset or skill category.

The resulting figure shows the overall strength of Lexus, Infiniti, and Mercedes. It also provides a summary of the profile of the strengths and weaknesses of each company. Two can be compared such as Ford and Lexus or BMW and Audi.

Analyzing Submarkets.   It is often desirable to conduct an analysis for submarkets or strategic groups and perhaps for different products. A firm may not compete with all other firms in the industry but only with those engaged in similar strategies and markets. For example, a competitive strength grid may look very different for the safety submarket—Volvo may have more strength, for example. Similarly, the handling submarket may also involve a competitive grid that will look different, with BMW having more strength.

The Analysis Process.   The process of developing a competitive strength grid can be extremely informative and useful. One approach is to have several managers create their own grids independently. The differences can usually illuminate different assumptions and information bases. A reconciliation stage can disseminate relevant information and identify and structure strategic questions. For example, different opinions about the quality reputation of a competitor may stimulate a strategic question that justifies marketing research. Another approach is to develop the grid in a group setting perhaps supported by preliminary staff work. When possible, objective information based on laboratory tests or customer perception studies should be used. The need for such information becomes clear when disagreements arise about where competitors should be scaled on the various dimensions.

Obtaining Information on Competitors

Information on competitors is usually available from a variety of sources. Competitors usually communicate extensively to their suppliers, custom-

FIGURE 4.7 Luxury Car Competitors in the U.S. Market

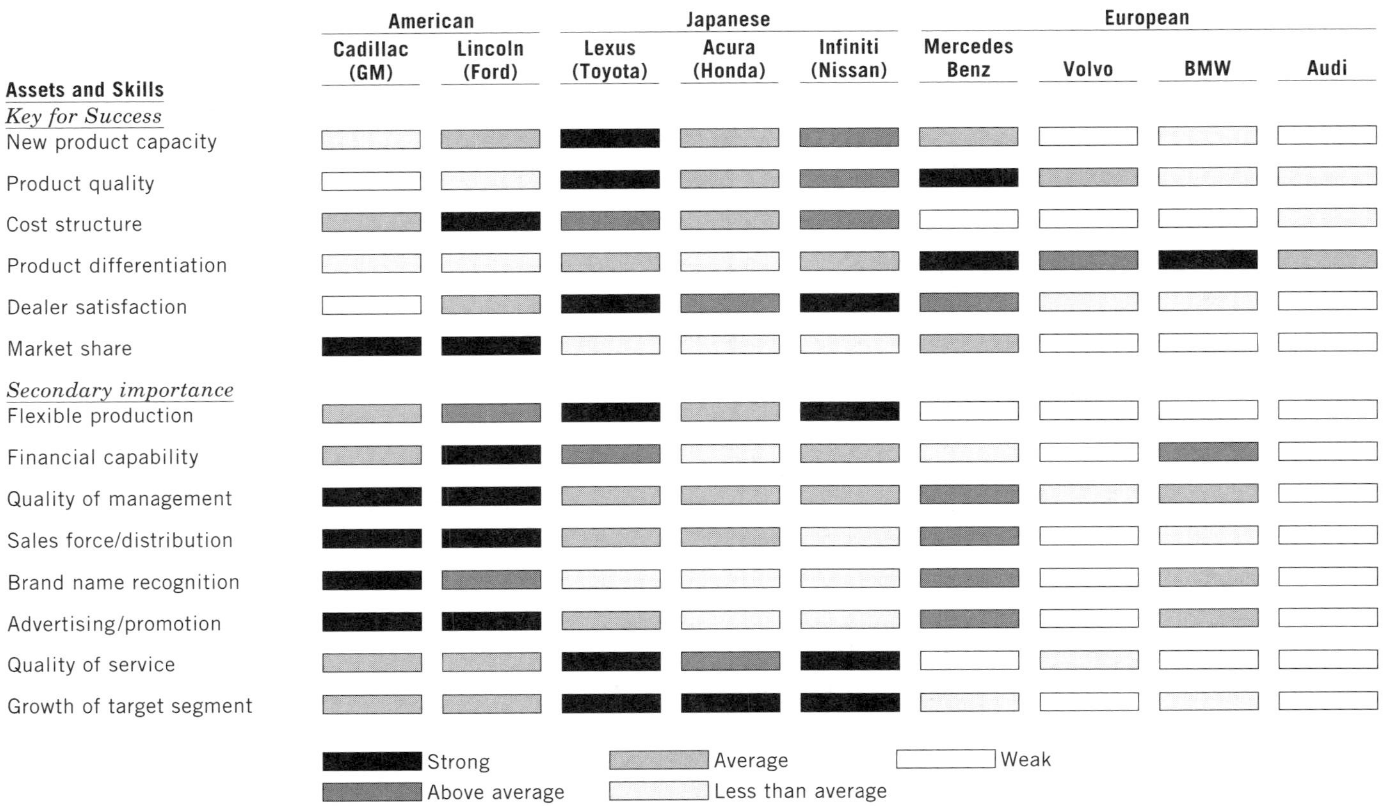

	American		Japanese			European			
Assets and Skills	Cadillac (GM)	Lincoln (Ford)	Lexus (Toyota)	Acura (Honda)	Infiniti (Nissan)	Mercedes Benz	Volvo	BMW	Audi
Key for Success									
New product capacity									
Product quality									
Cost structure									
Product differentiation									
Dealer satisfaction									
Market share									
Secondary importance									
Flexible production									
Financial capability									
Quality of management									
Sales force/distribution									
Brand name recognition									
Advertising/promotion									
Quality of service									
Growth of target segment									

Legend: Strong · Above average · Average · Less than average · Weak

83

ers, and distributors; to security analysts and stockholders; and to government legislators and regulators. Contact with any of these can provide information. Monitoring of trade magazines, trade shows, advertising, speeches, annual reports, and the like can be informative. Technical meetings and journals can provide information about technical developments and activities. Thousands of databases accessible by computer are now available from which detailed information on competitors and facilities can be obtained.

One way to secure detailed information about a competitor's standing with its customers is to use market research. For example, regular telephone surveys could provide information about the success and vulnerabilities of competitor strategies. Respondents could be asked questions such as the following. Which store is closest to your home? Which do you shop at most often? Are you satisfied? Which has the lowest price? Best specials? Best customer service? Cleanest stores? Best-quality meat? Best-quality produce? and so on. Those chains that were well positioned on value, on service, or on product quality could be identified, and tracking would show whether they were gaining or losing position. The loyalty of their customer base (and thus their vulnerability) could be indicated in part by satisfaction scores and the willingness of customers to patronize stores even when they were not the most convenient or the least expensive.

SUMMARY

The first step in competitor analysis is to identify groups of competitors. One approach is customer-based and considers customer choice, the set of competitors from which the customer selects; another is based on product-use associations, the set of competitors whose products are used in the same use situation. In nearly all industries, competitors can be portrayed in terms of how intensely they compete with a reference business.

A second approach is to identify strategic groups, groups of competitive firms that pursue similar strategies and have similar assets, skills, and other characteristics. Mobility barriers between strategic groups are strategically important because they can protect a profitable strategy. It is also important to identify potential competitors—firms with the motivation and ability to enter an industry.

To gain an understanding of competitors, it is useful to analyze them on the basis of several dimensions. Their size, growth, and profitability provide a gross measure of their relative importance. Their image and positioning strategy provide strategic insights. An analysis of objectives and of past and current strategies can provide insights into intentions and commitment. Organizational factors such as culture and exit barriers can point out strategic constraints. Cost structures can be clues to likely price strategies.

The first step in analyzing competitor strengths and weaknesses is to identify the relevant assets and skills in an industry. Toward that end it is useful to consider the characteristics of successful and unsuccessful businesses, key customer motivations, large cost components, mobility barriers, and the value chain. The competitive strength grid, in which competitors or strategic groups are scaled on each of the relevant assets and skills, provides a compact summary of key strategic information.

Information on competitors can be obtained from market research and from a variety of other sources such as trade magazines, trade shows, customers, and suppliers.

FOOTNOTES

[1] David Halberstam, *The Reckoning*, New York: William Morrow, 1986, p. 310.

[2] Halberstam, *Reckoning*, p. 310.

[3] George S. Day, Allan D. Shocker, and Rajendra K. Srivastava, "Customer-Oriented Approaches to Identifying Product Markets," *Journal of Marketing* 43, Fall 1979, pp. 8–19.

[4] John Foraker, Daisuke Kawanami, Dan Norton, Hiroshi Ohkubo, Vincent Weller, "Strategic Marketing Analysis of the U.S. Pet Food Industry," unpublished paper, 1993.

[5] Briance Mascarenhas and David A. Aaker, "Mobility Barriers and Strategic Groups," *Strategic Management Journal*, September–October 1989, pp. 475–485.

[6] Sharon Oster, "Intraindustry Structure and the Ease of Strategic Change," *The Review of Economics and Statistics* 3, August 1982, pp. 376–383.

[7] Mascarenhas and Aaker, op. cit.

[8] Donald C. Waite III, "Deregulation and the Banking Industry," *Bankers Magazine* 163, January–February 1982, pp. 76–85.

[9] Michael E. Porter, *Competitive Strategy*, New York: The Free Press, 1980, pp. 20–21. The concept of exit barriers will be discussed again in Chapter 14.

[10] Michael E. Porter, *Competitive Advantage*, New York: The Free Press, 1985, Chapter 2.

5

MARKET ANALYSIS

As the economy, led by the automobile industry, rose to a new high level in the twenties, a complex of new elements came into existence to transform the market: installment selling, the used-car trade-in, the closed body, and the annual model. (I would add improved roads if I were to take into account the environment of the automobile.)

Alfred P. Sloan, Jr., General Motors

Market analysis builds on customer and competitor analyses to make some strategic judgments about a market (and submarket) and its dynamics. One of the primary objectives of a market analysis is to determine the attractiveness of a market (or submarket) to current and potential participants. Market attractiveness, the market's profit potential as measured by the long-term return on investment achieved by its participants, will provide important input into the product-market investment decision. The frame of reference is all competitors. Whether or not a market is appropriate for a particular firm is a related but very different question. It will depend not only on the market attractiveness but also on how the firm's strengths and weaknesses match up against competitors'.

A second objective of market analysis is to understand the dynamics of the market. The need is to identify emerging key success factors, trends, threats, and opportunities and to develop strategic questions that can guide information gathering and analysis. A key success factor is an asset or skill that is needed to "play the game." If a firm has a strategic weakness in a key success factor that isn't neutralized by a well-conceived strategy, its ability to compete will be limited. The market trends can include those identified in customer or competitor analysis, but the perspective here is broader and others will usually emerge as well.

DIMENSIONS OF A MARKET ANALYSIS

The nature and content of an analysis of a market and its relevant product markets will depend on context. However, it will often include the following dimensions:

- Actual and potential market size
- Market growth
- Market profitability
- Cost structure
- Distribution systems
- Trends and developments
- Key success factors

Figure 5.1 provides a set of questions structured around these dimensions that can serve to stimulate a discussion identifying opportunities, threats, and strategic questions. Each of these dimensions will be addressed in turn, starting with an assessment of the market size. The chapter concludes with a section discussing the risks of growth markets.

FIGURE 5.1   Questions to Structure a Market Analysis

SIZE AND GROWTH

• What are the important and potentially important submarkets? What are their size and growth characteristics? What submarkets are declining or will soon decline? How fast? What are the driving forces behind sales trends?

PROFITABILITY

• For each major submarket consider the following: Is this a business area in which the "average firm" will make money? How intense is the competition among existing firms? Evaluate the threats from potential entrants and substitute products. What is the bargaining power of suppliers and customers? How attractive/ profitable are the market and its submarkets both now and in the future?

COST STRUCTURE

• What are the major cost and value-added components for various types of competitors?

DISTRIBUTION SYSTEMS

• What are the alternative channels of distribution? How are they changing?

TRENDS

• What are the trends in the market?

KEY SUCCESS FACTORS

• What are the key success factors, assets, and skills needed to compete successfully? How will these change in the future? How can the assets and skills of competitors be neutralized by strategies?

Actual and Potential Market Size

A basic starting point for the analysis of a market or submarket is the total sales level. If it becomes reasonable to believe that a successful strategy can be developed that will gain a 15 percent share, it is important to know the total market size. Knowledge of the submarkets is often critical. The value of the total beer market may not be very helpful if market dynamics are occurring at the level of submarkets such as non-alcohol, super-premium, microbreweries, dry, and imports.

Estimates of market size can be based on government sources or trade association findings. For example, such sources provide a breakdown of wine sales over time by type of wine, imported versus domestic, geographic markets, and even by competitor. Another approach is to obtain information on competitor sales from published financial sources, customers, or competitors. A more expensive approach would be to survey customers and project their usage to the total market.

Potential Market—The User Gap

In addition to the size of the current, relevant market, it is often useful to consider the potential market. A new use, new user group, or more frequent usage could change dramatically the size and prospects for the market.

There is unrealized potential for the cereal market in Europe and among institutional customers in the U.S.—restaurants and schools/daycare facilities.[1] All these segments have room for dramatic growth. In particular, Europeans buy only about 25 percent as much cereal as their U.S. counterparts. Furthermore, if technology allowed cereals to be used more conveniently away from home by providing shelf-stable milk products, usage could be further expanded. Of course, the key is not only to recognize the potential, but also to have the vision and program in place to exploit it. A host of strategists have dismissed investment opportunities in industries because they lacked the insight to see the available potential and take advantage of it.

Ghost Potential

Sometimes an area becomes so topical and the need so apparent that potential growth seems assured. As a Lewis Carroll character observed, "What I tell you three times is true." However, this potential can have a ghostlike quality caused by factors inhibiting or preventing its realization. For example, a huge demand for educational equipment exists in underdeveloped countries and in many sectors of developed countries, but a lack of funds inhibits buying. Artificial intelligence and pen-based PCs were both the beneficiaries of considerable hype but the promise never really materialized.

Small Can Be Beautiful

Some firms have investment criteria that prohibit them from investing in small markets. Coca-Cola and Procter & Gamble, for example, have historically looked to new products that would generate large sales levels within a few years. The problem is that in an era of micromarketing much of the action is in smaller niche segments. If a firm avoids them, it can lock itself out of much of the vitality and profitability of a business area. Furthermore, most substantial business areas were small at the outset, sometimes for many years. Avoiding the small market can thus often mean that a firm is always overcoming the first-mover advantage of others.

MARKET GROWTH

After the size of the market and its important submarkets have been estimated, the focus turns to growth rate. What will be the market's size in the future? If all else remains constant, growth means more sales and profits even without increasing market share. It can also mean less price pressure when demand increases faster than supply, and firms are not engaged in "experience curve" pricing, anticipating future lower costs. Conversely, declining market sales can mean reduced sales and often increased price pressure, as firms struggle to hold their shares of a diminishing pie.

The nominal strategy is thus to identify and invest in growth contexts and identify and avoid or disinvest in declining situations. Of course, the reality is not that simple. In particular, declining product markets can represent a real opportunity for a firm, in part because competitors may be exiting and disinvesting, instead of entering and investing for growth. The firm may attempt to become a profitable survivor by encouraging others to exit and by becoming dominant in the most viable segments. The pursuit of this strategy is considered in detail in Chapter 14.

The other half of the conventional wisdom, that growth contexts are always attractive, can also fail to hold true. In fact, growth situations can involve substantial risks. Because of the importance of correctly assessing growth contexts, a discussion of these risks is presented at the end of this chapter.

Identifying Driving Forces

In many contexts, the most important strategic question involves the prediction of market sales. A key strategic decision, often an investment decision, can hinge on not only being correct but also understanding the driving forces behind market dynamics.

Addressing most key strategic questions starts with asking on what does the answer depend. In the case of projecting sales of a major market, the need is to determine what forces will drive those sales. It is often helpful to visualize several sales scenarios, like those shown in Figure 5.2. The following questions can then be posed. What has to happen if pattern C is to occur? What could cause pattern B? Answers usually provide the identity of strategic subquestions that may be pivotal in strategy development.

In the minidisk market of the mid-1990s, for example, the rate of growth could be driven by machine cost, the costs of the disks, the emergence of an industry standard, the acceptance of the product in educational applications, and whether or not alternative technologies emerge. A key

FIGURE 5.2   Sales Patterns

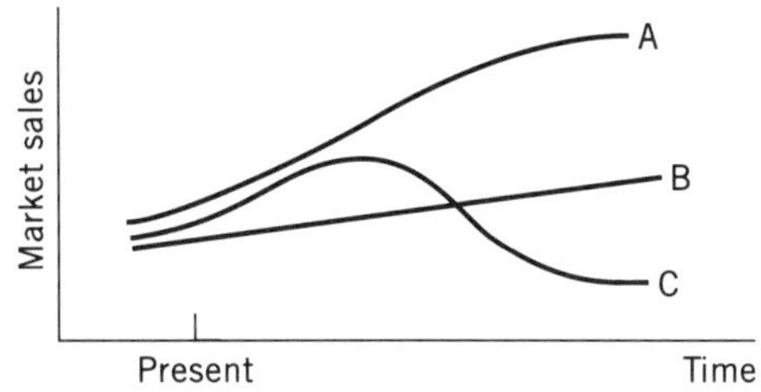

subquestion could then be what are the cost/price projections? A strategic subquestion can provide guidance for information search and analysis directions and can suggest scenario analyses. For example, scenarios based upon different assumptions as to cost could be explored.

In the wine market, the impact of anti-alcohol movements (like MADD), the tax policy, the relationship of wine to health, and the future demand for premium reds might be driving forces. One strategic subquestion might then focus on the likely strength of the anti-alcohol movements.

Forecasting Growth

Historical data can provide a useful perspective and help to separate hope from reality, but they need to be used with care. Apparent trends in data can be caused by random fluctuations or by short-term economic conditions, and the urge to extrapolate should be resisted. Furthermore, the strategic interest is not on projections of history but rather the prediction of turning points, times when the rate and perhaps direction of growth change.

Sometimes leading indicators of market sales can be identified that may help in forecasting and predicting turning points. Examples of leading indicators include

- Demographic data. The number of births is a leading indicator of the demand for education, and the number of people reaching age 65 is a leading indicator of the demand for retirement facilities.
- Sales of related equipment. Personal computer and printer sales provide a leading indicator of the demand for supplies and service needs.

Market sales forecasts, especially of new markets, can be based on the experience of analogous industries. The trick is to identify a prior market with similar characteristics. The sales of color televisions might be expected to have a pattern similar to that of black-and-white televisions, for example. The sales of a new type of snack might look to the history of other previously introduced snack categories or of other consumer products such as liquid diet products, granola cereal, or breakfast bars. The most value will be obtained if several analogous product classes can be examined and the differences in the product class experiences related to their characteristics.

Methods now exist to provide remarkably accurate forecasts of sales patterns for durable products such as appliances, cameras, and VCRs. They are based, in part, on decomposing sales into first purchases and replacement sales.

Detecting Maturity and Decline

One particularly important set of turning points in market sales is when the growth phase of the product life cycle changes to a flat maturity phase, and when the maturity phase changes into a decline phase. These transitions are important to the health and nature of the market. Often they are accompanied by changes in key success factors. Historical sales and profit patterns of a market can help to identify the onset of maturity or decline, but the following often are more sensitive indicators:

- *Price pressure caused by overcapacity and the lack of product differentiation.* When growth slows or even reverses, capacity developed under a more optimistic scenario becomes excessive. Furthermore, the product-evolution process often results in most competitors matching product improvements. Thus, it becomes more difficult to maintain meaningful differentiation.

- *Buyer sophistication and knowledge.* Buyers tend to become more familiar and knowledgeable as the product matures and thus become less willing to apply a premium price to obtain the security of an established name. Computer buyers over the years have gained confidence in their ability to select computers—as a result, the value of big names like IBM has receded.

- *Substitute products or technologies.* The sales of CD players provide an indicator of the decline in tape players.

- *Saturation.* When the number of potential first-time buyers declines, market sales should mature or decline.

- *No growth sources.* The market is fully penetrated and there are no visible sources of growth from new uses or users.

- *Customer disinterest.* A reduction in the interest of customers in applications, new product announcements, and so on.

Looking for Growth Submarkets

A payoff usually comes from understanding the dynamics within an industry. What submarkets are growing? Consider coffee.[2] Per capita consumption fell from over 3 cups per day in the early 1960s to under 1.7 cups per day in 1990 but then started a modest rebound in the 1990s. However, this rebound occurred in the face of a decline of the major supermarket brands, Maxwell House (Kraft), Hills Bros (Nestlé), and Folgers (P&G). The growth came from coffeehouses such as Starbucks (which has a chain of 250 stores and is growing fast), from consumers who buy specialty beans for their electric coffee grinders, and from gourmet brands. The major brands are struggling to participate, with entrants such as Maxwell House Rich French Roast, Folgers Gourmet Supreme, and Kraft's Cappio. Their names introduce a credibility problem: Can a supermarket brand really produce a gourmet coffee that is as interesting and appealing as that of a specialty firm like Starbucks?

MARKET PROFITABILITY ANALYSIS

Economists have long studied why some industries or markets are profitable and others are not. Michael Porter, a Harvard economist, applied his theories and findings to the business strategy problem of evaluating the investment value of an industry or market.[3] The problem is to estimate how profitable the average firm will be. It is hoped, of course, that a firm will develop a strategy that will bring above-average profits. If the average profit level is low, however, the task of succeeding financially will be much more difficult than if the average profitability were high.

Porter's approach to estimating the profitability of a market is called industry structure analysis, but it can be applied to a market or submarket within an industry. The basic idea is that the attractiveness of an industry or market as measured by the long-term return on investment of the average firm depends largely on five factors that influence profitability as shown in Figure 5.3:

- The intensity of competition.
- The existence of potential competitors who will enter if profits are high.
- Substitute products that will attract customers if prices become high.
- The bargaining power of customers.
- The bargaining power of suppliers.

Each plays a role in explaining why some industries are historically more profitable than others. An understanding of this structure can also suggest

FIGURE 5.3 Five-Factor Model of Market Profitability

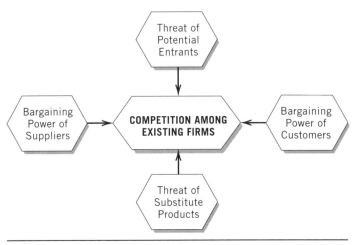

SOURCE: Adapted from Michael E. Porter, "Industry Structure and Competitive Strategy: Keys to Profitability," *Financial Analysis Journal*, July–August 1980, p. 33.

which key success factors are necessary to cope with the competitive forces.

Competitors

The intensity of competition from existing competitors will depend on several factors, including

- The number of competitors.
- Their relative size.
- Whether or not their product offerings and strategies are similar.
- The existence of high fixed costs.
- The commitment of competitors.
- The size and nature of exit barriers

As a first approximation, the more competitors, the more competitive intensity. However, the nature of the competitors will make a great deal of difference. The relative size of the competitors will affect competitive intensity, for example. If a ten-firm market is dominated by a few firms, the level of competition will usually be much less than if ten competitors of equal size are present. Furthermore, if the competitors have more highly differentiated products and employ different strategies, the pressure on prices will be less than in a commodity market such as steel. The existence of high fixed costs, as in the airline market, will stimulate price competition to improve capacity utilization.

Of particular importance in this analysis phase is to understand the commitment and exit barriers of the competitors. To what extent will they be motivated to spend whatever is needed to maintain position? In general, a firm that is undiversified and has made major commitments to facilities or sources of supply will be highly committed. Gallo, for example, has nearly all its sales tied to wine and has extensive vertical integration. It thus has a high level of commitment. A commitment to a business can also be created when that business supports other parts of a firm. A retailer may need to remain in several undesirable sites to maintain a critical mass regionally.

Another related consideration is the exit barriers such as specialized assets, long-term contracts, commitments to customers and distributors, and relationships to other parts of a firm. Exit barrier analysis (discussed further in Chapter 14) provides a tool for predicting the extent to which exiting will occur.

Potential Competitors

Chapter 4 discusses identifying potential competitors that might have an interest in entering an industry or market. Whether potential competitors, identified or not, actually do enter, however, depends in large part on the size and nature of barriers to entry. Thus, an analysis of barriers to entry is important in projecting the likely competitive intensity and profitability levels in the future. Entry barriers have helped the cereal market restrict entry for many decades so that Kellogg's, General Mills, Post (General Foods), and Quaker Oats control the market. Entry barriers include

- *Capital investment required.* Industries like mining or automobiles require large investments that increase risk.
- *Economies of scale.* If scale economies exist in production, advertising, distribution, or other areas, it becomes necessary to obtain a large volume quickly. In the cereal market, for example, it has been estimated that production economies of scale occur at approximately 5 percent of U.S. sales. Since a successful brand may gain only a 1 percent share, a new firm would need to score five winners, which is virtually impossible.
- *Distribution channels.* Gaining distribution in some markets can be extremely difficult and costly. Even large established firms that sell products with substantial marketing budgets have trouble obtaining space on the supermarket shelf. The cereal firms have encouraged stores

to allocate shelf space according to historical share, making it hard for a newcomer to break in.

- *Product differentiation.* Established firms may have high levels of customer loyalty caused and maintained by protected product features, a brand name and image, advertising, and customer service. Markets in which product differentiation barriers are particularly high include cereal, soft drinks, beer, cosmetics, over-the-counter drugs, and banking.

Substitute Products

Substitute products are represented by those sets of competitors that are identified as competing with less intensity than the primary competitors. They are still relevant, however, and can influence the profitability of the market and, in fact, can be a major threat or problem. Thus, plastics, glass, and fiber-foil products exert pressure on the metal can market. Electronic alarm systems are substitutes for the security guard market. Fax machines and electronic mail provide a serious threat to the express delivery market pioneered by Federal Express. Substitutes that show a steady improvement in relative price/performance and for which the customer's cost of switching is minimal are of particular interest.

Customer Power

When customers have relatively more power than sellers, they can force prices down or demand more services, thereby affecting profitability. A customer's power will be greater when its purchase size is a large proportion of the seller's business, when alternative suppliers are available, and when the customer can integrate backward and make all or part of the product. Thus, tire manufacturers face powerful customers in the automobile firms. The customers of metal can manufacturers are large packaged-goods manufacturers who have over time demanded price and service concessions and who have engaged in backward integration. Cereal firms face a supermarket industry that has become strong and assertive in part because of its developing strengths in information technology. Soft-drink firms sell to fast-food restaurant chains and athletic teams that have strong bargaining power.

Supplier Power

When the supplier industry is concentrated and sells to a variety of customers in diverse markets, it will have relative power that can be used to influence prices. Power will also be enhanced when the costs to customers of switching suppliers are high. Thus, the highly concentrated oil industry is often powerful enough to influence profits in customer industries that find it expensive to convert from oil. However, the potential for regeneration whereby industries can create their own power, perhaps by recycling waste, may have changed the balance of power in some contexts.

COST STRUCTURE

An understanding of the cost structure of a market can provide insights into present and future key success factors. The first step is to conduct an analysis of the value chain presented in Figure 4.5 to determine where value is added to the product (or service). As suggested in Figure 5.4, the proportion of value added attributed to one value chain stage can become so important that a key success factor is associated with that stage. It may be possible to develop control over a resource or technology as the OPEC oil cartel did. More likely, competitors will aim to be the lowest-cost competitor in a high value-added stage of the value chain. Advantages in lower value-added stages will simply have less leverage. Thus, in the metal can business, transportation costs are relatively high and a competitor that can locate plants near customers will have a significant cost advantage.

Of course, it may not be possible to gain an advantage at high value-added stages. For example, a raw material such as flour for bakery firms may represent a high value added, but because the raw material is widely available at commodity prices, it will not be a key success factor. Nevertheless, it is often useful to look first at the highest value-added stages.

It is very important, especially in fast-moving growth markets, to be able to anticipate changes in key success factors. One approach is to examine the changes in the relative importance of the value-added stages.

FIGURE 5.4 Value Added and Key Success Factors

Production Stage	Markets that Have Key Success Factors Associated with the Production Stage
• Raw material procurement	• Gold mining, wine making
• Raw material processing	• Steel, paper
• Production fabricating	• Integrated circuits, tires
• Assembly	• Apparel, instrumentation
• Physical distribution	• Bottled water, metal cans
• Marketing	• Branded cosmetics, liquor
• Service back-up	• Software, automobiles
• Technology development	• Razors, medical systems

For example, the cement market was very regional when it was restricted to rail or truck transportation. With the development of specialized ships, however, waterborne transportation costs dropped dramatically. Key success factors changed from local ground transportation to access to the specialized ships and production scale. For many electronics goods, the largest value-added item changed from assembly to components, as more of the product was integrated into components.

Another market cost structure consideration is the extent to which experience curve strategies are feasible. Can firms develop sustainable cost advantages based on volume? Are there large, fixed costs that would generate economies of scale? The experience curve concept and approaches to determine whether the context is compatible with such a strategy are presented in Chapter 11.

DISTRIBUTION SYSTEMS

An analysis of distribution systems should include three types of questions:

- What are the alternative distribution channels?
- What are the trends? What channels are growing in importance? What new channels have emerged or are likely to?
- Who has the power in the channel and how is that likely to shift?

Access to an effective and efficient distribution channel is often a key success factor. Channel alternatives can vary in several ways. One is the degree of directness. Some companies—such as Avon, Tupperware, and many industrial businesses—sell directly through their own sales force. Dell, Gateway, and L.L. Bean sell primarily through mail order. Others, such as Radio Shack and several shoe firms, sell through their own retail stores. Still other firms sell directly to retailers, sell through distributors or other intermediaries, or use some combination of channels. The firms closest to the end user have the most control over marketing and usually assume the highest risk.

Sometimes the creation of a new channel form can lead to a sustainable competitive advantage. A dramatic example is the success that L'eggs hosiery achieved by its ability to market hosiery in supermarkets. L'eggs, of course, supported the idea of using supermarkets with a comprehensive program that addressed a host of issues. The L'eggs program involved selling on consignment, packaging the hosiery in a container that made it relatively difficult to shoplift, using a space-efficient vertical display, providing a high-quality, low-priced product supported by national advertising, and performing in-store functions such as ordering and stocking. Thus, it is useful to consider not only existing channels but potential ones.

An analysis of likely or emerging changes within distribution channels can be important in understanding a market and its key success factors. The increased sale of wine in supermarkets made it much more important for wine makers to focus on packaging and advertising. The decision by Levi Strauss to move beyond department and specialty stores and sell its products in Sears affected the channels for boys' and menswear. The emergence of home shopping, the growth of convenience food stores in gas stations, the success of Wal-Mart, and the growth of specialty catalog retailing illustrate trends that have strategic importance to firms affected by the channels involved.

Related to customer power in market profitability analysis is channel power. In industries without strong brand names, such as furniture, retailers usually have relatively high power and can hold down the price that manufacturers are paid. The enhanced power of supermarkets, caused in large part by the explosion of transaction information and the importance of promotions, has altered the way packaged goods are marketed. The influence that P&G and other packaged goods firms once had on promotions, stocking, and display decisions has been significantly reduced. The ability of pharmacists to substitute generic drugs has altered power in that industry.

MARKET TRENDS

Often one of the most useful elements of external analysis comes from addressing the question, what are the market trends? The question has two important attributes: it focuses on change and tends to identify what is important. As a result, strategically useful insights almost always result. A discussion of market trends can serve as a useful summary of customer, competitor, and market analyses. It is thus helpful to identify trends near the end of market analysis.

The soft-drink industry has been affected by three trends. First, there is an increased consumer price sensitivity that has affected how brands are competing in the store. Second, there is increased concern for health and nutrition among all age categories. Third, there is increased demand for exotic flavors and variety that reflects boredom and a greater exposure to foreign cultures. The two latter trends are partially responsible for the dramatic increase in the consumption of non-cola beverages, including citrus-based sodas, flavored iced teas, New Age beverages, and bottled water.

The luxury car market faces four trends with strategic implications. There is a shift in customer motivations from prestige and comfort to value and safety. Second, there is an increasing emphasis on the lower end of the segment, with the European manufacturers all participating with smaller cars. A third trend is the increasing importance of good customer service as a competitive tool. Lexus and Infiniti set new standards for the industry. A fourth trend is toward leasing; more than 50 percent of the luxury car market is accounted for by leasing.

One trend in the workstation market is a progressively blurring distinction between personal computers and workstations.[4] Personal computers are becoming more powerful and workstation manufacturers are moving into the office market. Workstation manufacturers are developing "server" computers that can provide data-sharing and networking capabilities with some of the graphics that are needed for advanced engineering applications. An implication for the personal computer market is that a major new strategic group is emerging.

KEY SUCCESS FACTORS—BASES OF COMPETITION

An important output of market analysis is the identification of key success factors for strategic groups in the market. They are assets and skills that provide the bases for competing successfully. There are two types. First, there are the strategic necessities, which do not necessarily provide an advantage because others have them, but their absence will create a substantial weakness. Second, there are the strategic strengths, those at which a firm excels, the assets or skills that are superior to those of competitors and provide a base of advantage. The set of skills and assets developed in competitor analysis provides a base set from which key success factors can be identified. The questions to consider are which are the most critical skills and assets now and, more important, which will be most critical in the future.

One study of six mature product industries shows that the key success factors (KSFs) will differ by industry in predictable ways—a capital goods maker will have different KSFs than an operating supplies firm—and those firms that have strengths matching the KSFs perform substantially better than other firms.[5] The failure of firms such as Philip Morris and P&G to crack the soft-drink market because they lack the KSF of "access to bottlers" provides an illustration of the concept in action.

In the recording market, where hit records need to be created and managed, the key success factors include[6]

- An inventory of artists with a balance of developing artists and established mainstream acts.
- The skill of managing an artist's career to maximize the attractiveness of the firm to the artist and to create successful labels.

- The ability to control fixed and marginal costs and to obtain scale economies by producing other labels if necessary.
- Quick response systems to exploit a hit when it occurs.

An analysis of the wine market in the early 1990s identified seven key success factors:[7]

- Access to a quality grape supply (50 percent of the variable cost), especially for those in the premium segments.
- Access to technology both in the vineyard and winery so that costs can be controlled.
- The achievement of adequate scale, perhaps with a set of brands.
- Expertise in wine making.
- Name recognition—a sense of tradition and a "California connection" are very helpful.
- Strong relationships with distributors.
- The financial resources to compete in a capital-intensive business.

An analysis will be needed for each strategic group, because the required skills and assets for each will likely be different. For example, the bulk wineries such as JFJ Bronco Wine Company make and sell wine in bulk to other wineries and to private labelers such as the major supermarkets and liquor-store chains. Key success factors for bulk wine include the ability to make wine at acceptable quality using modern production facilities and scale economies so that sustainable cost advantages can be achieved. These key success factors are very different from those for the wine market in general.

It is important not only to identify KSFs, but also to project them into the future and, in particular, identify emerging KSFs. Many firms have faltered when KSFs changed and the skills and assets on which they were relying became less relevant. For example, for industrial firms, technology and innovation tend to be most important during the introduction and growth phases, whereas the roles of systems capability, marketing, and service backup become more dominant as the market matures. In consumer products, marketing and distribution skills are crucial during the introduction and growth phases, but operations and manufacturing become more crucial as the product settles into maturity and decline phases.

In the auto parts industry, the successful firms in the past were those that could supply a part such as a door handle reliably and at low cost.[8] However, automobile firms now want suppliers to design and build entire door systems complete with armrests, interior trim, latches, and wiring design instead of stamping out door handles. As a result, successful suppliers will need to have a design capability and to become experts on the relevant technologies.

RISKS IN HIGH-GROWTH MARKETS

AT&T in 1994 picked five key marketing and technology areas for investment largely on the basis of their dramatically high growth—networked computing, wireless communications, messaging, visual communications, and voice and audio processing.[9] Each can be justified in part because of its link to the AT&T core strategy of developing and exploiting its ability to build and manage networks and in part because AT&T has the technology to compete in those areas. However, there are risks inherent in these growth areas.

The conventional wisdom that the strategist should seek out growth areas often overlooks a substantial set of associated risks. As shown in Figure 5.5, there is the risk that[10]

- The number and commitment of competitors may be greater than can be supported by the market.
- A competitor may enter with a superior product or low-cost advantage.
- Key success factors might change and the organization cannot adapt.
- Technology might change.
- The market growth may fail to meet expectations.
- Resources might be inadequate to maintain a high growth rate.
- Adequate distribution may not be available.

FIGURE 5.5   Risks of High-Growth Markets

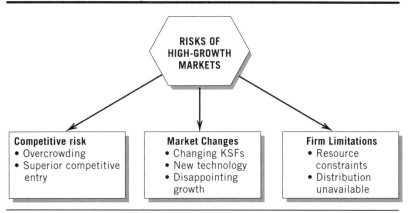

Competitive Overcrowding

Perhaps the most serious risk is that too many competitors will be attracted by a growth situation and enter with unrealistic market share expectations. The reality may be that sales volume is insufficient to support all of them. Consider, for example, the hundreds of participants in the personal computer market in the early 1990s. The Japanese damaged the value of many high-growth markets by quickly entering in large numbers and building excessive capacity.

The following conditions are found in markets in which a surplus of competitors is likely to be attracted, and a subsequent shakeout is highly probable:

1. The market and its growth rate have high visibility; as a result, strategists in related firms are encouraged to consider the market seriously and, in fact, may fear the consequences of turning their backs on an obvious growth direction.

2. Very high forecast and actual growth in the early stages are pointed to as evidence confirming high market growth as a proven phenomenon.

3. Threats to the growth rate are not considered or are discounted—little exists to dampen the enthusiasm surrounding the market. In fact, the enthusiasm may be contagious when venture capitalists and stock analysts become advocates.

4. Few initial barriers to entry exist to prevent firms from entering the market.

5. Products employ an existing technology rather than a risky or protected technology. Technology sometimes provides a more obvious and formidable barrier than, for example, a finance or marketing barrier. The true significance of a marketing barrier to entry, such as limited retail space, may be evident only after the market is overcrowded.

6. Some potential entrants have low visibility and their intentions are unknown or uncertain; thus, the quantity and commitment of competitors are likely to be underestimated.

The shakeout itself often occurs during a relatively short period of time. The trigger is likely to be a combination of (1) an unanticipated slowing of market growth, either because the market is close to saturation or a recession has intervened; (2) aggressive late entrants buying their way into the market by cutting prices; (3) the market leader attempting to stem the erosion of its market position with aggressive product and price retaliation; or (4) the key success factors in the market changing as a consequence of technological development, perhaps shifting the value-added structure. Each of these possible triggering events introduces additional sources of risk.

A Superior Competitive Entry

The ultimate risk is that a position will be established in a healthy growth market and a competitor will enter late with a product that is demonstrably superior or that has an inherent cost advantage. Thus, although IBM entered the personal computer market late, it established a strong if not dominant position by capitalizing on its name, its assurance of being a survivor, software availability, and service backup. The late entry of low-cost products from the Far East has occurred in countless industries, including radios, TVs, semiconductors, VCRs, and computer peripherals and components.

Changing Key Success Factors

A firm may be successful at establishing a strong position during the early stages of market development, only to lose ground later when key success factors change. One forecast is that the surviving personal computer makers will be those able to achieve low-cost production through vertical integration or exploitation of the experience curve, those able to obtain efficient, low-cost distribution, and those able to provide software for their customers—capabilities not necessarily critical during the early stages of market evolution. Many product markets have experienced a shift over time from a focus on product technology to process technology. A firm that might be capable of achieving product-technology-based advantages may not have the resources, skills, and orientation/culture needed to develop the process-technology-based advantages that the evolving market demands.

Changing Technology

Developing first-generation technology can involve a commitment to a product line and production facilities that may become obsolete, and to a technology that may not survive. A safe strategy is to wait until it becomes clear which technology will dominate and then attempt to improve it with a compatible entry. When the principal competitors have committed themselves, the most promising avenues for the development of a sustainable competitive advantage become more visible. In contrast, the early entry has to navigate with a great deal of uncertainty. For these reasons, most large computer companies were slow to make significant commitments to advanced office systems. They were uncertain what interconnecting software and hardware would be the basis for the systems adopted.

Disappointing Market Growth

Many shakeouts and price wars occur when market growth—even though it may still be healthy—falls below expectations, because competitors have built capacity to match the expectations. Demand for electronic banking took decades longer than expected to emerge, and demand for big-screen television took many years longer than expected to materialize. Forecasting is difficult, especially when the product market involved is new and dynamic and glamorized by popular euphoria.

The difficulty in forecasting is graphically illustrated by an analysis of more than 90 forecasts of significant new products, markets, and technologies that appeared in *Business Week, Fortune,* and the *Wall Street Journal* from 1960 to 1979.[11] Forecast growth failed to materialize in about 55 percent of the cases cited. Among the reasons were overvaluation of technologies (e.g., three-dimensional color TV and tooth-decay vaccines) or consumer demand (e.g., two-way cable TV, quadraphonic stereo, and dehydrated foods) or a failure to consider the cost barrier (e.g., the SST and moving sidewalks) or political problems (e.g., marine mining). The forecasts for "roll-your-own" cigarettes, small cigars, Scotch whiskey, and CB radios suffered from shifts in consumer needs and preferences.

Resource Constraints

The substantial financing requirements associated with a rapidly growing business are a major constraint for small firms. Royal Crown's Diet-Rite cola lost its leadership position to Coca-Cola's Tab and diet Pepsi in the mid-1960s when it could not match the advertising and distribution clout of its larger rivals. Even large, well-financed firms such as Apple and AT&T may have problems if they face heavy competing demands on available investment resources. Furthermore, financing requirements frequently are increased by higher than expected product development and market entry costs and by price erosion caused by aggressive or desperate competitors.

The organizational pressures and problems created by growth can be even more difficult to predict and deal with than financial strains. Many firms have failed to survive the rapid-growth phase because they were unable to obtain and train people to handle the expanded business or to adjust their systems and structures. Tandem Computers, which has justifiably prided itself on its ability to manage growth, believes its ability to grow is limited by its capacity to hire and train people. It is careful to avoid allowing growth to outstrip its personnel resources. Tandem has also attempted to have systems and structures in place in anticipation of future growth. In contrast, Korvette was an extremely successful pioneer discount chain until it failed to digest a growth spurt that saw sales and store size triple from 1962 to 1966. It simply was not able to develop the systems, structure, and personnel needed to cope with a much larger scale of operations.

Distribution Constraints

Most distribution channels can support only a small number of brands. For example, few retailers are willing to provide shelf space for more than four or five brands of a houseware appliance. As a consequence, some competitors, even those with attractive products and marketing programs, will not gain adequate distribution, and their marketing programs will become less effective.

Distribution limitations fueled the shakeout already appearing in the software business in the mid-1980s. More than 120 firms were making financial spreadsheet programs, whereas the market and distribution channels could not support more than a handful. Ultimately, only a few may survive. The beta format lost its position in video stores when the customer base became too small to support the inventory.

A corollary of the scarcity and selectivity of distributors, as market growth begins to slow, is a marked increase in distributor power. Their willingness to use this power to extract price and promotion concessions from manufacturers or to drop suppliers is often heightened by their own problems in maintaining margins in the face of extreme competition for their own customers. Many of the same factors that drew in an overabundance of manufacturers also contribute to overcrowding in subsequent stages of a distribution channel. The eventual shakeout at this level can have equally serious repercussions for suppliers.

SUMMARY

Market analysis is intended to help determine the attractiveness of a market to current and potential participants and to understand that market's structure and dynamics. A market analysis is often conducted along the following seven dimensions:

1. *Actual and potential market size.* The potential market includes the usage gap, which can be penetrated by creating increased use frequency, a greater variety of uses, new users, and new uses.

2. *Market growth.* To forecast growth patterns, it can be helpful to consider the forces driving sales, leading indicators, analogous industries, pressure on prices, and the existence of substitute products.

3. *Market profitability.* The competitive intensity of a market or any submarket will depend on five factors—existing competitors, supplier power, customer power, substitute products, and potential entrants. Barriers to entry include capital investment, economies of scale, access to distribution channels, and product differentiation.

4. *Cost structure.* One way to detect key success factors is to analyze the value added by the production stage and observe how it is changing. Another consideration is whether or not the market setting makes an experience curve strategy appropriate or even feasible.

5. *Distribution systems.* The need is to identify alternative channels and trends in their relative importance and to analyze the power relationships in each channel and how they might be changing.

6. *Market trends.* What trends in the market will affect future profitability of participant firms and key success factors?

7. *Key success factors.* What skills and assets are needed to compete in a strategic group now and in the future?

Growth market contexts involve a set of risks, the prime one being the threat of more competitors than the market can support. Other risks include the failure to gain distribution, inadequate resources, changing key success factors, changing technologies, the entry of superior products, and a failure of the market to meet growth expectations.

FOOTNOTES

[1] Greg Stanger, Clark Newby, Todd Andrews, Rob Wamer, Presley Stokes, and Lisen Stromberg, "The Ready to Eat Cereal Market," unpublished paper, 1991.

[2] Kathleen Deveny, "For Coffee's Big Three, A Gourmet-Brew Boom Proves Embarrassing Bust," *Wall Street Journal,* November 4, 1993, B1.

[3] This section draws on Michael E. Porter, *Competitive Advantage,* New York: The Free Press, 1985, Chapter 1.

[4] Anjali Grover, Per Lindberg, Paul Roberts, and Barbara Swales, "A Marketing Analysis of the Workstation Industry," unpublished paper, 1991.

[5] Jorge Alberto Souse De Vasconcellos and Donald C. Hambrick, "Key Success Factors: Test of a General Theory in the Mature Industrial-Product Sector," *Strategic Management Journal,* July–August 1989, pp. 376–382.

[6] Joe Brand, Lavon Eldemir, Ellen Ablow, and Stephen Ramirez, "The Record Industry," unpublished paper, 1990.

[7] John Dougery, Tomas Fabregas, Christan Koch, Lars Kogstad, and Aiexis Nasard, "The California Wine Industry Report," unpublished paper, 1991.

[8] Brian O'Reilly, "The Perils of Too Much Freedom," *Fortune,* January 11, 1993, p. 79.

[9] AT&T 1993 Annual Report.

[10] John Dougery, Tomas Fabregas, Christan Koch, Lars Kogstad, and Aiexis Nasard, "The California Wine Industry Report," unpublished paper, 1991.

[11] Steven P. Schnaars, "Growth Market Forecasting Revisited: A Look Back at a Look Forward," *California Management Review* 28(4), Summer 1986.

6

ENVIRONMENTAL ANALYSIS

There is something in the wind.

William Shakespeare, The Comedy of Errors

A poorly observed fact is more treacherous than a faulty train of reasoning.

Paul Valery, French philosopher

In this chapter, the focus changes from the market to the environment surrounding the market. The interest is in environmental trends and events with the potential to affect strategy, either directly or indirectly. Environmental analysis should identify such trends and events and estimate their likelihood and impact.

Although environmental analysis is one step removed from the market or industry, it is only one step. When conducting environmental analysis, it is very easy to get bogged down in an extensive, broad survey of trends. However, it is necessary to restrict the analysis to those areas relevant enough to have a significant impact on strategy.

Environmental analysis can be divided usefully, as shown in Figure 6.1, into five areas: technological, governmental, economic, cultural, and demographic. Each area is discussed and illustrated. Then, methods to forecast trends and events are presented. Clearly, an ability to anticipate important changes will be helpful. Scenario analysis—ways of creating and using future scenarios to help generate and evaluate strategies— follows. The question of identifying and ranking information-need areas is then addressed.

Dimensions of Environmental Analysis

Technology

One dimension of environmental analysis is technological trends or technological events occurring outside the market or industry that have the potential to impact strategies. They can represent opportunities to those in a position to capitalize. A new alternate technology could also pose a significant threat. For example, the cable TV industry, with its massive investment in the wiring of homes, is rightfully concerned with systems that allow customers to obtain signals directly from orbiting satellites. Express delivery services such as Federal Express have been affected by new forms of communication such as fax and e-mail.

Impact of New Technologies. Certainly it can be important, even critical, to manage the transition to a new technology. The appearance of a new technology, however, even a successful one, does not necessarily mean that businesses based on the prior technology will suddenly become unhealthy.

A group of researchers at Purdue studied 15 companies in five industries in which a dramatic new technology had emerged:[1]

- Diesel-electric locomotives versus steam.
- Transistors versus vacuum tubes.

FIGURE 6.1   Environmental Analysis

TECHNOLOGY

- To what extent are existing technologies maturing?
- What technological developments or trends are affecting or could affect the industry?

GOVERNMENT

- What changes in regulation are possible? What will their impact be?
- What tax or other incentives are being developed that might affect strategy?
- What are the political risks of operating in a governmental jurisdiction?

ECONOMICS

- What are economic prospects and inflation outlets for the countries in which the firm operates? How will they affect strategy?

CULTURE

- What are the current or emerging trends in lifestyles, fashions, and other components of culture? Why? What are their implications?

DEMOGRAPHICS

- What demographic trends will affect the market size of the industry or its submarkets? What demographic trends represent opportunities or threats?

GENERAL EXTERNAL ANALYSIS QUESTIONS

- What are the significant trends and future events?
- What threats and opportunities do you see?
- What are the key strategic questions—areas of uncertainty as to trends or events that have the potential to impact strategy? Evaluate these strategic questions in terms of their impact.

SCENARIOS

- What scenarios are worth being the basis of a scenario analysis?

- Ballpoint pens versus fountain pens.
- Nuclear power versus boilers for fossil-fuel plants.
- Electric razors versus safety razors.

Several interesting conclusions emerged that should give pause to anyone attempting to predict the impact of a dramatic new technology. First, the sales of the old technology continued for a substantial period, in part because the firms involved continued to improve it. Safety-razor sales have actually increased 800 percent since the advent of the electric razor. Thus, a new technology may not even signal the end of the growth phase of an existing technology. In all cases, firms involved with an old technology had a substantial amount of time to react to a new technology.

Second, it is relatively difficult to predict the outcome of a new technology. The new technologies studied tended to be expensive and crude at first. Furthermore, they started by invading submarkets. Transistors, for example, were first used in hearing aids and pocket radios. In addition, new technologies tended to create new markets instead of simply encroaching on existing ones. Throw-away ballpoint pens and many of the transistor applications were completely new-market application areas.

Forecasting New Technologies. One study indicated that past efforts to forecast technology had been remarkably successful. Richard N. Farmer looked back at the efforts to forecast environmental trends and events as represented by 21 articles that appeared in *Fortune* magazine during the 1930s and 1940s.[2] He found articles written prior to 1940 that made predictions about synthetic vitamins, genetic breakthroughs, the decline of railroads, the likelihood of TVs in all homes, the house-trailer explosion, and the advent of superhighways. A 1946 article accurately predicted the advent of the automated factory and the associated systems-analysis technology. Although Farmer found positive evidence of success at forecasting the impact of individual technologies, the record was much less impressive when it involved the cross-impact of one technology on another. For example, the impact of television on movies or the impact of diesel locomotives on steam locomotives was not considered. One implication of this study is that it is necessary to be more sensitive to the impact of a possible technological development on other technologies. We will return to cross-impact analysis shortly.

Government

The addition or removal of legislative or regulatory constraints can pose major strategic threats and opportunities. For example, the ban of some ingredients in food products (e.g., cyclamates) or cosmetics has dramatically affected the strategies of numerous firms. The impact of governmental efforts to reduce piracy in industries such as software (more than one-fourth of all software used is copied), audiocassettes, and movie videos is of crucial import to those affected. Deregulation in air travel, banking, railroads, and other industries has had enormous implications for the firms involved. The automobile industry is affected by fuel economy standards and by the luxury tax on automobiles costing over $32,000. The medical industry has been forced to justify investments in expensive equipment.

Information Technology

In nearly every industry, it is useful to ask what potential impact new information technology based on computer systems and new databases will have on strategies. How will it create SCAs and key success factors? Apparel manufacturers such as Levi Strauss, drug wholesalers such as McKesson, and retailers such as The Limited all have developed systems of inventory control, ordering, and shipping that represent substantial SCAs with which competitors have had to deal. Federal Express has stayed ahead of competitors by investing heavily in information technology. It was the first to have the ability to track packages throughout its systems and the first to link its systems with customers' computers. Merrill Lynch's Cash Management Account provided substantial customer benefits.

In supermarket retailing, the use of "smart cards," cards that customers present during checkout to pay for purchases, has been tested. Their use provides a record of all purchases that would allow

- Stores to build loyalty by rewarding cumulative purchase volume.
- Promotions to target individual customers based on their brand preferences and household characteristics.
- The use of cents-off coupons without the customer or store having to handle pieces of paper; the purchase of a promoted product would be discounted automatically.
- The store to identify buyers of slow-moving items to predict the impact on the store's choice of dropping an item.
- Decisions as to shelf space allocation, special displays, and store layout to be refined based on detailed data of customer shopping.

In the Farmer study mentioned earlier, forecasting in the 1930s and 1940s was extremely poor when international political events were involved. Thus, a mid-1930s article did not consider the possibility of American involvement in a European war. A 1945 article incorrectly forecast a huge growth in trade with Russia, not anticipating the advent of the Cold War. A Middle East scenario failed to forecast the emergence of Israel. International political developments, which can be critical to multinational firms, are still extremely difficult to forecast. A prudent strategy is one that is both diversified and flexible, so that a political surprise will not be devastating.

Economics

The evaluation of some strategies will be affected by judgments made about the economy, particularly inflation and general economic health as measured by unemployment and economic growth. Heavy investment in a capital-intensive industry might need to be timed to coincide with a strong economy to avoid a damaging period of losses. Usually it is necessary to look beyond the general economy to the health of individual industries. In the early 1980s, for example, the depression in the automobile market and related industries such as steel was much greater than in the economy as a whole.

A forecast of the relative valuations of currencies can be relevant for industries with multinational competitors. Thus, an analysis of the balance of payments and other factors affecting currency valuations might be needed. For example, in most developed countries, the automobile industry is extremely sensitive to changes in currency valuation.

Culture

Cultural trends can present both threats and opportunities for a wide variety of firms, as the following examples illustrate.

A dress retailer conducted a study that projected women's lifestyles. It predicted that a more varied lifestyle would prevail, that more time would be spent outside the home, and that those who worked would be more career-oriented. There were several implications relevant to the dress designer's product line and pricing strategies. For example, a growing number and variety of activities would lead to a broader range of styles and larger wardrobes, with perhaps somewhat less spent on each garment. Furthermore, more independence financially and socially would probably reduce the number of "follow-the-leader" fashions and the perception that certain outfits were required for certain occasions.

General Mills detected a set of consumer trends that influenced its expansion plans, including increased concern about the quality of food, diet, physical fitness, and "naturalness." Food-consumption patterns had shifted to increased away-from-home eating and staggered meals, because of more active lifestyles.[3] In response, General Mills

- Developed a chain of "Good Earth" restaurants specializing in natural foods.
- Entered the market for "healthy" eat-on-the-run products with Yoplait and Nature Valley Granola Bars.
- Developed a high-fiber cereal, "natural" cereals, and a series of vitamin-fortified cereals.
- Used more contemporary values in the advertising for threatened traditional brands like Cheerios and Wheaties.

The interest in health and nutrition has extended to pet food; there is concern for fat, calories, sodium, and preservatives, which has resulted

---

"Yesbuts"

Some trends such as the increases in the number of working women, interest in health, and single-person households are well known and their implications seem obvious. However, William Wells of the advertising agency DDB Needham suggests that when such trends are examined more closely, their character and implications can change.[4] By using an annual, large-sample national survey with hundreds of questions on diverse subjects such as shopping, nutrition, fashion, eating out, jogging, movies, products, and services used, it was possible to qualify some of these trends with some "yesbut" statements. For example:

YES, the number of working women in the population is and has been increasing BUT

- The increase is more glacial and long-term than explosive, as the percent of women in the work force has changed as follows:

1950	1960	1970	1980	1990
34	38	43	52	57

- Only about 4 percent of these women fit the image of a young MBA with a tailored suit and Coach briefcase; they are those in the top professional and managerial occupations.
- These women are not unusually convenience-oriented; they are not heavy users of cold cuts, packaged cookies, cake mix, frozen pizza, or other "convenience" items.

YES, there is an increased interest in exercise and harmful elements in food, BUT

- A relatively small percent of people engage in strenuous physical activities. On an average day, only about 8 percent participate in an active sport such as jogging or tennis.
- Those doing strenuous exercise are younger and not necessarily worried about harmful elements in food such as sugar, salt, or cholesterol.

YES, "single-person" households are increasing, BUT

- The "swinging singles" image is a bit deceptive. Only 25 percent of all singles are under 25, and 26 percent are over 65.

---

in significant opportunities and new product activity. In addition, many pet owners tend to think of their pets as people. The fact that there are more singles and nontraditional households contributes, because the pet takes on a new role in the living unit. There are implications as to the role of specialty stores and veterinarians in distributing product and in how a brand should relate to the user.

Demographics

Demographic trends can be a powerful underlying force in a market. Among the influential demographic variables are age, income, education, and geographic location.

The baby boomers, 77 million strong or 31 percent of U.S. population, have been making themselves felt as they move through their life cycle. In general, the population is aging. By the year 2000, consumers over 45 will increase by nearly 50 percent over 1990.

Teens are back as the baby boomers age. The 13- to 19-year-old population in the United States will peak at 31 million in the year 2010.[5] Teens mirror the age in which they live. They take for granted the consumer electronics spectrum, deal with adult issues such as AIDS and abortion, and have been called the MTV generation because of the MTV-influenced culture to which they have been exposed. Reaching them can be profitable as retailers such as The Gap and Wings and brands like Clearasil and Levi's have found.

Ethnic populations are rising rapidly and support whole firms and industries, as well as affect the strategies of mainline companies. Hispanic populations, for example, are growing about five times faster than non-Hispanic populations and are gaining in income as well. By the year 2000 they will be the largest minority group. The Asian-American population, currently five million in the United States, will increase 165 percent by the year 2000.

Responding to a Fading Yuppie Culture?

Yuppie culture and lifestyle has faded. The Yuppie generation has aged and found that possessions such as portable telephones, exercise machines, BMWs, and designer clothing have not brought the fulfillment that was promised. Some former Yuppies are looking toward lifestyles and values not based on possessions. Simplicity, naturalness, value, recycling, and relationships are among the new keywords. This change has presented challenges to firms like BMW that were well-positioned in the Yuppie era. BMW has responded by focusing upon the value represented by the German workmanship and design. But its legacy, once such an asset, has become something of a liability.

The movement of businesses and populations into different areas of the country has implications for many service organizations such as brokerage houses, real-estate ventures, and insurance companies. Furthermore, the revival of downtown urban areas has had considerable implications for retailers and real-estate developers, just as the earlier development of suburbia had.

One study has pointed out the strong and continuing trend toward the population growth of women over the age of 60. This group has a higher per capita income, more free time, and fewer family responsibilities than younger women. In addition, these women seem less reluctant to spend money than in the past. The study further indicates that such women are dissatisfied with available product selection, because relatively few products are positioned for their age group. This may suggest a real opportunity for products that focus on the mature woman.

FORECASTING ENVIRONMENTAL TRENDS AND EVENTS

There is obviously a large potential payoff in being able to detect current trends or events and, even better, to forecast future ones. But, how does one go about it?

Asking the Right Questions

The first basic step is simply to ask the right questions. What trends or events in the environment will affect industry size, our strategies, or those of our competitors? Figure 6.1 illustrates some questions that can form the basis for environmental analysis. Usually, those involved in developing a strategy are capable of formulating substantially complete answers to these questions if they simply take the time to consider them.

Trend Extrapolation

A simple method of forecasting is trend extrapolation. Demographic trends that are slow-moving are usually projectable. Some technological developments, like the cost of a unit of computer memory, can simply be extrapolated. In strategic decision making, however, it is often departures from an extrapolated trend that are of interest. Even in these cases, trend extrapolation provides a baseline from which a judgment can be made about turning points.

Asking Experts

An effective and efficient way to gain information about environmental trends and events is to ask questions of those who are experts in the various areas involved. Thus, in one study, retail merchants in the gourmet cookware business determined that the trend was toward basics and value, away from gadgets and gimmicks. Those knowledgeable in personal computers or in key application areas can make informal judgments about software trends for emerging computers.

There are several ways to obtain information from experts. One is to survey systematically their judgments as reported in trade and professional magazines. Another is to interview, perhaps by telephone, a set of experts. The interviews would usually be guided by an agenda but not a formal questionnaire. Cooperation can be encouraged by sharing study results. A variant would be to conduct group discussions with 6 to 10 experts; the resulting personal interchange can stimulate ideas.

Group discussions can be costly and difficult to organize. Furthermore, group dynamics can sometimes stifle views that depart from conventional wisdom, views that often are the most useful. The Delphi approach attempts to retain the advantages of group feedback without requiring group meetings. In a Delphi study, a questionnaire would be sent to a group of experts; they might be asked to predict the size of the solar-energy market and the nature of its composition 20 years hence, for example. The results would be summarized and tabulated and returned to the respondents, who would then be given a chance to change their opinions or to provide the rationale for their judgments. A third iteration would provide a new summary of the results, as well as arguments and rationales provided by the respondents.

Decomposing the Task

Predictions can often improve dramatically if the task is decomposed. Thus, instead of attempting to learn about the size of the solar-energy market in the year 2000, it might actually be easier to predict the demand for solar-energy use in swimming pools, water heaters, home heating, municipal power, and so on. Similarly, the demand for a new-technology medical-diagnostic instrument might be decomposed into first-time buyers, those buying a second unit, and those buying a replacement unit.

Cross-Impact Analysis

Cross-impact analysis is a set of methodologies designed to forecast an interrelated group of events. For example, consider Event A, that wind becomes an important energy source in the year 2000. Experts could estimate the probability of this event occurring. Using cross-impact analysis, they would consider simultaneously other events such as

- **Event B**—a breakthrough in which solar-energy cells become economical by the year 2000.
- **Event C**—the large-scale production of shale oil by 2000.
- **Event D**—the widespread use of solar energy for homes by 2000.
- **Event E**—the cost of oil triples (in constant dollars) by 2000.

The most interesting aspect of cross-impact analysis is determining the impact of one event on the probability of another. Thus, estimates of the probability that Event A will occur are obtained both under the assumption that Event B occurs and under the assumption that it does not. Similarly, Event A probabilities are estimated by assuming Event C occurs and by assuming it does not. With probability theory, the probability of patterns of technologies (or other environmental events) can be determined even though those providing judgments consider only two events at a time.

Whether or not this methodology is accessed, it is often worthwhile to consider the possible indirect impact of an environmental trend or event on a market. For example, what could be the impact on the health-food market of a further increase in people eating outside the home?

IMPACT ANALYSIS—ASSESSING THE IMPACT OF STRATEGIC QUESTIONS

An important objective of external analysis is to rank the strategic questions and decide how they are to be managed over time. Recall that a strategic question differs from a strategic decision in that it involves an area of uncertainty with implications for strategy. Which strategic questions merit intensive investment in information gathering and in-depth analysis, and which merit only a low-key monitoring effort?

The problem is that dozens of strategic questions, many with subquestions, are often generated. These questions can lead to an endless process of information gathering and analysis that can absorb resources indefinitely. A publishing company may be concerned about cable TV, lifestyle patterns, educational trends, geographic population shifts, and printing technology. Any one of these issues involves a host of subfields and could easily spur limitless research. For example, cable TV might involve a variety of pay-TV concepts, suppliers, technologies, and viewer reactions. Unless distinct priorities are established, external analysis can become descriptive, ill-focused, and inefficient.

The extent to which a strategic question should be monitored and analyzed depends on its impact and immediacy.

1. The impact of a strategic question is related to the following:

   • The extent to which it involves trends or events that will impact existing or potential SBUs (strategic business units).
   • The importance of the involved SBUs.
   • The number of involved SBUs.

2. The immediacy of a strategic question is related to
   - The probability that the involved trends or events will occur.
   - The time frame of the trends or events.
   - The reaction time likely to be available, compared with the time required to develop and implement appropriate strategy.

Impact of a Strategic Question

Each strategic question involves potential trends or events that could have an impact on present, proposed, and even potential strategic business units (SBUs). For example, a strategic question for a beer firm could be based on the future prospects of the microbrewery market. If the beer firm has both a proposed microbrewery entry and an imported beer positioned in the same area, trends in the microbrewery beer market could have a high impact on the firm. The trend toward "natural" foods may present opportunities for a sparkling water product line for the same firm and be the basis for a strategic question.

The impact of a strategic question will depend on the importance of the impacted SBU to a firm. Some SBUs are more important than others. The importance of established SBUs may be indicated by their associated sales, profits, or costs. However, such measures might need to be supplemented for proposed or growth SBUs in which present sales, profits, or costs may not reflect their true value to a firm. Finally, because an information-need area may affect several SBUs, the number of involved SBUs can also be relevant to a strategic question's impact.

Immediacy of Strategic Questions

Events or trends associated with strategic questions may have a high impact but such a low probability of occurrence that it is not worth actively expending resources to gather or analyze information. Similarly, if occurrence is far in the future relative to the strategic-decision horizon, then it may be of little concern. Thus, the harnessing of tide energy may be so unlikely or may occur so far into the future that it is of no concern to a utility.

Finally, there is the reaction time available to a firm, compared with the reaction time likely to be needed. After a trend or event crystallizes, a firm needs to develop a reaction strategy. If the available reaction time is inadequate, it becomes important to better anticipate emerging trends and events so that a reaction strategy can be initiated sooner.

Managing Strategic Questions

Figure 6.2 suggests a categorization of strategic questions for a given SBU. If both the immediacy and impact are low, then a low level of monitoring

FIGURE 6.2 Strategic Question Categories

Immediacy

		Low	High
Impact	**High**	Monitor and analysis; contingent strategies considered	In-depth analysis; strategy development
	Low	Monitor	Monitor and analysis

may suffice. If the impact is thought to be low but the immediacy is high, the area may merit monitoring and analysis. If the immediacy is low and the impact high, then the area may require monitoring and analysis in more depth, and contingent strategies may be considered but not necessarily developed and implemented. When both the immediacy and potential impact of the underlying trends and events are high, then an in-depth analysis will be appropriate, as will be the development of reaction plans or strategies. An active task force may provide initiative.

SCENARIO ANALYSIS

The essence of strategy development is to become creative; to surface new, effective strategies; and to view existing strategies from different perspectives. In fact, most strategic planning efforts are constrained by an existing mental model of the business and its environment. Strategies that emerge tend to be extrapolations of the past. How can new perspectives be introduced so that new alternatives are generated and old ones challenged? One answer is scenario analysis, an underused but powerful methodology. Consider the following examples:[6]

- A pharmaceutical company developed and examined scenarios based upon competitive new products. The conclusion that their investment plan was risky led to one of the largest mergers in U.S. history.

- The marketing organization of a bank analyzed scenarios based upon the future of U.S. interest and concluded that major geographic areas needed to be managed differentially in order to meet goals.

- An innovative European chemicals processor used alternative product and process R&D scenarios to identify contradictions in its long-range planning assumptions. As a result, alternatives were considered and $100 million in new investment was deferred until several competing R&D projects had played out.

- A software and services company developed three possible competitor scenarios with strategies for each. The result was the acceptance of a strategy which was a major departure from the past.

Scenarios provide a way to deal with complex environments where many other relevant trends and events interact with and affect one another. When a set of micro trends and events are aggregated into one, two, or three total scenarios of what the future environment will contain, the analysis is more manageable.

Scenarios also help deal with uncertainty. Instead of investing in information to reduce uncertainty (often an expensive and futile process), the possibility as opposed to the certainty of a scenario will be accepted. The strategist can then deal with the reality that it might not come to pass.

One key to scenario analysis is to have a strategist conduct the analysis. The process of developing scenarios and using those scenarios to consider new strategies and test existing ones will change mind-sets, challenge assumptions, create innovative options, and legitimize new directions. If the process is conducted by planners, experience shows that the necessary learning simply will not take place.

Scenario analysis as suggested by Figure 6.3 can be divided into four elements, the first of which is to identify the key scenarios.

Identify Scenarios

Strategic questions can drive scenario development because they address key areas of uncertainty. The impact analysis will serve to identify the

FIGURE 6.3 Scenario Analysis

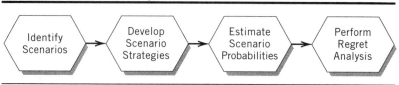

strategic question with the highest priority for a firm. A manufacturer of a medical imagery device may want to know whether or not a technological advance will allow its machine to be made at a substantially lower cost. A farm equipment manufacturer or ski area operator may believe that the weather—whether or not a drought will continue, for example—is the most important area of uncertainty. A workstation firm may want to know whether or not a single software standard will emerge or multiple standards will coexist. The question could then stimulate two or more scenarios.

When a set of scenarios is based largely on a single strategic question, the scenarios themselves can usually be enriched by related events and circumstances. Thus, an inflation-stimulated recession scenario would be expected to generate a host of conditions for the appliance industry.

It is sometimes useful to generate scenarios based on probable outcomes: optimistic, pessimistic, and most likely. The consideration of a pessimistic scenario is often useful in testing existing assumptions and plans. The aura of optimism that often surrounds a strategic plan may include implicit assumptions that competitors will not aggressively respond, the market will not fade or collapse, or technological problems will not surface. Scenarios analysis provides a nonthreatening way to consider the possibility of clouds or even rain on the picnic.

Often, of course, several variables are relevant to the future period of interest. The combination can define a relatively large set of scenarios. For example, a large greeting card firm might consider three variables important: the success of small "boutique" card companies, the life of a certain card type, and the nature of future distribution channels. The combination can result in a large number of possible scenarios. Experience has shown that two or three scenarios are the ideal number with which to work; any more and the process gets unwieldy and any value is largely lost.[7] Thus, it is important to reduce the number of scenarios by identifying a small set that ideally includes those that are plausible/credible, and those that represent departures from the present substantial enough to affect strategy development.

Develop Scenario Strategies

After scenarios have been developed, the next step is to relate them to strategies—both existing strategies and new options. A strategy tailored to an optimistic scenario might imply an aggressive effort to build capacity and to establish a strong market position. A pessimistic scenario could, conversely, suggest a strategy of avoiding investment and attempting to stabilize prices. A scenario based on a technological breakthrough could lead to an R&D program in that technology.

Estimate Scenario Probabilities

To evaluate alternative strategies, it is useful to determine the scenario probabilities. The task is actually one of environmental forecasting, except that the total scenario may be a rich combination of several variables. Experts could be asked to assess probabilities directly. A deeper understanding will often emerge, however, if causal factors underlying each scenario can be determined. For example, the construction equipment industry might develop scenarios based on three alternative levels of construction activity. These levels would have several contributing causes. One would be the interest rate. Another could be the availability of funds to the home-building sector, which in turn will depend on the emerging structure of financial institutions and markets. A third cause might be the level of government spending on roads, energy, and other areas.

Perform Regret Analysis

The final step is to compare the expected outcomes of each strategy if the wrong scenario emerges. What will happen if a strategy predicated on an optimistic scenario was pursued and the pessimistic scenario actually emerged? This exercise generates a feeling for and perhaps even a quantification of the risk associated with a strategy option. If such an evaluation can be quantified and the probability of each scenario can be estimated, the expected value of each strategy can be determined—it will be simply the sum of the outcomes under each scenario multiplied by the scenario probability.

SUMMARY

The role of environmental analysis is to detect, monitor, and analyze those current and potential trends and events that will create opportunities or threats to a firm. Environmental analysis can be divided, as shown in Figure 6.1, into five areas: technological, governmental, economic, cultural, and demographic.

Expert opinions often are helpful in environmental forecasting. It is usually worthwhile to consider the cross-impact of one environmental development on others. Impact analysis can help identify and evaluate strategic questions. The approach is to systematically assess the impact and immediacy of the trends and events that underlie each strategic question. Scenario analysis, a vehicle to explore different assumptions about the future, involves the creation of two to three plausible scenarios, the development of strategies appropriate to each, the assessment of scenario probabilities, and the evaluation of the resulting strategies across the scenarios.

FOOTNOTES

[1] Arnold Cooper, Edward Demuzilo, Kenneth Hatten, Elijah Hicks, and Donald Tock, "Strategic Responses to Technological Threats," *Academy of Management Proceedings,* 1976, pp. 54–60.

[2] Richard N. Farmer, "Looking Back at Looking Forward," *Business Horizons,* February 1973, pp. 21–28.

[3] Sandra D. Kresch, "The Impact of Consumer Trends on Corporate Strategy," *Journal of Business Strategy* 3, Winter 1983, pp. 58–63.

[4] William D. Wells, "YESBUTS," Chicago: DDB Needham, unpublished paper, 1990.

[5] Laura Zinn, "Teens," *Business Week,* April 11, 1994, pp. 76–84.

[6] Mason Tenaglia and Patrick Noonan, "Scenario-Based Strategic Planning: A Process for Building Top Management Consensus," *Planning Review,* March–April 1992, pp. 13–18.

[7] Robert E. Linneman and Harold E. Wein, "The Use of Multiple Scenarios by U.S. Industrial Companies," *Long-Range Planning* 12, February 1979, p. 84.

PART THREE

INTERNAL
ANALYSIS

7

SELF-ANALYSIS

We have met the enemy and he is us.

Pogo

Self-conceit may lead to self-destruction.

"The Frog and the Ox," Aesop

The fish is last to know if it swims in water.

Chinese proverb

In addition to external threats and opportunities, strategy development must be based on the objectives, strengths, and capabilities of a business. For example, Grand Met in the mid-1980s was involved in 28 different businesses including hotels, dairies, betting, gaming, childcare, pubs, and nursing services.[1] After self-analysis led to the conclusion that its strengths were marketing branded food and drink products and managing worldwide operations, Grand Met divested operations and focused on branded food and drink businesses with significant international potential.

Understanding a business in depth is the goal of self-analysis. A business self-analysis is similar to a competitor analysis, but it has a greater focus on performance assessment and is much richer and deeper. It is more detailed because of its importance to strategy, and because much more information is available. The analysis is based on detailed, current information on sales, profits, costs, organizational structure, management style, and other factors.

Just as strategy can be developed at the level of a firm, a group of strategic business units (SBUs), an SBU, or a business area within an SBU, self-analysis can be conducted at each of these levels. Of course, such analyses will differ from each other in emphasis and content, but their structure and thrust will be the same. The common goal is to identify organizational strengths, weaknesses, constraints, and, ultimately, responsive strategies, either exploiting strengths or correcting or compensating for weaknesses.

Self-analysis begins by examining the financial performance of a business, its profitability and sales. Indications of unsatisfactory or deteriorating performance might stimulate strategy change. In contrast, the conclusion that current or future performance is acceptable can suggest the old adage, "If it ain't broke, don't fix it." Of course, something that is not broken may still need some maintenance, refurbishing, or vitalization. Performance analysis is especially relevant to the strategic decision of how much to invest in or disinvest from a business.

The first section of this chapter considers shareholder value analysis. The next section discusses financial performance, as measured by sales, return on assets, and the economic value-added concept. The third section covers other performance dimensions linked to future profitability, such as customer satisfaction, product quality, brand associations, cost, new products, and employee capability. Chapter 8, "Portfolio Analysis," extends the material of this chapter by focusing on the performance of business units relative to each other and on the attractiveness of the external context of each.

Another perspective on self-analysis considers those business characteristics that limit or drive strategy choice. The fourth section examines five issues: past and current strategy, strategic problems, organizational capabilities and constraints, financial resources and constraints, and organizational strengths and weaknesses.

SHAREHOLDER VALUE ANALYSIS

Perhaps the most visible and influential development in strategy during the 1980s was the concept of shareholder value analysis (SVA). The interest in SVA is reflected in the many books and articles devoted to it and the number of consulting firms basing their practice on it. A host of major companies have applied SVA not only to place value on firms to be divested or acquired, but also to evaluate business units and their strategy options within a firm. SVA can be directly applied to evaluate a business or a strategy, and it provides a basis to understand business evaluation more generally.

SVA is simple, straightforward, and compatible with well-established concepts in finance.[2] A business is evaluated with respect to the value it creates for shareholders. Attaching a value to a business involves

1. Estimating the annual after-tax cash flows for a planning horizon:

$$\text{annual unit sales} \times \text{gross margin} - \begin{array}{l} \text{taxes,} \\ \text{fixed costs (advertising, R\&D, etc.),} \\ \text{investments in plant and working} \\ \text{capital} \end{array}$$

2. Obtaining the discounted value of this profit stream by applying the cost of capital for the business, the average of the cost of equity, and the cost of debt weighted by the relative size of the two.[3] The cost of equity is the cost of a risk-free investment (such as government bonds) plus an increment to account for the risk of the investment which is normally about 6 percent for a firm with average risk. The capital asset pricing model (CAPM) suggests that the only relevant risk is the "systematic" risk associated with the business area, that area of uncertainty caused by economy-wide fluctuations.

3. Estimating the residual value of the business unit, its value after the planning horizon. One approach is to assume that the profit level achieved during the end of the planning horizon will continue indefinitely or will grow or contract at a known rate.

4. Determining the total shareholder value, which is the sum of the present values of future cash flows and residual value less the market value of any debt associated with the business. A positive value means that the business is creating shareholder value. A negative value means that shareholder value is being eroded.

Shareholder Value Analysis at Coca-Cola

An SVA at Coca-Cola led to the conclusion that its entertainment business was not contributing positively to shareholder value.[4] As a result, it was spun off to a new firm called Columbia Pictures Entertainment. Coke's entries into pasta, instant tea, plastic cutlery, desalinization equipment, and wine all had ROI numbers around 8 percent, far below the cost of capital, and were therefore dumped.

SVA applied to the existing SBUs revealed that Coca-Cola's soda fountain business was not contributing to shareholder value because the business was very capital-intensive. Its return was only 12.5 percent, whereas the company's cost of capital was estimated at the time to be 16 percent. Switching from an expensive, five-gallon, stainless steel container to a disposable bag-in-a-box and to a 50-gallon container for large customers reduced the assets employed and increased return to 17 percent. The cost of capital was subsequently decreased from 16 to 12 percent by adding debt. As a result, Coke earned 29.4 percent on capital in 1993, almost 2.5 times its cost.

If a new strategy is to be considered, its value will be the difference between the value without the strategy option and the value with it.

SVA offers solutions to many of the problems associated with an analysis of business profitability using return on assets (ROA) as a standard. First, a focus on cash flow eliminates many accounting problems such as distortions caused by depreciation and asset book values. Second, and perhaps more important, SVA looks to future measures of profitability to evaluate a business. ROA considers current/past profits that are likely caused by investments years ago. The profits due to current investments and strategies are ignored unless there is a willingness to rely on the assumption that the present is a good predictor of the future.

SVA theoretically helps reduce the tendency of managers to be driven by the short-term pressures of the stock market because of its forward-looking thrust.[5] However, it does stress and reinforce the dominance of shareholder interest over that of other stakeholders such as employees, suppliers, customers, and communities. In that sense, it could, especially for those who do not employ it carefully, actually inhibit movements from the short-term financials that appear to influence investors.

SVA also focuses attention on financial analysis and a stream of numbers rather than on the development of creative, innovative strategic options and the underlying SCAs that must exist to generate future success. In general, strategy focuses on customers and competitors, whereas SVA focuses on shareholders. In the long run, of course, customer value and competitive advantage will generate shareholder value, but an undue emphasis on the shareholder and financial analysis may inhibit the convergence of the two.

Of course, SVA is fundamentally based on the ability of managers to provide good objective estimates of future profits, including residual value. Providing such estimates is extremely difficult. There is a pervasive tendency to be overly optimistic about market acceptance of new ventures and underestimate the time and investment required. In addition, there are numerous sources of uncertainty, including competitor reactions. In fact, as the uncertainty goes up, so does the potential to make the numbers match the managerial instinct that they are supposed to replace.

Of special concern is the ability to properly evaluate strategic options associated with a strategy. A move into a new market, for example, provides the possibility of developing new products for that market or engaging in geographic expansion. When, for instance, Black & Decker bought GE's small appliance business, it really bought an option to develop other products for that market. Usually a tendency exists to underestimate or even ignore the value of such strategic options. Even when they are included, estimation problems are substantial.

FINANCIAL PERFORMANCE—SALES AND PROFITABILITY

Self-analysis often starts with an analysis of current financials, measures of sales and profitability. Changes in either can signal a change in the market viability of a product line and the ability to produce competitively. Furthermore, they provide an indicator of the success of past strategies and thus can often help in evaluating whether strategic changes are needed. In addition, sales and profitability at least appear to be specific and easily measured. As a result, it is not surprising that they are so widely used as performance evaluation tools.

Most firms have sales and profitability targets as key elements of their objectives. Y. K. Shetty, a management professor and consultant, obtained a statement of corporate objectives from 82 large companies from four basic industrial groups and found that 89 percent used a profitability measure and 82 percent included a sales target.[6] Objectives such as market share, social responsibility, employee welfare, product quality, and research and development were found in fewer than two-thirds of the firms.

Sales and Market Share

A sensitive measure of how customers regard a product or service can be sales or market share. After all, if the relative value to a customer changes, sales and share should be affected, although there may be an occasional delay caused by market and customer inertia.

Sales levels can be strategically important. Increased sales can mean that the customer base has grown. An enlarged customer base, if we assume that new customers will develop loyalty, will mean future sales and profits. Increased share can provide the potential to gain SCAs in the form of economies of scale and experience curve effects. Conversely, decreased sales can mean decreases in customer bases and a loss of scale economies.

A problem with using sales as a measure is that it can be affected by short-term actions such as promotions by a brand and its competitors. Thus, it is important to separate changes in sales that are caused by tactical actions from those that represent fundamental changes in the value delivered to the customer. It is therefore important to couple an analysis of sales or share with that of customer satisfaction, which will be discussed shortly.

Profitability

Profits are certainly important indicators of business performance. They provide the basis for the internally or externally generated capital needed to pursue growth strategies, to replace obsolete plants and equipment, and to absorb market risk.

One basic profitability measure is return on assets, which is calculated by dividing the profits by the assets involved:

$$ROA = \frac{profits}{assets}$$

Equivalently, the following formula, developed by General Motors and DuPont in the 1920s, can be used to decompose ROA to return on sales and asset turnover:

$$ROA = \frac{profits}{sales} \times \frac{sales}{assets}$$

Thus, return on assets can be considered as having two causal factors. The first is the profit margin, which depends on the selling price and cost structure. The second is the asset turnover, which depends on inventory control and asset utilization.

The determination of both the numerator and denominator of the ROA terms is not as straightforward as might be assumed. Substantial issues surround each, such as the distortions caused by depreciation and the fact that book assets do not reflect intangible assets such as brand equity or the market value of tangible assets. These issues are discussed further in the appendix to this chapter.

What Is Good Performance?

What should the target projected ROA be for existing businesses? What rate of return or hurdle rate should be expected from a proposed strategic move? The term "hurdle rate" is used because it is the hurdle that must be cleared before an investment is considered viable. The hurdle rate will also be the discount rate used to determine the net present value of a proposed investment, the present value of the net stream of cash that flows from the investment.

Each business should earn an ROA that meets or exceeds the cost of capital, the weighted average of cost of equity and cost of debt.

In a provocative and influential article, Hayes and Garvin suggest that U.S. firms tend to set pretax hurdle rates artificially high, in the range of 25 to 40 percent, even when the ROA of their existing business might be much lower.[7] The high hurdle rates seem to be "safe" in that they are appropriate for the riskiest investments. The problem is that they are not adjusted down for investments such as upgrading capital equipment in existing businesses, which represent relatively safe investments. The result is bias against modernizing current business operations, and this has had an adverse effect on productivity in the United States.

Economic Value Added

Economic value added (EVA) provides an SVA perspective to the evaluation of business performance that takes into account profits, cost of capital, and capital employed.[8] The formula is

$$EVA = \text{net operating profit} - (\text{costs of capital} \times \text{capital employed})$$

$$\text{where net operating profit} = \text{operating profit} - \text{taxes}$$

The concept is that every business will employ capital in the form of plant, inventory, working capital, and other assets. Further, capital has a cost. To then get a measure of the firm's financial performance, an amount needs to be deducted from the net operating profit to reflect the cost of capital employed. If the result is positive, then the business has contributed positively to the shareholder value. If it is negative, the shareholder lost value during the year.

For example, 1993 calculations for Anheuser-Busch were as follows:

Operating profit	$1,756 million
−Taxes	617 million
	$1,139 million
Net operating profit	$1,139 million

Weighted cost of capital	11.3%
(67% equity @ 14.3%; debt @ 5.2%)	
×Total capital employed	$8,000 million
	$ 904 million

− Cost of capital in dollars	904 million
EVA	$ 235 million

Thus, Anheuser Busch added shareholder value by $235 million, a very good result.

The key to the analysis is the total capital employed. Prior to the introduction of EVA, capital employed looked like a free good and there was no incentive to reduce it. With EVA in place, however, great pressure is brought to reduce capital employed. Thus, CSX, a transportation company, has learned to operate very differently under EVA. It has reduced the number of containers it uses from 18,000 to 14,000, and they no longer sit in terminals for weeks between runs. Slower trains are pulled by three locomotives instead of four, saving fuel as well as reducing capital further. Quaker Oats has reduced its number of warehouses and inventory by completely changing the way it plans production.

An intriguing refinement of EVA is to capitalize expenditures on intangible assets such as people and brand equity. They can be amortized over three, five, or seven years, or whatever makes most sense. The reality is that for many businesses, intangible assets are the key to the future of the business, and it is worthwhile to handle them as such. The analysis is not tied to accounting rules. An extension would be to actually measure the value of intangibles instead of simply adding expenditures. Human assets might be measured by replacement cost and brand equity might be measured by the price premium it commands in the market.

The routes to increasing EVA are clear:

1. Earn more profit by reducing costs or increasing revenue without using more capital.
2. Invest in high return products—this, of course, is what strategy is all about.
3. Reduce the cost of capital by increasing the debt ratio or by reducing the risk of the portfolio of businesses.

4. Use less capital. This route has been a source of dramatic improvements in performance for many businesses which had previously considered capital a free good.

PERFORMANCE MEASUREMENT—BEYOND PROFITABILITY

One of the difficulties in strategic market management is developing performance indicators that convincingly represent long-term prospects. The temptation is to focus on short-term profitability measures and to reduce investment in new products and brand images that have long-term payoffs.

The concept of net present value represents a long-term profit stream, but it is not always operational. It often provides neither a criterion for decision making nor a useful performance measure. It is somewhat analogous to preferring $6 million to $4 million. The real question involves determining which strategic alternative will generate $6 million and which will generate $4 million.

Thus, it is necessary to develop performance measures that will reflect long-term viability and health. The focus should be on the assets and skills that underlie the current and future strategies and their SCAs. What are the key assets and skills for a business during the planning horizon?

Japanese versus U.S. Managers

Japanese managers differ sharply from U.S. managers with respect to their priorities.[9] The following table illustrates this point by showing that Japanese managers place almost no value on stockholder capital gain in assessing objective priorities. Shown are the average objective importance ratings in which three points are assigned to the objective considered most important (from a set of nine objectives), two points for the second-most important, and one point for the third-most important. The rank order is shown in parentheses.

| | Objective Importance | |
Objectives	U.S. Firms	Japanese Firms
ROI	2.43 (1)	1.24 (2)
Stockholder capital gain	1.14 (2)	0.02 (9)
Increase in market share	0.73 (3)	1.43 (1)
New product ratio	0.21 (7)	1.06 (3)
Number of firms responding	227	255

What strategic dimensions are most crucial: to become more competitive with respect to product offerings, to develop new products, or to become more productive? These types of questions can help identify performance areas that a business should examine. Answers will vary depending on the situation, but, as suggested by Figure 7.1, they will often include customer satisfaction/brand loyalty, product/service quality, brand/firm associations, relative cost, new product activity, and manager/employee capability and performance.

Customer Satisfaction/Brand Loyalty

Perhaps the most important asset of many firms is the loyalty of the customer base. Measures of sales and market share are useful but crude indicators of how customers really feel about a firm. Such measures reflect market inertia and are noisy, in part, because of competitor actions and market fluctuations. Measures of customer satisfaction and brand loyalty are much more sensitive and provide diagnostic value as well.

Guidelines for Measuring Satisfaction and Loyalty. First, problems and causes of dissatisfaction that may motivate customers to change brands or firms should be identified. Second, often the most sensitive and insightful information comes from those who have decided to leave a brand or firm. Thus, "exit interviews" for customers who have abandoned a brand can be very productive. Third, there is a big difference between a brand or firm being liked and the absence of dissatisfaction. The size and intensity of the customer group that truly "likes" a brand or firm should be known.

FIGURE 7.1 Performance Measures Reflecting Long-Term Profitability

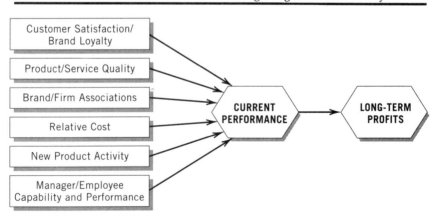

Fourth, measures should be tracked over time and compared with those of competitors. Relative comparisons and changes are most important.

Product and Service Quality

A product (or service) and its components should be critically and objectively compared both with the competition and with customer expectations and needs. How good a value is it? Can it really deliver superior performance? How does it compare with competitor offerings? How will it compare with competitor offerings in the future given competitive innovations? One common failing of firms is to avoid tough comparisons with a realistic assessment of competitors' current and potential offerings.

Product and service quality are usually based on several critical dimensions that can be identified and measured over time. For example, an automobile manufacturer can measure defects, ability to perform to specifications, durability, repairability, and features. A bank might be concerned with waiting time, accuracy of transactions, and the quality of the customer experience. A computer manufacturer can examine relative performance specifications and product reliability as reflected by repair data. A business that requires better marketing of a good product line is very different from one that has basic product deficiencies.

Brand/Firm Associations

An often overlooked asset of a brand or firm is what customers think of it. What are its associations? What is its perceived quality? Perceived quality, of course, can be very different from actual quality. It can be based on experience with past products or services and on quality cues such as retailer types, pricing strategies, packaging, advertising, and typical customers. Is a brand or firm regarded as expert in a product or technology area (such as designing and making sailboats)? Innovative? Expensive? For the country club set? Is it associated with a country, a user type, or an application area (like racing)? Such associations can be key strategic assets for a brand or firm.

The word-processing software firm WordPerfect is known for helpful, efficient product support. WordPerfect pioneered the practice of toll-free telephone backup in the software industry. Others can match this service but will find it hard to dislodge WordPerfect in the customers' minds on this dimension. The image of customer support is an enduring asset for WordPerfect.

Associations can be monitored by regularly asking customers in focus groups to describe their use experiences and to tell what a brand or firm means to them. The identification of changes in important associations will likely emerge from such efforts. Structured surveys using a representative sample of customers can provide even more precise tracking information.

Relative Cost

A careful cost analysis of a product (or service) and its components, which can be critical when a strategy is dependent on achieving a cost advantage or cost parity, involves tearing down competitors' products and analyzing their systems in detail. The Japanese consultant, Ohmae, suggested that such an analysis, when coupled with performance analysis, can lead to one of the four situations shown in Figure 7.2.[10]

If a component such as the braking system in a car or a bank's teller operation is both more expensive and inferior to that of the competition, a strategic problem requiring change may exist. An analysis could show, however, that the component is such a small item both in terms of cost and customer impact that it should be ignored. If the component is competitively superior, however, a cost-reduction program may not be the only appropriate strategy. A value analysis, in which the component's value to the customer is quantified, may suggest that the point of superiority could support a price increase or promotion campaign. If, on the other hand, a component is less expensive than that of the competition, but inferior, a value analysis might suggest that it be de-emphasized. Thus, for a car with a cost advantage but handling disadvantage, a company might de-emphasize its driving performance and position it as an economy car. An alternative is to upgrade the relative rating with respect to this component. Conversely, if a component is both less expensive and

FIGURE 7.2 Relative Cost vs. Relative Performance—Strategic Implications

superior, a value analysis may suggest that the component be emphasized, perhaps playing a key role in positioning and promotion strategies.

Sources of Cost Advantage. The many routes to cost advantage will be discussed in Chapter 11. They include economies of scale, the experience curve, product design innovations, and the use of a no-frills product offering. Each provides a different perspective to the concept of competing on the basis of a cost advantage.

Average Costing. In average costing, some elements of fixed or semi-variable costs are not carefully allocated but instead are averaged over total production. Thus, a plant may contain new machines and older machines that differ in the amount of support required to operate them. If support expenses are averaged over all output, the new machines will appear less profitable than they are and some inappropriate decisions could be precipitated.

Average costing can provide an opening for competitors to enter an otherwise secure market. For example, the J. B. Kunz Company, a maker of passbooks for banks, created a situation in which large-order customers were subsidizing small-order customers because of average costing.[11] The cost system inflated the costs of processing very large orders and thus provided an opportunity for competitors to underbid Kunz on the very profitable large orders. A product line that is subsidizing other lines is vulnerable, representing an opportunity to competitors and thus a potential threat to a business.

New Product Activity

Does the R&D operation generate a stream of new product concepts? Is the process from product concept to new product introduction well managed? Is there a track record of successful new products that have affected the product performance profile and market position?

The key self-analysis at Xerox that led to a remarkable turnaround in the 1980s showed that a critical problem was the company's inability to compete successfully in several major new product efforts.[12] The result was a product line that was at a growing performance disadvantage and increasingly vulnerable to competition. This assessment led to a restructuring of the organization to remove impediments to the new product process. For example, multifunctional new product teams were created and the approval process was streamlined.

Manager/Employee Capability and Performance

Also key to a firm's long-term prospects are the people who must implement strategies. Are the human resources in place to support current and

---

Benchmarking

Comparing the performance of a business component with others is called *benchmarking*. Xerox used benchmarking in the early 1980s to help correct a serious cost deficiency.[13] As part of the program, Xerox tore apart the machines of its competitors. Finding that its costs were excessive in comparison to other companies, Xerox established cost reduction as a prime design goal. To obtain other cost-reduction ideas, Xerox attempted to identify organizations in other industries that were particularly good in functional areas similar to those of Xerox.

L. L. Bean, the outdoor sportswear retailer and mail-order house, became one of the models for Xerox warehouse operations. Like the Xerox system, the L. L. Bean system involved products diverse in size, shape, and weight, which precluded the use of automation. The L. L. Bean warehouse system was computerized and included the following characteristics:

- Fast-moving items were stocked closest to the picking route. (An order is filled by "picking" the needed items from the warehouse inventory.)
- Incoming items were stored randomly to maximize space utilization and to minimize forklift travel distance.
- Orders were sorted to minimize picker travel distance.
- Incentive bonuses were based on picking productivity adjusted for errors.

Five other warehouse benchmark studies were also made. An electrical components manufacturer, for example, used bar-code labeling and a label scanner, and an appliance manufacturer developed an efficient way to maximize the forklift operation. These benchmark studies helped Xerox improve its annual productivity gains in the logistics and distribution area from 3 to 5 percent to around 10 percent. Company-wide efforts of this type helped Xerox to overcome a cost gap with respect to Japanese manufacturers that many felt was insurmountable.

---

future strategies? Do those who are added to the organization match its needs in terms of types and quality? Or are there gaps that are not being filled? Tandem Computers sustained rapid growth by deliberately staffing and organizing for the next growth phase. In contrast, Osborne Computer, which enjoyed huge sales in the early 1980s with a low-cost system that included popular software programs, could not develop the systems, people, and structure to cope with growth. It subsequently failed.

An organization should be evaluated not only on how well it obtains human resources but also how well it nurtures them. A healthy organization will consist of individuals who are motivated, challenged, fulfilled, and growing in their professions. Each of these dimensions can be observed and measured by employee surveys and group discussions. Certainly the attitude of production workers was a key factor in the quality and cost advantage that the Japanese automobile firms enjoyed throughout the 1970s. In service industries such as banking and fast foods, the ability to sustain positive employee performance and attitude is usually a key success factor.

DETERMINANTS OF STRATEGIC OPTIONS

Another perspective on self-analysis is to consider the determinants of strategic options. What characteristics of a business make some options infeasible without a major organizational change? What characteristic will be pivotal in making a choice between strategic options? Again, the answers to these questions will depend on the situation, but as noted in Figure 7.3, five areas warrant close scrutiny.

Past and Current Strategies

To understand the bases of past performance and attempt to sort out new options, it is important to be able to make an accurate profile of past and current strategies. Sometimes the strategy has evolved into something very different from what was assumed. For example, a firm positioned itself as an innovator and spent heavily on R&D to repeat its early break-through innovation. However, an honest analysis of its operations over the past two decades indicated that its success was based on manufacturing strengths and scale economies. In reality, others had introduced almost all the meaningful innovations in the industry during that period. A recognition that the R&D effort had been successful in improving product features, reliability, and cost, but not in developing any technological breakthroughs, was helpful in structuring strategic options.

FIGURE 7.3 Determinants of Strategic Options and Choices

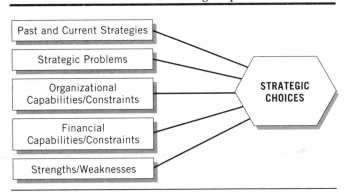

Strategic Problems

Another relevant and helpful construct is the strategic problem, a problem with strategic implications, such as the package tampering of Tylenol capsules or a delay in bringing a computer-based ordering system online. A strategic problem differs from a weakness or liability, which is the absence of an asset (e.g., good location) or skill (e.g., new product introduction skills). A business copes over time with a weakness or liability by adjusting strategies. Strategic problems, in contrast, need to be addressed and corrected even if the fix is difficult and expensive.

For example, U.S. automobile firms in the late 1970s decided that they had a quality (or "fit and finish") problem with respect to their Japanese and German competitors. Such a problem could and did precipitate some important strategic moves involving product design and production decisions.

Organizational Capabilities/Constraints

The internal organization of a company—its structure, systems, people, and culture—can be an important source of both strengths and weaknesses. The flexible, entrepreneurial organizational structure of 3M, in which new business teams and divisions are continually spun off, is a key to its growth. The systems of McDonald's and some other fast-food chains are important strengths. The background of Texas Instruments' management, largely engineering and manufacturing, has been a source of strength in its semiconductor businesses, but it has been a weakness in its consumer products efforts. The productive, low-cost culture at Dana and White has allowed it to pursue a low-cost strategy.

Internal organization can affect the cost and even the feasibility of some strategies. There must be a "fit" between a strategy and the elements of an organization. If the strategy does not fit well, it might be expensive or even impossible to make it work. For example, an established centralized organization with a background oriented to one industry may have difficulty implementing a diversification strategy requiring a decentralized organization and an entrepreneurial thrust. Internal organization is considered in more detail in Chapter 16, which discusses strategy implementation and the concept of fit.

Financial Resources and Constraints

Ultimately, judgments need to be made about whether or not to invest in an SBU or withdraw cash from it. A similar decision needs to be made about the aggregate of SBUs. Should a firm increase its net investment or decrease it by holding liquid assets or returning cash to shareholders or debtholders? A basic consideration is the firm's ability to supply investment resources.

A financial analysis to determine probable, actual, and potential sources and uses of funds can help provide an estimate of this ability. A cash flow analysis projects the cash that will be available from operations and depreciation and other assets. In particular, a growth strategy, even if it simply involves greater penetration of the existing product market, usually requires working capital and other assets, which may exceed the funds available from operations. The appendix to this chapter provides a discussion of how to conduct a cash flow analysis.

In addition, funds may be obtained either by debt or equity financing. To determine the desirability and feasibility of either option, an analysis of the balance sheet may be needed. In particular, the current debt structure and a firm's ability to support it will be relevant. The appendix also reviews some financial ratios that are helpful in this regard.

A division or subsidiary may need to consider how much support and involvement it can expect from a parent organization, particularly in regard to its investment proposals. The scenario of multiple SBUs all planning investments that, in the aggregate, are far beyond a firm's willingness and ability to support, is all too common. A realistic appraisal of a firm's resources can make strategy development more effective.

Organizational Strengths and Weaknesses

A key step in self-analysis is to identify the strengths and weaknesses of an organization that are based on its assets and skills. In fact, much of self-analysis is motivated by the need to detect strengths and weaknesses. There are, of course, many possible sources of strengths and weaknesses. In Chapter 4, methods to identify such sources of strengths and weaknesses are presented. In Chapter 9, we discuss how assets and skills become the bases of sustainable competitive advantages.

FROM ANALYSIS TO STRATEGY

In self-analysis, organizational strengths and weaknesses need to be not only identified but also related to competitors and the market. Strategic market management, as noted in Chapter 1, has three interrelated elements. The first is to determine areas in which to invest or disinvest. Investment could go to growth areas such as new product markets or programs designed to create new strength areas or to support existing ones. The second is the specification and implementation of functional area strategies involving product policy, manufacturing strategy, distribution choices, and so on. The third element of strategic market management is to develop assets and skills, bases of sustainable competitive advantage in the product markets where a firm competes.

In making strategic decisions, inputs from a variety of assessments are relevant, as the last several chapters have already made clear. However, the core of any strategic decision should be based on three types of assessments. The first concerns organizational strengths and weaknesses. The second evaluates competitor strengths, weaknesses, and strategies, because an organization's strength is of less value if it is neutralized by a competitor's strength or strategy. The third assesses the competitive context, the customers and their needs, the market, and the market environment. These assessments focus on determining how attractive the selected market will be, given the strategy selected.

The goal is to develop a strategy that exploits business strengths and competitor weaknesses and neutralizes business weaknesses and competitor strengths. The ideal is to compete in a healthy growing industry with a strategy based on strengths that are unlikely to be acquired or neutralized by competitors. Figure 7.4 summarizes how these three assessments combine to influence strategy.

FIGURE 7.4   Structuring Strategic Decisions

GE's decision to sell its small appliance division illustrates these strategic principles.[14] Small appliances were a part of GE's legacy and were linked to its lamp and major appliance product lines in the minds of retailers and customers. The small appliance industry was not profitable, however, in part because of overcapacity and the power of the retailer. Also, cost pressures contributed to a reduction in product performance and reliability. Further, GE's strengths, such as its technological superiority and financial resources, were not leveraged in the small appliance business. Anyone could knock off any innovation. Thus, GE decided that a strategic fit did not exist, and it sold the small appliance business to Black & Decker in the mid-1980s.

PRODUCT PORTFOLIO ANALYSIS

A very useful part of self-analysis is a product portfolio analysis in which the various business units are examined to determine the attractiveness of the market involved, the strength of a firm's position in that market, and whether or not the businesses have been generating or using cash. The analysis then suggests some strategies for deciding how the various businesses should be treated—whether cash should be invested into or withdrawn from them. Product portfolio analysis uses several well-developed models and techniques. Chapter 8 is devoted to their description. Some of the product portfolio models are based on experience curve theories that are discussed in Chapter 11.

SUMMARY

Shareholder value analysis uses discounted present value to understand cash flows associated with a strategy. It is theoretically sound and appropriately forward-looking (as opposed to current financials that measure the results of past strategies). However, it focuses attention on financial measures rather than other indicators of strategic performance. Developing the needed estimates, particularly the cash flow projections, is difficult and subject to a variety of biases.

Sales and profitability analysis provides an evaluation of past strategies and an indication of the current market viability of a product line. Return on assets, a basic measure, can be distorted by the limitations of accounting measures. An appropriate target rate of return should reflect a return premium over the prevailing risk-free interest rate to reflect the systematic risk of the business, the variation in profits driven by economy-wide fluctuations.

Economic value added (EVA) provides an SVA perspective to the evaluation of business performance. The concept is that every business will employ capital and that capital has a cost. To get a measure of a business's financial performance, an amount needs to be deducted from the net operating profit to reflect the cost of capital employed. If the result is positive, then the business has contributed positively to the shareholder value.

Performance should also be evaluated along other dimensions relevant to a business and its strategy. Included are customer satisfaction/brand loyalty, product/service quality, brand/firm associations, relative cost, new product activity, productivity, manager/employee capability, and performance.

Another perspective considers the business characteristics that limit or drive strategic choice, factors such as past and current strategy, strategic problems, organizational capabilities and constraints, financial resources and constraints, and organizational strengths and weaknesses. The final strategy choice attempts to employ organizational strengths in a context in which competitor strengths are either nonexistent or neutralized.

FOOTNOTES

[1] Grand Metropolitan Annual Report, 1993.

[2] For descriptions of SVA see Alfred Rappaport, *Creating Shareholder Value*, New York: The Free Press, 1986; David L. Wenner and Richard W. Leser, "Managing for Shareholder Value—From Top to Bottom," *Harvard Business Review*, November–December 1989, pp. 52–68; Roger A. Kerin, Vijay Mahajan, and P. Rajan Varadarajan, *Strategic Market Planning*, Boston: Allyn & Bacon, 1990; Chapter 9; Enrique R. Arzac, "Do Your Business Units Create Shareholder Value?" *Harvard Business Review*, January–February 1986, pp. 121–126; Shawn Tully, "The Real Key to Creating Wealth," *Fortune*, September 20, 1993, pp. 38–50.

[3] The formula is

$$\text{Cost of capital} = r_D(1 - T)\, D/(D + E) + r_E\, E/(D + E)$$

where: r_D = the interest rate associated with the debt
r_E = the rate of return on an equity investment in the business
D = the size of the debt
E = the size of the equity in the business
T = the corporate tax rate

[4] Bernard C. Reimann, "Managing for the Shareholders: An Overview of Value-Based Planning," *Planning Review*, January–February 1988, pp. 10–22, and Shawn Tully, "The Real Key to Creating Wealth," *Fortune*, September 20, 1993, pp. 38–50.

[5] For an excellent discussion of the limitations of SVA and the problems of implementing the concept, see George S. Day and Liam Fahey, "Putting Strategy into Shareholder Value Analysis," *Harvard Business Review*, March–April 1990, pp. 156–162.

[6] Y. K. Shetty "New Look at Corporate Goals," *California Management Review* 22, Winter 1979, pp. 71–79.

[7] Robert H. Hayes and David A. Garvin, "Managing as if Tomorrow Mattered," *Harvard Business Review*, May–June 1982, pp. 70–79.

[8] Shawn Tully, "The Real Key to Creating Wealth," *Fortune*, September 20, 1993, pp. 38–50.

[9] Tadao Kagono, Ikujiro Nonaka, Kiyonori Sakakibara, and Akihiro Okumura, *Strategic vs. Evolutionary Management—A U.S.–Japan Comparison of Strategy and Organization*, New York: North-Holland, 1985, p. 28.

[10] Kenichi Ohmae, *The Mind of the Strategist*, New York: Penguin Books, 1982, p. 26.

[11] J. B. Kunz Company A, Case 9-577-115, Boston, Mass.: Intercollegiate Case Clearing House.

[12] Gary Jacobson and John Hillkirk, *Xerox: An American Samurai*, New York: Macmillan, 1985.

[13] Frances G. Tucker, Seymour M. Zivan, and Robert C. Camp, "How to Measure Yourself Against the Best," *Harvard Business Review*, January–February 1987, pp. 8–10.

[14] Robert Slater, *The New GE*, Homewood, Ill.: Irwin, 1993, p. 101.

APPENDIX
THE ANALYSIS OF FINANCIAL RESOURCES

This appendix is designed to discuss some basic accounting issues and methods that affect the self-analysis of a business. The first two sections detail the problems of two key accounting constructs: book assets and accounting profits. The third provides a description of how to conduct an analysis of the sources and uses of funds that are the basis for cash flow projections.

Book Assets

The most accessible estimate of both existing and future asset values is usually the book value, the original cost less accumulated depreciation. Book value, however, is usually a distorted measure of assets employed.

Sometimes a major business investment does not appear on a balance sheet as a book asset. For example, new product development requires R&D effort, marketing research expenditures, and market introduction costs, all of which are expensed. The asset created, a new brand and most of what is associated with it, does not appear as a book asset. Advertising, which can create a strong brand name and associated image, is also expensed. The most important assets of many businesses, particularly services, are their human assets, but they are rarely reflected in book assets. Even when physical assets such as a building are a major asset component, their book value will depend on the depreciation schedules, which are driven by tax considerations. As a result, book asset value may bear little resemblance to either replacement cost or liquidation value.

Thus, book assets must be examined when interpreting ROA measures. It is sometimes possible to adjust book assets to reduce distortions. Book assets can be replaced with liquidation values or replacement costs. Investments in new products or advertising can be considered assets for the purposes of ROA analysis. Another approach is to supplement ROA with other profitability measures such as the profit margin, the profit per person (for a law firm), or profit per square foot of selling space (for a retailer).

Accounting Profits

There are several problems with accounting profits. One is allocated costs over which the business unit may have little control, costs such as corporate executives and corporate staff. In that context, it may be useful to use contribution margin, which is the gross profit prior to allocating costs, to represent profits in the numerator. Another issue arises when several SBUs share activities or assets such as sales forces, staff activities, production facilities, or distribution activities. It is important that these costs be properly and consistently divided among the SBUs so that what appear to be changes in performance are not simply based on changes in cost allocations.

Depreciation is another potential source of misinterpretation. It can, for example, understate the investment needed to maintain a business at its present level. A seemingly profitable business can be mortgaging its future if investment necessary to maintain the business is not forthcoming. If depreciation is inadequate to fund this necessary investment level, the investment needs to be funded either from profits or other sources, or the business will decline. For example, Chrysler, by reducing investment in the late 1960s, provided short-term profits at the expense of long-term business health. The concept of the investment level needed to maintain a current business, if it differs markedly from the depreciation level, may be useful.

Sometimes cash flow is of more interest than profitability because cash flow is not affected by depreciation. Cash flow is the basis of the shareholder value analysis.

Projecting Cash Flow—Sources and Uses of Funds

A projection of cash flow during the strategy horizon is essential to determine what base of cash resources is available and what cash needs will be required. At the outset, a reasonable baseline assumption might be made that current strategies and trends will extend into the near future.

It can be helpful also to project the flow of funds given both optimistic and pessimistic scenarios. The impact of changes in strategies and the introduction of new strategies can then be determined.

Figure 7A.1 shows a simplified balance sheet and the major categories of sources and uses of funds. It will provide a context in which to discuss the principal elements of a cash flow analysis. As the sources and uses of funds items are presented, some useful balance sheet ratios will be introduced. They provide measures of the financial health of a firm in terms of its assets and debt structure. As such, they are helpful in making judgments concerning the desirability and feasibility of raising money through debt or equity financing.

The first item under the source and use of funds in Figure 7A.1 is changes in net working capital. Working capital is defined as current assets less current liabilities (generally liabilities under one year). The

FIGURE 7A.1 Balance Sheet and Sources and Uses of Funds Statement

Balance Sheet, December 31 (Millions)

Current Assets		6.0	Current Liabilities		3.0
• Cash, receivables, investments	3.5		• Accounts payable	2.0	
• Inventory	2.5		• Other	1.0	
			Long-term Liabilities		2.0
Fixed Assets		6.0			
• Property, plant, and equipment	10.0		Equity		7.0
• Less accumulated depreciations	4.0		• Capital stock	4.0	
			• Retained earnings and other	3.0	
Total Assets		12.0	Total Liabilities		12.0

Projected Sources and Uses of Funds

Sources of Funds		Uses of Funds	
• Decrease in net working capital	0	• Increase in networking capital	1.0
• Sale of fixed assets	0	• Purchase of fixed assets	2.5
• Issue L. T. liabilities	2.0	• Retire L. T. liabilities	0
• Sell capital stock	0	• Buy back capital stock	0
• Operations: net income	1.0	• Operations: net losses	0
• Depreciation	.5	• Dividends	0
Total Sources of Funds	3.5	Total Uses of Funds	3.5

current ratio is one way of measuring the adequacy of working capital:

$$\text{current ratio} = \frac{\text{current assets}}{\text{current liabilities}}$$

The most desirable ratio will depend, of course, on the nature of a business. In particular, firms with large amounts of assets in inventories may require a higher ratio. Another ratio that deletes inventories is called the quick or acid-test ratio:

$$\text{quick ratio} = \frac{\text{current assets less inventory}}{\text{current liabilities}}$$

As sales grow, of course, working capital will have to grow also so that it will continue to be adequate for supporting operations.

The second item concerning the sources and uses of funds in Figure 7A.1 is the sale or purchase of fixed assests. The acquisition of fixed assets might be divided into that necessary for maintaining current operation levels and that for more discretionary expenditures to generate growth.

Again, the analysis of the sources and uses of funds should reflect the implications of any proposed growth strategy.

The third funds-flow category is the issue or retirement of long-term debt. In determining the appropriate debt level, useful ratios are

$$\text{debt-to-equity ratio} = \frac{\text{long-term liabilities}}{\text{equity}}$$

$$\text{total debt-to-equity ratio} = \frac{\text{total liabilities}}{\text{equity}}$$

Of course, the higher these ratios are, the larger the interest burden in a downturn and the lower the ability to obtain new debt in an emergency. The optimal level will depend on the ability of the earnings to carry added interest expense, the policy of a firm toward debt and its associated risk, the return expected on future investment, and the debt-to-equity ratio of competing firms. The use of funds obtained from debt financing will be relevant for determining how much debt to undertake. If the funds are to be used to buy a firm, the structure of the resulting combined balance sheet and funds flow must be considered.

The fourth category shown in Figure 7A.1 is changes in capital stock. To what extent is it feasible and desirable to raise capital through the sale of stock? Conversely, it may be beneficial to use funds to buy stock if the stock is undervalued, as compared with alternative investments.

Finally, there are the sources of funds from operations, which provide the base from which investment planning will begin. To net income, depreciation expense is added, and dividends to be paid are subtracted. Depreciation is an expense item that does not involve cash outflow. Thus, depreciation is actually a source of funds. Obviously, the net income from operations will interact with other sources. For example, increasing debt will increase interest expense, which will reduce the funds available from future operations. And, the ability to raise stock may depend on dividend policy. Furthermore, investment or disinvestment in assets will affect depreciation in future years.

In evaluating the balance sheet, considerable judgment and reservation may be appropriate. There may be bad debts among the reported receivables, the depreciation may not reflect plant deterioration, and assets and liabilities may have market values that differ substantially from their reported book value. Inflation effects contribute to the interpretation difficulties. Thus, it might be appropriate to interpret or adjust the ratios and cash flow projection accordingly.

8

PORTFOLIO ANALYSIS

A little neglect may breed great mischief
. . . for want of a nail the shoe was lost; for
want of a shoe the horse was lost.

Benjamin Franklin

Dig a well before you are thirsty.

Chinese proverb

A key element of self-analysis is the assessment of the strength of a business position in the market. Portfolio analysis, which has had a rich and colorful history in strategy management, extends strength assessment in three directions.

First, portfolio analysis combines the assessment of business position with a market attractiveness evaluation, which emerges from external analysis in general and market analysis in particular. One output of portfolio analysis is thus a compact summary representation of the two most important assessments of any business.

Second, portfolio analysis includes multiple strategic business units (SBUs) in the same analysis and addresses the SBU investment decision—which organizational units should receive resources, which should have resources withheld, and which should be resource generators. The basic resource allocation problem is created as follows. A firm has a variety of SBUs, each needing cash and each able to generate cash. In a decentralized organization, it is natural for the manager of a cash-generating SBU to control the available SBU cash. The basic incentive of an SBU manager, after all, is profitable growth, and any SBU manager will have ready investment opportunities that will stimulate growth for his or her SBU. However, the result is that a fast-growing SBU, which may have low profit or even losses but enormous potential, with a huge need for cash, will often be starved of needed cash. The culprit is the decentralization policy that requires or encourages SBUs to fund their own growth. The irony is that SBUs involving mature products may have inferior investment alternatives, but because cash flow is plentiful in these SBUs, their investments still get funded. The net effect is to channel available cash to low-potential areas and to withhold it from the most attractive areas. The portfolio models force the issue of which SBUs should receive the available cash.

Third, portfolio analysis offers baseline recommendations concerning the investment strategies for each SBU based on an assessment of business position and market attractiveness. These baseline recommendations can serve to introduce strategic options that might not otherwise be considered.

Of course, the strategic investment-allocation decision can occur at several levels. For example, at the corporate level, a decision might be needed regarding investment in or allocation to divisions, groups of SBUs, or individual SBUs. At the SBU level, the choice might be between multiple products. At the product level, managers might need to decide which market to enter. As will be seen, some of the portfolio models are more appropriate for certain levels than others and each model must be interpreted differently for various levels of analysis.

Portfolio analysis exploded on the scene in the mid-1960s with colorful labels such as dogs, stars, and cash cows, which have since become part of the strategy vocabulary. However, it was at first oversold as the method that provided strategy recommendations which should always be followed. In the 1970s, when it became clear that the model assumptions did not always hold, there was a tendency to discredit the portfolio models and dismiss them as being at best useless and at worst dangerous, leading to disastrous strategies. In the 1980s and 1990s a realization emerged that the models are useful but should be considered only a part of internal analysis. Their role is thus to summarize information and to suggest strategy options, particularly with respect to the resource allocation decision, rather than to dictate strategy choices.

In this chapter, two portfolio models are discussed: the BCG (Boston Consulting Group) growth-share matrix and the industry attractiveness-business position matrix associated with General Electric. The chapter concludes with a discussion of risk assessment and the experience of managers with portfolio analysis.

THE BCG GROWTH-SHARE MATRIX

The BCG concept of the experience curve evolved during the 1960s into a highly visible portfolio model termed the growth-share matrix. The BCG growth-share matrix, being both simple and easily quantifiable, is often a useful first step in portfolio analysis. It suggests that the desirability of the market can best be expressed by the market growth rate, and that the best summary indication of a firm's strength in a market is its relative market share. Thus, the growth-share matrix positions the various SBUs within a firm in terms of these two dimensions, as Figure 8.1 illustrates.

The Growth Dimension

Of all the characteristics of a market, why select growth as the single indicator of its desirability? The reasons include the following:

- Growth is perhaps the best measure of the product life cycle, a key strategic consideration.
- Market share is assumed to be more easily gained in a growth context when new users with no developed loyalties are attracted to the product class. Furthermore, competitors may react less aggressively to the loss of new customers than to the loss of their base of existing customers.
- Share gain is important, in part, because of its link to the experience curve, a point that will be discussed in more detail when the second dimension of the growth-share matrix is introduced.

FIGURE 8.1   The Growth-Share Matrix

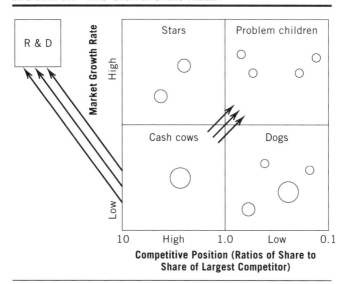

• A market position in a growth market will be worth more in the future as the market grows, if we assume the position can be retained. It is normally easier to retain market share than to gain it.

• In a growth market, demand often exceeds supply; excess demand will support premium prices and profit levels.

• By aggressively entering into a growth market and establishing a sustainable competitive advantage, a firm can discourage competitors from entering the market.

The midpoint of the growth dimension is somewhat arbitrary but is usually set at a 10 percent annual growth rate. Thus, markets growing in excess of 10 percent are considered to be high-growth markets, whereas those growing below 10 percent are low-growth markets.

The Market-Share Dimension

The second dimension of the growth-share matrix is market share. Actually, the horizontal axis in Figure 8.1 is a relative competitive position, as defined by the ratio of market share to the share of the largest competitor. The log scale is used so that the midpoint of the axis is 1.0, the point at which a firm's market share is exactly equal to that of its largest competitor. Anything to the left of the midpoint indicates that the firm has the leading market-share position.

Relative market share is selected as the single indicator of a firm's position for several reasons:

- The largest-share firm will very likely enjoy advantages of size such as economies of scale, high brand recognition, channel dominance, and the strongest bargaining position with customers and suppliers.
- The market leader is in the best position to exploit the experience curve because it will accumulate experience faster than competitors. The experience curve model, to be discussed in detail in Chapter 11, suggests that cumulative production experience will result in lower unit costs because of learning effects, technological improvements in production/operations, and product redesign.
- Empirical evidence indicates that market share is related to profitability.

A host of empirical studies suggest that profitability is related to market share. One of the most relevant, because of the extensive database involved, is the PIMS (profit impact of market strategy) study. The PIMS database, its background, some empirical findings, and the ways in which firms can draw on it to help evaluate strategy are described in the boxed insert.

One of the dramatic PIMS findings is the relationship between ROI and market share, as shown in Figure 8.2. On average, a difference of 10 percent in market share is accompanied by a difference of about 5 percent in pretax ROI.

The relationship shown in Figure 8.2 reflects differences among businesses and should not be interpreted as predictive of the change in ROI that a firm would enjoy if it increased its market share. The fact is that a share increase might be costly. High-market-share firms may differ from a low-share business on a host of dimensions besides market share. In particular, they may simply have better management and may be luckier. Having the good fortune or skill to be in the right market with the right product may have caused both market share and profits to increase. In fact, Jacobson and Aaker, also using the PIMS database, found that when an effort was made to control for management quality and luck, a 10-point change in market share by itself would result in only a 1-point improvement in ROI.[1]

The market share to ROI relationship will also depend on context. Another PIMS study determined that high-market-share businesses with relatively low ROI tended to have low-quality reputations, charge higher prices, share marketing resources with other businesses, and be in regional and fragmented markets.[2]

The Matrix and Its Cast of Characters

The position of a set of SBUs is shown in Figure 8.1. The size of each circle represents the sales level of the SBU. The matrix is divided into

FIGURE 8.2   Relationship Between Market Share and Pretax ROI

Number of businesses: approximately 2,000

four quadrants, and the products or SBUs in each have been given colorful labels. Each is associated with baseline policy implications.

Stars.   The upper left quadrant contains the high-share SBUs operating in high-growth markets. Because they are in growth contexts, the model predicts that they will have a heavy need for cash to support that growth. However, because they are in a strong competitive position (they are, in fact, the highest-share competitors), it is assumed they will be farthest down the experience curve, and should therefore have high margins and be generating large amounts of cash. Thus, they will be both users and providers of large cash flows. On balance they should generally be self-supporting with respect to their cash needs. If cash is required for a star to maintain its share position, however, then it should be provided. Any temptation to net out large amounts of cash, sacrificing position, should be resisted.

Cash Cows.   Cash cows are high-share SBUs operating in a low-growth market. Because of their market position, their cash generation should be high. Because the market is mature, the cash investment needs should be

The PIMS Program[3]

In the early 1960s, General Electric embarked on an internal project to attempt to explain the differences in profitability among its various SBUs. This project was later expanded through a nonprofit research group to include SBUs from many diverse companies. The PIMS database now contains data from over 3000 SBUs representing more than 450 firms. Some of these SBUs have been in the database since 1970. Each SBU supplies to the PIMS database detailed information such as:

- ROI (return on investment)
- Market share
- Investment intensity—the ratio of investment to sales
- R&D expenditures
- Marketing expenditures
- Perceived product quality—the percent of offerings that were superior to those of competitors, and the percent perceived by the SBU managers as inferior

Analysis of these data has revealed that highly capital-intensive businesses tend not to have high ROI because of the high investment and because capital-intensive industries tend to be characterized by vigorous price competition. Another finding, discussed in Chapter 10, is that high-quality products can be more profitable than low-quality products, regardless of whether or not a low or high price is charged.

In addition to general findings and observations, the PIMS project provides member firms with reports that indicate what ROI an average SBU "should" be expected to make, given its characteristics in terms of the PIMS variables. These reports can be used to evaluate SBU performance.

Also available is a PIMS-based prediction of how the SBU's ROI would change if a policy change were made, such as increasing expenditures on R&D. Although such predictions are suggestive and provide an inexpensive way to explore policy changes, taking them too seriously is foolish. They are based largely on relationships between SBUs. The problem is that firms that spend more on R&D are different in many ways from firms that spend little on R&D—in particular, each has an R&D organization and a philosophy that is unique. It is unrealistic to think that if a firm increases its R&D expenditures, it will suddenly be similar to the firm with the large R&D expenditures and actually perform as well.

The PIMS data and analysis are not without problems. The key market-share variable is sensitive to the product-market definition used by the SBU manager. Other variables such as perceived product quality depend on subjective judgments. In cross-section analysis, differences in ROI that appear to be caused by market share or other variables could actually be caused by differences among industries or among strategic groupings of firms. Also, the sample of firms in the PIMS database is likely to be biased toward larger firms that are industry leaders.

small and these businesses should therefore be a source of substantial amounts of cash that can be channeled to other areas.

Dogs.   Low-share SBUs that are in low-growth markets are called dogs. Because of their weak share, it is assumed that their progress on the experience curve is slow and thus their profits will be low or nonexistent. Furthermore, because growth is low, expansion of share is assumed to be very costly. Dogs are often cash users and possibly even "cash traps"— products that perpetually absorb cash, in part because of the investment required to maintain position.

Problem Children.   Low-share businesses in high-growth markets, problem children (sometimes called question marks or wildcats) are assumed to have heavy cash needs because, although they need to fund growth, they generate little cash because they are not far down the experience curve. If a problem child's market share cannot be changed, it will continue to absorb cash. As its market matures, it will become a cash-absorbing dog, a cash-trap scenario. If market share can be adequately improved, however, a question mark can be converted into a star. Usually such a strategy will require heavy influxes of cash during the short run. Improved position should eventually enable it to generate cash, become a star, and then, ultimately, a cash cow.

Strategy Implications

As Figure 8.1 indicates, the general strategy is to take cash from the cash cows to fund R&D, the source of future SBUs, and those problem children that have the potential to gain share to achieve star status. The cash cows should receive a maintenance investment level, but any tendency to automatically reinvest the cash they are generating should be avoided. Stars, on the other hand, should be managed to maintain share; current profitability should be of lesser concern. Given that the stars are adequately financed, a limited number of the most promising problem children can be selected for investment to try to improve their shares. The other problem children should not receive investment. They should be sold, abandoned, or milked for whatever cash they can produce.

The dogs, usually the most prevalent category, present a challenge. Several alternatives are available. First, a dog can sometimes become very profitable through the pursuit of a "focus" segmentation strategy, in which the business specializes in a small niche where it can dominate. In effect, it would then be the star or cash cow of the redefined market. Second, investment can be withheld and the business milked or harvested of whatever cash is forthcoming until the business dies. Third, the business can be sold or simply liquidated. Managers should be wary of "turnaround" plans for dogs, particularly when there is no fundamental change in the market or environment.

One of the most dramatic examples of a strategy being driven by market share and related considerations is that of Jack Welch, the chairman of General Electric.[4] His policy is to compete only in those industries in which GE has a competitive advantage that will support its being either in the first or second position. During ten years as CEO, Welch reduced GE's portfolio of major businesses from about 100 businesses to 14 with commanding market shares. GE is first in the United States and the world in aircraft engines, broadcasting (NBC), circuit breakers, electric motors, engineering plastics, industrial and power systems, lighting, locomotives, and medical diagnostic imaging. In major appliances and lighting, GE is second in the world market. Among the businesses that did not meet Welch's criteria and were thus sold were computer chips, TV sets, small appliances, and coal mines.

In summary, the BCG growth-share portfolio model is a scheme for managing cash. It suggests that overt decisions need to be made regarding whether or not an SBU is to be a cash generator or cash user. It further suggests that the number of SBUs selected to be cash users should be limited so that enough resources will be available to improve each one's position. Similarly, some SBUs, namely, the cash cows and those dogs and problem children selected for milking, should generate cash and be allowed only minimal investment. It is also helpful to apply this analysis to competitors as a means of predicting what they might do, especially if the competitors are known to be using a portfolio model. The general strategies of divestment, milking, and holding position are discussed in more detail in Chapter 14. Chapters 12 and 13 cover growth strategies.

Assumptions and Limitations

The BCG growth-share matrix is usually easy to develop, because measures on the two dimensions are often readily available and the baseline conclusions usually clear. The fact that the model is so simple also means that its assumptions are both evident and vulnerable in many contexts.[5]

The Assumption That Market Share Affects Cost. The motivation for using relative share to describe competitive position is based on the assumption that market share will affect costs because of scale economies and experience curve effects, both discussed in Chapter 11. Thus, the growth-share-matrix logic is unlikely to apply when a business consists of a variety of products, each with its own manufacturing operation and operating on its own experience curve. Thus, it is rarely helpful in allocating investment over divisions or groups of SBUs. Furthermore, an experience-curve-based, low-cost strategy is only one of several ways to compete. Relative market share will not be as likely to be relevant to differentiation or focus strategies, for example.

Even if the experience curve is relevant for all the organizational units involved, there may be difficulties in applying it. In particular, SBUs may not be operating on the same experience curve because one SBU

- Is better able to share experience with other SBUs.
- Has different overhead structures.
- Uses a different technology.
- Benefits from vendor experience or from knowledge of production-method developments.
- Is less capable of reducing costs via product redesign, automation, or other approaches.

The Growth Dimension. A basic premise of the growth-share matrix and, indeed, of much business strategy writing and practice is that growth markets are attractive investment areas. As the discussion in Chapter 5 makes clear, such a premise and its underlying assumptions should be carefully examined in each specific context.

Furthermore, it may not be easy to accurately forecast future growth. Past growth, which is usually available, may not be a good predictor of future growth.

The Product-Market Definition. The whole analysis is highly sensitive to the definition of the product market. As noted in Chapter 5, there are almost always several levels of market definition that, although defensible, would each generate very different strategy implications. Is the appropriate market "laptop computers" or "all personal computers?" A firm such as Toshiba might be strong in the laptop market but very weak in desktop computers. Should the market be only the market served? A California maker of beer or furniture, or a California seller of insurance could define its market as including only California, the West, or the whole United States. A refrigerator firm could define its market as apartment dwellers and ignore homeowners. An SBU manager can rather easily "change" his or her problem child into a star by suitably redefining its product market.

The Cash-Flow Focus. The growth-share matrix focuses on cash flow. However, the SBU is usually also interested in ROI, sales growth, and risk. It is not at all clear that the recommended investments in stars and selected question marks will maximize ROI. Furthermore, the recommendations could lead to investments clustered in a single technology, market, or production facility that would inherently involve relatively high risk. A consideration of risk could lead to investments in multiple technologies even if that meant investing in dogs.

Implementation. Increasing the market share of a problem child can involve unacceptable amounts of cash, especially if a competitor has a similar strategy or is protecting a star. Furthermore, antitrust laws can inhibit growth. Xerox and IBM, for example, have both been restricted by antitrust action from combining service contracts with product sales. Others have been prevented from increasing share through acquisition. Government regulation or labor power, particularly in Europe, can make it difficult for a firm to withdraw from a market. Even the niche-strategy alternative for dogs and problem children can be difficult to implement. If a product line requires full-service backup, it might not be feasible to carve out a small product or market niche. These problems and others are discussed further in Chapter 14.

THE MARKET ATTRACTIVENESS–BUSINESS POSITION MATRIX

The BCG portfolio model is deliberately simplistic in that it focuses on cash flow and uses two variables, growth and share. General Electric planners, in reacting to the limitations of the BCG model, developed the market attractiveness–business position matrix, drawing on portfolio approaches used by the consulting firm, McKinsey.[6] The structure of this matrix is shown in Figure 8.3.

Consider first market attractiveness, the horizontal axis. Instead of being based only on market growth, it is based on as many relevant factors as are appropriate in a given context. Nine factors that could be used are shown in Figure 8.3. The managers involved need to select the most appropriate factors, weight them as to relative importance in terms of context, evaluate a market on each factor, and then combine the evaluation into a summary measure. Thus, the analysis has the potential of being richer and more valid than one using only growth.

The evaluation of a market with respect to the factors selected is made on the basis of the prospective ROI. Thus, the focus is on ROI prospects rather than cash flow even though the analysis is usually more qualitative than quantitative.

Consider next the business-position assessment as shown on the vertical axis. Instead of using only market share as a criterion, as many factors as are appropriate for the given context are employed. A partial list of potentially useful factors is shown in Figure 8.3. Again, specific factors need to be selected, their relative appropriateness assessed, the SBU needs

FIGURE 8.3   The Market Attractiveness–Business
Position Matrix

Market Attractiveness

		High	Medium	Low
	High	1	1	2
Business Position; Its Ability to Compete	**Medium**	1	2	3
	Low	2	3	3

1. Invest/grow
2. Selective investment
3. Harvest/divest

Evaluating the Ability to Compete	**Evaluating Market Attractiveness**
• Size	• Size
• Growth	• Growth
• Share by segment	• Customer satisfaction levels,
• Customer loyalty	• Competition; quantity, types,
• Margins	effectiveness, commitment
• Distribution	• Price levels
• Technology skills	• Profitability
• Patents	• Technology
• Marketing	• Governmental regulations
• Flexibility	• Sensitivity to economic
• Organization	trends

to be rated on each factor, and finally, the ratings need to be combined
into an overall assessment of a firm's ability to compete in the market.

Applying the Matrix

The market attractiveness–business position matrix is a formal, structured
way to attempt to match a firm's strengths with market opportunities. It
is therefore similar to the ideas presented in Chapter 7 about developing
strategy to reflect firm strengths and weaknesses, competitor strengths
and weaknesses, and market attractiveness. In this context, the competitors' strengths and weaknesses are made a part of the market attractiveness assessment.

One implication is that when both firm position and market attractiveness are positive, as in the boxes marked 1 in Figure 8.3, then a firm
should probably invest and attempt to grow. When the assessment is more
negative, as in the boxes marked 3, however, the nominal recommendation

would be to either harvest or divest. For the three boxes marked 2, an investment decision would be made only selectively, when there was a specific reason to believe the investment would be profitable.

A useful exercise is to attempt to predict whether either your position or the attractiveness of the market will change if it is assumed the current strategy is followed. A predicted movement to another cell can signal the need to consider a change in strategy.

In structuring strategies, the following are among the logical alternatives:

- *Invest to hold.* Attempt to stop erosion in position by investing enough to compensate for environmental and competitive forces.
- *Invest to penetrate.* Aggressively attempt to move the position up, even at the sacrifice of earnings.
- *Invest to rebuild.* Attempt to regain a previously held position that has been lost by a milking strategy that, for whatever reason, is no longer appropriate.
- *Selective investment.* Attempt to strengthen position in some segments and let position weaken in other segments.
- *Low investment.* Attempt to harvest the business, drawing cash out and cutting investment to a minimum.
- *Divestiture.* Sell or liquidate the business.

The industry attractiveness–business position matrix is much richer than the growth-share matrix. As a result, it is not limited to "volume" industries, but can be applied in other competitive settings as well. Furthermore, its structure can be adapted more easily to higher-level investment-allocation decisions such as those across divisions. A business-position and a market-attractiveness rating may both represent averages of several component businesses. However, such average ratings can still have conceptual meaning for the purpose of structuring an allocation decision. They become a way to evaluate the extent to which an organizational unit has been able to match organizational strengths with competitive weaknesses in attractive markets. Recall the discussion at the end of Chapter 7 covering this underlying aim of strategy development.

Limitations

Although the market attractiveness–business position matrix is indeed much richer and more broadly applicable than the BCG growth-share matrix, its measures can also be more subjective and ambiguous, especially across business units. The selection and weighting of factors and the subsequent development of both a firm's position and market attractiveness are highly subjective processes. They can be unduly influenced by historical perspectives and performance and by individual biases and backgrounds. The final evaluations are bound to be somewhat unreliable in that different people will obtain different evaluations. Furthermore, different business units will undoubtedly require consideration of different factors, both in assessing business positions and in determining market attractiveness. The fact that two businesses have been evaluated with respect to different criteria adds ambiguity to the analysis.

As is true of the growth-share matrix, the results can be very sensitive to the definition of the product market. The analyses of market attractiveness and business position can both be dramatically affected if the market is luxury cars instead of all cars, stout instead of beer, or greeting cards sold through drugstores instead of all greeting cards.

THE RISK MATRIX

Portfolio analysis as applied by Shell Chemicals U.K. introduces environmental risk into the model.[7] The logic is that the risk from environmental forces affecting a business area may not be easily integrated into the "business-sector-prospects" axis because it involves a very different type of analysis. The risk matrix approach considers environmental risk as a separate axis in the model. Figure 8.4 shows an environmental-risk axis added to the business-sector-prospects axis.

The risk position is based on the seriousness of environmental threats and the probability of their occurrence. The inclusion of the environmental-risk dimension allows the baseline strategy recommendations to be adjusted for the risk factor. A moderate to high risk level will cause the appraisal of the market to be reduced.

PORTFOLIO MODELS IN PRACTICE

Philippe Haspeslagh, a business policy professor at INSEAD in France, conducted a study of firms drawn from the Fortune "1000" industrial firms that had used portfolio models.[8] About one-third of the respondents in the study felt that the most important benefit of using portfolio models was achieving a better understanding of their businesses, which in turn, they felt, led to better strategic decision making. In part, the analysis contributed by providing a vocabulary and graphic tools that aided communication. Another one-third felt that the key benefits were improved resource allocation, strategic reorientation, and exit and entry decisions. The balance of firms had developed no opinion or focused on the objectivity and commitment that emerged from the process.

FIGURE 8.4 The Risk Matrix

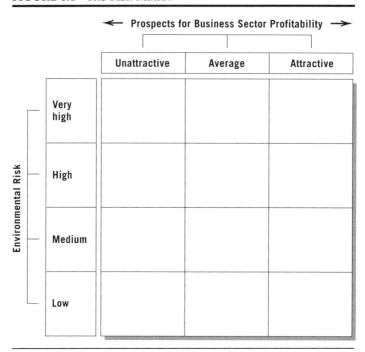

The decision as to which portfolio model to use was not regarded as critical. In fact, the labels commonly used, such as dog, cash cow, and star, were often found to be irrelevant and even the source of problems. The implication is that the models tended to be used qualitatively and that the experience curve thrust of the growth-share matrix was not a dominant part of the use of the models. Considered fundamental to portfolio planning were

1. Defining the SBUs for purposes of strategic decisions.
2. Classifying those SBUs on a portfolio grid according to their competitive positions and the attractiveness of their markets.
3. Considering the implications of using this framework to assign growth and financial objectives to each SBU and to allocate resources accordingly.

SUMMARY

Portfolio models can help firms that are operating diverse businesses to understand their group of businesses and to allocate resources among them. The BCG growth-share matrix rates markets on the basis of their growth rate, the assumption being that growth markets are more attractive investments than mature markets (an assumption discussed in Chapter 5). Market position is indicated by relative market share, which is related to ROI in the PIMS studies, and is also crucial to an experience-curve-based strategy. The resulting matrix has four quadrants that define SBUs as stars, cash cows, dogs, or problem children. The baseline strategy is to use cash generated by cash cows and selected dogs and problem children to fund embryonic businesses, promising problem children, and any stars requiring investment in excess of their own cash flow. Among the model's limitations are the fact that the experience curve is not always relevant or easy to work with, the inadequacy of the growth dimension to reflect market attractiveness, measurement issues, sensitivity to product-market definitions, the focus on cash flow, and the difficulty of implementing implied strategies.

The market attractiveness-business position matrix is richer and therefore potentially more valid but also more ambiguous and less reliable. Both market-attractiveness and business-position assessments are made on the basis of as many factors as appear relevant in a given context. The risk matrix adds an environmental-risk dimension to the analysis.

FOOTNOTES

[1] Robert Jacobson and David A. Aaker, "Is Market Share All That It's Cracked Up to Be?" *Journal of Marketing* 49, Fall 1985, pp. 11–22.

[2] Carolyn R. Woo, "Market-Share Leadership—Not Always So Good," *Harvard Business Review*, January–February 1984, pp. 50–53.

[3] Robert D. Buzzell and Bradley T. Gale, *The PIMS Principles*, New York: The Free Press, 1987.

[4] Stratford P. Sherman, "The Mind of Jack Welch," *Fortune*, March 27, 1989, pp. 39–50.

[5] George S. Day, "Diagnosing the Product Portfolio," *Journal of Marketing*, April 1977, pp. 29–38.

[6] One description emphasizing the determination of matrix positions is in William E. Rothschild, *Putting It All Together*, New York: AMACOM, 1976, Chapter 8; another is in Sidney Schoeffler, "In Defense of PIMS, GE and BCG," *Marketing News*, February 9, 1979, p. 8.

[7] S. Q. Robinson, R. E. Hichens, and P. P. Wade, "The Directional Policy Matrix Tool for Strategic Planning," *Long-Range Planning* 11, April 1978, pp. 8–15.

[8] Philippe Haspeslagh, "Portfolio Planning: Uses and Limits," *Harvard Business Review*, January–February 1982, pp. 58–73.

PART FOUR

ALTERNATIVE BUSINESS STRATEGIES

9

OBTAINING A SUSTAINABLE COMPETITIVE ADVANTAGE

Vision is the art of seeing things invisible.

Jonathan Swift

All men can see the tactics whereby I conquer, but what none can see is the strategy out of which great victory is evolved.

Sun-Tzu, Chinese Military Strategist

What are the strategic alternatives that should be considered? Which one is optimal? These questions have remained in the background but now become the focus—in this chapter and in Chapters 10 through 15. One goal of these chapters is to widen the scope of available strategic alternatives in order to increase the likelihood that the best alternatives will be considered. A good decision among inferior alternatives is much less desirable than a poor decision among superior alternatives.

Chapters 12 and 13 consider growth strategies involving the product-market investment decision. Chapter 12 discusses market penetration, product-market expansion, and vertical integration. Diversification, another growth option, is the subject of Chapter 13. Chapter 14 focuses on mature and declining markets and discusses industry revitalization, being the profitable survivor, and the hold, milk, and exit decisions. In Chapter 15, global strategies, of increasing importance to many firms, are analyzed.

This and the following two chapters focus on how to develop a sustainable competitive advantage (SCA), the key to a successful strategy, and how to understand and neutralize the SCAs of competitors. According to Stephen South, Corporate Planning Director of Clark Equipment, "The process of strategic management is coming to be defined, in fact, as the management of competitive advantage—that is, as a process of identifying, developing, and taking advantage of enclaves in which a tangible and preservable business advantage can be achieved."[1]

THE SUSTAINABLE COMPETITIVE ADVANTAGE

A strategy can involve a variety of functional area strategies such as positioning strategies, pricing strategies, distribution strategies, global strategies, and on and on. Infinite ways of competing exist. As illustrated by Figure 9.1, however, how you compete is not the only key to success. At least three other factors are requisite for the creation of an SCA and thus a strategy that will be successful over time.

Basis of Competition—Assets and Skills

The first factor is the basis of competition. The strategy needs to be based on a set of assets, skills, and capabilities. Without the support of assets or skills, it is unlikely that the SCA will be enduring. There is no point in pursuing a quality strategy without the design and manufacturing capability to deliver quality products. For instance, a department store premium service positioning strategy will not succeed unless the right people and culture are in place. Who you are is as important as what you do.

FIGURE 9.1   The Sustainable Competitive Advantage

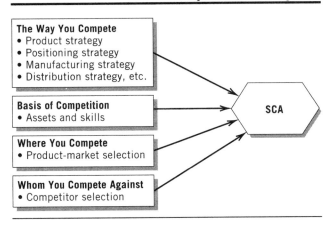

Furthermore, the activities of a business, such as positioning a product line as one of high quality, are usually easily imitated. What is less easy to imitate, however, is the actual delivery of high quality; that can require specialized assets and skills. Anyone can distribute cereal or detergent through supermarkets, but few have the assets and skills needed to do it effectively.

As discussed in Chapter 4, several questions can help to identify relevant assets, skills, and capabilities. What assets and skills are possessed by successful businesses and lacking in unsuccessful businesses? What are the key motivations of the major market segments? What are the large value-added components? What are the mobility barriers? What elements of the value chain can generate advantage?

Where You Compete

The second important determinant for an SCA is the choice of the target product market. A well-defined strategy supported by assets and skills can fail because it does not work in the marketplace. Thus, a strategy and its underlying assets and skills should involve something valued by the market. If distribution is to be an SCA for Heublein's wine operation, for example, distribution should be important to success in the industry. Procter & Gamble's Pringle's potato chips had a host of assets such as a consistent product, long shelf life, a crush-proof container, and national distribution and advertising, but these assets adversely affected taste perception, which was the most important attribute according to the market. Kingsford Charcoal failed in the barbeque sauce market because there was no room for a third entrant in the premium segment.

Whom You Compete Against

The third requirement for an SCA involves the identity of competitors. Sometimes an asset or skill will form an SCA only given the right set of competitors. Thus, it is vital to assess whether a competitor or strategic group is weak, adequate, or strong with respect to assets and skills. The goal is to engage in a strategy that will match up with that of competitors who lack strength in relevant assets and skills.

In general, for an asset or skill to be the basis of an SCA, it should help create either a cost advantage over competitors or a point of difference from competitors. For example, flight safety is important to airline passengers, so if a strategic group such as the economy airlines is perceived to be weak on safety, or if some airlines are superior with respect to antiterrorist security, then an SCA could indeed exist.

Additional Characteristics of SCAs

Thus, an effective SCA will be created when a strategy has at least three characteristics. It should be supported by assets and skills. It should be employed in a competitive arena containing segments that will value the strategy. Finally, it should be employed against competitors who cannot easily match or neutralize the SCA. In addition, an effective SCA should

1. **Be substantial** enough to make a difference. A modest edge on competitive dimensions may not provide an advantage that will affect the marketplace. For example, an ability to produce marginally superior quality carpeting may not be valued adequately by the market.

2. **Be sustainable** in the face of environmental changes and competitor actions. A high-tech market such as that for personal computers can change over time to the point that the importance of technological advantage is reduced as the product becomes more of a commodity. Name recognition in some contexts may be easily countered with clever advertising or by the choice of distribution channels. A cost advantage enjoyed by Toyota in making automobiles may be compromised by Korean manufacturers who have developed cost advantages of their own. Some information technology innovations such as Merrill Lynch's Cash Management Account were replicated by followers and were not as much of an advantage as first perceived. If a strategy by design or accident confronts competitors who can neutralize or overcome the assets and skills, there will not be a sustainable advantage.

3. When possible, **be leveraged** into visible business attributes that will influence customers. The key is to link an SCA with the positioning of a business. Thus, skills and assets that relate to ensuring reliability in products may not be apparent to customers. If they can be made

visible through advertising or a product design, however, then they can support a reliability positioning strategy. Maytag is known as a reliability firm because its advertising is supported by product design and product performance that makes the reliability claim believable.

In practice, an SCA can take a wide variety of forms. A study of SCAs identified by business managers illustrates this variety.

What Business Managers Name as Their SCAs

Managers of 248 distinct businesses in the service and high-tech industries were contacted and asked to name the SCA of their business.[2] The objectives were to identify frequently employed SCAs, to confirm that managers could articulate them, to determine whether different managers from the same strategic business unit (SBU) would identify the same SCAs, and to find how many SCAs would be identified for each SBU. The responses were coded into categories. The results, summarized in Figure 9.2, provide some suggestive insights into the SCA construct.

Figure 9.2 indicates the wide variety of SCAs mentioned, each representing distinct competitive approaches. The top few by no means dominated the list. Of course, the list did differ by industry. For high-tech firms, for example, name recognition was less important than technical superiority, product innovation, and installed customer base. The next two chapters discuss several SCAs in more detail.

Most of the SCAs in Figure 9.2 reflect assets or skills. Customer base, quality reputation, good management and engineering staff, for example, are business assets, whereas customer service and technical superiority usually involve sets of skills.

For a subset of 95 of the businesses involved, a second SBU manager was independently interviewed. The result suggests that managers can identify SCAs with a high degree of reliability. Of the 95 businesses, 76 of the manager pairs gave answers that were coded the same and most of the others had only a single difference in the SCA list.

Another finding is instructive—the average number of SCAs per business was 4.65, suggesting that it is usually not sufficient to base a strategy on a single SCA. Sometimes a business is described in terms of a single skill and asset, implying that being a "quality-oriented" business or a "service-focused" business explains success. This study indicates, however, that it may be necessary to have several skills and assets.

Strategic Thrusts—Routes to an SCA

There are a host of strategic thrusts that can underlie an SCA. Each SCA may be based on one or a combination of them. Five of the most notable,

FIGURE 9.2 Sustainable Competitive Advantages of 248 Businesses

	High-Tech	Service	Other	Total
1. Reputation for quality	26	50	29	105
2. Customer service/product support	23	40	15	78
3. Name recognition/high profile	8	42	21	71
4. Retain good management and engineering staff	17	43	5	65
5. Low-cost production	17	15	21	53
6. Financial resources	11	26	14	51
7. Customer orientation/feedback/ market research	13	26	9	48
8. Product-line breadth	11	23	13	47
9. Technical superiority	30	7	9	46
10. Installed base of satisfied customers	19	22	4	45
11. Segmentation/focus	7	22	16	45
12. Product characteristics/ differentiation	12	15	10	37
13. Continuing product innovation	12	17	6	35
14. Market share	12	14	9	35
15. Size/location of distribution	10	11	13	34
16. Low price/high-value offering	6	20	6	32
17. Knowledge of business	2	25	4	31
18. Pioneer/early entrant in industry	11	11	6	28
19. Efficient, flexible production/ operations adaptable to customers	4	17	4	26
20. Effective sales force	10	9	4	23
21. Overall marketing skills	7	9	7	23
22. Shared vision/culture	5	13	4	22
23. Strategic goals	6	7	9	22
24. Powerful well-known parent	7	7	6	20
25. Location	0	10	10	20
26. Effective advertising/image	5	6	6	17
27. Enterprising/entrepreneurial	3	3	5	11
28. Good coordination	3	2	5	10
29. Engineering research and development	8	2	0	10
30. Short-term planning	2	1	5	8
31. Good distributor relations	2	4	1	7
32. Other	6	20	5	31
Total	315	539	281	1136
Number of businesses	68	113	67	248
Average number of SCAs	4.63	4.77	4.19	4.58

shown in Figure 9.3, are discussed explicitly in this chapter and the two chapters that follow. Among other thrusts that could be important in some contexts are being innovative, thinking globally, having an entrepreneurial style, or exploiting information technology.

Two of the most important strategic thrusts are differentiation and low cost. Michael Porter has suggested that all strategies will provide either a low-cost or differentiation advantage.[3] Differentiation means that there is an element of uniqueness about a strategy that provides value to the customer. For example, firms differentiate their offerings by enhancing performance, quality, reliability, prestige, or convenience. In the following chapter, several differentiation strategies that appear in the Figure 9.2 SCA study are presented which have a particular emphasis on providing superior quality and creating strong brand equity. A low-cost strategy can be based on a cost advantage that can be used to invest in the product, support lower prices, or provide high profits. Low-cost strategies are discussed in Chapter 11.

Strategies can have other thrusts in addition to differentiation and low cost. Three of these thrusts appear in Figure 9.3. Focus strategies focus on a market segment or part of a product line. Preemptive strategies are strategies that employ first mover advantages to inhibit or prevent competitors from duplicating or countering. Synergistic strategies rely on the synergy between a business and other businesses in the same firm; its role is considered in the next section. In Chapter 11, focus and preemptive strategies are discussed in addition to low-cost strategies.

Several other strategic thrusts could be considered. Treacy and Wiersema have suggested that three paths lead to market leadership.[4] The first, illustrated by Dell Computer, is operational excellence, which leads to customer convenience and cost efficiencies. Dell created a radically different and efficient delivery system for personal computers based upon build-to-order manufacturing and mail-order marketing. The second is customer intimacy in which firms such as Home Depot and Nord-

FIGURE 9.3   Strategic Thrusts

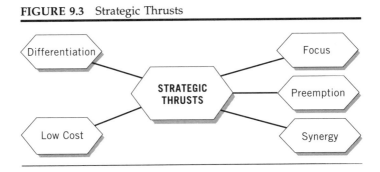

strom excel at individual personalized service. The third is product leadership where companies such as Johnson & Johnson and 3M strive to produce a continuous stream of state-of-the-art products and services.

THE ROLE OF SYNERGY

Synergy between SBUs can provide an SCA that is truly sustainable because it is based on the characteristics of a firm that are probably unique. A competitor might have to duplicate the organization in order to capture the assets or skills involved.

A core element in the GE strategic vision is to achieve synergy across many businesses.[5] GE's Jack Welch calls it "integrated diversity." The concept is that a GE business can call upon the resources of the firm and of other GE businesses to create advantage. For example, the SCAs of General Electric in the CT scanner (an x-ray-based diagnostic system) business are in part based on its leadership in the x-ray business, where it has a huge installed base and a large service network, and in part based on the fact that it operates other businesses involving technologies used in CT scanners. In the following chapters, a variety of strategies are discussed, most of which have the potential for synergy.

A cornerstone of the IBM strategy under Lou Gerstner is to create synergy by pushing core technologies across more product lines.[6] The intent is to leverage the IBM size, scale, and technologies. This vision is a far cry from his predecessors who planned to break IBM up into autonomous business units.

Synergy means that the whole is more than the sum of its parts. In this context, it means that two SBUs (or two product-market strategies) operating together will be superior to the same two SBUs operating independently. In terms of products, positive synergy means that offering a set of products will generate a higher return over time than would be possible if each of the products was offered separately. Similarly, in terms of markets, operating a set of markets within a business will be superior to operating them autonomously.

As a result of synergy, the combined SBUs will have

1. Increased customer value and thus increased sales
2. Lower operating costs
3. Reduced investment

Generally the synergy will be caused by exploiting some commonality in the two operations such as

- Sharing a channel or sales force
- Sharing a brand name and image
- Products combining to form a system that provides customer value
- Sharing customers
- Sharing a plant or operating process
- Sharing R&D

Synergy is not difficult to understand conceptually, but it is slippery in practice, in part because it can be difficult to predict whether synergy will actually emerge. Often two businesses seem related, and sizable potential synergy seems to exist but is never realized. Sometimes the perceived synergy is merely a mirage or wishful thinking, perhaps created in the haste to put together a merger. Other times, the potential synergy is real, but implementation problems prevent its realization. Perhaps there is a cultural mismatch between two organizations, or the incentives are inadequate. The material on implementation in Chapter 16 is directly relevant to the problem of predicting whether potential synergy will be realized.

Obtaining instant synergy is a goal of alliances and joint ventures. Pairing McDonald's with Texaco, for example, has provided traffic and added value for Texaco and valuable locations for McDonald's. Sega has surged ahead of Nintendo in part because it has been able to gain access to new technology and to exploit its own core graphics technology through alliances.[7] Sega has partnered with AT&T in communications, Hitachi in chips, Yamaha in sound, JVC in game machines, and Microsoft in software.

Core Competencies

A firm's asset or skill that is capable of being the competitive basis of many of its businesses is termed a core competence and can be a synergistic advantage. Prahalad and Hamel suggest a tree metaphor in which the root system is core competence, the trunk and major limbs are core products, the smaller branches are business units, and the leaves and flowers are end products.[8] You may not recognize the strength of a competitor by simply looking at its end products and failing to examine the strength of its root system. Core competence represents the consolidation of firm-wide technologies and skills into a coherent thrust. The key to strategic management can be the management of core competencies rather than business units because the SCAs of business units are, in fact, based on core competencies.

Consider, for example, the core competencies of Sony in miniaturization, 3M in sticky-tape technology, Black & Decker in small motors, Honda in vehicle motors and power trains, NEC in semiconductors (which underlies its attack on both the computer and communications businesses), and Canon in precision mechanics, fine optics, and microelectronics. Each of these competencies underlies a large set of businesses and has the potential to create more. Each of these firms invests in competence in a variety of different ways and contexts. Each would insist on keeping its primary work related to the core competence in-house. Outsourcing would risk weakening the asset, and each firm would rightfully insist that there is no other firm that could match its state-of-the-art advances.

Capabilities-Based Competition

Capabilities-based competition suggests that the key building blocks of business strategy are not products and markets but, rather, business processes.[9] Investment in building and managing a process that outperforms competition can lead to a sustainable advantage. Therefore, strategy development must identify the most important processes within the organization, specify how they should be measured, identify target performance levels, relate performance to achieving superior customer value and competitive advantage, and assign cross-functional teams to implement.

One such process is the new product development and introduction process. Japanese automobile firms that have reduced the process from five years to three years while making it more responsive to the needs of the market have achieved a huge advantage. Another is the management of international operations, considered an SCA by IDV, the spirits subsidiary of Grand Metropolitan. Still another is the order and logistics process in retailing. By developing dramatic improvements in its order and logistics process through warehouse innovations, a dedicated trucking system, and computerized ordering, Wal-Mart developed huge cost and inventory handling advantages over its competition.

Developing superior capabilities in key processes involves strategic investments in people and infrastructure to gain advantage. True process improvement does not occur without control and ownership of the parts of the process. Thus, the virtual corporation, where pieces are drawn from many sources in response to the organizational task at hand, is not a good model for capabilities-based competition.

STRATEGIC VISION VERSUS STRATEGIC OPPORTUNISM

There are two very different approaches to the development of successful strategies and sustainable competitive advantages. Each can work but may require very different systems, people, and culture. Strategic vision takes a long-term perspective; the focus is on the future in both strategy development and the supporting analysis. Strategic opportunism emphasizes strategies that make sense today. The implicit belief is that the best way to have the right strategy in place tomorrow is to have it right today.

Strategic Vision

To successfully manage a strategic vision, a firm should have four characteristics:

1. **A clear future strategy** with a core driving idea and a specification of the competitive arena, functional area strategies, and competitive advantage that will support the business.
2. **Buy-in throughout the organization.** There should be a belief in the correctness of the strategy, an acceptance that the vision is achievable and worthwhile, and a real commitment to making that vision happen.
3. **Assets, skills, and resources to implement** the strategy should be in place, or a plan to obtain them should be under way.
4. **Patience.** There should be a willingness to stick to the strategy in the face of competitive threats or enticing opportunities that would divert resources from the vision.

A strategic vision provides a sense of purpose. Saturn's commitment to building a world-class car and respecting customers' intelligence has the potential to inspire. In contrast, it is hard to get energized to increase ROI by 2 points or sales by 10 percent so shareholders will be wealthier. Strategic vision also provides the rationale for investment that may require years to achieve a payoff. The ability of ARCO to stick to a price-value position throughout its operations is one reason it has developed effective programs and resources.

Managing a strategic vision requires a certain kind of organization and management style, as summarized in Figure 9.4. A strategic vision is based on a forward-looking, long-term perspective—the planning horizon extends into the future two, five, or more than ten years, depending on the business involved. The goal of the supporting information system and analysis effort is thus to understand the likely future environment. Experts who have insights into key future events and trends can be helpful. Scenario analysis, delphi techniques, technological forecasting, and trend analysis should be part of the analysis phase of strategy development.

The organization needs to be capable of building assets that may not have immediate payoff. A top-down, centralized structure with a reward system that supports the vision is helpful, as is a strong, charismatic leader who can sell the vision to relevant constituencies inside and outside the organization.

FIGURE 9.4   Organizational Differences

Organizational Characteristics	Strategic Vision	Strategic Opportunism
Perspective	• Forward looking	• Present
Strategic Questions	• Trends affecting the future	• Current threats and opportunities
Environmental Sensing	• Future scenarios	• Change sensors
Information System	• Forward looking • Analysis strengths	• On-line • Current
Orientation	• Commitment • Build assets • Vertical integration	• Flexibility • Adaptability • Fast response
Leadership	• Charismatic • Visionary	• Tactical • Action-oriented
Structure	• Centralized • Top-down	• Decentralized • Fluid
People	• Eye on the ball	• Entrepreneurial
Economic Advantage	• Scale economies	• Scope economies
Signaling	• Strong signals sent to competitors	• Surprise moves

A vision of a synergistic, technology-driven firm has helped Corning develop from a consumer products firm to a leader in such areas as fiber optics and liquid-crystal displays.[10] Corning's strategy involves investing heavily in technology, sharing the technology across business units, and forming technology and marketing alliances. The goal is to leverage technological developments to maximize the impact on the whole organization.

A strategic vision can take many forms. Jack Welch of GE had a vision of being the first or second competitor in each business area and he dramatically changed GE as a result. Mercedes, Tiffany, and Nordstrom at one point were guided by a vision of being the best in their field in terms of delivering quality products and services. The vision of Sharp is to succeed by being a technological innovator, especially in optoelectronic technologies.[11] The firm has already been the first to market flat screen TVs, double-cassette recorders, solid-state calculators, color desktop fax machines, and HDTV projection systems, and is the leading supplier of electroluminescent displays for computers.

Strategic Stubbornness

The risk of the strategic vision route, as suggested by Figure 9.5, is that the vision may be faulty and its pursuit may be a wasteful exercise in

FIGURE 9.5   Vision versus Opportunism

	Strategic Approach	Strategic Risk
Focus on Future	Strategic vision	Strategic stubbornness
Focus on Present	Strategic opportunism	Strategic drift

strategic stubbornness. There are a host of pitfalls that could prevent a vision from being realized. Three stand out.

First, the picture of the future may be substantially accurate, but the firm may not be able to implement the strategy required. That was, in part, the problem with the efforts of GE and others to crack the computer market in the 1960s and with the attempt of Sony to promote its Beta VCR format as the industry standard.

Second, the vision might be faulty because it is based on faulty assumptions about the future. For example, the concept of a one-stop financial services firm that drove the vision of American Express, Sears, Merrill Lynch, and others was based, in part, on the erroneous assumption that customers would see value in a one-stop financial service. It turned out that consumers preferred to deal with specialists. GE's concept of factory automation was similarly faulty, as it discovered after some big losses. Customers wanted hardware and software components, not a factory system.

A third problem occurs when there is a paradigm shift. A scenario might change meaningfully from what was assumed, the market might not emerge as expected, or new operators might enter and change the game. For example, the environment envisioned by Businessland was affected by new forces that emerged. Businessland built a dominant retail chain with a vision of attaining economies of scale while providing name computers (IBM, Compaq, and Apple) and valued-added service to large companies.[12] However, storefronts turned from assets to liabilities when large companies began to prefer to interact with vendors through personal contact and even mail-order sales. These unanticipated distribution dynamics, together with weak operations (especially computer control, ironically) and some product errors (attempting a private label brand and mismanaging the Compaq relationship), led the company into serious trouble in the early 1990s. Businessland's founder was quoted as saying, "You don't get to live on visions forever."

The power of a vision is based on the commitment that accompanies it. This commitment, together with a focus on the future instead of the past, can result in pursuing a faulty vision beyond the point at which the probability of success is high. The trick, of course, is to maintain the commitment and patience in the face of adversity, while at the same time not allowing a failed vision to use up resources on a futile attempt at a miracle recovery.

Strategic Opportunism

Strategic opportunism, in contrast, is driven by a focus on the present. The premise is that the environment is so dynamic and uncertain that it is not feasible to aim at a future target. Unless a business is structured to have strategic advantages in the present, it is unlikely to ever be strategically successful in the future.

Strategic opportunism provides several advantages. One is that the risk of missing emerging business opportunities is reduced. Firms such as General Mills in cereals, Ralston Purina in pet foods, and Ziff Communications in special interest computer publishing all seek emerging niche segments and develop brands tailored to specialty markets. Thus, Ralston brands such as Deli-Cat, Kitt'N Kaboodle, and Mature, and General Mills brands like Triangles, Oatmeal Crisp, Sprinkle Spangles, and Cinnamon Toast Crunch are all designed to appeal to a current taste or trend. Ziff is continuously introducing niche computer magazines. Further, the risk of strategic stubbornness is also reduced.

Strategic opportunism tends to generate a vitality and energy that can be healthy, especially when a business has decentralized R&D and marketing units that generate a stream of new products. Within 3M, for example, new businesses are continually created and evaluated with respect to their prospects. A global strategic vision rarely inhibits. HP is another firm that believes in decentralized entrepreneurial management. These decentralized firms are often close to the market and technology and are willing to pursue opportunities.

Strategic opportunism results in economies of scope, where assets and skills are supported by multiple product lines. Nike, which applies its brand assets and skills in product design and customer sensing to a wide variety of product markets, is a good example. A key part of the Nike strategy is to develop strong emotional ties and relationships with focused segments through its product design and brand name strengths. The organization is extremely sensitive to emerging segments (such as outdoor basketball) and the need for product refinements and product innovation. Nike has strategic flexibility, which characterizes successful strategic opportunistic firms.

As Figure 9.4 suggests, the prototypical business driven by strategic opportunism is very different from a business guided by a strategic vision. The strategic questions posed are very different. What trends are most active and critical now? What is the current driving force in the market? What are the strategic problems facing the business that need immediate correction? What technologies are ready to be employed? What are current strategic opportunities and threats? What are competitors doing in the market and in the lab? What strategy changes are occurring or will soon occur?

The supporting information system and analysis are also different. To support strategic opportunism, companies must monitor customers, competitors, and the trade to learn of trends, opportunities, and threats as they appear. Information gathering and analysis should be both sensitive and on-line. Frequent, regular meetings to analyze the most recent developments and news may be helpful. The organization should be quick to understand and act on changing fundamentals.

The hallmark of an organization that emphasizes strategic opportunism is strategic flexibility and the willingness to quickly respond to strategic opportunities as they emerge. The organization is adaptive, with the ability to adjust its systems, structure, people, and culture to accommodate new ventures. The strategy is dynamic and change is the norm. New products are being explored or introduced and others are de-emphasized or dropped. New markets are entered and disinvestment occurs in others. New synergies and assets are being created. The people are entrepreneurial, sensitive to new opportunities and threats, and fast to react.

Strategic Drift

The problem with the strategic opportunism model is, as suggested by Figure 9.5, that it can turn into strategic drift. Investment decisions are made incrementally in response to opportunities rather than being directed by a vision. As a result, a firm can wake up one morning and find that it is in a set of businesses for which it lacks the needed assets and skills and which provides few synergies.

At least three phenomena can turn strategic opportunism into strategic drift. First, a short-lived transitory force may be mistaken for one with enough staying power to make a strategic move worthwhile. If the force is so short-lived that a strategy does not pay off or does not even have a chance to get into place, the result will be a strategy that is not suitable for the business or the environment.

Second, opportunities to create immediate profits may be rationalized as strategic when, in fact, they are not. For example, an instrumentation firm might receive many requests from some of its customers for special-purpose instruments that could conceivably be used by other customers but that, in fact, have little strategic value for the company. Opportunities like this might result in a sizable initial order but then they could divert R&D resources from more strategic activities.

Third, expected synergies across existing and new business areas may fail to materialize because of implementation problems, perhaps due to culture clashes or because the synergies were only illusions in the first place. A drive to exploit core competencies might not work. As a result, new business areas would be in place without the expected sustainable advantages.

Strategic drift not only creates a business without needed assets, but it can also result in a failure to support a core business that does have a good vision. Without a vision and supporting commitment, it is tempting to divert investment into seemingly sure things that are immediate—strategic opportunities. Thus, strategic opportunism can be an excuse to delay investment or divert resources from a core vision.

One example of strategic drift is a firm that designed, installed, and serviced custom equipment for steel firms. Over time, steel firms became more knowledgeable and began buying standardized equipment mainly on the basis of price. Gradually, the firm edged into this commodity business to retain its market share. The company finally realized it was pursuing a dual strategy for which it was ill-suited. It had too much overhead to compete with the real commodity firms, and its ability to provide upscale service had eroded to the point that it was now inferior to some niche players. Had there been a strategic vision, the firm would not have fallen into such a trap.

Korvette, the first major successful discounter, started with a walk-up hard goods store in New York that offered name brands at $5 over wholesale cost.[13] Its low-cost image allowed it to expand into other locations and become a major retailing force. One industry spokesperson called Korvette's founder one of the most influential retailers of the century. Over time, however, it moved into soft goods, furniture, and food and aggressively expanded geographically. The firm's hands-on management style became ineffective in an organization with major coordination and communication problems. Worse, the basis of Korvette's low-cost image was undercut. It eventually drifted into a business requiring assets it did not have and its resulting decline, culminating in bankruptcy, was as spectacular as its rise.

Vision Plus Opportunism

Many businesses attempt to have the best of both worlds by engaging in strategic vision and strategic opportunism at the same time. Strategic opportunism can supplement strategic vision by managing diversification away from the core business and by managing the route to achievement of a firm's vision. Thus, if Weight Watchers' vision is to exploit brand associations by extending its name to other product categories, strategic opportunism can describe the process of selecting the extensions and the order in which they are pursued.

The combination can and does work. However, there are obvious risks and problems. One is that strategic vision requires patience and investment and is vulnerable to the enticements represented by the more immediate return that is usually associated with strategic opportunism. It is difficult to maintain the persistence and discipline required by strategic vision in any case, even without distractions by alternative strategies that have been blessed as part of the thrust of the organization.

The organizational problems are worse. It is difficult for one organization to use both approaches well because the systems, people, structure, and culture that are best for one approach are generally not well-suited for the other. To create an organization that excels at or even tolerates both is not easy.

A Dynamic Vision

A model to avoid strategic stubbornness is to have a dynamic vision that can change when the situation evolves. Of course, visions that are excessively dynamic are no longer visions at all, and identifying when a vision should change is most difficult. It is like the Irishman who, when asked how to get to a tourist site outside of Dublin, replied: "Just go straight until you reach Red's bar just over a bridge. Half a mile before you get there turn right." The role of strategic management is to periodically review the vision and to consider creating a new direction for the business. The result will be a vision-driven organization which has a vision that is consistent with whatever situation evolves.

STRATEGIC INTENT

Hamel and Prahalad have suggested that some firms have strategic intent, which couples strategic vision with a sustained obsession with winning at all levels of the organization.[14] They note that this model explains the successful rise to global leadership of companies such as Canon, Komatsu, Samsung (see insert), and Honda. Thus, Canon was out to "beat Xerox," Komatsu to "encircle Caterpillar," and Honda to become a "second Ford."

A strategic intent to achieve a successful strategy has several characteristics in addition to having a strategic vision and an obsession with success. First, it should recognize the essence of winning. Coca-Cola's strategic intent has included the objective of putting a Coke within "arm's reach" of every consumer in the world because distribution and accompanied visibility are the keys to winning. NEC decided it needed to acquire the technologies that would allow it to exploit the convergence of computing and telecommunications. That became its guiding theme.

Second, strategic intent involves stretching an organization with a continuing effort to identify and develop new SCAs or to improve those that exist. Thus, it has a dynamic, forward-looking perspective. What will our advantage be next year and two years after that? Consider Matsushita, Toshiba, and the other Japanese television manufacturers. They first relied on low-labor-cost advantages. By servicing private label needs, they added economies of scale. The next step was to build advantages in quality, reliability, features, brand name, and distribution. In contrast, an analysis of their strengths and weaknesses might have led to the conclusion that they should focus on a low-cost niche.

Third, strategic intent often requires real innovation, a willingness to do things very differently. Savin entered the U.S. copier market with a product that could be sold through dealers instead of being leased and was simple, low-priced, and reliable. As a result, Xerox's huge advantage in sales and service and its ability to finance leased equipment was neutralized. Honda made real advances in motor design in order to attack the large motorcycle market.

An obsession with winning can be created even without a competitor. Peter Johnson told how he created phantom competitors when running two companies—Trus Joist, a maker of structural components for buildings that had a patent-based monopoly, and a legal power administration monopoly.[15] In each case, the phantom competitor would develop low-cost options and generate creative options for breaking into the business. As a result, Trus Joist was prompted to innovate in a companion market and the power agency shut down two partially completed atomic power plants.

Strategic intent provides a long-term drive for advantage that can be essential to success. It provides a model that helps break the mold, getting a firm away from just doing the same things a bit better and working a bit harder than the year before. It has the capability to elevate and extend an organization, helping it reach levels it would not otherwise attain.

The focus on winning and sales volume that is a hallmark of strategic intent can be self-destructive, as Kenichi Ohmae observes.[16] He criticizes the "winning by working harder" obsession of Japanese firms, claiming that it has made many industries less profitable than they might have been. For example, Japanese firms have created enormous overcapacity in shipbuilding, automobiles, and other industries and have engaged in

---

Samsung and Microwave Ovens

In 1977, Samsung decided to make microwave ovens despite the fact that there were major established competitors with seemingly unbeatable SCAs who were making millions of ovens per year.[17] During the next four years, it saw its first two prototypes melt down, redesigned its product again and again, bought the last magnetron factory from the United States, and received its first order for 240 ovens from Panama. In 1980, a J.C. Penney order requiring Samsung to build a unit 25 percent less expensive than existing ones necessitated still another redesign. In 1983, GE, under pressure from Japanese firms, turned to Samsung to source some of its products. Samsung's labor costs of $1.47 contrasted sharply with GE's $52.00. By the late 1980s, Samsung was building more than 4 million units per year and had cornered more than one-third of the U.S. market.

It is clear that Samsung had a strategic intent to enter the microwave oven market. Its goals during the first decade were production and meeting whatever customer needs were required to gain sales. Financial return was of no consequence. An enormous investment was made in design, manufacturing, and engineering. To make it happen, a large, competent staff carefully analyzed how competitors had solved problems and what customers expected. The firm was very responsive to customer needs even when it met sizable losses. It capitalized on its cost advantage and the willingness of production and engineering personnel to work 68-hour weeks. Samsung virtually willed its own remarkable success.

---

destructive price competition in order to "win." Those in the whaling industry created an excess whale-killing capacity that resulted in negative public opinion which finally affected their business.

STRATEGIC FLEXIBILITY

Strategic intent usually represents a commitment to attaining an SCA. However, in some dynamic industries, an SCA can be a moving target that is difficult to attain proactively because there are too many uncertainties to make the necessary predictions about customer needs, technology, competitive posture, and so on. In those contexts, the answer is to attain strategic flexibility, so that the business will be ready when a window of opportunity arises.

Strategic flexibility is the ability to adjust or develop strategies to respond to external or internal changes. As Aaker and Mascarenhas have noted, there are three ways to achieve strategic flexibility: diversifying, investing in underused resources, and reducing commitment of resources to a specialized use.[18]

Diversification can involve participation in multiple-product markets, technologies, plant locations, or countries. It can also involve organizational forms like decentralized units, which are more responsive to the environment, and alliances. The concept is to reduce the impact of a localized undesirable event or trend and to increase the chances that a firm will participate in a desirable event or trend. An objective might be, for example, to participate in three technologies, including an important emerging one.

Flexibility can also be obtained by investing in underused assets. An obvious example is to maintain liquidity so that investment can be quickly funneled to opportunity or problem areas. Less obvious is the maintenance of excess capacity in manufacturing, organization staffing, or R&D in order to increase a firm's ability to react quickly. Thus, one objective could be to develop the capability to double production within three months' time.

Flexibility can be enhanced by reducing business area exit barriers. Reducing the commitment of resources to specialized uses can minimize the adverse impact of an undesirable event or trend. Thus, asset purchase (versus leasing), vertical integration, and technological leadership might be avoided. Conversely, entering foreign markets through exporting or licensing, subcontracting, and using temporary workers (an important part of the strategy of many Japanese firms) might be encouraged.

Lessons from U.S. Business Blunders

An analysis of some egregious business blunders revealed four fatal misconceptions:[19]

1. Labor costs are killing us. In fact, the labor content is often only a small percentage of value added. Furthermore, the most efficient factories have more costly labor input; they just use and motivate it better.

2. You can't make money at the low end. Actually, last year's low end, from radios to semiconductors, often forms the technological, manufacturing, and marketing basis for next year's high end.

3. We can't sell it. U.S. firms attempted to sell products, from microwave ovens (the major appliance firms) to fax machines (Xerox first introduced the fax), using marketing methods familiar to them, rather than approaches attuned to the innovation.

4. It's cheaper to buy it (a new business area) than grow it. Treating SBUs as stand-alone units to be bought or sold discourages unit synergy, diverts attention to external investment (the grass is always greener on the other side), and treats investment needed for survival as just another capital budgeting decision.

SUMMARY

A strategy needs three characteristics to have a sustainable competitive advantage. It must be supported by assets and skills. It should be employed in a competitive arena that contains segments which will value the strategy. Finally, it should face competitors who cannot easily match or neutralize the SCA. A wide variety of SCAs are available to a business. More than 30 are identified in the Figure 9.2 study, with perceived quality at the head of the list. Among the possible strategic thrusts are differentiation, low cost, focus, preemption, and synergy.

Synergy has the potential to provide an SCA that is truly sustainable because it is based on the unique characteristics of an organization. A concern is to make sure potential synergy actually exists and that any implementation problems can be overcome.

In developing strategies, it is useful to consider the concepts of strategic vision, strategic stubbornness, strategic opportunism, strategic drift, strategic intent, and strategic flexibility. A strategic vision, based on a future focus, is a vision of what the strategy of the future should be. Strategic opportunism focuses on the present and emphasizes current opportunities and strategy choices, allowing a strategy to emerge from a set of incremental decisions. Strategic intent couples strategic vision with an obsession with winning in a particular product market even if innovation and organizational stretch are involved. Strategic flexibility is the ability to adjust or develop strategies to respond to external or internal changes and can be achieved by diversifying, maintaining underused assets, and avoiding commitment.

FOOTNOTES

[1] Stephen E. South, "Competitive Advantage: The Cornerstone of Strategic Thinking," *The Journal of Business Strategy* 4, Spring 1981, p. 16.

[2] David A. Aaker, "Managing Assets and Skills: The Key to a Sustainable Competitive Advantage," *California Management Review*, Winter 1989, pp. 91–106.

[3] Michael E. Porter, *Competitive Advantage*, New York: *The Free Press*, 1985, Chapter 1.

[4] Michael Treacy and Fred Wiersema, "Customer Intimacy and Other Value Disciplines," *Harvard Business Review*, January–February 1993, pp. 83–93.

[5] Noel M. Tichy, "Revolutionize Your Company," *Fortune*, December 13, 1993, pp. 114–118.

[6] Ira Sager, "Lou Gerstner Unveils His Battle Plan," *Business Week*, April 4, 1994, pp. 58–60.

[7] Neil Gross and Robert D. Hof, "Sega!," *Business Week*, February 21, 1994, pp. 66–71.

[8] C. K. Prahalad and Gary Hamel, "The Core Competence of the Corporation," *Harvard Business Review*, May–June 1990, pp. 79–91.

[9] George Stalk, Philip Evans, and Lawrence E. Shulman, "Competing on Capabilities: The New Rules of Corporate Strategy," *Harvard Business Review*, March–April 1992, pp. 57–69.

[10] Keith H. Hammonds, "Corning's Class Act," *Business Week,* May 13, 1991, pp. 68–76.

[11] Neil Gross, "Sharp's Long-Range Gamble on Its Innovation Machine," *Business Week,* April 29, 1991, pp. 84–86.

[12] G. Pascal Zachary, "Businessland Teeters on the Edge," *San Francisco Chronicle,* March 24, 1991, p. D-1.

[13] Robert F. Hartley, *Marketing Mistakes,* 5th ed., New York, Wiley, 1992, Chapter 13.

[14] Gary Hamel and C. K. Prahalad, "Strategic Intent," *Harvard Business Review,* May–June 1989, pp. 63–76.

[15] Peter T. Johnson, "Why I Race Against Phantom Competitors," *Harvard Business Review,* September–October 1988, pp. 106–112.

[16] Kenichi Ohmae, "Companyism and Do More Better," *Harvard Business Review,* January–February 1989, pp. 125–132.

[17] Ira C. Magaziner and Mark Patinkin, "Fast Heat: How Korea Won the Microwave War," *Harvard Business Review,* January–February 1989, pp. 83–92.

[18] David A. Aaker and Briance Mascarenhas, "Flexibility: A Strategic Option," *Journal of Business Strategy,* Fall 1984, pp. 74–82.

[19] Thomas A. Stewart, "Lessons from U.S. Business Blunders," *Fortune,* April 23, 1990, pp. 128–138.

10

DIFFERENTIATION STRATEGIES

Ever since Morton's put a little girl in a
yellow slicker and declared, "When it rains,
it pours," no advertising person worth his or
her salt has had any excuse to think of a
product as having parity with anything.

Malcolm MacDougal
Jordan Case McGrath

If you don't have a competitive advantage,
don't compete.

Jack Welch, GE

The secret of success is constancy to
purpose.

Benjamin Disraeli

A differentiation strategy is one in which a product offering is different from that of one or more competitors in a way that is valued by the customers. The value added should affect customer choice and ultimate satisfaction. Most successful strategies that are not based entirely on a low-cost advantage will be differentiated in some way.

There are many ways to differentiate by adding value. There might be something that can be done much better than competitors or an extra product feature or service that can be included. Value can be added to any aspect of a business. Consider the following examples:

Ingredient or Component

- Pepperidge Farm uses more expensive ingredients than do competitors.
- Mercedes uses better materials both in the body and in the interior than others.

Product Offering

- The Apple PowerBook has a superior embedded mouse design that adds value.
- Pringles offers a package that protects the potato chips.

Combining Products

- DowBrands adds value with Spiffits, which augments cleaning products by putting them into premoistened towels.

Added Service

- Milliken shop towels, an industrial rag business, provides its customers—industrial laundries—with a wide variety of services such as computer-based order-entry systems, freight optimization systems, market research assistance, data systems, sales leads, and even seminars on telecommunications, selling skills, and production.[1]
- An airline offers a club for frequent flyers that provides access to airport facilities.

Breadth of Product Line

- CompUSA provides a one-stop-shopping computer store.
- An audio equipment firm that makes a complete line offers customers total system design.

Service Backup

- Saturn provides a high level of dealer service, in part because they have a well-designed dealer network, and in part because the car was designed from a service view.

Channel

- L'eggs hosiery created a big business by providing quality and reliability in hosiery conveniently available in supermarkets.

SUCCESSFUL DIFFERENTIATION STRATEGIES

Clearly there are a variety of ways to differentiate. Whatever the route, the successful differentiation strategy should have three characteristics:

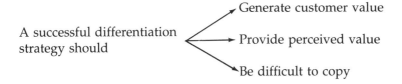

A successful differentiation strategy should
- Generate customer value
- Provide perceived value
- Be difficult to copy

Provide Value

First, a differentiation strategy needs to add value for the customer. A distinction is needed between apparent value and actual value. Too often a point of difference with apparent value is not valued by the customer. The one-stop financial service vision was not valued by customers—they wanted excellence and competence from investment managers, and convenience was relatively unimportant. Having the Bayer name on non-aspirin products had much less value in the market than was hoped. The value of the Bayer name did not transfer to new product classes.

One key to a successful differentiation strategy is to develop the point of differentiation from the customer's perspective rather than from the perspective of the business operation. How does the point of differentiation affect the customer's experience of buying and using the product? Does it serve to reduce cost, add performance, or increase satisfaction? The concepts of unmet needs and customer problems outlined in Chapter 3 are relevant.

Another method for differentiating a product is to employ market research to systematically understand the customer and to test ideas and assumptions. One role of market research is to insure that the value added will justify the price premium involved. A differentiation strategy is often associated with higher price, because it usually makes price less critical to the customer and because differentiation usually costs something. The question is whether that price premium works in the marketplace.

Provide Perceived Value

Second, the added value must be perceived by the customer. If that is not the case, the problem may be that the value added has not been communicated at all or has not been communicated effectively. Thus, the customer may be unaware that Burger King has a convenient ordering system or that Subaru has a superior braking system. The customer may not have been exposed to the information, or the information may not have been packaged in a memorable, believable way.

Branding the added value is one way to help make it more memorable, meaningful, and believable. The Mr. Goodwrench brand helps GM communicate its service program. Resolution Enhancement is a brand name that helps HP describe a rather esoteric product improvement for its LaserJet printer.

The perceived value problem is particularly acute when the customer is not capable of evaluating the added value. Consider airline safety or the skill of a dentist. The customer is unable to evaluate them without investing significant time and effort. Rather than expend such effort, the customer will look for signals such as the appearance of the aircraft or the professionalism of the dentist's front office. The task is then to manage the signals or cues of value added. User association and endorsements can help. Oral B is the toothbrush recommended by dentists, and Air Jordan is endorsed by Michael Jordan.

Be Difficult to Copy

Finally, the point of differentiation needs to be sustainable. A value added such as 24-hour support is relatively easy to copy if it proves successful. The challenge is to create differentiation strategies that are difficult to copy. One reason to identify two strategic thrusts—synergy from the previous chapter and first mover advantage in the next—is that when they are combined with a differentiation thrust, sustainability is more likely.

When the point of differentiation involves a total organizational effort with a complex set of assets and skills, it will be difficult and costly to copy, especially if there is a dynamic, constantly evolving quality to it. A creative organization with heavy R&D investment, such as that of Microsoft, will inhibit duplication. As discussed below, the quality option and building strong brands can also require a total organizational effort.

Duplication by competitors requires not only ability but will. Increasing the investment or risk involved will discourage competitors. If, for example, multiple points of differentiation are involved, duplication will be more expensive. Saturn has no-haggle pricing, a reliable car, safety features, a committed company, and the Spring Hill, Tennessee (made in the Unites States), connection. Duplicating only one aspect of this differentiation strategy would be inadequate. Overinvestment in a value-added activity may pay off in the long run by discouraging competitors from duplicating a strategy. For example, the development of a superior service back-up system might discourage competitors. The same logic can apply to a broad product line. Some elements of that line might be unprofitable, but if they plug holes that competitiors could use to provide value, then the analysis looks different.

Two Approaches to Differentiation

A host of approaches or strategic orientations can lead to sustainable differentiation strategies, including using strategic information systems, thinking globally, being innovative, being customer driven, or using a unique distribution system. Most successful strategies will involve the total organization, its structure, systems, people, and culture. The quality option and building strong brands will be discussed in detail in this chapter. They are important in their own right in that many successful differentiated firms employ one or of both of these approaches. Further, a discussion of each allows several issues of differentiation strategies to emerge.

THE QUALITY OPTION

The prototype of differentiation is a "quality" strategy in which a business will deliver and be perceived to deliver a product or service superior to that of competitors. A reputation for quality was the most frequently mentioned sustainable competitive advantage (SCA) in Figure 9.2.

A quality strategy can mean that the brand, whether it is a hotel, car, or computer, will be a premium brand as opposed to a value or economy entry. Thus, Marriott Hotels, Mercedes-Benz automobiles, and IBM computers offer enhanced customer benefits, command a price premium, and are top of the line.

A brand can also be the quality option within a group of value or economy brands. Thus, although Kmart does not deliver the same level of personal service, the same quality merchandise, and the same store ambience as Nordstrom, it can still have high quality with respect to those in its strategic group. It will simply be judged on a different set of criteria:

Redefining Quality in Automobiles[2]

Throughout the 1970s and 1980s, the primary quality objective was to be defect-free—the J. D. Powers rating based on customer experience provided a credible measure. By this measure, Japanese cars were far superior to those of competitors. However, in the late 1980s, U.S. cars began to catch up, to the point that the differences were of reduced consequence. Now the problem for U.S. car makers is that the Japanese car makers have now changed the quality game.

The new quality concept is called *miryokuteki hinshitsu* (literally meaning "things gone right")—it takes for granted defect-free manufacturing and changes the focus to making cars that fascinate and delight. The idea is to engineer extraordinary levels of look, sound, and feel into cars, the cumulative effect of which will alter the personality of a car. The whole concept is implemented with the *kaisen* (continuous improvement) philosophy, a research-based concern about customer desires and strong conceptualizations of what a car's personality should be.

Examples are not hard to find. Nissan developed the first computer-driven "active suspension" to smooth the ride of the Infiniti without compromising handling, and placed a counterbalanced lid on its Maxima to help people juggling groceries. Lexus developed its soft, comfortable interior based on extensive human engineering research. The Miata was designed to have the look and feel of classic sports cars. Honda developed the same feel for buttons and a system to reduce vibration.

---

perhaps ease of parking, waiting time at checkout, courtesy of the checkout person, and whether or not desired items are in stock. Dell was regarded as the quality option for mail-order computer firms, at least until Compaq and IBM decided to enter the fray. Gillette's "Good News" is the quality option among disposable blades.

Total Quality Management

To be the quality option, a business must distinguish itself with respect to delivering quality to customers. What is required is a quality-focused management system that is comprehensive, integrative, and supported throughout the organization. Such systems are well developed in Japan and are known in the United States as Total Quality Management (TQM).[3] They consist of a host of tools and precepts, including

- The commitment of senior management to quality as evidenced by substantial time commitment and an emphasis on TQM values.

- Cross-functional teams that focus on quality improvement projects and are empowered to make changes. These teams are sometimes called quality circles, but that phrase is associated with early quality efforts and is too limiting. There should be team-oriented recognition or rewards.

- A process (rather than results) orientation. The focus is on developing and improving processes that will lead to improved quality. Teams should use problem-solving tools and methods to develop programs. An example is the pareto chart, a bar graph that ranks causes of process variation by the degree of impact on quality.

- A set of systems such as suggestions systems, measurement systems, and recognition systems.

- A focus upon the problems and underlying causes of customer complaints and areas of dissatisfaction. One approach used in TQM is to explore a problem in depth by repeatedly asking, "Why?" This process has been dubbed "the five whys."

- The tracking of key quality measures. Benchmarking (performance comparisons) are made with other firms inside and outside the industry and inside and outside the country. Ambitious goals are set. Successes are recognized.

- The involvement of suppliers in the system with supplier audits, ratings, and recognition, as well as joint team efforts.

- The importance of the customer—quality is defined in terms of customer satisfaction.

A Customer Focus

The quality option is designed ultimately to improve customer satisfaction. It follows that a customer focus will be part of a successful effort. A customer focus is something that many organizations profess to have. The problem is to distinguish between lip service and a culture and set of programs that together represent a meaningful SCA.

One indicator of a customer focus is the involvement of top management. A hallmark of most customer-driven organizations is that top executives have regular and meaningful one-on-one contact with customers. When Lou Gerstner took over IBM in 1993, one of his top priorities was to spend time with customers. In fact, he required his top managers to visit five customers a week for a three-month period and send him a report on each. He was trying to change a culture.

Another indicator is a link to the compensation and measurement system. An additional change initiated by Lou Gerstner was in the compensation of the IBM sale force.[4] Commissions are now based 60 percent on profitability, 40 percent on customer satisfaction, and 0 percent on sales. Customers are surveyed to determine if they are happy with the local sales team and if the sales representative has helped them achieve their business objectives.

A third indicator of a customer focus is a knowledge of what drives customer choice, satisfaction, and dissatisfaction. In Chapter 3, Customer Analysis, a discussion of how to develop a list of customer motivations, group them into coherent sets, and then assess their relative importance to the customer was presented.

Figure 10.1 lists eight dimensions of product quality suggested by Harvard's Garvin and five dimensions of service quality that emerged from a series of customer perception studies of service quality involving industries such as retail banking and long-distance telecommunications. Of course, any specific context will have a very different and usually much larger list. One challenge is to reduce the list to a manageable and relevant set and then to select those most important to customers. Another is to convert the customer vocabulary into measures that the business manager can understand and use. If a friendly attitude is important to customers, what operational elements of the business will contribute and how should they be measured?

FIGURE 10.1   Quality Dimensions

PRODUCT QUALITY[5]

1. **Performance.** How well does a washing machine clean clothes?
2. **Durability.** How long will a lawnmower last?
3. **Conformance to specifications.** What is the incidence of defects?
4. **Features.** Does an airline flight offer movies and dinner?
5. **Name.** Does the name mean quality? What is the firm's image?
6. **Reliability.** Will each visit to a restaurant result in similar quality?
7. **Serviceability.** Is the service system efficient, competent, and convenient?
8. **Fit and finish.** Does the product look and feel like a quality product?

SERVICE QUALITY[6]

1. **Tangibles.** Appearance of physical facilities, communication materials, equipment, and personnel.
2. **Reliability.** Ability to perform the promised service dependably and accurately.
3. **Responsiveness.** Willingness to help customers and provide prompt service.
4. **Competence.** Knowledge and skill of employees and their ability to convey trust and confidence.
5. **Empathy.** Caring, individualized attention that a firm provides its customers.

Quality Function Deployment (QFD)

A formal method to aid this translation from customer motivations to quality measures is termed quality function deployment or QFD.[7] The heart of QFD is a matrix. The columns represent the functional characteristics of a product. A pencil, for example, can be specified in terms of length, time between sharpening, lead dust, and shape. The rows of the matrix correspond to the customer motivations such as easy-to-hold, does not smear, point lasts, and does not roll. The cells of the matrix are evaluated to determine how relevant a functional characteristic is to customer motivation. For example, the lead dust is relevant to the does-not-smear benefit and the pencil length and shape are relevant to the easy-to-hold benefit. This becomes one input to the process of prioritizing the functional characteristics in the product development phase.

In transferring customer motivations to operational measures there is always the concern that a quality measure can be counterproductive. To improve the quality of a phone service, the percent of calls answered after the first ring was measured until it was found that the pressure to answer promptly caused agents to become abrupt and impatient and thus customer satisfaction suffered.

Signals of High Quality

Most of the quality dimensions such as performance, durability, reliability, and serviceability are difficult if not impossible for buyers to evaluate. As a result, consumers tend to look for signals of quality. The "fit-and-finish" dimension can be such a quality signal. Buyers assume that if a firm's products do not have good fit-and-finish, they probably will not have other more important quality attributes. An electronics firm found that its speed of responding to information requests affected perceived product quality. In pursuing a quality strategy, it is usually critical to understand what drives quality perception and to look to the "small" but visible elements. Research has shown that in many product classes a key dimension that is visible can be pivotal in affecting perceptions about more "important" dimensions that are very difficult to judge.[8] For example

- Stereo speakers. Larger size means better sound.
- Detergents. Suds mean cleaning effectiveness.
- Tomato juice. Thickness means high quality.
- Fruit-flavored children's drinks. Thickness means low quality.
- Cleaners. A lemon scent can signal cleaning power.

- Supermarkets. Produce freshness means overall quality.
- Cars. A solid door-closure sound implies good workmanship and a solid, safe body.
- Orange juice. Fresh is better than refrigerated, which is better than bottled. Bottled is followed by frozen, canned, and finally, dry-product forms.
- Clothes. Higher price means higher quality.

In the service context, the most important attributes, such as the competence of those providing the service, are extremely difficult to evaluate—consider evaluating surgeons, librarians, airline pilots, dentists, or bankers. Customers cope by looking at those dimensions that are easily evaluated such as the physical appearance of personnel or a facility. The chairman of one airline was quoted as saying, "Coffee stains on the flip-down trays mean (to the passengers) that we do our engine maintenance wrong."[9] It is thus crucial to understand not only what is important with respect to quality, but also what drives those quality perceptions.

Perceived Quality and Financial Performance

The PIMS database of some 3,000 businesses has been analyzed in hundreds of studies, most trying to find clues to strategic success. Perhaps the most definitive finding from this research is that the most important strategic factor affecting the performance of a business unit is the perceived quality of its products. In fact, businesses in the lowest twentieth percentile with respect to relative perceived quality averaged 17 percent ROI, whereas those in the top twentieth percentile earned nearly twice as much.

A detailed examination by Jacobson and Aaker of the relationships between perceived quality and other key strategic variables in addition to ROI provides insights into how perceived quality creates profitability.[10] Perceived quality affects ROI directly because the cost of retaining customers is reduced, and also indirectly because it allows a higher price to be charged and enhances the market share. The higher price not only provides margin dollars but also serves as a quality cue reinforcing perceptions. The higher share suggests that a "quality strategy" does not have to involve high costs. Enhancing quality helps the Kmarts as well as the Tiffanys of the world.

Finally, perceived quality does not increase costs. The conventional wisdom that there is a natural association between a quality/prestige niche strategy and high cost is not reflected in data. The concept that "quality is free" may be part of the reason. In fact, enhanced quality may lead to reduced defects and lowered manufacturing costs. John Young of Hewlett-Packard noted that a focus on quality is one of the best ways to control costs, and mentioned one study that demonstrated fully 25 percent of its manufacturing costs resulted from responses to bad quality.[11]

Perceived Quality and Stock Return

Perceived quality has also been shown by Aaker and Jacobson to drive stock return, a measure that truly reflects long-term performance.[12] They analyzed annual measures of perceived quality obtained from the Total Research EquiTrend database for 35 brands such as IBM, Hershey, Pepsi, and Sears for which brand sales were a substantial part of firm sales. Perceived quality had a significant impact on stock return, comparable with that of ROI. Given that ROI is an established and accepted influence on stock return, the performance of perceived quality is noteworthy. It means that investors are able to detect and respond to programs that affect intangible assets such as perceived quality. Figure 10.2 shows the dramatic relationship between perceived quality and stock return.

The Schlitz Story

The Schlitz story provides a dramatic illustration of the strategic power of perceived quality.[13] From a strong number 2 position in 1974 (selling 17.8 million barrels of beer annually) supported by a series of well-regarded "Gusto" ad campaigns, Schlitz fell steadily until the mid-1980s when it had all but disappeared (with sales of only 1.8 million barrels). The stock market value of the brand fell more than a billion dollars.

FIGURE 10.2   Stock Market Reaction to Changes in Perceived Quality and ROI

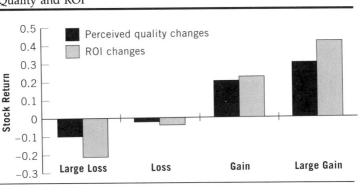

Quality at Sheraton

A team of two dozen people developed a service improvement program at Sheraton labeled the Sheraton Guest Satisfaction System.[14] The system has several elements:

- Customer-satisfaction goals. Employees are expected to be friendly, acknowledge guests' presence, answer guests' questions, and anticipate guests' problems and needs. Staff performance in these areas is measured, and good employees are rewarded with prizes and recognition.

- Hiring. Responses to videos of potentially problematic incidents help personnel select a staff that really empathizes with people.

- Training. A series of training programs including role-playing help staff cope with difficult situations.

- Measurement. Quarterly reports are based on guest questionnaires that rate factors such as bed comfort and lighting, as well as interactions with employees.

- Ongoing meetings. Performance is assessed, problems are corrected, and improvement programs are developed.

- Rewards. Ten percent of the top performing and most improved hotels each quarter become members of the Sheraton's "Chairman's Club."

The collapse can be traced to a decision to reduce costs by converting to a fermentation process that took 4 days instead of 12, substituting corn syrup for barley malt, and using a different foam stabilizer. Word of these changes got into the marketplace. Then, in early 1976, "flaky, cloudy" beer appeared on the shelves, a condition eventually traced to the new foam stabilizer. Worse still, in early summer of that same year, an attempted fix caused the beer to go flat after a short time on the shelf. In the fall of 1976, 10 million bottles and cans of Schlitz were "secretly" recalled and destroyed. Despite a return to its original process and aggressive advertising, Schlitz never recovered.

BUILDING STRONG BRANDS

Another way to differentiate is to build strong brands, to create brand equity. A strategy based on strong brands is likely to be sustainable because it creates competitive barriers. The value of brands is reflected by the financial community where the strategic asset value of brands is recognized. Kraft was purchased for nearly $13 billion, more than 600 percent over its book value, because of the value of the brand names it controls.

Brand equity generates value to the customer that can emerge either as a price premium or enhanced brand loyalty. Brands add customer value in several ways. Brands can

- Help interpret and process information. A brand such as Kodak can be a mechanism to organize and remember a large quantity of information accumulated over time.
- Provide confidence in the purchase decision. Purchasing an HP LaserJet is a lower risk than buying from a firm that is less established in the printer business.
- Add meaning and feelings to the product. A family-time association with McDonald's can change the nature and quality of the use experience, for example.

What Is Brand Equity?

Brand equity is a set of assets and liabilities linked to a brand's name and symbol that add to or subtract from the value provided by a product or service to a firm and/or that firm's customers.[15] The assets and liabilities on which brand equity is based differ from context to context. They can be usefully grouped into four categories, however. As shown in Figure 10.3, one, perceived quality, has already been discussed. The remaining three are brand awareness, brand identity, and brand loyalty. These three, like perceived quality, need to be actively managed. It should be recog-

FIGURE 10.3   Brand Equity

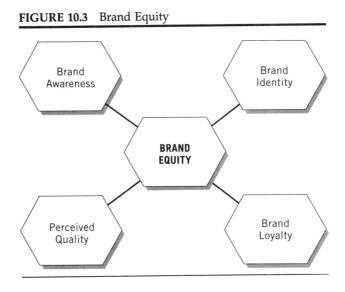

nized that they can require investment in order to be created or maintained. Furthermore, people and systems need to be in place so that programs that will damage them can be identified and resisted.

Brand Awareness

Brand awareness is often taken for granted but, in fact, it can be a key strategic asset. In some industries where there is product parity, awareness provides a sustainable competitive difference. In such cases, awareness, the third most mentioned SCA (see Figure 9.2), serves to differentiate the brands along a recall/familiarity dimension.

Brand awareness can provide a host of competitive advantages. First, awareness provides the brand with a sense of familiarity, and people like the familiar. For low-involvement products such as soap or chewing gum, familiarity can drive the buying decision. In fact, taste tests of products like colas and peanut butter show that a recognized name can affect evaluations even if the brand has never been purchased or used.

Second, name awareness can be a signal of presence, commitment, and substance, attributes that can be very important even to industrial buyers of big-ticket items and consumer buyers of durables. The logic is that if a name is recognized, there must be a reason. This logic is in large part behind the successful efforts to brand components such as NutraSweet and Intel.

Third, the salience of a brand will determine if it is recalled at a key time in the purchasing process. For instance, the initial step in selecting an advertising agency, a car to test drive, or a computer system is to decide on which brands to consider. The extreme case is name dominance, where the brand is the only one recalled when a product class is cued. Consider Kleenex tissue, Clorox bleach, Band-Aid adhesive bandages, Jell-O gelatin, Crayola crayons, Morton salt, Lionel trains, Philadelphia cream cheese, V-8 vegetable juice, and A-1 steak sauce. In each case, how many other brands can you name? How would you like to compete against the dominant brand?

Brand awareness is an asset that can be remarkably durable and thus sustainable. It can be very difficult to dislodge a brand that has achieved a dominant awareness level. The Datsun name was as strong as that of Nissan four years after its name change.[16] In the mid-1980s, an awareness study on blenders was conducted. In this study people were asked what brand of blender they preferred, and GE was the number 2 brand even though it had not made blenders for 20 years.[17] Another study of brand-name familiarity involved homemakers who were asked to name as many brands as they could.[18] On the average, they came up with 28 names each. The age of the brands named was most remarkable—more than 85 percent were over 25 years old and 36 percent were over 75 years old.

What are the implications? One is that the establishment of a strong name anchored by high recognition creates an enormous asset. Furthermore, the asset becomes stronger and stronger over the years as the number of exposures and experiences grow. As a result, a challenging brand, even with an enormous advertising budget and other points of advantage, may find it difficult to enter the memory of the customer.

Brand Identity

A key enduring business asset can be its identity, the associations attached to a firm and its brands.[19] A brand association is anything that is directly or indirectly linked in memory to a brand. Thus, McDonald's could be linked to Ronald McDonald, kids, golden arches, having fun, fast service, family outings, or Big Macs. The most common association is that of product attributes or customer benefits—Heinz is the slowest pouring catsup, Volvo is durable and safe, Snapple is relatively healthy and thirst quenching, and Kleenex is soft.

In addition to product attribute and customer benefit associations, brands gain strategic positon by association with

- Use or application (Gatorade is for football games)
- Product class (Carnation Instant Breakfast is a breakfast food)
- Product user (Miller is for the blue-collar, heavy beer drinker)
- Lifestyle and feelings (the Pepsi Generation)
- Personality (Harley is a macho, male, free spirit)
- Symbol (the Prudential Rock)

A brand's associations are assets that can differentiate, provide reasons to buy, instill confidence and trust, affect feelings toward a product and the use experience, and provide the basis for brand extensions. In doing so, they can create a sustainable advantage.

Associations can provide an important basis for differentiation, especially in product classes such as wines, perfumes, and clothes where it is difficult to distinguish objectively between various brands. The personality of Cher, for example, is unique and so therefore is the brand that bears her name. A differentiating association can be a sustainable advantage. A strong position such as that held by Nordstrom in service or Gatorade in athletics is not easily overcome by competitors. The competitive advantage can be substantial when the association is based on an intangible such as technological leadership, health food, style, or perceived value. It is difficult for a competitor to demonstrate superiority or even parity on such an attribute.

Many brand associations involve product attributes or customer benefits that provide a specific reason to buy and use a brand. They represent a basis for purchase decisions and brand loyalty. Thus, Crest is a cavity-prevention toothpaste, Colgate represents clean, white teeth, and Close-Up generates fresh breath. "Miller time" provides a reason to buy Miller's beer—a cold Miller can be a well-deserved reward. Bloomingdale's is a fun place that carries high-fashion merchandise.

Some associations influence purchase decisions by ascribing credibility and confidence to a brand. If a Wimbledon champion uses a certain tennis racket or a professional hair stylist uses a particular hair-coloring product, consumers may feel more comfortable with those brands. An Italian name and accompanying Italian associations may lend credence to a pizza maker.

Other associations stimulate positive feelings that are then transferred to a brand and to its use experience. Celebrities like Bill Cosby, symbols such as the jolly Green Giant, or slogans like "reach out and touch someone" can all stimulate positive feelings. The associations and their companion feelings then become linked to the brand. One of the roles of the Charlie Brown characters as spokespersons for Metropolitan Life is to soften the image of an otherwise large, impersonal organization with a serious message by linking Metropolitan with Charles Schulz's well-liked characters and the warm, positive feelings they engender.

Associations can create positive feelings during the use experience, serving to transform a product into something different from what it might otherwise be. Advertising, for example, can make the experience of drinking Pepsi seem more fun and driving a Bronco more adventuresome than without the advertising. For many, opening a Tiffany box and wearing Tiffany jewelry are accompanied by a different set of feelings than if the same jewelry had been presented in a Macy's box.

An association can provide the basis for an extension. Honda's experience in small motors makes extensions from motorcycles to outboard motors and lawn mowers plausible. Sunkist is associated with healthy, outdoor activities as well as oranges; this has boosted its image in a variety of other products, including fruit bars, soft drinks, and vitamin C tablets.

The power of a strong association is illustrated by the Weight Watchers business, which was purchased by the H. J. Heinz Co. in the late 1970s for approximately $120 million. What was purchased was the strategic potential of the Weight Watchers association with a professional approach to weight control. As Anthony O'Reilly, the president of Heinz, noted, "You can say light and you can say very light and you can say extra light and trimline or slimline, but at the end of the day, Weight Watchers has an authority about it that will win."[20]

The Heinz vision was that the weight control associations linked to the Weight Watchers program and customer base would provide the basis for a sustainable competitive advantage not only in the core frozen-dinner area but in numerous other extensions as well. During the 1980s, Heinz, in fact, exploited these associations by extending the name relentlessly to new products. By 1989, it was marketing 60 frozen-food items and more than 150 nonfrozen food items. Each extension not only exploited the Weight Watchers name and its associations, but reinforced them as well. In the 1970s, observers were questioning the wisdom of buying such a mature, unexciting business. In 1989, however, Weight Watchers had profits which exceeded $100 million, close to its total acquisition price—all because the potential of a strong association had been recognized.

Brand Loyalty

A customer orientation will lead to a concern for existing customers and programs to generate brand loyalty. A prime enduring asset for some businesses is the loyalty of the installed customer base (listed as item 10 in Figure 9.2). Competitors may duplicate or surpass a product or service, but they still face the task of making customers switch brands. Brand loyalty, or resistance to switching, can be based on simple habit (there is no motivation to change from the familiar gas station or supermarket), preference (there is genuine liking of the brand of cake mix or its symbol, perhaps based on use experience over a long time period), or switching costs. Switching costs would be a consideration for a software user, for example, when a substantial investment has already been made in training employees to learn a particular software system.

An existing base of loyal customers provides enormous sustainable competitive advantages. First, it reduces the marketing costs of doing business, since existing customers usually are relatively easy to hold—the familiar is comfortable and reassuring. Keeping existing customers happy and reducing their motivation to change is usually considerably less costly than trying to reach new customers and persuading them to try another brand. Of course, the higher the loyalty, the easier it is to keep customers happy.

Second, the loyalty of existing customers represents a substantial entry barrier to competitors. Excessive resources are required when entering a market in which existing customers must be enticed away from an established brand that they are loyal to or even just satisfied with. The profit potential for the entrant is thus reduced. For the barrier to be effective, however, potential competitors must know about it; they cannot be allowed to entertain the delusion that customers are vulnerable. Therefore, signals of strong customer loyalty, such as advertisements about documented customer loyalty or product quality, can be useful.

Third, brand loyalty provides trade leverage. Strong loyalty toward brands like Nabisco Premium Saltines, Cheerios, or Tide will ensure preferred shelf space because stores know that customers include such brands on their shopping lists. At the extreme, brand loyalty may determine a customer's store choice. Unless a supermarket carries such brands as Weight Watchers frozen dinners, Paul Newman's salad dressing, Asahi Super-Dry beer, or Grey Poupon mustard, for example, some customers will switch stores.

Fourth, a relatively large, satisfied customer base provides an image of a brand as an accepted, successful, enduring product that will include service backup and product improvements. For example, in 1988, Dell Computer, a mail-order computer firm, advertised an installed base of 100,000 customers, including over 50 percent of the Fortune 500 companies, to reassure prospective customers wary of buying a mail-order computer.

Finally, brand loyalty provides the time to respond to competitive moves—it gives a firm some breathing room. If a competitor develops a superior product, a loyal following will allow the firm the time needed to respond by matching or neutralizing. For example, some newly developed high-tech markets have customers who are attracted by the most advanced product of the moment; there is little brand loyalty in this group. In contrast, other markets have loyal, satisfied customers who will not be looking for new products and thus may not learn of an advancement. Furthermore, they will have little incentive to change even if exposed to the new product. With a high level of brand loyalty, a firm can allow itself the luxury of pursuing a less risky follower strategy.

Many firms have taken their customers for granted, only to see them dissipate when competitors attack. Micropro's Wordstar, which dominated the full-featured word processing industry in the early 1980s, lost its position to WordPerfect and others when it turned its back on its customer base.[21] Wordstar failed to provide adequate product support to its customers and, perhaps worse, introduced a new-generation product, Wordstar 2000, which was not backward compatible. Thus, customers could switch to WordPerfect as easily as learning Wordstar 2000. As a result, Micropro's position eroded until its stock was probably worth less than 1 percent of that of the upstart WordPerfect in 1990. Had it only upgraded its basic Wordstar product and offered competitive product support, Micropro might have held its position and WordPerfect might have been a minor player in the software scene.

The management of brand loyalty is a key to achieving strategic success. It involves

- Placing a value on the future purchases expected from a customer so that existing customers receive appropriate resources.
- Measuring the loyalty of existing customers. Measurement should include not only sensitive indicators of customer satisfaction but also measures of the relationship between the customer and the brand. Is the brand respected, considered a friend, liked, and trusted?
- Conducting exit interviews with those who leave the brand to locate points of vulnerability.
- Generating a customer culture, where people throughout the organization are empowered and motivated to keep the customer happy.

SUMMARY

A successful differentiation strategy will provide customers with perceived and actual value that is difficult for competitors to copy. Differentiation can stem from a focus on quality or building strong brands, or from other features such as being innovative or customer-driven or using a unique distribution system.

The quality option implies that the customer will receive greater value with respect to comparably priced alternatives. In other words, the products and services will simply be better. The foundation of a quality option is often a total quality management program that systematically guides the organization toward delivering quality. Quality is defined with respect to customer satisfaction, so a customer focus needs to be in place, including a way to detect and respond to customer needs and concerns. Quality cues need to be managed because perceived quality is as important as actual quality. Studies show that a quality strategy, on the average, results in a larger ROI and enhances stock return.

Building brand equity, another approach to differentiation, involves developing perceived quality, brand awareness, brand identity, and brand loyalty. Brand awareness provides a sense of familiarity, a signal of substance, and brand recall when a purchase is being considered. A brand's identity is an asset that can differentiate, provide reasons to buy, instill confidence and trust, affect feelings toward a product and use experience, and provide the basis for brand extensions. Brand loyalty reduces marketing costs, creates barriers to competitors, provides trade leverage, affects the brand image, and provides time to respond to competitive threats.

FOOTNOTES

[1] Tom Peters, *Thriving on Chaos*, New York: Knopf, Chapter C-1.

[2] Drawn in part from David Woodruff, "A New Era for Auto Quality," *Business Week*, October 22, 1990, pp. 84–96; Alex Taylor III, "Why Toyota Keeps Getting Better and Better and Better," *Fortune*, November 19, 1990, pp. 66–79.

[3] For an excellent summary of Total Quality Management in the United States see the special issue on TQM in *California Management Review*, Spring 1993.

[4] Ira Sager, "IBM Leans on Its Sales Force," *Business Week*, February 7, 1994, p. 110.

[5] David A. Garvin, "What Does 'Product Quality' Really Mean?" *Sloan Management Review*, Fall 1984, pp. 25–43.

[6] Valarie A. Zeithaml, Leonard L. Berry, and A. Parasuraman, "Communication and Control Processes in the Delivery of Service Quality." *Journal of Marketing*, April 1988, pp. 35–48; A Parasuraman, Leonard L. Berry, and Valaries A. Zeithaml, "Guidelines for Conducting Service Quality Research," *Marketing Research*, December 1990, pp. 34–44.

[7] Robert Neff, "Quality: Overview—Japan," *Business Week*, October 25, 1991, pp. 22–23; John R. Hauser and Don Clausing, "The House of Quality," *Harvard Business Review*, May–June 1988, pp. 63–73.

[8] Zeithaml, Berry, and Parasuraman, "Communication and Control Processes" and Parasuraman, Berry, and Zeithaml, "Guidelines."

[9] Tom Peters and Nancy Austin, *A Passion for Excellence*, New York: Random House, 1985, p. 77.

[10] Robert Jacobson and David A. Aaker, "The Strategic Role of Product Quality," *Journal of Marketing*, October 1987, pp. 31–44.

[11] John Young, "The Quality Focus at Hewlett-Packard," *The Journal of Business Strategy*, 5, Winter 1985, p. 7.

[12] David A. Aaker and Robert Jacobson, "The Financial Information Content of Perceived Quality," *Journal of Marketing Research*, May 1994.

[13] The Schlitz story is described in David A. Aaker, *Managing Brand Equity*, New York: The Free press, 1991.

[14] David Walker, "At Sheraton, the Guest Is Always Right," *Adweek's Marketing Week*, October 23, 1989, pp. 20–21.

[15] Aaker, *Managing Brand Equity*, Chapter 2–6.

[16] Aaker, *Managing Brand Equity*, p. 57.

[17] "Shoppers Like Wide Variety of Houseware Brands," *Discount Store News*, October 24, 1988, p. 40.

[18] Leo Bogart and Charles Lehman, "What Makes a Brand Name Familiar?" *Journal of Marketing Research*, February 1973, pp. 17–22.

[19] Aaker, *Managing Brand Equity*, Chapter 5.

[20] Anthony O'Reilly, "What's on His Plate?" *Advertising Age*, February 26, 1990, p. 16.

[21] The Wordstar material was drawn in part from Kate Bertrand, "Can MicroPro Catch Its Fallen 'Star'?" *Business Marketing*, May 1989, pp. 55–66, and Aaker, *Managing Brand Equity*.

11

OBTAINING AN SCA— LOW COST, FOCUS, AND THE PREEMPTIVE MOVE

Never follow the crowd.

Bernard M. Baruch

The first man gets the oyster, the second man gets the shell.

Andrew Carnegie

A business strategy can be usefully characterized by one or more strategic thrusts—combinations of functional area strategies and bases of SCAs (sustainable competitive advantages) that represent the essence of the strategy. Five types of strategic thrusts were introduced in Chapter 1 and discussed in Chapter 9: differentiation, low cost, focus, the preemptive move, and synergy. Most strategies involve either differentiation or low cost, and some involve both, although organizational realities make the successful implementation of both difficult. The other three types are not so frequently present, but are often pivotal when they are relevant.

Differentiation was the subject of Chapter 10, and synergy was introduced in Chapter 9 and is a recurring theme in the next two chapters. In this chapter, the other three strategic thrusts are covered: low cost, focus, and the preemptive move.

LOW-COST STRATEGIES

Although there is a tendency to think of low cost as a single approach such as scale economies, low-cost labor, or production automation, it is important to recognize that there are many methods of obtaining a low-cost advantage. The successful low-cost firms are those that can harness multiple approaches such as those shown in Figure 11.1 and discussed below.

No-Frills Product/Service

A direct approach to low cost is simply to remove all frills and extras from a product or service. For example, the membership warehouses such as Price Club and Sam's all provide warehouse settings, usually in low-cost areas, without amenities like the ability to charge on a credit card and personal service. No-frills airlines, legal services clinics, discount brokers, and the Hyundai automobile company have followed the same general principle.

A major risk, especially in the service sector, is that competitors will add just a few features and position themselves against a no-frills firm. Motel 6 pioneered the concept of spartan lodging in the early 1960s by giving the world the $6 hotel room with no phone or TV set. The economy lodging industry in the last decade has attracted a host of competitors, most of which aim to offer a bit more than Motel 6 at a comparable or slightly higher price. The result can be feature war.

The goal is to generate a no-frills cost advantage that is sustainable for one of two reasons. First, competitors cannot easily stop offering services that their customers expect. Second, competitors' operations and

FIGURE 11.1 The Low-Cost Strategic Thrust

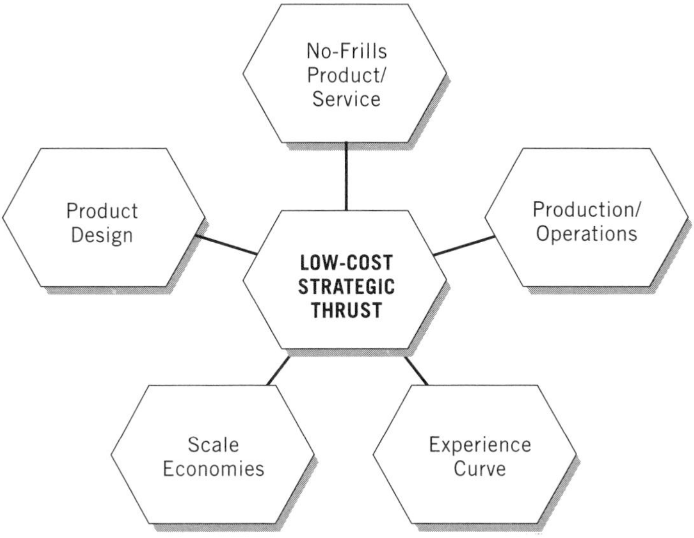

```
                    ┌─────────────┐
                    │  No-Frills  │
                    │  Product/   │
                    │  Service    │
                    └─────────────┘

  ┌──────────┐       ┌──────────┐       ┌────────────┐
  │ Product  │       │ LOW-COST │       │ Production/ │
  │ Design   │───────│ STRATEGIC│───────│ Operations │
  └──────────┘       │ THRUST   │       └────────────┘
                     └──────────┘

       ┌──────────┐       ┌────────────┐
       │  Scale   │       │ Experience │
       │Economies │       │   Curve    │
       └──────────┘       └────────────┘
```

facilities have been designed for such services and cannot be easily changed.

A case in point is Southwest Airlines. Founded in 1971 with three planes serving three Texas cities, Southwest had no assigned seats, peanuts-only meal service, low overhead, and below-industry-average wages.[1] The company shunned fancy hubs, reservation systems, and global schedules. Because of the reduced service, Southwest could turn around planes more quickly, which resulted in more trips and scale economies. Competitors such as Delta and American could not cut services that their customers expected. Further, their strategy, which was based upon a hub/reservation system, could not be adapted. As a result, the no-frills strategy propelled Southwest from a struggling survivor to the industry winner. The ultimate compliment was the emergence of imitators such as Morris Air and UltrAir.

A firm with an inherent cost advantage has a good chance of making a no-frills approach stick. Arco made a move in the early 1980s to eliminate costly credit card service and substantially reduce its gasoline price. One reason that Arco was able to hold the new price difference during a subsequent price war was a cost advantage in its Alaskan crude sources and its low-cost culture which its competitors could not match. Another was that the elimination of credit card service provided a logic to the new price strategy and reduced the pressure on competitors to retaliate.

Product Design

A product's design or composition can create cost advantages. For example, Masonite developed a line of pressed-wood alternatives to wood that use sawdust, wood chips, branches, and twigs. The resulting products cost less than half as much as their wood competitors.

Japanese competitors have entered several established industries, including copiers, by designing reliable, simple products involving relatively few, readily available (as opposed to customized) parts. A U.S. firm, Fadal, has reversed the tables in the machine tool industry by using the same strategy to retain 20 percent of the metalworking machine market under attack from the Japanese.[2] Fadal produces the Volkswagen Beetle of the industry—a functional, durable machine that is easy to operate and fix. The key is keeping its organization focused on cost and simplicity.

A variant is to augment a product with relatively high-margin accessories or extra features and thus provide a higher perceived value to customers. Several computer firms have achieved a low systems price by including software or printers.

Product downsizing is another approach that can be helpful when price pressures inhibit alternatives. It is termed the "Hershey's solution" because Hershey downsized its chocolate bar when confronted with increases in the price of cocoa.

Production/Operations

Raw Material Cost Advantage. A firm's access to raw materials can provide a sustainable cost advantage. For example, a firm might buy undeveloped oil or coal resources, anticipating a time when access would be limited. Fort Howard Paper achieved a cost advantage by being the only major paper maker to use recycled pulp exclusively.[3] Although it is not considered as good as virgin material, recycled pulp provides a key edge in the away-from-home market for toilet paper and other products used in hotels, restaurants, and office buildings.

Low-Cost Distribution. When a major cost component is distribution, the use of a different channel can create substantial cost advantages. In the computer hardware industry, for example, mail-order firms such as Dell, Northgate, Gateway, and Zeos have natural cost advantages because they have none of the fixed costs of a sales force nor the expense of compensating retailers. They are especially well-suited for those who know what they want and do not need hand-holding. As the computer industry matures and its products become more user-friendly, the percentage of people who are comfortable with a mail-order alternative increases.

Labor Cost Advantage.   In some labor-intensive industries, a sustainable cost advantage, at least with respect to some strategic groups, can be based on access to inexpensive labor. The apparel industry, in which labor accounts for about 27 percent of cost, has seen importers make substantial inroads because of their cost advantage, particularly in the area of less fashion-sensitive apparel where a long lead time can be tolerated. A key success factor in many apparel industries is the ability to work with offshore sources.

Government Subsidy.   Some firms receive government subsidies or other special treatment that effectively provides a direct or indirect sustainable cost advantage. For example, steel companies in Europe and Japan are heavily subsidized by their governments. Many national airlines are subsidized and, in addition, they receive help in terms of access to routes. Furthermore, countries like Ireland and states such as Virginia can provide substantial incentives to locate there, which can translate into a cost advantage.

Location Cost Advantage.   Sometimes the best retail locations are obtained on favorable terms by those who enter early into a market. The competitors are then faced with paying more and perhaps being shut out of some locations. Certainly, one reason for McDonald's success is its long-standing policy of buying real estate. This practice has not only given McDonald's a cost advantage, but it has also contributed significantly to its profits.

Production Innovation and Automation.   Innovations in the production process, including automation, can provide the basis of a competitive advantage. The problem often is to make the advantage sustainable. One approach is to attempt to keep the innovations secret by providing plant security and incentives for employees to stay. A second is to keep improving them so that the competitors must match a moving target. The third is to make capacity expansion decisions visible to discourage competitors, as DuPont did in the titanium oxide business when it developed a unique production process.[4]

Purchase of Inexpensive Capital Equipment.   Firms sometimes are motivated to divest a business even at a price far below replacement cost or

---

COMPAQ

Compaq had a winning strategy in the PC business during the 1980s, which involved maintaining a technology leadership over IBM, targeting Fortune 500 firms, using limited distribution, and supporting high prices and high margins.[5] In the face of competitive pressures from mail-order firms, Compaq in late 1991 realized that its vision was obsolete. The result is a rare case of a company that reinvented itself totally to create a new vision.

The cornerstone of the new vision was a low-cost focus which required radical changes in the whole company and its operations. Instead of providing a price ceiling for the industry, Compaq was almost overnight an aggressive price leader. It saw its share of the $35-billion-a-year market jump from 3.8 to 10 percent in only two years.

To accommodate its new low-cost vision, Compaq made the following changes:

- Created a new culture. One observer felt that the atmosphere at Compaq went from Camelot to the South Bronx.

- Aggressively reduced manufacturing costs and ran factories 24 hours a day.

- Reversed a long-standing policy of manufacturing in-house and outsourced assembly work.

- Went to a build-on-order, just-in-time manufacturing system that reduced inventory and made the system more responsive to demand.

- Exploited economies of scale—in 1993 as volume doubled from 1.5 million to 3 million computers, total manufacturing costs actually fell. Compaq bailed out of printers when it realized that inadequate volume would not allow the company to compete.

- Added retailers, including Wal-Mart, that required lower margins—the number was quintupled from 2,000 to more than 10,000.

- Added new products such as Presario, a line of home computers with built-in software.

---

book value. In an industry with significant fixed costs, obtaining low-cost capacity can provide considerable competitive leverage. The opportunity to buy competitors occurs most frequently in mature or declining industries and is discussed in more detail in Chapter 14.

Reduction of Overhead. A firm, especially in a mature, established industry, can find itself with a bloated work force and excessive overhead that was created over time, perhaps in part during more demanding growth periods. Such a context provides opportunities for cost reductions, especially for a new owner or CEO.

White Industries provides an excellent example of a firm that first acquired low-cost assets, then moved in to reduce overhead and an excess work force. During the late 1960s and 1970s, White bought the appliance brands Franklin (Studebaker), Kelvinator (American Motors), Westinghouse, Philco (Ford), and Frigidaire (GM) from firms that were losing money in the mature appliance industry.[6] As a result, White became one of the major firms in the appliance industry, together with Whirlpool, General Electric, and Maytag.

Each of the brands acquired by White had been a division of a large company with heavy overhead that had become a cash trap. White was able to turn each business around within months, in large part because of a very different cost culture and much less overhead. Some overhead was reduced by streamlining the product line and by consolidating production; much of the rest was obtained simply by running an extremely lean operation. The old firms, with strong union presences and established cultures, would have been incapable of doing something similar even if they had recognized the need to do so.

Scale Economies

The scale effect reflects the natural efficiencies associated with size. Fixed costs such as advertising, sales force overhead, R&D, staff work, and facilities upkeep can be spread over more units. Furthermore, a larger operation can support specialized assets and activities such as market research, legal staff, and manufacturing-engineering operations dedicated to a firm's needs.

The key to scale economies is to determine the optimal size for an operation. When the size is below optimal, a firm can suffer a severe competitive disadvantage. The advertising expenditures of the smaller beer brands, for example, suffer from scale economies enjoyed by larger competitors. In some industries such as cereal, however, it has been shown that only a small market share is required to attain scale economies.

A common mistake is to assume that scale economies will occur even when a firm's volume is based on multiple products or brands. For example, Quaker Oats bought Gaines (Gainesburgers, Cycle, and Gravy Train) to add to its dog food brands (Ken-L-Ration and Kibbles'n Bits) in order to attain a substantial number 2 position in the dog food market and a commanding 75 percent share in the semimoist segment.[7] One problem was that the five brand names required their own marketing and production so that there were few resulting scale economies. Furthermore, the larger market presence stimulated a vigorous response by the market leader Ralston—it launched a semimoist entry to undercut what Quaker thought was its cash cow.

The Experience Curve

The experience curve suggests that as a firm accumulates experience in building a product, its costs in real dollars (net of inflation) will decline at a predictable rate. Figure 11.2 shows the experience curve for the Model T Ford as reflected by its price. An 85 percent experience curve means that cost will be reduced by 15 percent each time the cumulative experience doubles. Literally thousands of cost studies by the Boston Consulting Group (BCG) and others provide empirical support. The implication is that the first entry into a market that attains a large market share will have a continuing cost advantage.

The experience curve may be in part caused by economies of scale but it is primarily based on the following:

- *Learning.* The basic idea is that people learn to do tasks faster and more efficiently simply by repetition. Furthermore, with a higher volume extending over a longer time period, it becomes worthwhile to improve task processes. Learning has links to the time and motion studies of the early 1900s, the learning curve of the 1930s, and more recently, to quality circles popularized by Japanese firms.

- *Technological Improvements in Production/Operations.* The installation of new machinery, computer/information systems, or other capital

FIGURE 11.2   Price of Model T, 1909–1923 (Average List Price in 1958 Dollars)

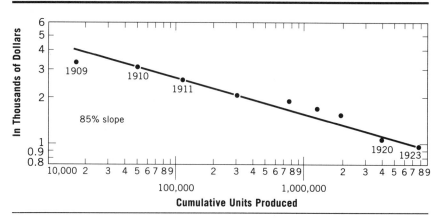

equipment to improve production or operations can dramatically affect costs, especially for capital-intensive industries. Furthermore, as experience accumulates, people will learn to use such equipment to its full capability and may even modify it to extend its performance.

- *Product Redesign.* Simplifying products can sharply reduce costs. For example, the number of parts in a door-lock mechanism on a U.S. automobile declined from 17 in 1954 to 4 in 1974.[8] The cost of the mechanism in real dollars fell almost 75 percent during that period. The decrease in cost was credited to as many as 20 individual product improvements, including improvements in metallurgy and casting techniques.

Several issues need to be addressed in working with the experience curve concept. First, multiple products can complicate. For example, when several products share a component such as a motor or field service operation, that component will have the benefit of enhanced volume and will advance along the experience curve faster than other components. Consequently, there may be several experience curves to analyze.

Second, the experience curve is not automatic. It must be proactively managed with efficiency-improvement goals, quality circles, product design targets, and equipment upgrading. Further, a late entry can access the most recent design and thus gain the same advantage as the more experienced vendors.

Third, if the technology or market changes, the experience curve may become obsolete. As Walter Kiechel put it, "There you are contentedly making glass bottles for milk, making quite a lot of bottles in fact. You get better at it all the time, producing bottles for less and less per unit, and just rocketing down the old you-know-what. All of a sudden, from out of nowhere, comes some bozo with a wax-paper carton. This character has never even heard of your experience curve, but three years later wax cartons are everywhere and your glass bottle factory is in cobwebs."[9]

Fourth, the experience curve model implies that cost improvements, whatever their source, should be translated into low prices and higher share so that the business can stay ahead on the experience curve. However, it is possible that lower costs should be accompanied by price stability to avoid price wars and to improve profitability.[10] The Japanese use of the low price, improve-share logic has degraded such industries as consumer electronics and is not necessarily a model to be emulated.

A key to strategy development is recognizing when the experience curve model will apply. When an industry is mature, the experience curve becomes flat, and because it takes so long to double cumulative experience, the experience curve is less useful. If the value added is low, the experience curve will also have little impact. If a purchased raw material such as wheat or sulfur is 80 percent of the cost, there is very little role for

---

Ford's Model T

The experience of the Ford Motor Company from 1908 to 1923 illustrates how an experience curve strategy can lead a firm to focus obsessively on costs and thus ignore trends, fail to innovate, and end up with an obsolete product.[11] A very well-defined 85 percent experience curve is shown in Figure 11.2. It is worth noting that the steady cost reduction did not just happen. It was caused, in part, by the building of the huge River Rouge plant, a reduction in the management staff from 5 to 2 percent of all employees, extensive vertical integration, and the creation of the integrated, mechanized production process paced by conveyors.

However, in the early 1920s, consumers began to request heavier, closed-body cars that offered more comfort. As Alfred P. Sloan, Jr., the head of General Motors during this time, noted, "Mr. Ford . . . had frozen his policy in the Model T . . . preeminently an open-car design. With its light chassis, it was unsuited to the heavier closed body, and so in less than two years (by 1923) the closed body made the already obsolescent design of the Model T noncompetitive."[12]

As a result, in May of 1927, Henry Ford was forced to shut down operations for nearly a year at a cost of $200 million to retool so that he could compete in the changed marketplace. It seems clear that the very decisions that allowed Ford to march down the experience curve made it difficult for the company to react to the changing times and to competition. The standardized product, extensive vertical integration, and single-minded devotion to production improvements all tended to create an organization that was ill-suited to respond to the changing environment—indeed an organization whose goals and thrust were intimately involved with preserving the status quo, the existing product.

---

experience to play. Some of the most successful applications of the experience curve have been in continuous-process manufacturing contexts such as semiconductors or capital-intensive heavy industries like steel.

A Low-Cost Culture

A successful low-cost strategy is usually multifaceted, with costs attacked on several fronts and supported by a cost-oriented culture. Top management, rewards, systems, structure, and culture must all stress cost reduction. There needs to be a single-minded focus comparable to that achieved by the firms that successfully engage in total quality management. In other words, a commitment is required. Heinz, for example, became the low-cost producer in ketchup, frozen french fries, vinegar, and cat food by committing the organization to cost reduction.[13] It held a conference on low-cost operations for the firm's top 100 managers, developed new processes to peel potatoes and to reclaim heat from ovens, developed cost- and quality-control teams, shifted Star-Kist production off-shore, and automated soup production in England.

FOCUS STRATEGIES

The focus strategic thrust, whether it involves differentiation, low cost, or both, concentrates on one part of the market or product line. As suggested by Figure 11.3 focus strategies avoid diluting or distracting strategy implementation, provide a way to compete with limited resources, bypass assets and skills of larger competitors, provide positioning strategy, and reduce competitive pressures.

A focus strategy avoids strategy dilution or distraction and is thus more likely to lead to a sustainable advantage. When the internal investments, programs, and culture have all been directed toward a single end and there is "buy-in" on the part of everyone in the organization, the result will be assets, skills, and functional strategies that match market needs. In most cases, as the product line or market is expanded, compromises will be made in advertising, distribution, manufacturing, and so on, and the SCA and associated entry barriers will be diluted. It is no accident that specialized retailers such as The Limited, The Gap, Benetton, Toys "R" Us, Victoria's Secret, and the Foot Locker have been much more

FIGURE 11.3 A Focus Strategy

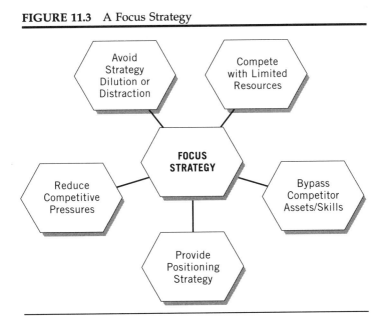

successful than department stores and others that are spread thin. One reason is the strategic and operational advantages of focusing.

A business that simply lacks the resources to compete in a broad product market must focus in order to generate the impact that is needed to compete effectively. Such a limitation can occur, for example, when an automobile or airplane manufacturer faces heavy product development and tool costs or a consumer products firm cannot afford to support multiple brands.

A focus strategy provides the potential to bypass competitor assets and skills. For example, in the cereal and other packaged foods industries, the ability to establish brand names and distribute branded products is a key success factor. However, firms that focus on private-label manufacture in which cost-control considerations dominate can also do well. These firms insulate themselves from the major manufacturers who would compromise their own brands by producing private labels.

A focused strategy may also provide a positioning device. The association of a business with a narrow product line, segment, or geographic area can serve to provide a useful identity. For example, Neiman Marcus competes only in the very high-priced end of its industry and therefore appeals to a very narrow segment. Any effort to compete in a broader product market, even if feasible, would risk damaging the exclusive image it has developed for its existing stores. The Raymond Corporation is known for its limited product line of "narrow-aisle" lift trucks suitable for navigating the narrow spaces in warehouses.

Although the payoff of a small niche may be less than that of a large, growing market, the competition may often also be less intense. The "majority fallacy" concept states that appraisals of fast-growing segments overlook or minimize the likelihood that many competitors will be attracted. This explains why growth areas often stimulate destructive overcapacity and why a more modest product-market scope may be a preferable choice.

The potential of enhancing an SCA by using a focus strategy must be balanced by the fact that it naturally limits the potential business. As a result, profitable sales may be missed. Furthermore, the focused business will often have to compete with larger companies that will enjoy scale economies. Thus, it is crucial that the focus involves a strategy with meaningful SCAs.

Discipline is required to pursue a focus strategy and bypass large markets. Consider the case of Fab 1 Shot, a Colgate-Palmolive product providing packets of detergent and fabric softener that would serve a single wash, thus offering convenience to the busy homemaker.[14] Instead of a focus strategy aimed at those for whom convenience was extremely important, such as college students, singles, and apartment dwellers, Colgate succumbed to the temptation to go after the large mainstream market with a mammoth promotional and advertising effort. The result was a failure, in part because the mainstream market wanted more control over the quantity of product used and thus did not value the convenience offered.

Focusing the Product Line

Focusing on part of a product line can enhance the line's technical superiority. In most businesses, the key people have expertise or interest in a few products. Those who are the driving force behind a fashion firm may be interested primarily in women's high fashion. A consumer electronics firm may be founded and run by someone who is very interested in audio quality. When the products of a firm capture the imagination of its key people, the products tend to be exciting, innovative, and of high quality. As the product line broadens, however, the products tend to be me-too products, which do not provide value and detract from the base business. In such a situation the willpower to maintain a focus and resist product expansion may pay off.

Targeting a Segment

Targeting a segment is another approach to a focus strategy. Michelin Tires, Calvin Klein clothes, and Portman Hotels all focus on the upscale segment, those consumers who want the highest quality and are not price-sensitive. Portman will pick up guests at the airport in a Rolls-Royce. An industrial distributor may focus on large-volume users. A clothing retailer

---

The Hernia Hospital

Shouldice Hospital near Toronto specializes in hernia operations.[15] The hospital and staff are thus tailored to the needs of the hernia patient. Patients walk to watch TV, to eat, and even to and from the operating room. Walking, it turns out, is good therapy. There is thus no need to deliver food to rooms or to have wheelchair facilities. The length of a hospital visit is around half of the norm elsewhere. No general anesthesia is administered because local anesthesia is safer and cheaper for hernia operations. Doctors at Shouldice are exceptionally skillful and productive because they do so many operations. Measured by how often repeat treatment is needed, Shouldice is ten times more effective than other hospitals.

By concentrating on one segment of the medical market, Shouldice has developed a hospital that is proficient, low-cost, and capable of delivering an extraordinary level of patient satisfaction. Ex-patients are so pleased that some 1500 "alumni" came to a reunion.

might serve only those needing large sizes. A ski manufacturer might serve only competitive skiers. Harley-Davidson focuses on bikers wanting powerful "macho" motorcycles. Armstrong Rubber has performed well over the years by focusing on replacement tires—Sears Roebuck is a major customer. Voyager MC makes two-piece golf clubs that can be taken on airplanes for golfers who travel.

Limited Geographic Area

A special type of segmentation variable is geographic location. Geographic segmentation can be effective when it is possible to tailor the product offering and its marketing program to the geographical area served. For example, a regional beer such as the Texas beer, Lone Star, can use local humor and dialects and local promotions such as a rodeo circuit in its marketing efforts. The resulting local associations can provide sustainable competitive advantages (SCAs) that are not easily overcome by national brands, which are constrained by a national program. A three-store supermarket chain may serve a very limited area with a product and service package suitable for its particular clientele.

Another rationale for geographic segmentation is to obtain cost advantages from operating within a geographic area. For example, such businesses as cement manufacturers, bakeries, and dairies, for which transportation costs are substantial, may benefit from being regional.

Low-Share Competitors

In many industries there is a dominant firm with substantial scale advantages. A key to competing against such a firm is usually to use some variant of a focus strategy. One approach is to look for a portion of the market in which the dominant firm is making high profits, which may be used to subsidize other parts of its business. Another is to focus on a part of the market that has been neglected and develop an offering and strategy to capture it.

Hamermesh and two colleagues studied low-share firms with good financial performance records and found that a focus strategy was a key to their success.[16] They all tended to (1) compete in a limited number of segments where their strengths were most highly valued, (2) work closely or jointly with customers on R&D, (3) invest in improvement of manufacturing and operations rather than development of breakthrough products, (4) have strong CEOs, and (5) emphasize profitability rather than growth.

THE PREEMPTIVE MOVE

A preemptive strategic move is an implementation of a strategy new to a business area that, because it is first, generates a skill or asset that competitors are inhibited or prevented from duplicating or countering.[17] A sustainable first-mover advantage can result from technological leadership, preemption of assets, and/or buyer switching costs. For example, when a retailer gains access to a set of prime locations in a community, other retailers are inhibited from competing because of the resulting location disadvantage. The advantage is not automatic, as will be shown, but requires active and continuing investment and management.

As shown in Figure 11.4, preemptive moves can be directed at supply systems, products, production systems, customers, or distribution and service systems.

Supply Systems

A business can gain advantage by preempting access to the best or least expensive sources of raw materials or production equipment. Interna-

FIGURE 11.4   Sources of Preemptive Opportunities

SUPPLY SYSTEMS

- Secure access to raw materials.
- Preempt production equipment.
- Dominate supply logistics.

PRODUCTS

- Preempt a position.
- Develop a dominant design.
- Secure superior product development personnel.

PRODUCTION SYSTEMS

- Develop production processes.
- Expand capacity.
- Vertically integrate.

CUSTOMERS

- Train customers in usage skills—become the familiar brand.
- Get customers to make long-term commitments.
- Gain specialized knowledge about a customer set.

DISTRIBUTION AND SERVICE SYSTEMS

- Occupy prime locations.
- Dominate key distributors or outlets.

tional Nickel and DeBeers based their firms on access to the raw materials nickel and diamonds, respectively. A key advantage of the Red Lobster restaurant chain was its access to the best seafood sources and seafood distribution. Airlines can place large orders for planes, thereby forcing competitors to remain years behind in obtaining the best equipment. Like many preemptive moves, those oriented toward the supply system are risky. If supply commitments are made and business does not materialize or other superior supply sources emerge, such a strategy could backfire.

Product Opportunities

The first product to be introduced in a market can enjoy the substantial advantage of occupying a desirable position. Frito-Lay's 99.5 percent service standard tends to preempt the position of providing the fastest, most reliable service. There simply is not much room for a competitor to exceed 99.5 percent. A competitor is almost forced into another positioning strategy.

The key in some industries is to become the "industry standard." Thus, in the personal computer industry, IBM became the industry standard mainly because of the clout of the IBM name and organization. In doing so IBM essentially created industry standards for the IBM hardware system, Intel's X86 microprocessor, and Microsoft's DOS operating system. Tragically for IBM, the hardware system turned out to be easily cloned, and the microprocessor and operating systems became the protected assets. Had IBM had more foresight, it could have owned or participated in both the Intel and Microsoft products. It thus would have controlled the PC business in the late 1980s and 1990s, instead of struggling to find profitable niches.

Production Systems

When a business can pioneer a production process that is effective at reducing cost, enhancing quality, or both, an SCA can be created. Japanese firms have been able to achieve such an SCA in industry after industry. A key to their success is their commitment to keep investing and improving over time, to be a moving target. Another approach is to aggressively expand capacity in order to discourage competitors from entering the market.

Customer Opportunities

A first mover can develop customer loyalty by creating switching costs, which is done in a variety of ways:

- **A customer can simply become familiar with the first mover's product or service.**[18] If it is satisfactory, there may be no incentive to try something different, the performance of which is uncertain. The familiarity switching cost is particularly relevant to low-cost convenience products where it is difficult for a customer to justify any search effort.

- **A customer may be enticed or required to make a long-term commitment.** For example, a hospital supply firm made substantial inroads against a dominant, established firm by offering to place computer terminals in hospitals to facilitate ordering emergency products. The terminals ultimately were used to order routine as well as emergency items. Because hospitals needed only one such terminal, the established firm found its belated effort to duplicate the service frustrated—it had been preempted.

- **A customer may invest by learning to use a first mover's product or service.** Switching would require the duplication of this learning investment. Many industrial equipment manufacturers, such as Texas Instruments in the area of oil field instrumentation, have generated customers with knowledge equity in their equipment.

- **A firm may gain specialized knowledge about a customer.** A law firm or advertising agency may become so intimate with a client that it would be disruptive for the client to attempt a new relationship. A computer firm such as NCR may gain such specialized knowledge about a retail chain that it would be risky and expensive for that chain to switch to another computer firm.

Distribution and Service Systems

A retail chain can preempt locations by committing early to an area and selecting prime outlets. The chain will not only have first choice of outlets, but will also discourage competitors by reducing their profit potential. In many industries, distribution-channel capacity limits exist. There is only so much shelf space or capacity in a distributor warehouse or sales representative organization. The firm that gets first access to this distribution-channel capacity will be hard to dislodge.

Implementing the Preemptive Move

Several threads run through the concept of a preemptive move. First, by definition it involves doing something novel. One does not get there by copying and improving on strategies already in place. Innovation is required. Thus, some mechanism must exist to allow ideas for preemptive actions to surface.

Second, the preemptive move often involves the substantial commitment of resources, which implies substantial risk. It is this very commitment, however, that helps make the resulting advantage sustainable, because competitors are reluctant to move against a committed firm. Profit potential for an entrant is always higher if it is likely that existing competitors will exit.

Third, a successful first-mover advantage assumes that a competitor will be inhibited or prevented from duplicating or countering. For example, a competitor's "quality prestige" brand could be cannibalized and weakened if it introduced a lower-priced brand as a reaction to a preemptive move at the low end of the market. A competitor might be committed to an existing distribution system or manufacturing process and thus be reluctant to follow a first mover. In deciding to invest in a preemptive move, companies need to consider the possible reaction of competitors and, when possible, reduce the likelihood that they will engage in damaging follower strategies such as those discussed below.

Research on Market Pioneers

Since pioneers and early entrants to a product category often use preemptive strategies, their performance gives a hint about the power of a preemptive move. There is substantial empirical evidence from several studies involving both consumer and industrial businesses that a preemptive move does, on the average, pay off.[19] For example, a study of more than 500 mature industrial businesses using the PIMS database showed that first-entrant firms averaged a market share of 29 percent, early followers averaged 21 percent, and late entrants averaged 15 percent. Another study of 18 consumer markets showed that the first firm to enter a market had a lasting market-share advantage that ranged from 6 market-share points (with 7 entrants) to 13 (with only 2 entrants).[20]

When all true market pioneers are considered in the analysis, including those first entrants that did not survive, the advantage of pioneers is reduced. Golder and Tellis used historical methods to identify the true market pioneers.[21] They included MITS in computers, Daguerrotype in cameras, Bright Star in batteries, Vernors in soft drinks, Hartford in tires, Ampex in video recorders, California Cooler in wine coolers and Kirsch's in diet cola. The research found that there was only a 50 percent survivor rate among the true pioneers and that the survivors averaged only a 19 percent market share, about two-thirds of the figure found in the PIMS study where the pioneer was defined as the earliest entry of the surviving firms. Clearly, a pioneer without the resources and ability to exploit an idea can be vulnerable.

Follower Advantages

There are a host of firms that have been successful in part because they were followers. In fact, Schnaars found 28 industries in which a historical analysis revealed that the innovator lost position to a follower.[22] The success of the follower was based on such factors as technological improvements, more resources for advertising, control of distribution channels, the ability to exploit a cost advantage, the selection of a different market segment, or superior positioning. For example,

- Kirsch's No-Cal (1952) and later Royal Crown's Diet Rite (1962) pioneered diet soft drinks, but they could not match the distribution advantages and the advertising budgets of diet Pepsi (1963) or Coke's Tab (1963).
- Cuisinart (1973) lost position to Black & Decker because it could not produce and market lower-priced units.
- MITS (1975) and Apple (1977) created computers for hobbyists but when the market turned to business users, IBM entered and quickly dominated.
- Wordstar (1979) was stuck with an obsolete standard when WordPerfect (1982) and Microsoft Word (1983) provided a technological advance and Wordstar failed to update.
- In VCRs, Ampex (1956) focused on selling broadcasters and never adapted a product for the home market. Sony's Betamax (1975) eventually lost out to the Matsushita VHS system (1976) because Sony was not able to create an industry standard.
- Leica (1925), a German brand, could not keep pace with the product improvements and low prices of the Japanese firms such as Canon (1934) and Nikon (1946).
- In commercial jet aircraft, deHavilland (1952) rushed to market with a jet that crashed frequently. Boeing (1958) followed with the much more reliable 707.

In fact, many firms deliberately engage in a strategy of being a follower, imitating competitors that are successful. Followers have real advantages. The most important advantage may be reduced new product failure rates. The fact is that most new products, especially those with radically new concepts, fail. The true pioneer must absorb that risk. It makes sense for a firm, especially a large one with resources to apply, to wait until a concept has been proved and the market developed before entering. Entering late will have costs and disadvantages, but a lot of resources will be saved by the reduced incidence of failure.

Followers are often imitators, and imitation requires substantially less investment in both R&D and in manufacturing. Further, it takes less time. After a pioneer has taken ten years to refine a concept and set up manufacturing, a follower may be able to accomplish the same task in one year or less.

Followers can benefit from watching the market evolve. The follower can improve on the design and perhaps participate in a second generation product or manufacturing process while the pioneer is stuck with an investment in a first generation product and operation. Further, the pioneers may be committed to a segment or positioning strategy that will be sub-optimal as the market evolves. The earliest computer buyers were basically hobbyists, a far cry from the mainstream business market that IBM targeted. Taster's Choice successfully followed Maxim in the freeze-dried coffee category by positioning along the taste dimension.

SUMMARY

Figure 11.5 provides a summary of the five strategic thrusts discussed. Differentiation, the subject of Chapter 10, provides customer value by

FIGURE 11.5 Alternative Strategic Thrusts—A Summary

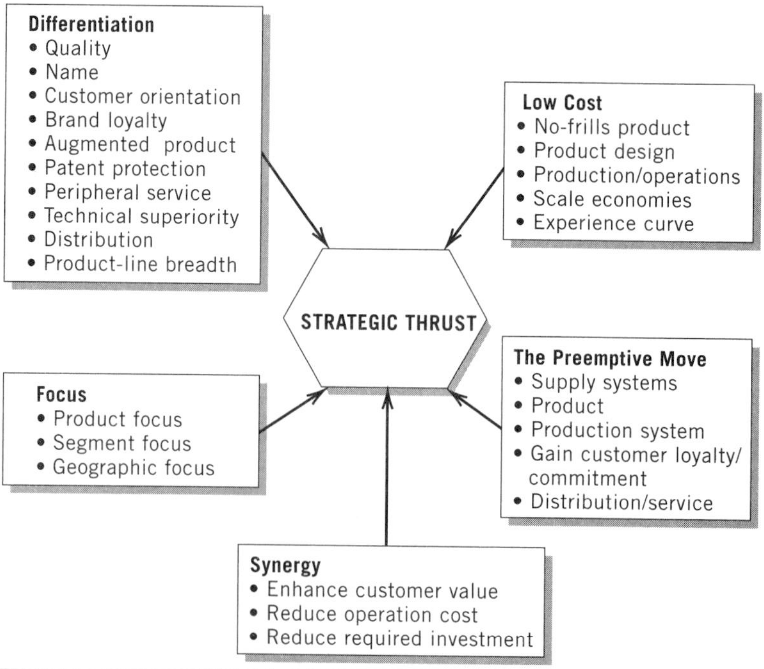

enhancing product or service characteristics. Synergy, introduced in Chapter 9, focuses on the advantages created by multiple businesses.

A low-cost thrust involves a sustainable cost advantage, which can be used to invest in the product, support lower prices, or provide high returns. Among many routes to a cost advantage are the no-frills product, product designs, the production/operations processes, scale economies, and the experience curve. The experience curve, which has been observed in thousands of studies, suggests that value-added costs will decline at a fixed percentage each time cumulative experience doubles, due in part to learning, capital investment, and product redesigns.

The focus strategy usually employs either differentiation or low cost, but another important element is the concept of a focus, usually involving a narrowing of either the product line or the market served.

A preemptive strategic move is an implementation of a strategy new to a business area that generates a skill or asset that followers are inhibited or prevented from duplicating or countering. A preemptive move can oocur throughout the organization, the supply system, the product, the production system, the customers, and the distribution system. A deliberate follower strategy has the advantage of avoiding many of the costs and risks of pioneering.

FOOTNOTES

[1] Herbert Kelleher, "Marketers of the Year," *Brandweek*, November 8, 1993, p. 41.

[2] Zachary Schiller, "Fadal's Attractions," *Business Week*, October 22, 1990, pp. 62–66.

[3] Bill Saporito, "Heinz Pushes to Be the Low-Cost Producer," *Fortune*, June 24, 1985, p. 54.

[4] *United States v. E. I. DuPont de Nemours & Company*, FTC Docket No. 9108, 1982. Interestingly, DuPont's plan to gain share was challenged by the FTC as being an illegal effort to monopolize. It was held, however, that DuPont's conduct was reasonable, not in violation of the antitrust statutes. DuPont had built excess capacity to respond to market opportunity rather than to deter entry. It did not price below cost, make false announcements of plant expansion, or lock up customers with long-term contracts.

[5] Stephanie Losee, "How Compaq Keeps the Magic Going," *Fortune*, February 21, 1994, pp. 88–92.

[6] 1981 Annual Report, White Consolidated Industries, Inc.

[7] Bill Saporito, "How Quaker Oats Got Rolled," *Fortune*, October 8, 1990, pp. 129–138.

[8] Walter Kiechel III, "The Decline of the Experience Curve," *Fortune*, October 5, 1981, p. 140.

[9] Kiechel, "The Decline of the Experience Curve," p. 144.

[10] William W. Alberts, "The Experience Curve Doctrine Reconsidered," *Journal of Marketing* 53, July 1989, pp. 36–49.

[11] William J. Abernathy and Kenneth Wayne, "Limits of the Learning Curve," *Harvard Business Review*, September–October 1974, pp. 109–119.

[12] Alfred P. Sloan, Jr., *My Years with General Motors*, New York: Doubleday, 1964, pp. 162–163.

[13] Saporito, "Heinz Pushes to Be the Low-Cost Producer," pp. 44–54.

[14] Cara Appelbaum, "Targeting the Wrong Demographic," *Adweek's Marketing Week*, November 5, 1990, p. 20.

[15] William H. Davidow and Bro Utal, "Service Companies: Focus or Falter," *Harvard Business Review*, July–August 1989, pp. 77–85.

[16] R. G. Hamermesh, M. J. Anderson, Jr., and J. E. Harris, "Strategies for Low Market Share Businesses," *Harvard Business Review*, May–June 1978, pp. 95–102.

[17] This section draws on Ian C. MacMillan, "Preemptive Strategies," *Journal of Business Strategy* 4, Fall 1983, pp. 16–26.

[18] Marvin B. Lieberman and David Montgomery, "First-Mover Advantages," *Strategic Management Journal*, Vol. 9, March–April 1988, pp. 41–58.

[19] William T. Robinson, "Sources of Market Pioneer Advantages: The Case of Industrial Goods Industries," *Journal of Marketing Research*, February 1988, pp. 87–94; William T. Robinson and Claes Fornell, "Sources of Market Pioneer Advantage in Consumer Goods Industries," *Journal of Marketing Research*, 22, August 1985, pp. 305–317.

[20] Glen L. Urban and Gurumurthy Kalyanaram, "Dynamic Effect of the Order of Entry on Market Share, Trail Penetration, and Repeat Purchases for Frequently Puchased Consumer Goods," Working Paper, MIT, Cambridge, Mass., January 1991.

[21] Peter N. Golder and Gerard J. Tellis, "Pioneer Advantage: Marketing Logic or Marketing Legend?" *Journal of Marketing Research*, May 1993, pp. 158–170.

[22] Steve P. Schnaars, *Managing Imitation Strategies*, New York: The Free Press, 1994.

12

GROWTH STRATEGIES: PENETRATION, PRODUCT-MARKET EXPANSION, AND VERTICAL INTEGRATION

Marketing should focus on market creation, not market sharing.

Regis McKenna

Results are gained by exploiting opportunities, not by solving problems.

Peter Drucker

An objective of most organizations is to grow—in terms of sales, value added, profits, personnel, and resources. Growth introduces vitality to an organization by providing challenges and rewards. In fact, it can be difficult to even survive with a no-growth scenario because competitors will attack and vulnerable areas will experience decline. With no compensating growth areas, an organization will wither. If a business is reduced below a critical mass and loses needed scale economies, it may no longer be viable. Thus, growth objectives may be not only healthy, but also necessary.

A host of different strategies can lead to growth. Mission statement development, discussed in Chapter 2, attempts to outline the type of growth strategy that seems most promising for a firm. At later stages of the planning process, growth strategies need to be considered at a more detailed, specific level.

Figure 12.1 provides a way to structure alternative growth strategies based, in part, on the product-market matrix introduced in Chapter 2. The first set of growth strategies involves existing product markets. The

FIGURE 12.1   Alternative Growth Strategies

	Present products	New products

Present markets	**I. Growth in existing product markets**
	• Increase market share
	• Increase product usage
	  – Increase the frequency used
	  – Increase the quantity used
	  – Find new application for current users
		II. Product development
		• Add product features, product refinement
		• Expand the product line
		• Develop a new generation product
		• Develop new products for the same market

New markets	**III. Market development** • Expand geographically • Target new segments	**V. Diversification involving new products and new markets** • Related • Unrelated

Vertical integration

IV. Vertical integration strategies
• Forward integration
• Backward integration

next two concern product development and market development. The fourth concerns integration strategies and the fifth diversification strategies, which will be covered in Chapter 13. The distinctions between some of these categories may be blurred, but the structure is still helpful in generating strategic options.

GROWTH IN EXISTING PRODUCT MARKETS

Existing product markets are often attractive growth avenues. An established firm has a base on which to build and momentum that can be exploited. Furthermore, the firm may have experience, knowledge, and resources (including human resources) already in place. Growth can be achieved in existing product markets by increasing share through capturing sales held by competitors. Alternatively, product usage among existing customers can be increased.

Increasing Market Share

Perhaps the most obvious way to grow is to improve market share. A share gain can be based on tactical actions such as advertising, trade allowances, promotions, or price reductions. The problem is that share gain obtained by such means can be difficult to maintain. A preferred approach is to generate a more permanent share gain by creating an SCA (sustainable competitive advantage) with enhanced customer value or by overcoming or neutralizing a competitor's SCA. Thus, the need is to create or enhance the assets and skills of the business and neutralize those of competitors. Growth in market share can be based on any of the strategic thrusts detailed in the previous two chapters.

Increasing Product Usage

Attempts to increase market share will very likely affect competitors directly and therefore precipitate competitor responses. The alternative of attempting to increase usage among current customers is usually less threatening to competitors.[1]

When developing programs to increase usage, it is useful to begin by asking some fundamental questions about the user and the consumption system in which the product is embedded. Why isn't the product or service used more? What are the barriers to increased use? Who are the light users, and can they be influenced to use more? What about the heavy users?

Heavy users are usually the most fruitful target. It is often easier to get a holder of two season football tickets to buy four or six than to get an occasional attendee of games to buy two. It is helpful to look at the extra-heavy user subsegment—special treatment might solidify and expand usage by a substantial amount. Consider United Airlines Executive Premier class (for those flying 75,000 miles per year), the special dinner parties and courier service offered by Chase Manhattan to the biggest accounts, or the first class treatment provided to high rollers by Las Vegas casinos.[2]

Light users should not be ignored, because there may be a way to unlock their potential. Who are the light users and why don't they use more? Hillside Coffee noted that people in their early twenties were light coffee users. Exploiting a sweet tooth in this segment, flavored coffees such as Vanilla Nut and Swiss Chocolate Almond were successfully introduced.

Increased product usage can be precipitated in three ways, as noted in Figure 12.1. First, the frequency of use can be increased. Second, the quantity used in each application can be increased. Finally, new applications can be sought. The first two methods are detailed in Figure 12.2.

FIGURE 12.2 Increasing Usage in Existing Product Markets

Approach	Strategy	Examples
Frequency of Use/ Consumption	• Provide reminder communications	• Jell-O Pudding
	• Position for frequent use	• Shampoo, car care
	• Position for regular use	• Flossing teeth after meals
	• Make the use easier or more convenient	• Dixie-cup dispenser, microwavable
	• Provide incentives	• Frequent-flyer plan
	• Reduce undesirable consequences of frequent use	• Gentle shampoo
	• Use at different occasions	• Cereal as snack versus breakfast
	• Use at different locations	• Radio in shower
Level of Use/ Consumption	• Provide reminder communications	• Increase insurance coverage
	• Provide incentives	• Special price for accessories
	• Influence norms	• Use of larger containers
	• Reduce undesirable consequences of increased use level	• Low-calorie candy
	• Develop positive associations with use occasions	• Frito-Lay: "Bet you can't eat just one."

Increasing the Frequency of Use

Provide Reminder Communications. For some use contexts, awareness, or recall of a brand, is the driving force. People who know about a brand and its use may not think to use it on particular occasions without reminders.

Reminder advertising may be necessary. Steak sauce and other condiment brands conduct reminder advertising campaigns to obtain more frequent usage. A manufacturer of canned spiced ham found that most customers kept the product in their pantry "just in case." The problem was to influence its use in recipes. The strategy used was a reminder advertising and promotion campaign. General Foods conducted a reminder campaign for Jell-O Pudding with Bill Cosby asking, "When was the last time you served pudding, Mom?"

Routine maintenance functions like dental checkups or car lubrication are easily forgotten and reminders can make a difference. An Arm & Hammer consumer survey revealed that people who use baking soda as a deodorizer in refrigerators thought that they changed the box every 4 months when actually they did so only every 14 months.[3] An advertising campaign geared to seasonal reminders about replacing the box resulted.

Position for Regular Use. The image of a product can change from that of occasional to frequent usage by a repositioning campaign. For example, the advertising campaigns for Clinique's "twice-a-day" moisturizer and "three glasses of milk per day" both represent efforts to change the perception of the products involved. The use of programs such as the Book-of-the-Month club, CD clubs, videotape clubs, and flower-of-the-month or fruit-of-the-month delivery can turn infrequent purchasers into "once-a-monthers."

Make the Use Easier. Asking why customers do not use a product or service more often can lead to approaches for easier product use. For example, a Dixie-cup or paper-towel dispenser encourages use by reducing the usage effort. Packages that can be placed directly in a microwave make usage more convenient. A reservation service can help those who must select a hotel or similar service. Frozen waffles and Stove Top stuffing are examples of product modifications that increased consumption by making usage more convenient.

Provide Incentives. Incentives can be provided to increase consumption frequency. Promotions such as double mileage trips offered by airlines with frequent-flyer plans can increase usage. A challenge is to structure the incentive so that usage is increased without creating a vehicle for debilitating price competition. Price incentives such as two for the price of one can be effective, but they also may stimulate price retaliation.

Reduce Undesirable Consequences of Frequent Use. Sometimes there are good reasons why a customer is inhibited from using a product more frequently. If such reasons can be addressed, usage may increase. For example, some people might believe that frequent hair washing may not be healthy. A product that is designed to be gentle enough for daily use might alleviate this worry and thereby stimulate increased usage. A low-calorie, low-sodium, or low-fat version of a food product may sharply increase the market. The brand that becomes associated with a product change will be in the best position to capitalize on the increased market.

Increasing the Quantity Used

Similar techniques can be employed to increase the quantity used on each use occasion:

- **Reminder communications.** An insurance customer can be reminded to consider increasing the coverage on a house if its replacement value has increased. A shirt buyer might be reminded to consider a tie or another accessory.

- **Incentives can be used.** A fast-food restaurant, for example, might attempt through pricing or promotion to increase the number of items purchased at a meal. A special price may be available if a drink and fries are ordered with a hamburger.

- **Efforts can be made to affect the usage level norms.** The size of a "normal" serving might change by creating a larger glass or container and influencing its acceptance.

- **The perceived undesirable consequences of heavy consumption might be addressed.** A "lite" beer or low-calorie salad dressing could remove a calorie-motivated reason to restrict the usage level. Life Savers candies have advertised that one piece has fewer calories than people think. Positive associations with the use occasion might be developed through advertising. Thus, a sense of fun and refreshment associated with Pepsi-Cola might encourage heavier usage. Frito-Lay has used the "bet you can't eat just one" tag line to emphasize taste pleasure. A computer equipment firm could associate efficiency with buying a larger system.

New Applications for Existing Product Users

The detection and exploitation of a new functional use for a brand can rejuvenate a business that has been considered a has-been for years. A classic example is Jell-O, which began strictly as a dessert product but found major sources of new sales in applications such as Jell-O salads. Another classic story is that of Arm & Hammer baking soda, which saw annual sales grow tenfold by persuading people to use its product as a refrigerator deodorizer. An initial 14-month advertising campaign boosted the use as a deodorizer from 1 to 57 percent. The brand subsequently was extended into other deodorizer products, dentifrices, and laundry detergent.

Other brands have found growth through new applications. For example,

- Grape-Nuts is served over yogurt or ice cream.

- A chemical process used by oil fields to separate water from oil is used by water plants to eliminate unwanted oil.

- Lipton soup includes recipes for new uses on boxes and in ads that suggest, "Great meals start with Lipton—recipe soup mix—soup." The recipe concept is emphasized even in the slogan.

New uses can best be identified by conducting market research to determine exactly how customers use a brand. From the set of uses that emerge, several can be selected to pursue. For example, users of external analgesics were asked to keep a diary of their uses.[4] A surprising finding was that about one-third of Ben-Gay's usage and more than one-half of its volume was for arthritis relief instead of muscle aches. A separate marketing strategy was developed for this use featuring dancers (Ann Miller) and football players (John Unitas) who now have arthritis, and the brand caught a wave of growth.

Another tactic is to look at the applications of competing products. The widespread use of raisins prompted Ocean Spray to create dried cranberries, which can be found in cookies and in cereal such as Muesli with a "made with real Ocean Spray cranberries" seal on the package. They are also being sold as a snack food called Ocean Spray Craisins.

Sometimes a large payoff will result for a firm that can provide applications not currently in general use. Thus, surveys of current applications may be inadequate. Firms such as General Mills have sponsored recipe contests, one objective of which has been to create new uses for a product by discovering a new "recipe classic." For a product such as stick-on labels that can be used in many ways, it might be worthwhile to conduct formal brainstorming sessions or other creative exercises.

If some application area is uncovered that could create substantial sales, it needs to be evaluated. First, a market survey or other forecasting device might be used to estimate the potential increase in sales. How many customers could use the product in that way? What level of product purchase would that application support for each customer? Arm & Hammer conducted more than 150 market research studies to support its development of new use applications and new products.

Second, the feasibility and costs of exploiting an application area need to be assessed. Some new applications can require substantial marketing programs. Angostura Bitters, a 160-year-old brand used primarily in Manhattans, decided to promote nonalcoholic drinks, starting with the Charger.[5] The Charger, a drink that had been sold in bars for decades, consisted of sparkling water, bitters, and lime. Canada Dry was enticed to promote it by putting a packet of bitters with a recipe on the necks of Canada Dry Seltzer bottles. Tastings were organized at museums and street fairs. Radio ads with a "Charger" theme were run. Other drinks, such as the Caribbean made with cranberry juice, pineapple juice, and bitters, followed.

Third, the possibility that a competitor will take over an application area by product improvement, heavy advertising, or other means, or will engage in price warfare, needs to be analyzed. The issue is whether or not a brand can achieve a sustainable advantage in its new application. Ocean Spray is associated with cranberries, which might protect its entry into a cranberry snack, but the firm's name will be less helpful in a processed application such as cookies and cereals.

PRODUCT DEVELOPMENT FOR THE EXISTING MARKET

As reflected in Figure 12.1, product development can occur in a variety of ways, and it is helpful to distinguish between them. They include the addition of product features, the expansion of a product line, the development of new generation technologies, and the development of new products for an existing market.

Product Feature Addition

One type of product development is simply the addition of features to a firm's current product. An automobile firm could add a transmission or sunroof option that would improve its penetration of an existing market. For some candy firms, the creation of novel packages provides a key to sales. A clothing firm could add accessories to its line of merchandise. A firm making personal computers could add memory or built-in software. Clearly, such line extensions involve almost total commonality of marketing, operations, and management. Because they represent such visible growth opportunities and are accomplished relatively easily, they can be very enticing. They still absorb resources, however, and should be resisted if the prospective ROI is unsatisfactory.

Line extension can also occur when high-tech or industrial firms are asked by a customer to produce a special-purpose version of a product. The resulting product will have a set of features that may only be useful to the requesting customer. Such development work can lead to substantial sales and even to new products, but the attraction of a visible customer need can be overly enticing. If this type of development activity is permitted to preempt more ambitious development programs, the long-term health of an organization can suffer.

Product-Line Expansion

A second type of product development activity aimed at existing markets is to expand or broaden a product line. The marketing and distribution effort and perhaps even much of the manufacturing will be common to the product-line extensions. A paint firm may want to add wood stains to its line. A cross-country ski firm could add a racing line for advanced-skier customers who may want to trade up. A book retailer could add children's books and a "how-to" section to its line. The product-line extension will be based on many factors, of course, but will often involve consideration of the following questions:

- **Will customers benefit from a systems capability or service convenience made possible by a broad product line?** The inclusion of a software line and printers with a line of computers provides the potential of offering a more complete system. However, customers may want not only systems design but also systems support.

- **Do potential manufacturing, marketing, or distribution cost efficiencies exist from an expanded product line?** To the extent that there are shared costs, the experience and scale effects on costs will be enhanced. The question is whether or not, even with this cost advantage, the proposed product-line extension will have a satisfactory ROI.

- **Can assets or skills be applied to a product-line extension?** Philip Morris underestimated the difficulty of transferring its marketing magic to the 7UP business and finally gave up.

- **Does a firm have the skill and needed resources in R&D, manufacturing, and marketing to add the various products proposed?** Sometimes an apparently simple line extension like adding wood stains to a line of paints can involve a totally new manufacturing effort, raw materials technology, or marketing effort and, thus, may not fit the capabilities of the firm.

- **Is the new product line compatible with the existing brand?** Maytag needed to expand its line in order to fully support the emerging large retailers that demanded a full line, so it bought the brands Magic Chef, Admiral, Norge, and Hoover.[6] These acquisitions gave Maytag its needed full line and presence at the lower end. However, the new brands were not comparable to Maytag in quality, often being at the bottom of *Consumer Reports'* ratings for such appliances, and thus they put the Maytag reputation at risk with both dealers and consumers.

Developing New Generation Products

Growth can be obtained in an existing market by creating new generation products. Such products can obsolete existing ones, thus providing a source of sales. Compact disks and stereo TV sets were part of the reason that the stagnant home audio market enjoyed a substantial spurt in sales in the late 1980s. The advent of low-fat ice cream such as Dreyer's Grand Light stimulated growth in the ice cream category.

Yamaha Pianos had gained 40 percent of the global piano market, but it was declining by 10 percent each year, and they also faced competition from Korean firms. Yamaha responded by developing the Disklavier that functioned and played like other pianos, except that it also included an electronic control system, thus creating a modern version of the old player piano. The system allowed a performance to be recorded with great accuracy and stored on a 3.5-inch disk. The new technology could be used by the professional player or composer, the student who wanted a built-in role model or accompanist, and those who wanted a great pianist to play in their home. The Disklavier allowed Yamaha to revitalize a business that was buried in a declining market. In addition, the company spawned a retrofit subindustry, as well as an industry to support the disks.

The decision to pursue new technologies is particularly tricky for a successful firm that has a vested interest in the old technology and thus faces competitive risks with a strategy of delay and disinterest. The Gillette experience of the early 1960s illustrates this point.[7] Gillette resisted the stainless steel blade technology because its durability meant that people would need far fewer blades and because the cost to change the firm's manufacturing and marketing efforts would be high. The company was making in excess of a 40 percent return on investment. As a result, the small British stainless innovator, Wilkinson, and its U.S. rivals, Eversharp and Schick, made major and permanent inroads into Gillette's share and profits. Gillette's share fell from 70 to 55 percent, and its return fell to below 30 percent.

While the outsider has nothing to lose and much to gain from pursuing an innovation that will disrupt the marketplace, the established competitor faces two forces that inhibit innovation. First, even if the new technology is successful, often the best result is that a significant investment will be required just to maintain the same level of sales and profits. And the new technology could present problems that add time and expense and reduce customer acceptance—hardly an attractive incentive. Second, the existing competitor needs to focus on improving costs, quality, and service for the existing offering, which leaves little time and effort to explore a totally new technology.

Although new technologies such as laser printers or minicomputers can disrupt an established business, they can also create profitable growth opportunities. Existing competitors should be aware of their biases against detecting and exploiting such opportunities. If the biases are visible, the chances that they will inhibit the organization from participating in a new technology will be reduced.

New Products for Existing Markets

A classic growth pattern is to exploit a marketing or distribution strength by adding compatible products that share customers with but are very different from existing products. Synergy is usually obtained at least in part by the commonality in distribution, marketing, and brand-name recognition and identity. Lenox, a maker of fine china, exploited its traditional, high-quality image and its distribution system by expanding into the areas of jewelry and giftware. H&R Block added legal services to its chain of income tax services, hoping to gain synergy by sharing office space and operations. A ski boot manufacturer added skis and then ski clothing.

A major vehicle for product expansion is brand extension, exploiting a brand with strong awareness and associations by extending it into another product category. Consider Duracell Durabeam flashlights, Gerber baby clothes, Sunkist vitamin C tablets, Pierre Cardin wallets, Benihana frozen entrées, Dole Frozen Fruit Bars, and Arm & Hammer oven cleaner, which capitalizes on Arm & Hammer's 97 percent name recognition. Each has strong name identification and associations that can drive success in the new category. Managers must make sure that the extension fits the brand, that it provides helpful associations, and that it does not damage or dilute associations of the brand.[9]

A rationale for product expansion is to achieve synergies. Sometimes, however, synergies are simply illusory. General Foods had little in common with a fast-food restaurant chain that it acquired, even though both involved food. More often, synergy exists, but its benefit is modest and does not overcome the costs and problems associated with the new area.

Toward Synergies in Financial Services[8]

During the 1980s, a variety of firms developed a broad range of financial services. Sears is the most dramatic example. It brought the real-estate company Coldwell Banker and the brokerage house Dean Witter into a firm that already had Allstate insurance, Allstate S&L, and 25 million active Sears charge-card users. Sears, to exploit the synergy represented by this array of financial services, opened more than 300 financial boutiques in its larger stores, where various combinations of Allstate salespeople, Dean Witter brokers, and Coldwell Banker agents were located. In addition, it introduced the Discovery Card. The final verdict is not in on the Sears effort, but its initial experience illustrates the problems of realizing synergies:

- The concept of leveraging store traffic by locating kiosks in the stores was oversold. The atmosphere and customer types did not lend themselves to Coldwell Banker or Dean Witter. One broker told of attempting to talk to a customer in the toy department with his kids yelling in the background. The profile of a Sears customer was very different from that of the asset-heavy profitable customer of a brokerage firm. Furthermore, the Sears name, which meant value and trust in tires and tools, may not have been an asset in securities. By the early 1990s, these brokerage units were in only 100 of the largest and most spacious stores.

- The concept of cross-selling is difficult to implement. It is much easier to get an organization behind its own products. Dean Witter achieved much of its profits from its own mutual funds. In the early 1990s, Dean Witter salespeople were selling annually around $1 billion of annuities managed by Sears' Allstate Insurance unit, but this was a modest amount compared to projections.

- Dean Witter suffered damaging losses in its mortgage banking operation after being acquired by Sears. Under Sears, Dean Witter focused on the retail business and turned its back on mortgage banking. Was this a good strategic move or simply an inevitable result of operating in the Sears culture?

American Express, another financial conglomerate, actively encouraged and managed efforts to exploit synergies such as cross-selling and sharing of office space, data-processing capabilities, and marketing expertise through its "one enterprise" program. Although the company had success in selling life insurance to its cardholders and to customers of its stock brokerage unit, Shearson-Lehman, the experience demonstrated that synergy is elusive. Problems with Fireman's Fund Insurance and Shearson-Lehman turned the whole venture into something of a disaster.

In contrast, State Farm Insurance has been dramatically successful, becoming one of the largest financial service firms by "sticking to its knitting," avoiding anything but its core insurance business.

The effort to combine United Airlines, Westin Hotel and Resorts, and Hertz into one organization was aborted, in part because the potential synergies, mostly involving a common reservation system and cross-selling, had substantial implementation problems and were not valued by the stock market.

Anheuser-Busch was disappointed in its efforts to expand into beverages other than beer, such as Baybry's Cooler, Dewey Stevens Premium Wine Cooler, Zeltzer Seltzer, and several wines and bottled drinks.[10] Ironically, Anheuser-Busch's greatest weakness was in distribution, an expected strength area. The firm had no problems with liquor retailers, where beer distributors were the key element. However, it was weak in the supermarket, where such distributors were bypassed. Because it was limited to its beer distribution network, the company had a difficult time keeping prices competitive.

There is significant risk to any new product venture, especially with respect to customer acceptance. Clairol failed with Small Miracle hair conditioner, which could be used through several shampoos, in part because customers could not be convinced that the product would not build up on their hair if it were not washed off with each use. Even the use of an established brand cannot prevent failure. The concept of a colorless cola, Crystal Pepsi, did not achieve acceptance. Rice-a-Roni's Savory Classics did not fit the consumer's notion of the role of Rice-a-Roni in the kitchen. The Arm & Hammer name also spawned two failures, a spray underarm deodorant, for which the Arm & Hammer name may have had the wrong connotations, and a spray disinfectant.

MARKET DEVELOPMENT USING EXISTING PRODUCTS

A logical avenue of growth is to develop new markets by duplicating the business operation, perhaps with minor adaptive changes. With market expansion, the same expertise and technology and sometimes even the same plant and operations facility can be used. Thus, there is potential for synergy and resulting reductions in investment and operating costs. Of course, market development is based upon the premise that the business is operating successfully. There is no point in exporting failure or mediocrity.

Expanding Geographically

Geographic expansion may involve changing from a regional operation to a national operation, moving into another region, or expanding to another country. KFC, McDonald's, Coca-Cola, Levi's, and VISA are businesses that have exported their operations to other countries successfully. Samuel Adams and other microbreweries have expanded their market from local to regional to national to global.

Expanding into New Market Segments

A firm can also grow by reaching into new market segments. There are, of course, a variety of ways to define target segments and therefore growth directions:

- **Usage.** The nonuser can be an attractive target. An audio electronics firm could target those who don't own an audio system.
- **Distribution channel.** A firm can reach new segments by opening up a second or third channel of distribution. A retail sporting goods store could market to schools via a direct sales force. A direct marketer such as Avon could introduce its products into department stores under another brand name.
- **Age.** Johnson & Johnson's baby shampoo was languishing until the company looked toward adults who wash their hair frequently.
- **Attribute preference.** An instrumentation firm might extend its line to include more precise equipment in order to serve a segment that requires greater accuracy.

A key to detecting new markets is to consider a wide variety of segmentation variables. Sometimes looking at markets in a different way will uncover a useful segment. It is especially helpful to identify segments that are not being served well, such as the women's calculator market or the fashion needs of older people. In general, segments should be sought for which the brand can provide value. Coming into a new market without providing any incremental customer value is very risky.

Evaluating Market Expansion Alternatives

Although synergy can potentially be high, several other considerations are involved in a market expansion:

- Is the market attractive? Will customers value the product or service? Does it really offer meaningful and distinctive value? How formidable and committed are competitors? Can their assets and skills be neutralized by the right strategy? Are market and environmental trends supportive?
- Do the resources and will exist to make the necessary commitment in the face of uncertainties? Does the move make strategic sense? Compaq bailed out of the printer business despite having a superior product

because the prospects of catching HP and the other leaders were too formidable. The commitment was lacking.

- Can the business be adapted to the new market? To the extent that conditions differ, is there a convincing plan to adapt the business to differing conditions? For example, Rheingold Beer, a New York company, failed in an attempt to enter the California market, in part because it tried to use a distribution channel unsuitable for California and in part because a promotion that was effective in New York fell flat in California.

- Can the assets and skills that are at the heart of business success be transferred into the new business environment? Procter & Gamble was unable to capitalize on its marketing and distribution assets in efforts to market soft drinks, and it experienced disappointment in cosmetics and fragrances as well.

The experience of Federal Express when it attempted to duplicate its concept in Europe illustrates the last two issues.[11] Setting up a hub-and-spoke system in Europe was inhibited by regulatory roadblocks at every turn. Attempts to short-circuit regulations by acquiring firms with related abilities resulted in something of a hodgepodge—Federal Express now owns a barge company, for example. The firm also lacked a first-mover advantage in Europe because DHL and others had employed the Federal Express concept years earlier. A reliance on the English language and a decision to impose a pickup deadline of 5 o'clock in Spain (where people work until 8) caused additional implementation problems.

VERTICAL INTEGRATION STRATEGIES

Vertical integration represents another potential growth direction. Forward integration occurs when a firm moves downstream with respect to product flow, such as a manufacturer buying a retail chain. Backward integration is moving upstream, such as when a manufacturer invests in a raw material source. A good way to understand when vertical integration should be considered and how it should be evaluated is to look at the possible benefits and costs of a vertical integration strategy:

Benefits	*Costs*
• Operating economies	• Operating costs
• Access to supply or demand	• Management of a different
• Control of the product system	business
• Entry into a profitable business	• Increase in risk
• Enhanced technological	• Reduced flexibility
innovation	• Cost of inward focus

Benefit: Operating Economies

Combining operations can result in improved production and related economies. Consider an integrated firm that designs and manufactures women's accessories to be distributed through its own chain of retail stores and mail-order catalog business. Compare it to a competitor who designs accessories but must deal with separate manufacturing, retailing, and mail-order firms. This simple example illustrates the following potential savings:

• **Steps in the production process can be combined, eliminated, or more closely coordinated.** The result can be savings in handling, transportation, and inventory costs. In particular, with uncertainty lessened by the communication between and control of the two operations, inventory can often be reduced.

• **Economies of scale are possible.** Combining two operations allows the sharing of warehouses, sales forces, accounting operations, computer facilities, and staff activities such as marketing research. To the extent that a larger operation is more efficient, economies will be observed.

• **Substantial transaction costs are involved in creating a contract between two separate firms.** A search for suppliers by one firm and customers by the other can be expensive. The transaction itself will often involve salespeople, purchasing agents, lawyers, technical staffs, purchase orders, invoices, and shipping documents. If the two organizations are combined, these transaction costs usually are either eliminated or substantially reduced. A high incidence of transactions can signal that vertical integration should be considered.

• **Economies related to information gathering are available.** Market research and industry data can be shared by both organizations. Furthermore, the supplying firm can have intimate access to its customer's applications and problems.

Benefit: Access to Supply or Demand

Access to Supply.   In some contexts, a key success factor is access to a supply of raw material, a part, or another input factor; backward integration can reduce the availability risk. A forest-products firm may thus acquire timberland. Hewlett Packard lost a crucial six months getting a workstation to the market when a key supplier of chips was six months late, whereas IBM, with internal sources, did not have that problem. Sometimes suppliers are not capable of or interested in providing the needed component. For example, when refrigerated boxcars and warehouses were first needed by meat packers, they had to develop them because there was no source.

Access to Demand. Similarly, forward integration could be motivated by a concern about product outlets. Thus, Kemper, an insurance firm, bought regional stock brokerage firms in order to provide sales outlets. A motivation to gain access to major buyers was behind the large automakers' investment in car rental firms—Ford has invested in Hertz and Budget, General Motors in Avis and National, whereas Chrysler owns Thrifty and Snappy. These vertical relationships not only provide sales but important exposure of their new models to prospective customers.

Idiosyncratic Products and Services. Whenever only one buyer and one seller exist for highly specialized products and services, there will be an incentive to consider vertical integration. The economist Oliver Williamson terms such products and services "idiosyncratic."[12] When such specialization occurs, a real danger exists that one party may "hold up" the other by taking opportunistic advantage of a change in either its circumstance or the environment. Of course, contractual arrangements can attempt to prevent hold-up problems. In reality, however, it can be very difficult to find a contract that will cover all eventualities in a long-term relationship embedded in a changing environment.

Four types of specialization can be identified:[13]

1. **Brand name.** If one party owns the brand name, the other may develop its equity without controlling the essence of the asset. Thus, Savin successfully pioneered the small copier in 1970 with a product manufactured by Ricoh. Because market power and profits were controlled by Savin, Ricoh decided to integrate forward by establishing its own brand name.

2. **Dedicated assets.** When a large asset investment is required, vertical integration may be useful. A can company will have to make a large investment to create a can factory near a brewery. If the contract is prematurely terminated, the investment would cause excess capacity.

3. **Technological.** A petroleum plant may be designed to use a high-grade ore that is available only from a few sources. If the raw material source is jeopardized, the plant may cease to be viable. The plant could be designed to accept a variety of grades of ore. Obtaining such flexibility would, however, require substantially more investment.

4. **Knowledge-based.** A supplier may acquire specialized knowledge and thus become the only practical source for an input factor. For example, a law firm or engineering contractor might become so familiar with

the involved product, service, and client firm that for practical purposes no competing suppliers would exist, even if there were several able competitors at the outset of the relationship. Vertical integration will prevent the supplier from making abnormal profits and perhaps further enhance the degree of knowledge transfer between the two firms.

Benefit: Control of the Product System

It may become necessary to integrate vertically in order to gain sufficient control over a product or service to maintain the integrity of a differentiation strategy. For example, a vital component may need to be made with precision, and outside contractors may be unable to provide it or unwilling to make an investment in the specialized assets needed. Vertical integration may be the only way to ensure that the desired quality is achieved.

Sony has lived with the memory of its superior Beta format being overrun by the consortium of VHS firms. The final nail was hammered in when the movie studios stopped producing films in the Beta format. Sony has since become a one-stop shop for entertainment so that in the future it can guarantee a supply of software for its hardware products. By buying Columbia Pictures, Tri-Star Pictures, Columbia Pictures Television, and CBS Records, Sony has substantial control over supplier decisions.

Benefit: Entry into a Profitable Business Area

A vertical integration decision can simply be motivated by an attractive profit potential. Thus, a chain of retail stores may simply be an attractive business investment, and the fact that it now is an outlet for a firm's product may be a relatively minor consideration.

Too often this rationale is faulty and is accompanied by an inadequate understanding of the customers and competitors in the new industry and of what it takes to be successful there. The attractiveness of a new source of sales makes it easy to minimize the difficulties.

Benefit: Enhanced Technological Innovation

Vertically integrated firms may have an advantage in achieving technological innovation. First, technical information is more readily shared between business units if they are in the same firm—thus, the R&D effort of an in-house supplier can be more focused. This contrasts with the usual inhibitions to the free exchange of information between two firms even if a positive, long-term relationship exists between them. Second, because the scale is larger, the potential is greater for innovation that can impact several stages of the production process, producing larger returns. Third, vertical integration can facilitate the implementation of new processes or the introduction of new products. When two separate organizations are involved, a selling job may be required to implement innovations, and many barriers can become established.

Five types of potential benefits associated with vertical integration have been discussed. We now turn to the possible costs and disadvantages.

Cost: Operating Costs

Vertical integration can create potential operating costs that may outweigh the operating economies:

- The added complexity and coordination required will put strains on the management system. There is no guarantee that associated costs will not exceed the transaction costs between two firms.

- The two integrated operations are unlikely to match exactly with respect to the capacity appropriate for efficient operation. As a result, one or the other will probably have excess capacity that will elevate costs.

- Without the discipline of outside price competition, there may be less incentive for cost control. After all, the supplying operation is assured of its customer.

- A transfer price simulating a market price is usually used to cover intrafirm transactions. The danger is that faulty information or organizational pressures can cause this transfer price to be either too high or too low. In either case, suboptimal decisions can easily result. For example, if the transfer price was artificially low, the downstream operation would appear more profitable than it actually was, and thus an inadvisable expansion decision might be precipitated.

Cost: Management of a Different Business

Vertical integration often involves adding an operation that requires organizational assets and skills which differ markedly from those of a firm's other business areas. As a result, the firm may not be suited to run the integrated operation effectively and competitively. Consider Pillsbury's efforts to manage Burger King. Part of the difficulty was caused by differences in culture, personnel, and operations.

Cost: The Risk of Increased Commitment to a Business

The classic way to reduce risk is to avoid having too many eggs in one basket—to diversify. Vertical integration tends to increase the commitment and investment that are tied to a certain market. If that market is healthy, then integration may enhance profits. On the other hand, if the market turns down, integration may cause profits to be more depressed. Integration also raises exit barriers. If the business becomes weak, the additional investment and commitment created by integration will inhibit consideration of an exit alternative. Furthermore, if one operation becomes dependent on the other, it may be awkward to try to exit from one.

Cost: Reduced Flexibility

Vertical integration usually means that a firm is committed to an in-house supplier or customer. Suppose that technology changes and it is necessary to change suppliers or suffer a substantial competitive disadvantage. The flexibility of changing suppliers may be limited because of a commitment made to an integration partner. Similarly, a decision to integrate into retailing may be regretted if customer preferences dictate that another channel is going to become dominant. There is often a trade-off between flexibility and commitment. Increased commitment provides the potential of higher profits but is associated with a reduction in the ability to adapt to changing circumstances.

Cost: Inward Focus

The process of actively dealing with suppliers or customers in the marketplace and of anticipating supplier technological developments and new customer applications can be extremely healthy. The integrated firm with captive supplier-customer units has a reduced need for that process. Furthermore, there is the previously mentioned reduced pressure on cost control.

Alternatives to Integration

Several alternatives to integration exist, such as long-term contracts, exclusive dealing agreements, asset ownership, joint ventures, strategic alliances, technology licenses, and franchising. For example, a winery can have a long-term contract with vineyards that protects both. Exclusive dealing agreements that link a manufacturer and a retail chain or distributor can provide the needed information transfer, strategy coordination, and transaction and distribution efficiency. Automobile firms that own the special tooling used by their suppliers provide a technological and financial link that helps insure reliable supply. Most of these alternatives involve difficulties, especially as circumstances and power relationships change over time, but they also provide many of the advantages of integration with fewer disadvantages. They should usually be considered before commitments to integration are pursued.

Are Integrated Firms More Profitable?

Robert Buzzell of Harvard studied 1649 businesses in the PIMS database to attempt to determine the impact on profitability of vertical integration, defined as value added as a percentage of sales.[14]

Figure 12.3 illustrates this relationship. Although net profit as a percent of sales does increase with vertical integration, the return on investment (ROI) does not. The increase in investment that accompanies vertical integration counters any increase in profit. The figure suggests the intriguing concept that the most profitable businesses are at the extremes of the vertical integration spectrum. There is a V-shaped relationship between vertical integration and profitability. Thus, manufacturers should be wary of taking a middle course. The business that puts together systems and farms out component production will tend to minimize investment, seek out low prices, and have maximum flexibility. The heavily integrated firm will maximize the benefits of vertical integration.

SUMMARY

One available growth strategy is to grow within an existing product market by increasing market share or product usage. Increased product usage occurs by increasing usage frequency or the quantity used, or by finding new applications. A second growth strategy is to develop new products for an existing market. Product development can be based on adding product features, expanding the product line, developing new

FIGURE 12.3 Vertical Integration and Profitability

Vertical Integration— Value Added as Percentage of Sales	Net Profit as Percentage of Sales	Net Profit as Percentage of Investment (ROI)	Number of Businesses
Under 40%	8%	26%	267
40–50%	8	22	341
50–60%	9	20	389
60–70%	10	22	338
Over 70%	12	24	314

SOURCE: Adaped from Robert D. Buzzell, "Is Vertical Integration Profitable?" *Harvard Business Review*, January–February 1983, p. 97.

generation technologies, or adding different products that are sold to the same market. A third growth direction is market development, expanding the market either geographically or by targeting new market segments. A key consideration in product or market expansion or diversification is determining whether synergy will be created.

Vertical integration represents another growth direction. It can provide operating economies, improved access to supply or demand, improved control over the product systems, an entry into a profitable business area, and a way to enhance the development and implementation of technological innovations. On the other hand, it can also create operating costs, problems associated with managing very different businesses, increased risk, reduced flexibility, and the costs of being excessively "ingrown." Alternatives to integration include long-term contracts, quasi-integration, and partial integration.

FOOTNOTES

[1] This section draws on the excellent paper by Philip E. Hendrix, "Product/Service Consumption: Implications and Opportunities for Marketing Strategy," Working Paper, Emory University, 1986.

[2] Robert E. Linneman and John L. Stanton, Jr., "Mining for Niches," *Business Horizons,* May–June 1992, pp. 43–51.

[3] Barnaby J. Feder, "Baking Soda Maker Strikes Again," *The New York Times,* June 16, 1990, p. 17.

[4] Linden A. Davis, Jr., "Market Positioning Considerations," *Product-Line Strategies,* New York: The Conference Board, 1991, pp. 37–39.

[5] Robert Hanson, "Angostura's Past Helps Revive Bitters," *Adweek's Marketing Week,* May 23, 1988, pp. 53–55.

[6] Robert L. Rose, "Image to Protect: Maytag's Acquisitions Don't Have the Reputation for Quality Enjoyed by Its Washers," *Wall Street Journal,* January 31, 1991, p. B-1.

[7] Robert F. Hartley, *Marketing Mistakes, 3rd ed.,* New York: Wiley, 1986, pp. 91–105.

[8] "The Peril in Financial Services," *Business Week,* August 20, 1984, pp. 52–56; "Sears Roebuck's Struggling Financial Empire," *Fortune,* October 14, 1985, pp. 40–43; "Synergy Works at American Express," *Fortune,* February 16, 1987, pp. 79–80; Michael Siconolfi, "Dean Witter Proves an Asset to Sears, Confounding Pundits," *Wall Street Journal,* March 15, 1991, p. 1–6.

[9] For a detailed treatment of brand extensions see chapter 9 in David A. Aaker, *Managing Brand Equity,* New York: The Free Press, 1991.

[10] "A-B Set to Can Beverage Unit?" *Adweek's Marketing Week,* December 7, 1987, pp. 1, 6.

[11] Daniel Pearl, "Federal Express Finds Its Pioneering Formula Falls Flat Overseas," *Wall Street Journal,* April 15, 1991, pp. A1–A6.

[12] See Oliver E. Williamson, "Comparative Economic Organization," *Administrative Science Quarterly,* September 1991, and Oliver E. Williamson, "Transaction-Cost Economics: The

Governance of Contractual Relations," *Journal of Law and Economics* 22, October 1979, pp. 233—261.

[13] David J. Teece, "Markets in Microcosm: Some Efficiency Properties of Vertical Integration," Working Paper, Stanford University, November 1981.

[14] Robert D. Buzzell, "Is Vertical Integration Profitable?" *Harvard Business Review*, January–February 1983, pp. 92–102.

13

DIVERSIFICATION

Tis the part of a wiseman to keep himself today for tomorrow, and not venture all his eggs in one basket.

Miguel de Cervantes

Put all your eggs in one basket and—WATCH THAT BASKET.

Mark Twain

A tobacco firm buys a frozen-food company, a cola firm enters the wine business, a chemical company goes into swimming pool supplies, or an aerospace firm starts making automobile parts. Such diversification moves represent both the opportunity for growth and revitalization and the substantial risk of operating an unfamiliar business in a new context.

Diversification is the strategy of entering product markets different from those in which a firm is currently engaged. Two growth strategies discussed in Chapter 12, product expansion and market expansion, usually involve entry into new product markets, thus representing diversification. However, diversification can also involve both new products and new markets. A diversification strategy can be implemented by either an acquisition (or merger) or a new business venture.

It is helpful to categorize diversification as "related" and "unrelated." A related diversification is one in which the new business area has meaningful commonalities with the core business. Meaningful commonalities provide the potential to generate economies of scale or synergies based on an exchange of skills or resources. The resulting combined business should be able to achieve improved ROI because of increased revenues, decreased costs, or reduced investment. As noted in Chapter 9, meaningful commonalities can involve similar

- Distribution channels
- Images and their impact on the market
- Sales or advertising efforts
- Facilities
- Production processes
- R&D efforts
- Operating systems
- Staff needs

The product expansion growth strategy normally involves the same market and distribution system, so it would qualify as a related diversification. The market expansion growth strategy is usually also a related diversification because it applies the same production technology and often involves a similar market and distribution system. Vertical integration is usually an unrelated diversification, however, because it typically lacks an area of commonality.

An important issue to consider in any diversification decision is whether, in fact, there is a real and meaningful area of commonality that will affect the ultimate ROI. An unrelated diversification (a diversification lacking meaningful commonalities) may still be justifiable, but a different rationale would be needed. Thus, the concept of related diversification is more than an issue of definition. In the following section we consider the rationale and risks of related diversification and then those of unrelated diversification.

RELATED DIVERSIFICATION

Exporting or Exchanging Assets and Skills

Related diversification provides the potential to attain synergies by sharing assets or skills across businesses. When related diversification is accomplished by internal expansion, the goal is to export assets or skills. When acquisition of or merger with another business is the vehicle, the goal is to combine two sets of complementary assets and skills, with each party contributing what the other lacks. In either case, a business exploring related diversification should consider several steps.

The first step is to inventory assets and skills in order to identify real strengths that are exportable to another business area. Recall the discussion in Chapter 4 on identifying assets and skills. Among exportable assets and skills (as noted in the section on Unrelated Diversification on page 268) are brand names, marketing skills, sales and distribution capacity, manufacturing skills, and R&D capabilities.

The second step toward related diversification is to find a business area where the assets and skills can be applied to generate an advantage. A line of greeting cards sold through drugstores might be able to use the distribution assets and skills of an over-the-counter drug marketer.

One fruitful exercise is to examine each asset for excess capacity. Are there assets that are underutilized? A tax firm which asked itself this question took advantage of excess office space to offer certain legal services. A supermarket chain with obsolete sites went into the discount liquor business. A cookie plant began making muffins. A sales force selling over-the-counter drugs to drug chains found that it could handle greeting cards as well. If a diversification can be found to use excess capacity, a substantial, sustainable cost advantage could result.

An example of synergy based, in part, on exploiting excess capacity, is the Los Angeles sports empire of Jerry Buss. Buss owns four sports teams, including the Lakers basketball team and the Kings hockey team, all of which play in his 17,500-seat Forum and appear on his Prime Ticket regional cable channel, which reaches nearly 1.6 million homes. The teams provide a product for the Forum and the cable channel, both of which have excess capacity. Furthermore, the cable channel helps generate interest in the teams and other Forum events such as rock concerts.

Finally, implementation problems need to be addressed. Assets and skills may require adaptations when applied to a different business. Further, new capabilities may have to be found or developed. When acquisitions are involved, two organizations with different systems, people, and cultures will have to be merged. Many efforts at achieving synergy falter because of implementation difficulties.

Brand Name

One common exportable resource is a strong, established brand name such as Hershey's, Sunkist, Coke, Puma, BMW, or Campbell Soup. A strong brand name can provide name familiarity that will help in the tasks of acquiring awareness, generating trial purchases, and gaining distribution for new products—tasks that can cost hundreds of millions of dollars in some consumer contexts.

Often more important than name recognition is what the name means, the brand associations. As Figure 13.1 indicates, four types of associations are relevant in making brand-extension decisions:[1]

- *An image of high (or low) perceived quality.* If the name IBM, Betty Crocker, or Heineken is attached to a new product, there will be a presumption that it will be a high-quality product, backed by a strong firm.
- *Attribute associations with the brand or product class that are helpful in the new context.* For example, Hiram Walker used the Häagen-Dazs name on one of its liquors to create associations with a product class (premium ice cream), which suggest it is rich and creamy and is used by upscale, discriminating consumers.
- *Attribute associations that would be negative in the new context.* For example, Heineken wine might be expected to taste like beer, Log Cabin

FIGURE 13.1   Brand Name Associations—
Häagen-Dazs Candy

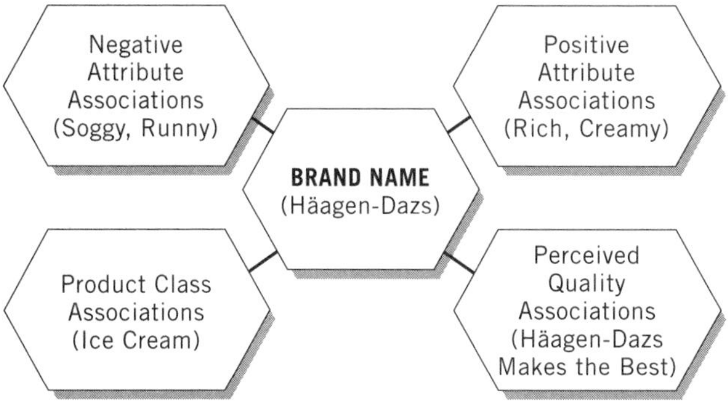

pancakes might be expected to be soggy, or a McDonald's Theme Park might be perceived as plastic, cheap, and dangerous.

- *Associations with a product class.* For example, to many people, Heineken means beer, whereas Kraft is linked to several product classes, including cheese and salad dressing. How feasible is it to attach a brand to another product class? Would it dilute the existing product class associations?

Three factors determine what associations will carry over into a new context:

1. *The strength of the attribute or quality associations in the existing context.* If these associations are weak to begin with, they will be weaker in the new context.

2. *The fit of a brand into the new context.* There needs to be a link such as a common use situation (hair care), user type (glamorous, upscale), functional benefits (speedy delivery), or attribute (salty). Vuarnet sunglasses are associated with skiing and fashion, and thus a skiwear line as a brand extension would make sense, because it would share a common use context and involve the fashion attribute.

3. *Whether or not it is plausible to consider the brand in the new context.* Would the makers of the brand be perceived as having the expertise to make the new product class? Thus, a "fashion-driven firm" like Vuarnet would probably be able to make skiwear, because a fashion touch is the key. A movement by Vuarnet into skis might be stretching it, however. To the extent that the new brand context is implausible, the positive attribute and quality associations will be weak and negative associations may emerge.

Developing brand extension options can start by finding out on what products a brand name would fit and what associations it would bring to the new product class. For example, when Bausch & Lomb found that many associated the firm with precision German engineering and that Bausch & Lomb hearing aids would be attractive, it bought Miracle Ear, a manufacturer with a thousand franchise outlets.[2] When it found that customer trust could be transferred, Bausch & Lomb also decided to leverage its Sensitive Eyes name to start a lotion and cream business.

A brand extension can provide substantial support for a brand name by increasing its awareness level and by reinforcing its associations. For example, the Sunkist associations with oranges, health, and vitality are reinforced by the promotion of Sunkist juice bars and Sunkist vitamin C tablets. However, extensions also have the potential to damage a core brand by creating undesirable attribute associations or weakening those that exist. Thus, the Sunkist health image may be weakened by Sunkist fruit rolls. The strong product-class associations of Kleenex and A-1 might be hurt if they were extended.

Perhaps the worst potential result of an extension is a foregone opportunity to create a new brand equity. Consider where P&G would be without Ivory, Camay, Dreft, Tide, Cheer, Joy, Pampers, Crest, Secret, Sure, Folger's, and Pringles, and its other 70 or so brands. P&G detergent, P&G toothpaste, P&G deodorant, P&G coffee, and P&G potato chips don't have the same impact.

Marketing Skills

A firm will often either possess or lack strong marketing skills for a particular market. Thus, a frequent motive for diversification is to export or import marketing skills. Black & Decker had developed and exploited throughout the 1980s an aggressive new products program (e.g., cordless screwdrivers and HandyChopper), effective consumer marketing (for names such as Spacemaker, Dustbuster, and ThunderVolt cordless tools), and intensive customer service and dealer relations.[3] The acquisition of Emhart with its branded door locks, decorative faucets, outdoor lighting, and racks provided Black & Decker with an opportunity to apply its marketing skills and distribution clout to a firm that lacked a marketing culture.

Applying marketing skills is not always as easy as it appears. Philip Morris, a successful marketer of Miller Lite among other brands, failed with 7UP, which it attempted to position as a caffeine-free soft drink in response to "health" interests of consumers. After a seven-year battle, Philip Morris gave up and sold the line to Pepsi-Cola. The problems that beset Philip Morris included the reaction of competitors who rushed caffeine-free drinks to the market, the power of existing distributors, and the limited appeal of lemon-lime drinks. Coca-Cola made a similar misjudgment when it created Wine Spectrum and failed in its efforts to overcome Gallo, in part because of Gallo's control over distribution. Coca-Cola eventually gave up, selling out to Seagram's. Even Procter & Gamble, one of the best at penetrating the grocery store, has had difficulty making Tropicana Orange Juice profitable because of industry overcapacity and overuse of promotions. The experiences of Philip Morris, Coca-Cola, and Procter & Gamble illustrate the uncertainty of applying skills even in industries that seem well-suited on the surface.

Capacity in Sales or Distribution

A firm with a strong distribution capability may add products or services that could exploit that capability. Thus, Black & Decker's distribution strength helped provide a boost to the Ernhart lines. A joint venture between Nestlé and Coca-Cola in the canned tea business combined Coke's distribution strength with the product knowledge and name of Nestlé.

A firm with capacity in its sales or service organization can look to diversify into products that can use that capacity. For example, one firm that sold cleaning products to auto supply retailers added a line of auto accessories that their sales force could handle. A small innovative company with interesting products but without the clout to gain exposure might be able to provide complementary assets and skills to a firm with excess sales capacity.

Manufacturing Skills

Manufacturing or processing ability can be the basis for entry into a new business area. The ability to design and make small motors helped Honda succeed in the motorcycle business and led to their entry into lawn equipment, outboard motors for boats, and a host of other products. The ability to make small products has been a key for Sony as it has moved from product to product in consumer electronics.

R&D Skills

Expertise in a certain technology can lead to a new business based on that technology. GE's early research has spawned very successful businesses. For example, its research on turbines for electricity generation provided the basis for its aircraft engine business, and its light bulb research provided the foundation for what became the medical instrumentation business. In general, breakthroughs in a business area tend to come from technologies "owned" by other industries. Creativity, often in short supply, is needed to provide opportunities for basic technology and the R&D capability that supports it.

Achieving Economies of Scale

Related diversification can sometimes provide economies of scale. Two smaller consumer products firms, for example, may not each be able to afford an effective sales force, new product development or testing programs, or warehousing and logistics systems. However, the combination of these firms may be able to operate at an efficient level. Similarly, two firms, when combined, may be able to justify an expensive piece of automated production equipment.

The Elusive Search for Synergy

The concept of a total communications firm that includes advertising, direct marketing, marketing research, public relations, and sales promotion was intended to generate synergy by effective cross-selling and by providing clients with more consistent coordinated communication efforts.[4] Young & Rubicam has the "whole egg," whereas the Ogilvy Group promises a harmonious blend of services with "Ogilvy orchestrations."

Although there are some successes—AT&T business systems has attained more consistency in communications with its "the right choice" theme—the difficulty of achieving hoped-for synergy is all too clear. Fewer than 10 percent of clients use more than one service and anecdotes about the problems abound. When Bristol-Myers used a Y&R direct marketing unit to help attack a problem with advertising, a competitive conflict between two Y&R units surfaced as each subtly hinted that the other was less effective and that the budget should be shifted accordingly. Also, Foote Cone referred a client to a sales promotion unit that did not coordinate or perform well. The client became upset, ending such referrals, for a time at least. A basic problem is that many organizations added to a communications firm are small, autonomous, not of comparable quality to the lead advertising firm, and without a culture of coordination.

Sometimes a critical mass is needed in order to be effective. For example, a specialized electronics firm may need an R&D effort, but R&D productivity may be low if it is not feasible to have several researchers who can interact.

Risks of Related Diversification

Even related diversification can be risky. There are three major problems:

- *Similarities and potential synergy simply do not exist.* Strategists often delude themselves that a synergistic justification exists by manipulating semantics. In 1968, for example, General Foods, frustrated with an FTC antitrust decision ordering it to avoid buying any firms marketing to supermarkets, bought Burger Chef, a chain of 700 fast-food restaurants.[5] The logic was that it was in a fast-growing industry and was "food-related." The fact was that this similarity was of little value. General Food's efforts to manage Burger Chef were a disaster. In 1972 alone, an $83 million write-off had to be taken, many times the purchase price of $16 million.

- *Potential synergy may exist but is never realized because of implementation problems.* This happens when a diversification move involves integrating two organizations that have fundamental differences and/or when one of the two organizations lacks the ability or motivation to undertake programs necessary to make the diversification work. In Chapter 16, the implementation issue is discussed in more detail.

- *Possible violations of antitrust laws create an additional risk when an acquisition or merger is involved.* Ironically, as the degree of commonality and potential synergy increases, so does the possibility of an antitrust problem.

- *An acquisition is overvalued.* Buying a business in another area, even a related one, can be risky. Borden engaged in an agressive acquisition program in the late 1980s involving 91 businesses costing some $2 billion.[6] Many were regional brands that never were able to successfully break out of the region. One of the most important was Laura Scudder's, a California snack food company that surprised Borden with a major union problem that closed its California plants. A plan to ship chips from Utah was too costly and damaged the chips. The brand was sold in 1993 at a disastrous $150 million loss.

UNRELATED DIVERSIFICATION

Unrelated diversification lacks enough commonality in markets, distribution channels, production technology, or R&D thrust to provide the opportunity for synergy through the exchange or sharing of assets or skills. The objectives are therefore mainly financial, to generate profit streams that are either larger, less uncertain, or more stable than they would otherwise be. Figure 13.2 summarizes the motivations for both unrelated and related diversification.

FIGURE 13.2 Motivations for Diversification

RELATED DIVERSIFICATION	UNRELATED DIVERSIFICATION
• Exchange or share skills or assets, thereby exploiting	• Manage and allocate cash flow.
• Brand name	• Obtain high ROI.
• Marketing skills	• Obtain a "bargain" price.
• Sales and distribution capacity	• Restructure a firm.
• Manufacturing skills	• Reduce risk by operating in multiple product markets.
• R&D and new product capability	• Tax benefits
• Economies of scale	• Obtain liquid assets.
	• Vertical integration.
	• Defend against a takeover.
	• Provide executive interest.

Manage and Allocate Cash Flow

Unrelated diversification can balance the cash flows of strategic business unit (SBU) entities. A firm which has many SBUs that merit investment might buy or merge with a cash cow to provide a source of cash. The acquisition of the cash cow may reduce the need to raise debt or equity over time, although if the cash cow is acquired, resources will need to be expended. ITT, for example, purchased Hartford Insurance in the 1970s in order to provide a source of cash for its many SBUs that had a net need for cash.

Conversely, a firm with a cash cow may enter new areas seeking growth opportunities or simply areas to generate future earnings if its core cash cow eventually falters. The tobacco firms of Philip Morris and Reynold's have used their enormous cash flows to buy a host of firms such as General Foods, Nabisco, and Del Monte. One motivation is to provide alternative core earning areas in case the tobacco cash cow is crippled by effective antismoking programs or by successful damage litigation.

Entering Business Areas with High ROI Prospects

A basic diversification motivation is to improve an ROI by moving into business areas with high growth and ROI prospects. The Heinz purchase of Weight Watchers in the late 1970s, discussed in Chapter 10, illustrates such a motivation.[7] The vision paid off. By 1989, Heinz was selling 210 different products under the Weight Watchers name, from salad dressings and yogurt to frozen desserts to pizza, and was making more than $100 million per year (nearly what Heinz had paid for the business ten years earlier).

The motivation to enter attractive businesses is understandable when the present core business is declining in the face of adversity. Thus, tobacco companies have moved into the area of packaged goods. Among the acquisitions of Philip Morris in its effort to diversify beyond tobacco are Miller Beer, Kraft, and General Foods. Seagram's, facing declining liquor sales, bought Tropicana Products even though it involved a completely different distribution system and retail environment.[8]

Obtaining a "Bargain" Price for a Business

Another way to improve ROI is to acquire a business at a "bargain" price so the investment is low and the associated ROI will therefore be high. As Chapter 14 discusses, bargains may indeed be available in declining industries when firms decide to exit at any price. However, there is substantial evidence in finance suggesting that when publicly traded stocks are involved, "bargain prices" are rare because the market is based on relatively detailed and dispersed information.

Numerous studies have explored the stock return payoff when an acquisition is made. One review of some 41 such studies concludes that the stock price of the acquired or target firm on average goes up about 22 percent within a month of the announcement of the acquisition.[9] Significantly, however, the return enjoyed by the acquiring firm is close to zero. This implies that the acquired firm on average commands a substantial premium and therefore is not a bargain. That premium tends to be larger when the transaction involves stock because more bidders tend to be attracted by the announcement of the impending stock transaction.

The Potential to Restructure a Firm

An acquisition can provide the basis for a restructuring of the acquired firm, the acquiring firm, or both.[10] The objective would be to change the thrust of a firm from one set of industries to another. For example, Esmark dramatically restructured by selling its oil and gas businesses and its Swift operation and concentrating the resulting assets on its consumer products businesses. Not incidentally, the thrust change may result in investors perceiving a firm to be in more attractive industries, thus causing its stock price to rise.

The key is to identify firms that are undervalued with respect to their potential after a restructuring. One approach suggested by Booz Allen acquisition specialists is to group a firm's businesses into four categories:[11]

1. *Core businesses.* A core business might represent 25 to 60 percent of sales. Strategically, the core business should be strong and have some sustainable competitive advantages on which to build. The core business has probably been used to attempt diversification.

2. *Successful diversifications.* These would be the firm's stars with strong positions in attractive markets.

3. *Unsuccessful diversifications.* An undervalued firm typically has a substantial proportion of sales in unsuccessful diversifications, which is a major drag on performance.

4. *Nonoperating investments.* These could be stock investments or physical assets carried below realizable market.

Unsuccessful diversifications and their effect on performance may generate associations and perceived risks that cause a firm to be undervalued. The core business, successful diversifications, and nonoperating investments may be worth much more than the current firm as a whole.

Liquidating or divesting the unsuccessful diversifications would be one way to realize that value. Another possibility would be to spin off the core business, which by itself may be valued relatively highly, and thereby use the successful diversifications as a base to generate a new core business. If the original core business is in an industry not highly regarded by the stock market, the revised core could be valued higher.

Restructuring has become controversial for two reasons. First, restructuring often is stimulated by outside investment interests that finance takeovers by having a firm assume a large debt. The surviving businesses are burdened with this debt and thus capacity to finance growth and change is greatly reduced. For example, Lucky stores went from being a firm with three healthy retail chains and little debt to one engaged only in food retailing with a massive debt load. Second, outside investors who restructure are accused of neglecting long-term business interests as they are driven to improve short-term performance and increase the price of a stock. Their short-run orientation may cause them to liquidate or milk portions of a business that are potential long-run assets. The takeover of a timber company, for example, resulted in a dramatic increase in tree cutting, which sharply enhanced profits at the expense, in some people's view, of the long-term value of the firm.

Reducing Risk

The reduction of risk can be another motivation for unrelated diversification. Heavy reliance on a single product line can stimulate a diversification move. Hershey was almost totally dependent on its candy and confectionery business, a business that was vulnerable to an increased interest in health and health foods. Hershey purchased Friendly Ice Cream, a chain of family restaurants based in Massachusetts, and the Skinner Macaroni Company with the goal of making nonconfection revenues a significant percent of sales. Of course, there is the real risk that the new business areas may be money-draining headaches, as Mobil discovered when it acquired Montgomery Ward.

Risk can also be reduced by entering businesses that will counter or reduce the cyclical nature of existing earnings, as when a general contractor and farm equipment maker purchased a specialty steel concern.

Stockholder Risk Versus Management Risk

Diversification may reduce the market risk facing a firm and thus protect the firm's employees, customers, and managers. Managers, in particular, face the loss of their job and reputation from a business downturn over which they may have no control, and thus they may be motivated to diversify. However, risk reduction obtained from unrelated diversification is of no value to stockholders, who are free to diversify by holding a portfolio of stocks. Based on the premise that stockholders are the only relevant stakeholders of a business, it can be argued that the reduction of risk is not a legitimate objective.

Even stockholders cannot diversify from "systematic risk," that portion of variation of the stock return correlated with general economic conditions and measured by the beta of a business. Thus, a diversification that would reduce a firm's systematic risk would be of value to stockholders. For example, an upscale chain of restaurants might acquire a set of Taco Bell outlets which would do well when the economy is down.

Tax Implications

Tax considerations can stimulate mergers or acquisitions of unrelated firms. Firms can accumulate large tax-loss carryovers, which they can exploit. Thus, a firm with a large series of losses from its automatic teller machines purchased a profitable sweater manufacturer, which could utilize the losses to reduce taxes. Mergers have also been motivated by firms that have underutilized tax incentives to make capital investments.

Obtaining Liquid Assets

A firm can become an attractive acquisition candidate because of substantial liquid assets that can be readily deployed or because of a low debt-to-equity ratio that provides the potential to support debt financing. Banks and insurance companies can be attractive acquisition targets because they provide access to money.

Vertical Integration Motivations

A vertical integration is usually an unrelated diversification. In Chapter 12, some of the motivations for vertical integration were discussed, such as obtaining operating economies, gaining access to or control of supply or demand, and enhancing technological innovation.

Defending Against a Takeover

The threat of an unfriendly takeover can lead to an acquisition. One firm bought a small banana company to generate an antitrust obstacle to a takeover by United Fruit. Martin Marietta responded to a takeover move by Bendix by attempting to buy Bendix with the help of a third firm, United Technologies. The complex and expensive maneuvering ended with a fourth company, Allied Corporation, buying Bendix, while Martin Marietta remained independent.

Providing Executive Interest

For the executives making the decision, diversification can be stimulating. It can also lead to the prestige of a larger organization. A study in which 14 merger experts were queried as to the motivations involved found that enhancement of personal power as measured by the sales volume controlled by a chief executive may be a moderately important motivation in merger decisions.[12] Another related conclusion was that the merger decisions were ultimately made by one person, the CEO.

Risks of Unrelated Diversification

The very concept of unrelated diversification suggests risk and difficulty because, by definition, there is no possibility of synergy. Many knowledgeable people have made blanket statements warning against unrelated diversification. Peter Drucker claims that all successful diversification requires a common core or unity represented by common markets, technology, or production processes.[13] He states that without such unity, diversification never works; financial ties alone are insufficient. Among the major risks are

• Attention may be diverted from the core business.
• Managing the new business may be difficult.
• The new business may be overvalued.

Unrelated diversification, if unsuccessful, may actually damage the original core business by diverting attention and resources from it. Quaker Oats embarked on an aggressive acquisition program in the early 1970s, going into toys and theme restaurants. In the process, however, the company allowed its core business areas to deteriorate. The new product effort suffered, and the market share and shelf facings fell as a result.

The potential for difficulties in managing a diversification is magnified when an unrelated business is acquired. The new business may require assets, skills, and an organizational culture that differ from those of the core business. Furthermore, a skilled, valued management team in the acquired company might leave and be difficult to replace.

A new business area might be incorrectly evaluated. For example, environmental threats may be overlooked or misjudged. If an acquisition is involved, its strategic liabilities, weaknesses, and problems may be undiscovered or miscalculated. General Host, a food store and baked goods firm, acquired Cudahy, the meat-packing firm, just before its plant and methods were made virtually obsolete by new packers with highly automated plants.[14] National Intergroup, with steel and oil as its core businesses, bought a drug wholesaler, only to find a price war was starting and that a project to sell computer services to druggists was a disaster.[15]

Performance of Diversified Firms

In the 1960s and early 1970s, a wave of acquisitions took place, the largest since the turn-of-the-century mergers for monopoly.[16] The typical transaction was a friendly merger involving a business unrelated to the business area of the acquiring firm. The result was a trend to unrelated diversification and conglomeration. The fraction of single-business companies in the Fortune 500 dropped from 23 to 15 percent from 1959 to 1969 and the percent of conglomerates with no dominant business rose from 7.3 to 19. The interest in unrelated diversification was fueled by high stock values (which meant funds to buy firms were available), tough antitrust regulation (which inhibited related diversification), and a belief that "management" was a skill owned by large companies that could be applied to acquired firms.

The consensus now is that the unrelated diversification of the 1960s was a mistake. Profitability of unrelated acquired companies did not, on average, improve. Further, most of them were subsequently divested. Porter examined 2,021 acquisitions made in new industries by 33 large diversified U.S. companies from 1950 to 1980 and found that more than half were divested by 1986.[17] Of the 931 acquisitions that were unrelated, 74 percent were divested.

There is some evidence that related acquisitions tend to perform better than unrelated ones. In a classic study, Rumelt, a UCLA professor, compared related diversification strategies (a common skill or asset applies to all of the component businesses) with less related (businesses are linked to each other within the firm) and unrelated diversification.[18] His study of a sample of Fortune 500 firms found that the related diversifications were the highest in performance, followed by the less related and finally the unrelated. Another study showed that 50 related diversifications in the 1975 to 1984 period had a significantly higher ROA than 20 unrelated diversified firms.[19]

In an interesting study reported in *Fortune*, the 10 largest mergers of 1971 were evaluated 10 years later.[20] With respect to estimated 1981 earnings per share, half of the firms would have been better off without the acquisitions. Furthermore, only three of the acquisitions had returns on investment exceeding 10 percent, as compared with the 13.8-percent median return for the Fortune 500 companies. It turned out that the acquiring firms were also, on the whole, bad investments during the same period; half actually had a negative return. This performance may reflect the quality of management decisions, or it may simply reflect unfavorable conditions that the acquisitions were designed to alleviate.

ENTRY STRATEGIES

When the decision is made to enter a new product market, the entry strategy becomes critical.[21] Figure 13.3 summarizes seven alternative strategies with their advantages and disadvantages.

The most common entry routes are internal development and acquisition. Developing a new business internally means that a concept, strategy, and team can be created without the limitations, liabilities, or acquisition cost represented by acquiring an existing business. An internal venture is a variant in which a separate entity within the existing firm is established, so that the new business will not be constrained by existing organizational culture, systems, and structure. For example, the IBM PC was developed and marketed by a separate organizational entity in a remarkably short time.

The acquisition route saves calendar time. An acquisition can mean that a firm becomes an established player in a matter of weeks instead of years. Perhaps more important, it means that substantial entry barriers such as distribution or brand-name recognition are overcome. A variant is an educational acquisition in which a small firm that is not established as a major force is acquired in order to obtain a window into a technology or market, as well as knowledge, experience, and a base from which to grow.

The other options shown in Figure 13.3 represent reduced risk and commitment, as well as a reduced chance that the route will lead to an established business supported by SCAs (sustainable competitive advantages). A joint venture will share the risk with others and provide one or more missing and needed assets and skills. For example, a small firm that possesses a new technology could enter into a joint venture with a larger firm that has financial resources and access to distribution. Licensing a technology from others provides a fast way to overcome one entry barrier, but makes it difficult to gain control of that same technology in the future. Both of these entry options are important in international business contexts and are discussed in detail in Chapter 15. An alternative to a joint venture is an alliance in which the parties share assets to attack a market. For example, Sony's cooperative technology-sharing arrangements with a host of small high-tech firms serve to keep Sony on the cutting edge of technology and also provide the small firms with access to Sony's production, engineering, and marketing assets.

FIGURE 13.3 Entry Strategies

Entry Strategy	Major Advantages	Major Disadvantages
Internal Development	• Uses existing resources • Avoids acquisition cost especially if unfamiliar with product/market	• Time lag • Uncertain prospects
Internal Venture	• Uses existing resources • May keep talented entrepreneurs	• Mixed success record • Can create internal stresses
Acquisition	• Saves calendar time • Overcomes entry barriers • Problem of integrating two organizations	• Costly—usually buy redundant assets
Joint Venture or Alliance	• Technological/marketing unions can exploit small/large firm synergies • Distributes risk	• Potential for conflict in operations between firms • Value of one firm may be reduced over time
Licensing from Others	• Rapid access to technology • Reduced financial risk	• Will lack proprietary technology and technological skills • Will be dependent on licensor
Educational Acquisition	• Provides window and initial staff	• Risk of departure of entrepreneurs
Venture Capital and Nurturing	• Can provide window on new technology or market	• Unlikely alone to be a major stimulus of firm growth
Licensing to Others	• Rapid access to a market • Low cost/risk	• Will lack knowledge/control of market • Will be dependent on licensee

SOURCE: Adapted from Edward B. Roberts and Charles A. Berry, "Entering New Businesses: Selecting Strategies for Success," *Sloan Management Review*, Spring 1985, pp. 317.

The lowest involvement options are licensing others to use and market a technology or entering into a business as a venture-capital investor. General Electric and Union Carbide are among firms that have made minority investments in young and growing high-tech enterprises in order to secure some relationship to a new technology. Both licensing and becoming a venture capital investor offer the potential to increase involvement over time if the business does well and to control any risk.

Selecting the Right Entry Strategy

Roberts and Berry suggest that the selection of the right entry strategy depends on the level of a firm's familiarity with the product market to be entered.[22] They define familiarity along two dimensions: (1) market and (2) technology or service embodied in the product.

With respect to market factors, three levels of familiarity are defined:

- *Base.* Existing products are sold within this market.
- *New/familiar.* The company is familiar with the market because of extensive research, experienced staff, or links with the market as a customer.
- *New/unfamiliar.* Knowledge of and experience with the market are lacking.

An analogous set of three levels of familiarity with the technologies or services embodied in the product is set forth:

- *Base.* The technology or service is embodied within existing products.
- *New/familiar.* The company is familiar with the technology because of work in related technologies, an established R&D effort in the technology, or extensive focused research in the technology.
- *New/unfamiliar.* Knowledge of and experience with the technology are lacking.

The basic suggestion is that as the level of familiarity on these two dimensions declines, the commitment level should be reduced. Figure 13.4 shows the baseline entry strategy recommendations that follow from a familiarity assessment. Of course, there will be contexts in which a high-commitment approach in the unfamiliar/unfamiliar cell will make sense. However, Roberts and Berry suggest, on the basis of experience and theory, that substantial risk is associated with such an approach and the option of gaining familiarity should be seriously considered.

SUMMARY

Related diversification involves the potential to attain synergies by exporting or exchanging assets or skills, whereas such potential is largely lacking in unrelated diversification. Figure 13.2 summarizes the motivations of each diversification route. The major risks of related diversification are (1) that implementation difficulties will prevent the synergies from being realized, or (2) that synergies do not exist in the first place. The management problems and potential for mistakes are magnified when an unrelated business is involved. Studies have found that firms engaged in

FIGURE 13.4 Optimal Entry Strategies

		Technologies or Services Embodied in the Product		
		Base	New familiar	New unfamiliar
Market Factors	New unfamiliar	Joint ventures	Venture capital or educational acquisitions	Venture capital or educational acquisitions
	New familiar	Internal market developments or acquisitions (or joint ventures)	Internal ventures or acquisitions or licensing	Venture capital or educational acquisitions
	Base	Internal base developments (or acquisitions)	Internal product developments or acquisitions or licensing	Joint ventures

SOURCE: Adapted from Edward B. Roberts and Charles A. Berry, "Entering New Businesses: Selecting Strategies for Success," *Sloan Management Review*, Spring 1985, pp. 3–17.

unrelated diversification tend, on the average, to underperform other firms.

Figure 13.3 illustrates a variety of ways to enter a market besides acquisition and internal development. When the market and technology are unfamiliar, it is especially risky to attempt an entry requiring a large commitment.

FOOTNOTES

[1] David A. Aaker, *Managing Brand Equity*, New York: The Free Press, 1991, Chapter 9.

[2] Myron Maget, "Let's Go for Growth," *Fortune*, March 7, 1994, pp. 60–72.

[3] Michael J. McDermott, "The House That Nolan's Building," *Adweek's Marketing Week*, August 14, 1989, pp. 20–22.

[4] Drawn, in part, from Joanne Lipam, "Ad Firms Falter on One-Stop Shopping," *Wall Street Journal*, December 1, 1988, p. B1.

[5] Robert F. Hartley, *Marketing Mistakes*, 5th ed., Columbus: Grid Publishing, 1992, pp. 258–276.

[6] Kathleen Deveny and Suein L. Hwang, "A Defective Strategy of Heated Acquisitions Spoils Borden Name," *Wall Street Journal*, January 18, 1994, B1.

[7] Aaker, *Managing Brand Equity*, Chapter 5.

[8] Nancy Youman, "So Far, So Good for Seagram's Beverage Shot," *Adweek's Marketing Week*, June 3, 1990, pp. 54–55.

[9] Deepak K. Datta, George E. Pinches, and V. K. Narayanan, "Factors Influencing Wealth Creation from Mergers and Acquisitions: A Meta-Analysis," *Strategic Management Journal* 13, 1992, pp. 67–84.

[10] Michael G. Allen, Alexander R. Oliver, and Edward H. Schwallie, "The Key to Successful Acquisitions," *Journal of Business Strategy* 2, Fall 1981, pp. 14–24.

[11] Michael G. Allen, Alexander R. Oliver, and Edward H. Schwallie, "The Key to Successful Acquisitions," *Journal of Business Strategy* 2, Fall 1981, pp. 14–24.

[12] Wayne I. Boucher, "The Process of Conglomerate Merger," prepared for the Bureau of Competition, Federal Trade Commission, June 1980.

[13] Peter Drucker, "The Five Rules of Successful Acquisition," *Wall Street Journal*, October 15, 1981, p. 16.

[14] Arthur M. Louis, "The Bottom Line on Ten Big Mergers," *Fortune*, May 3, 1982, pp. 84–89.

[15] Gregory L. Miles, "National Intergroup: How Pete Love Went Wrong," *Business Week*, March 6, 1989, pp. 56–64.

[16] Andrei Shleifer and Robert W. Vishny, "Takeovers in the 60s and the 80s: Evidence and Implications," *Strategic Management Journal* 12, 1991, pp. 51–59.

[17] Michael E. Porter, "From Competitive Advantage to Corporate Strategy," *Harvard Business Review*, May–June 1987, pp. 43–59.

[18] Richard Rumelt, "Diversity, Strategy and Profitability," *Strategic Management Journal* 3, 1982, pp. 359–369.

[19] Paul G. Simmonds, "The Combined Diversification Breadth and Mode Dimensions and the Performance of Large Diversified Firms," *Strategic Management Journal* 11, 1990, pp. 399–410.

[20] Louis, "The Bottom Line."

[21] Edward B. Roberts and Charles A. Berry, "Entering New Businesses: Selecting Strategies for Success," *Sloan Management Review*, Spring 1985, pp. 3–17.

[22] Roberts and Berry, "Entering New Businesses."

14

STRATEGIES IN DECLINING AND HOSTILE MARKETS

> Anyone can hold the helm when the sea is calm.
>
> *Publilius Syrus*
>
> Where there is no wind, row.
>
> *Portuguese proverb*

Strategic planning is often associated with a search for healthy, growing markets and the development of strategies to penetrate those markets. However, as the discussion in Chapter 5 makes clear, there are a variety of risks in high-growth contexts, including the possibility that a market can be crowded with competitors, each trying to find a niche. On the other hand, declining markets as well as mature markets can represent real opportunities for a business following the right strategy, in part because they are not as attractive to competitors. Thus, declining markets are not always to be avoided.

A declining market involves a fall in demand, often caused by an external event such as the creation of a competing technology, a change in customer needs or tastes, or a shift in government policy. Of course, a competitor in a declining market will attempt to obtain sustainable competitive advantages (SCAs) and compete successfully. In a market characterized by zero or negative growth, however, the options of milking and even exiting should be considered, as suggested by the portfolio models. Thus, it is important to understand these options as well.

In this chapter several strategic alternatives especially relevant to declining markets are considered:

1. Create a growth context by revitalizing the industry so that it becomes a growth industry or by focusing on a growth submarket.
2. Be the profitable survivor in the industry by dominating the market, thus encouraging others to exit.
3. Milk or harvest. Withdraw resources so that they can be invested elsewhere.
4. Exit or liquidate. Salvage existing assets.

Hostile markets are those with overcapacity, low margins, intense competition, and management in turmoil. Hostility has two primary causes. The first is a decline in demand. The second and most important cause of hostility is competitive expansion. During the 1980s, for example, the semiconductor, airline, minicomputer, and orange juice industries became hostile when the expansion of industry capacity exceeded the growth of demand. Thus, even a growing market can be hostile.

Hostile markets are all too common. In fact, out of thousands of executives in this author's executive programs, only one has admitted to competing in a market that was not hostile, and that person was the manager of the Panama Canal! It is thus important to understand the dynamics of hostile markets and why some competitors do better than others in such environments. In the final section of this chapter, the life cycle of a hostile market will be described and the strategies of above average performers will be discussed.

CREATING GROWTH IN DECLINING INDUSTRIES

It is usually assumed that existing industry participants have already fully exploited the market potential of a stagnant or declining industry. If that assumption is untrue, a dramatic opportunity exists for a business to participate in revitalizing the industry and assume a commanding position in the new growth context. As suggested by Figure 14.1, industry revitalization can be created by new markets, new products, new applications, revitalized marketing, government-stimulated growth, and the exploitation of growth submarkets.

New Markets

An obvious way to generate growth is to move into neglected or ignored market segments with the potential for new growth. Texas Instruments designed a calculator for women—a neglected market in a mature product category despite the fact that 60 percent of buyers were women. The new calculator, termed the Nuance, looked like a compact with a latch-key cover in either purple or soft beige. Its rubber keys were contoured for comfort and staggered so that long nails would not create double strokes. Some industries have seen international expansion fuel growth. Barbie, for example, found new market vitality in Europe and Japan.

New Products

Sometimes a dormant industry can be revitalized by a product that makes existing products obsolete and accelerates the replacement cycle. The consumer electronics market has seen color television, cassette tapes, CDs,

FIGURE 14.1 Revitalizing a Stagnant Market

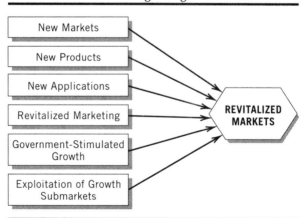

stereo television, and big screen television all generate growth spurts. A new product variant can add interest, such as the introduction of gourmet coffees or cranberry-based juices.

New Applications

A new application for a product can stimulate new industry growth. In Chapter 12, the graphic example of baking soda and its use as a deodorizer is given. The cranberry industry has created new growth by finding new recipes for its product and encouraging cranberry use outside holiday meals. Lysol Disinfectant Spray came out with a new scent and targeted day-care centers. The small refrigerator opened up new sources of sales in the office and student dormitory. A prime way to find promising applications is to learn how existing customers are using the product or service.

Revitalized Marketing

A product class may be revived by a fresh marketing approach such as changing the distribution channel by using new types of stores or direct selling, selling the product to firms to use as giveaway promotion items, changing the pricing structure, or perhaps changing the advertising. A dormant headache product was rejuvenated by linking it to its rural Southeastern roots. The original packaging and bitter taste were restored, advertisements were run featuring Southern spokespersons, and associations were developed with events such as bass-fishing tournaments and minor league baseball.

Government-Stimulated Growth

There is an old adage, "If all else fails, change the rules of the game." Strategically, the idea is to change the environment so that industry sales will be enhanced. A government body can provide incentives for change, such as tax incentives for installing home insulation or refurbishing low-income housing. Or a government might dictate that air bags be installed in cars, thus stimulating a new industry.

Exploitation of Growth Submarkets

Some firms have been successful in declining or mature industries because they have been able to focus on growth subareas, pockets of demand that are healthy and perhaps even growing nicely. The super-dry, nonalcoholic, and microbrewery brands are all growing in the mature beer market. Convertibles are again growth segments in the automobile industry.

Sometimes a growth submarket has the same visibility and risk as another growth market, but it is neglected because its parent industry is unattractive. As a result, it is likely to receive less competitive attention.

BE THE PROFITABLE SURVIVOR[1]

The conventional advice is to avoid investing in declining markets, to milk or exit businesses that are trapped in a declining situation. However, an aggressive alternative is to invest in order to obtain or strengthen a leadership position. A strong survivor may be profitable, in part because there may be little competition and in part because the investment might be relatively low. The cornerstone of this strategy is to encourage competitors to exit. Toward that end a firm can

- Be visible about its commitment to be the surviving leader in the industry.

- Raise the costs of competing by price reductions or increased promotion.

- Introduce new products and cover new segments, thereby making it more difficult for a competitor to find a profitable niche. Thus, the major coffee manufacturers such as Maxwell House and Folgers have introduced gourmet coffees to make sure that this relatively small but growing niche is not left to others.

- Reduce competitors' exit barriers by assuming their long-term contracts, supplying spare parts and servicing their products in the field, or by supplying them with products. For example, a regional bakery could supply private-label products to a local retailer, thus enabling the retailer to exit from doing its own baking.

- Create a national, dominant brand in a declining industry that is fragmented. Chesebrough-Ponds, for example, bought Ragu Packing, a regional spaghetti-sauce maker and created a major national brand, thereby generating economies of scale in both marketing and manufacturing.

- Purchase a competitor's market share and/or its production capacity. This is the ultimate removal of a competitor's exit barriers and ensures that a tired competitor won't be taken over by a more vigorous organization. In the late 1980s Kunz, which made passbooks for financial institutions, was able to buy competitor assets so far under book value that the payback period was measured in months. As a result Kunz had record years in a business area others had written off as all but dead decades earlier. As noted in Chapter 11, White Industries has become the third largest appliance manufacturer by buying such names as Kelvinator, Westinghouse, Philco, and Frigidaire from firms that were strongly motivated to exit.

MILK OR HARVEST

A milk or harvest strategy aims to generate cash flow by reducing investment and operating expenses, even if that causes a reduction in sales and market share. The underlying assumptions are that the firm has better uses for the funds, that the involved business is not crucial to the firm either financially or synergistically, and that milking is feasible because sales will decline in an orderly way.

It is useful to distinguish between a fast and a slow milking plan. Fast milking involves sharp reductions in operating expenditures and perhaps price increases to maximize short-term cash flow and to minimize the possibility that any additional money will be invested in the business. A fast milking strategy accepts the risk of a sharp sales decline that could precipitate a market exit. Slow milking involves sharply reducing long-term investment in plant, equipment, and R&D, but only gradually reducing expenditures in operating areas such as marketing and service. Slow milking attempts to maximize the flow of cash over time by prolonging and slowing the decline.

A classic example of a slow milking strategy was that of Chase & Sanborn coffee.[2] In 1879, Chase & Sanborn became the first American company to pack roasted coffee in sealed cans. In 1929, it combined with Royal Baking Powder and Fleischmann to form a company called Standard Brands. During the 1920s and 1930s, Chase & Sanborn advertised heavily and dominated the coffee industry. The "Chase & Sanborn Hour," starring Edgar Bergen and Charlie McCarthy, was one of the most popular radio shows of its time. After World War II, instant coffee and General Foods' Maxwell House both appeared. Instead of fighting the heavy advertising of Maxwell House, Chase & Sanborn chose a milking strategy. Over the years, advertising support for the brand was reduced until, finally, advertising was stopped entirely. In 1981, Standard Brands merged with Nabisco, which then sold off the coffee business for about $15 million to a small Miami firm, General Coffee. Standard Brands also followed the slow milking strategy with Royal Pudding when that product was faced with another General Foods brand, Jell-O.

Conditions Favoring a Milking Strategy

There are several conditions which would support a milking strategy rather than a hold or exit strategy:

- The decline rate is pronounced and unlikely to change but not excessively steep, and pockets of enduring demand ensure that the decline rate will not suddenly become precipitous.
- The price structure is stable at a level that is profitable for efficient firms.
- The business position is weak but there is enough customer loyalty, perhaps in a limited part of the market, to generate sales and profits in a milking mode. The risk of losing relative position with a milking strategy is low.
- The business is not central to the current mission of the firm.
- A milking strategy can be successfully managed.

Implementation Problems

Implementation of a milking strategy can be difficult. One of the most serious problems is that if employees and customers suspect that a milking strategy is being employed, the resulting lack of trust may upset the whole strategy. As the line between a milking strategy and abandonment is sometimes very thin, customers may lose confidence in the firm's product and employee morale may suffer. Competitors may attack more vigorously. All these possibilities can create a sharper-than-anticipated decline. To minimize such effects, it is helpful to keep a milking strategy as inconspicuous as possible.

Another serious problem is the difficulty of placing and motivating a manager in a milking situation. Most SBU managers do not have the orientation, background, or skills to engage in a successful milking strategy. Adjusting performance measures and rewards appropriately can be difficult for both the organization and the managers involved. It might seem reasonable to use a manager who specializes in milking strategies, but that is often not feasible simply because such specialization is rare. Most firms rotate managers through different types of situations, and career paths simply are not geared to creating milking specialists.

When the Premises Are Wrong

One advantage of milking rather than divesting is that a milking strategy can often be reversed if it turns out to be based on incorrect premises regarding market prospects, competitor moves, cost projections, or other relevant factors. A resurgence in product classes that were seemingly dead or in terminal decline gives pause. Oatmeal, for example, has experienced a sharp increase in sales because of its cost and associations with nutrition and health. In men's apparel, suspenders and pocket watches have shown signs of growth. Fountain pens, invented in 1884, were virtually killed by the appearance in 1939 of the ballpoint. However, the combination of nostalgia and a desire for prestige has provided a major comeback for the luxury fountain pen. As a result, the industry has seen years in which sales doubled.

The Hold Strategy

A variant of the milking strategy is the hold strategy, in which growth-motivated investment is avoided but an adequate level of investment is employed to maintain product quality, production facilities, and customer loyalty. A hold strategy is appropriate when an industry is declining in an orderly way, pockets of enduring demand exist, price pressures are not extreme, a firm has exploitable assets or skills, and a business contributes by its presence to other business units in the firm. A hold strategy would be preferable to an invest strategy when an industry lacks growth opportunities and a strategy of increasing share would risk triggering competitive retaliation. The hold strategy can be a long-term strategy to manage a cash cow or an interim strategy employed until the uncertainties of an industry are resolved.

A problem with the hold strategy is that if conditions change, reluctance or slowness to reinvest may result in lost market share. The two largest can manufacturers, American and Continental, failed to invest in the two-piece can process when it was developed because they were engaged in diversification efforts and were attempting to avoid investments in their "cash cow." As a result, they lost substantial market share.

DIVESTMENT OR LIQUIDATION

As Figure 14.2 suggests, when a business environment and business position are both unfavorable, then the final alternative, divestment or liquidation, is precipitated. Among the conditions that would suggest an exit decision rather than a milking decision are the following:

- The decline rate is rapid and accelerating, and no pockets of enduring demand are accessible to the business.

- The price pressures are expected to be extreme, caused by determined competitors with high exit barriers and by a lack of brand loyalty and product differentiation. Thus, a milking strategy is unlikely to be profitable for anyone.

- The business position is weak; one or more dominant competitors have achieved irreversible advantage. The business is now losing money and future prospects are dim.

FIGURE 14.2 Strategies for Declining or Stagnant Industries

		Business Position in Key Segments	
		Strong	**Weak**
Industry Environment • Rate of decline • Pockets of demand • Price pressure	**Favorable**	Invest or hold	Milk or exit
	Unfavorable	Milk or exit	Exit

SOURCE: Adapted from Kathryn Rudie Harrigan and Michael E. Porter, "End-Game Strategies for Declining Industries," *Harvard Business Review*, July–August 1987, p. 119.

- The firm's mission has changed, and the role of the business has become superfluous or even unwanted.
- Exit barriers can be overcome.

A set of exit barriers can inhibit an exit decision. In particular

- Specialized assets such as plant and equipment may have little value to others.
- Long-term contracts with suppliers and with labor groups may be expensive to break.
- The business may have commitments to provide spare parts and service backup to retailers and customers. For example, in the 1960s, many vacuum-tube manufacturers such as RCA also made TV sets that used specialized tubes. The customers' assumption that RCA would supply parts provided a substantial exit barrier for the RCA vacuum-tube business.
- An exit decision may affect the reputation and operation of other company businesses. Thus, GE was concerned about the impact its decision to discontinue small appliances would have on its lamp and large appliance business retailers and consumers.
- Government restrictions can effectively prohibit an exit decision. Rail service, for example, cannot simply be terminated.

Managerial pride may also be a factor. Professional managers often view themselves as problem-solvers and are reluctant to admit defeat. Several anecdotes describe firms that have sent a series of executives to close down a subsidiary, each of whom convinced him- or herself after arriving that a turnaround was possible, only to subsequently fail at the effort. Furthermore, there may be an emotional attachment to a business that has perhaps been in the "family" for many years and that may even have been the original business on which the rest of the firm was based. It is difficult to turn your back on such a valued friend.

SELECTING THE RIGHT STRATEGY FOR THE DECLINING ENVIRONMENT

The spectrum of investment alternatives ranges from invest to hold to milk to exit. In order to determine the optimal alternative in a declining environment, a firm needs to consider strategic questions in the five areas summarized in Figure 14.3 and discussed below.

FIGURE 14.3   The Investment Decision in a Declining Industry

---

SOME STRATEGIC QUESTIONS

Market Prospects
1. Is the rate of decline orderly and predictable?
2. Are there pockets of enduring demand?
3. What are the reasons for the decline—is it temporary?

Competitive Intensity
4. Are there dominant competitors with unique skills or assets?
5. Are there many competitors unwilling to exit or contract gracefully?
6. Are customers brand-loyal? Is there product differentiation?
7. Are there price pressures?

Performance/Strengths
8. Is the business profitable? What are its future prospects?
9. What is the market-share position and trend?
10. Does the business have some SCAs with respect to key segments?
11. Can the business manage costs in the face of declining sales?

Interrelationship with Other Businesses
12. Is there synergy with other businesses?
13. Is the business compatible with the firm's current strategic thrust?
14. Can the firm support the cash needs of the business?

Implementation Barriers
15. What are the exit barriers?
16. Can the organization manage all the investment options?

Market Prospects

A basic consideration is the rate and pattern of decline. A precipitous decline should be distinguished from a slow, steady decline. One determining factor is the existence of pockets of enduring demand, segments that are capable of supporting a core demand level. The cigar industry decline has been slow and steady in part because the premium segment is stable and loyal. The vacuum-tube industry had replacement demand even after vacuum tubes had all but disappeared from new products. In the leather industry, leather upholstery is still a healthy market.

Another factor affecting the decline rate, particularly in dynamic industries, is product obsolescence. When disposable diapers were introduced, the sale of rubber panties for babies dramatically declined.

A related issue is the predictability of the pattern. If the pattern is based on demographics such as the size of the teen population, then it may be predictable. In contrast, fashion and technology can change quickly, and therefore predictions based on them are riskier. A slow decline may accelerate, or a declining market may suddenly be revived. For example, the natural food trend has revived oatmeal, and an inflation-stimulated price sensitivity at one point gave Kool-Aid a resurgence.

Competitive Intensity

A second consideration is the level of competitive intensity created by the industry structure. Are there one or more dominant competitors that have substantial shares and a set of unique assets and skills that form formidable sustainable competitive advantages? Is there a relatively large set of competitors that is not disposed either to exit or to contract gracefully? If the answer to either of these questions is yes, the profit prospects for others may be dismal.

One consideration is whether or not competitors agree about the decline of an industry. The competitors in the baby food industry in the 1960 to 1978 period simply did not believe that the rate would decline as much as it did (42 percent) or for as long as it did (20 years).[3] Overcapacity in the industry and substantial pressure on prices resulted.

Another perspective comes from customers. A key to making a profit in a declining industry is price stability. Are customers relatively price-insensitive, such as buyers of premium cigars or replacement vacuum tubes? Is there a relatively high level of product differentiation and brand loyalty? Or has the product become a commodity? Are there costs involved in switching from one brand to another?

Performance/Strengths

A business position appraisal should focus on business strengths and capabilities, as well as current performance. Sources of strength in a declining environment are usually quite different from those in other contexts. The strengths must reflect the reality that there are fewer products to make and fewer customers to serve. Thus, sources of strength such as economies of scale, vertical integration, and technological leadership may actually be liabilities. Helpful strengths in a declining industry are

- Strong established relationships with profitable customers, especially those in pockets of enduring demand.

- A strong brand name. At this stage it will be difficult for competitors to alter their images significantly. Thus, the nature of an established image can be most important.

- The ability to operate profitably with underutilized assets.

- The ability to reduce costs as business shrinks. Flexibility in applying assets and resources.

- A large market share if economies of scale are present.

An analysis of current profitability is important to the assessment of future position, but care is needed, especially if an exit decision is involved. Book assets, for example, may be overstated, because their market value may be small or even negative if they have associated obligations. Some overhead items that would have to be shifted to other businesses under an exit alternative might be properly omitted from some analyses.

Interrelationships with Other Businesses

Interrelationships between businesses should be considered in a firm's investment decision. A business may support other businesses within the firm by providing part of a system, by supporting a distribution channel, or by using excess plant capacity or a by-product of another production process. If the firm is vertically integrated, a decision to leave a particular business may affect the other components.

Visibly closing down a business may generate a credibility problem for the parent corporation, especially if a large write-off is involved. Closing down could affect access to financial markets and influence the opinion of dealers, suppliers, and customers about the firm's other operations. When Texas Instruments closed its digital watch and magnetic bubble memory groups—areas it had pioneered—shock waves were felt among customers, suppliers, and other stakeholders.

Implementation Barriers

Finally, the possible implementation problems associated with each option must be considered. Exit barriers affect the exit option. The milk option presents difficult management problems in that both the managers and customers involved will have to accept a disinvest context. The hold option is also a delicate issue, because a passive investment strategy can inadvertently lead to a loss of position.

HOSTILE MARKETS

Declining markets can create hostile markets, markets usually associated with overcapacity, low margins, intense competition, and management in turmoil. However, hostile markets can also occur in growth contexts if there is overcapacity caused by too many competitors. It is not an exaggeration to say that most industries are either in hostility or are in danger of becoming hostile. It is thus useful to take a close look at hostility. Fortunately, a major study is available to provide insights.

Windemere Associates, a management consulting firm, has systematically studied more than 40 hostile industries, and its findings are reported in two articles by Don Potter.[4] These reports suggest that hostility can be precipitated by competitors who are attracted to—and who tend to minimize the risks of—growth contexts in which margins and profits are high. Therefore, high prices and profits should be a cause for concern as well as celebration, and it might be worthwhile in the long run to forego them or to build other barriers in order to discourage competitors from entering the market.

A Hostile Industry—Six Phases

The Windemere study identified six phases of hostile markets (shown in Figure 14.4) that could span decades. Although they don't always occur in the order set forth, most do occur. An understanding of this six-phase life cycle can help firms prevent or manage hostile environments.

Phase 1—Margin Pressure. Predatory pricing to gain share, stimulated in part by overcapacity, leads to margin erosion; the prime beneficiaries

---

FIGURE 14.4 Six Phases of Hostility

Phase 1—Margin pressure
Phase 2—Share shifts
Phase 3—Product proliferation
Phase 4—Self-defeating cost reduction
Phase 5—Consolidation and shakeout
Phase 6—Rescue

are large customers. As a result, competitors attempt to create or find protected niches. However, others eventually will encroach on attractive niches. Note that efforts to isolate Japanese companies in the low end of copiers, cars, motorcycles, and semiconductors failed as they eventually moved their product lines up, attacking the high-margin niche markets.

Phase 2—Share Shifts. Each year, one to five percent of share in a hostile market will shift from one group of companies to another. One cause is a leader's trap, where a leading company, often the biggest and best firm, will not match discounting in its market, believing that a superior product and customer loyalty will support a large price premium. This strategy rarely works. The leader's prices eventually fall, but only after share (which is difficult to regain) is lost and customers have become convinced that the leader's prices before the adjustment were excessive. The experience of IBM and Compaq, who clung to high prices long after competitors such as Dell had established lower price points, is illustrative. Another cause of share shift is a flight to quality, where a company such as Federal Express simply delivers more reliability or has more accessible distribution. A third cause is acquisitions, which occur when competitors become desperate to achieve economies of scale.

Phase 3—Product Proliferation. Competitors compete for share by attempting to generate value for the customer through product proliferation. The product might be upgraded by bundling additional features or functions such as a suite hotel room, color-tinted cement, or not-from-concentrate orange juice. A soup company might add new lines such as low-sodium soups or new recipes. A bank might add new checking accounts with service variants. Others might unbundle and offer stripped versions of the product, such as Marriott's Fairfield Inn or Southwest Airlines. Product proliferation rarely results in winners but, rather, just raises the ante for all.

Phase 4—Self-Defeating Cost Reduction. A pressure to maintain margins leads to self-defeating cost reductions. A company intent on limiting investments may fail to match product and quality improvements of competitors, which can be costly in terms of share. For example, some organic-felt shingle roofing manufacturers were slow to invest in improved glass fiber shingles until a major share shift occurred. Even more serious is the failure to keep pace with rising industry quality standards. As General Motors, Schlitz, and many others have learned, it is hard to recover from a damaged reputation. Attempting to squeeze margins out of the distribution channel or sales force may provide illusory short-term savings at the expense of market position.

Phase 5—Consolidation and Shakeout. Consolidation, generally geared to reducing overhead, occurs in three waves. The first is internal and involves reducing the workforce, closing facilities, and pruning businesses. The second involves mergers and acquisitions, where stronger firms buy weaker ones in part to reduce overhead. The third is global in scope, with combinations of international players being formed, such as when Bridgestone bought Firestone Tires.

Phase 6—Rescue. Industries can emerge from hostility, some in as few as five years, but most after a decade or longer. One route is consolidation, where three or four key players control more than 80 percent of the market and all players have given up trying to win share through price competition. Procter & Gamble and Kimberly Clark have achieved such a consolidation in the disposable diaper market. However, it can take 15 to 20 years (as it did in appliances) for consolidation to play out. Industries may emerge from hostility more quickly if demand grows enough to soak up overcapacity. The necessary growth in demand may be fueled by expanded customer markets or shifts in the value of international currencies that stimulate export demand.

Strategies that Win in Hostile Markets

The Windemere study identifies two types of firms that have achieved above-average sales growth and profitability within the hostile industries. The first type, termed Gold competitors, holds the number 1 or 2 position and includes such firms as Federal Express, American Airlines, Alcoa Aluminum, Canon Copiers, Owens/Corning Fiberglass roofing, Yellow Freight trucking, and Paccar trucks. The second, termed Silver competitors, includes firms such as Airborne Express, Alaska Airlines, Pitney Bowes copiers, Tamko roofing, and Freightline trucks. Silver competitors are smaller and occupy number 3 slots or lower in sales.

An examination of how these two types of firms have succeeded in hostile conditions is illuminating. Their recipe for success has five basic ingredients.

Focus on Large Customers. Volume, which is crucial because it drives the cost structure, comes from a relatively small subset of customers. Gold competitors are the prime suppliers to the industry's largest customers, although they serve others as well. Their weapons are strong brand identity with end users and close relationships with the large-volume distribution channels. They adapt well to channel shifts. Owens/Corning Fiberglass, for example, added a strong retail marketing program to its wholesale distributions when retail channels became important. In industries without channels of distribution, Gold customers will attempt to create a large customer out of medium-sized firms. Federal Express, for example, created a "parts bank program," in which Federal Express maintained an inventory of parts for firms in order to expedite shipment.

Because Silver companies rarely possess the infrastructure to serve the largest customers as well as the Gold competitors, they focus instead on developing strong relationships with medium-sized customers. Freightline focuses on selling its trucks to small fleet owners, for example. These second-tier customers tend to emphasize good service and reasonable prices to their own end-user customers. Silvers can thus service their customers without sacrificing margins. To attract these customers, Silvers often adopt industry specialties. Ball, for example, has become the major supplier of wide-mouth jars to the food industry.

Differentiate on Reliability. The top firms tend to differentiate on intangibles such as reliability and a relationship of trust and confidence rather than on product features and attributes, which are easier to copy. The focus is on providing the end user with a product or service that works consistently and the channel member with efficient and reliable delivery.

Gold companies use widespread physical presence and advertising to create a large share of mind and a strong brand identity with end users. With channel customers, Golds reduce costs by investing in information technology.

Silvers offer service levels that are higher and more consistent than their rivals. Pitney Bowes guarantees a four-hour response time on a copier service call, for example. Silvers tend to have strong channels and often offer exclusivity of territories to protect them.

Cover Broad Spectrum of Price Points. Golds will offer a broad array of products covering the high, medium, and low ends of the market. They avoid leaving niches available to others and end up with a product mix that mirrors the market. Silvers will usually participate in the high-end market but will not feel constrained by a niche segment. Rather, they will introduce products that are responsive to their largest customers.

Turn Price into a Commodity. In the early stages of hostility, price differences can be as large as 10 to 15 percent. However, price differentials eventually converge to within 5 percent and become less important. Golds such as Federal Express in air express, Roadway in the less-than-truckload trucking, and IBM in personal computers drop their price umbrella so that smaller competitors can grow and price "at the market." They basically match the price of peers, thereby removing price from the customers' buying criteria. Their superior performance is rewarded by customer loyalty rather than premium prices. Silvers gain share initially by discounting, but eventually their discount level is reduced and their focus shifts to delivering superior performance for key customers.

Have an Effective Cost Structure. The most successful companies in hostile markets have an effective cost structure. Golds such as Gallo in table wine and John Deere in farm equipment achieve high productivity not only by exploiting economies of scale but also by investing in automation and information systems to reduce costs. Silvers target the high end of the market where returns are better and focus intently on key customers. They are also customer-focused in their R&D, and they stretch their marketing budgets by concentrating on existing customers and avoiding advertising directed at gaining new customers.

Golds Versus Silvers. In summary, the companies that outperform others in hostile industies tend to focus attention on large customers, differentiate on reliability, cover a wide spectrum of price points, turn price into a commodity, and have effective cost structures. However, the Golds compete very differently from the Silvers. Golds enjoy significant economies of scale, have a broad presence in share of shelf and share of mind, and offer efficiencies to channel partners. Silver firms are smaller, offer above-standard service, compete at higher price points, protect the margins of their channel partners, and focus on low unit cost with key customers.

SUMMARY

One strategic option in a declining or stagnant industry is to create a growth context by revitalizing an industry. Such efforts can involve new markets, technologies that obsolete existing products, new applications, revitalized marketing, government-stimulated demand, and growth submarkets. A second option is to be the profitable survivor by strengthening a leadership position and encouraging others to exit, perhaps by buying their assets.

A milk or harvest strategy aims to generate cash flow by reducing investment and operating expenses, even if that causes a reduction in sales and market share. The underlying assumptions are that the firm has better uses for the funds, that the involved business is not crucial to the firm either financially or synergistically, and that milking is feasible because sales will decline in an orderly way. The exit alternative is often inhibited by exit barriers such as commitments to customers and specialized assets.

The investment decision in declining markets should rely on an analysis of market prospects, competitive intensity, business strengths, interrelationships with other businesses in the firm, and implementation barriers. The strategic questions in Figure 14.3 summarize the decision process. Hostile markets are caused by too many competitors as well as declining demand. Hostile markets typically go through phases—margin pressures, share shifts, product proliferation, self-defeating cost reductions, consolidation, and rescue. Two strategies to gain above-average returns are represented by Golds, number 1 or 2 firms with economies of scale and substantial presence, and by Silvers, number 3 or lower firms, that focus on a smaller segment, usually at the high end of the market.

FOOTNOTES

[1] Some excellent research has been done on strategy development in declining industries, on which the balance of this chapter draws. It has been reported in Michael E. Porter, *Competitive Strategy*, New York: The Free Press, 1980, Chapter 8; Kathryn Rudie Harrigan, *Strategies for Declining Businesses*, Lexington, Mass.: Lexington Books, 1980; and Kathryn Rudie Harrigan and Michael E. Porter, "End-Game Stategies for Declining Industries, "*Harvard Business Review*, July–August 1983, pp. 111–120.

[2] Milton Moskowitz, "Last Days of Chase & Sanborn," *San Francisco Chronicle*, February, 22, 1982, p. 56.

[3] Kathryn Rudie Harrigan, *Strategies for Declining Businesses*, Lexington, Mass.: Lexington Books, 1980, p. 153.

[4] Donald V. Potter, "Success Under Fire: Policies to Prosper in Hostile Times," *California Management Review*, Winter 1991, pp. 24–38; Donald V. Potter, "Strategies that Win in Hostile Markets, *California Managment Review*, Fall 1994.

15

GLOBAL STRATEGIES

Most managers are nearsighted. Even though today's competitive landscape often stretches to a global horizon, they see best what they know best: the customers geographically closest to home.

Kenichi Ohmae

A powerful force drives the world toward a converging commonality, and that force is technology. . . . The result is a new commercial reality—the emergence of global markets for standardized consumer products on a previously unimagined scale of magnitude.

Theodore Levitt

My ventures are not in one bottom trusted, nor to one place.

William Shakespeare, The Merchant of Venice

Many firms find it necessary to develop global strategies in order to compete effectively. A global strategy is different from a multidomestic or multinational strategy in which separate strategies are developed for different countries and implemented autonomously. Thus, a retailer might develop different store groups, in several countries, that are not linked and that operate autonomously. A multidomestic operation is usually best managed as a portfolio of independent businesses where separate investment decisions are made for each country.

A global strategy, in contrast, is conceived and implemented in a worldwide setting and involves the following decisions:

1. In which countries should products be marketed and at what market-share level in each?
2. To what extent should products and services be standardized across countries?
3. Where should the value-added activities such as research, production, and service be located?
4. To what extent should the brand name and marketing activities such as brand position, advertising, and pricing be standardized across countries?
5. Should competitive moves in individual countries be part of a global strategy and, if so, what should that strategy be?

A global strategy can result in strategic advantage or neutralization of a competitor's advantage. For example, products or marketing programs developed in one market might be used in another. Or a cost advantage may result from scale economies generated by the global market or from access to low-cost labor or materials. Operating in various countries can lead to enhanced flexibility as well as meaningful sustainable competitive advantages (SCAs). Investment and operations can be shifted to respond to trends and developments emerging throughout the world or to counter competitors that are similarly structured. Plants can be located in order to gain access to markets by bypassing trade barriers.

Even if a global strategy is not appropriate for a business, making the external analysis global may still be useful. A knowledge of competitors, markets, and trends from other countries may help a business identify important opportunities, threats, and strategic questions. A global external analysis is more difficult, of course, because of the different cultures, political risks, and economic systems involved.

The motivations for global strategies are presented next, followed by discussions of the standardization versus customization issue and the use of alliances in developing global strategies.

MOTIVATIONS UNDERLYING GLOBAL STRATEGIES

A global strategy can result from several motivations in addition to simply wanting to invest in attractive foreign markets. The diagram of these motivations shown in Figure 15.1 provides a summary of the scope and character of global strategies.

Obtaining Scale Economies

An analysis of three British industries in the 1970s showed the power of scale economies resulting from a global perspective.[2] The British firms—British Leyland in automobiles, ICL in computers, and Ferranti in semiconductors—all had dominant positions in the British market, at times about twice that of their U.S. competitors—Ford, IBM, and Texas Instruments. The U.S. firms operated globally, however, and, unlike the British firms, had only a small percentage of their sales in England but substantially larger shares in Europe. As a result, the U.S. firms far exceeded their British competitors in terms of performance as measured by ROI.

Scale economies can occur from product standardization. The Ford world-car concept, for example, allows product design, tooling, parts production, and product testing to be spread over a much larger sales base. However, standardization of the development and execution of a marketing program can also be an important source of scale economies. Consider Coca-Cola, which since the 1950s has employed a marketing strategy—the brand name, concentrate formula, positioning, and advertis-

FIGURE 15.1 Motivations for Global Strategies

ing theme—that has been virtually the same throughout the world.[3] Only the artificial sweetener and packaging differ across countries. McCann-Erickson claims to have saved $90 million in advertising production costs over 20 years by producing worldwide Coca-Cola campaigns such as "It's the real thing" and "Can't beat the feeling."

Several influential observers have suggested that the SCAs emerging from worldwide scale economies are becoming more important and that in many industries they are becoming a necessary aspect of competition. Theodore Levitt, in a visible article on the globalization of markets, posits that worldwide communications have caused demand and fashion patterns to be similar across the world, even in less developed countries.[4] Kenichi Ohmae, longtime head of McKinsey in Japan, cites a litany of products that are virtually identical in Japan, Europe, and the United States, including Nike footwear, Pampers diapers, Band-Aid bandages, Cheer detergent, Nestlé coffee, Kodak film, Revlon cosmetics, and Contac paper.[5] He notes that people from different countries, from youths to businesspeople, wear the same fashions.

Ohmae also suggests that the long-accepted waterfall model of international trade is now obsolete.[6] In the waterfall model, a firm first establishes itself in a domestic market. It then penetrates the markets of other advanced countries before moving into less developed countries. The experience of Honda in motorcycles is representative. After creating a dominant position in Japan with considerable scale economies, it entered the U.S. market by convincing people that it was "fun" to ride its small, simple motorcycle and by investing in a 2,000-dealer network. With its scale economies thus increased, Honda expanded its line to include larger cycles and then moved into the European market.

The new model, according to Ohmae, is that of a "sprinkler," where a product is exposed all over the globe at once. He points to products such as the Sony Walkman, Canon's AE-1, and the Minolta A-7000, which exploded onto the worldwide market in a matter of months. The Walkman actually first took off in California. Under the sprinkler model, a firm introducing a new product doesn't have time to develop a presence and distribution channel in a foreign market. Instead, it forms a consortium with other firms that have already established distribution in other countries. This allows the new product to go global immediately. The resulting economies of scale can allow lower prices, often a key to creating markets and a barrier to competitors.

In order to achieve maximum scale economies, a manufacturer would need to make all units in its home country. Yet, for many reasons, companies spread component production and final assembly throughout the world. Matsushita, which has 150 plants in 38 countries, has developed "export centers" as a way to gain the advantages of politically hospitable, low-cost host countries close to regional markets that will support substantial economies of scale.[7] The export center does more than simply manufacture a product. It controls the product from the drawing board to the loading dock. The Malaysian export center, one of the first, produces one quarter of Matsushita's air conditioner and TV volume.

Desirable Global Brand Associations

Brand names linked to global strategies can have useful associations. For customers and competitors, a global presence automatically symbolizes strength, staying power, and the ability to generate competitive products. Such an image can be particularly important to buyers of expensive industrial products or consumer durables such as cars or computers because it can lessen concern that the products may be unreliable or rendered obsolete by technological advances. Japanese firms such as Yamaha, Sony, Canon, and Honda operate in markets where technology and product quality are important, and they have benefited from a global brand association.

Access to Low-Cost Labor or Materials

Another motivation for a global strategy is the cost reduction that results from access to the resources of many countries. Substantial cost differences can arise with respect to raw materials, R&D talent, assembly labor, and component supply. Thus, a computer manufacturer may purchase components from Korea and Singapore, obtain raw materials from South America, and assemble in Mexico and five other countries throughout the world in order to reduce labor and transportation costs. Access to low-cost labor and materials can be an SCA, especially when it is accompanied by the skill and flexibility to change when one supply is threatened or a more attractive alternative emerges.

Access to National Investment Incentives

Another way to obtain a cost advantage is to access national investment incentives which countries use to achieve economic objectives for target industries or depressed areas. Unlike other means to achieve changes in trade, such as tariffs and quotas, incentives are much less visible and objectionable to trading partners. Thus, the British government has offered Japanese car manufacturers a cash bonus to locate a plant in Britain. Ireland, Brazil, and a host of other governments offer cash, tax breaks, land, and buildings to entice factories to locate in their particular country.

Cross-Subsidization

A global presence allows a firm to cross-subsidize, to use the resources accumulated in one part of the world to fight a competitive battle in another.[8] Consider the following: One firm uses the cash flow generated in its home market to attack a domestically oriented competitor. For example, in the early 1970s Michelin used its European home profit base to attack Goodyear's U.S. market. The defensive competitor (i.e., Goodyear) can reduce prices or increase advertising in the United States to counter, but by doing so, it will sacrifice margins in its largest markets. An alternative is to attack the aggressor in its home market where it has the most to lose. Thus, Goodyear carried the fight to Europe to put a dent in Michelin's profit base.

The cross-subsidization concept leads to two strategic considerations:[9]

- To influence an existing or potential foreign competitor, it is useful to maintain a presence in its country. The presence should be large enough to make the threat of retaliation meaningful. If the share is only 2 percent or so, the competitor may be willing to ignore it.

- A home market may be vulnerable even if a firm apparently controls it with a large market share. A high market share, especially if it is used to support high prices and profits, can attract foreign firms that realize the domestic firm has little freedom for retaliation. A major reason for the demise of the U.S. consumer electronics industry was that American firms were placed at a substantial disadvantage compared with global competitors that had the option to cross-subsidize.

Dodge Trade Barriers

Strategic location of component and assembly plants can help gain access to markets by penetrating trade barriers and fostering goodwill. Peugeot, for example, has plants in 26 countries from Argentina to Zimbabwe. Locating final assembly plants in a host country is a good way to achieve favorable trade treatment and goodwill because it provides a visible presence and generates savings in transportation and storage of the final product. Thus, Caterpillar operates assembly plants in each of its major markets, including Europe, Japan, Brazil, and Australia, in part to bypass trade barriers. An important element of the Toyota strategy is to source a significant portion of its car cost in the United States and Europe to deflect sentiment against foreign domination.

Access to Strategically Important Markets

Some markets are strategically important because of their market size or potential or because of their raw material supply, labor cost structure, or technology. It can be important to have a presence in these markets even if such a presence is not profitable. Because of its size, the U.S. market is critical to those industries in which scale economies are important, such as automobiles or consumer electronics.

Sometimes a country is important because it is the locus of new trends and developments in an industry. A firm in the fashion industry may benefit from a presence in countries that have historically led the way in fashion. Or a high-tech firm may want to have operations in a country that is in the forefront of the relevant field. For example, an electronics firm without a Silicon Valley presence will find it difficult to keep abreast of technology developments and competitor strategies. Sometimes adequate information can be obtained by observers, but those with design and manufacturing groups on location will tend to have a more intimate knowledge of trends and events.

STANDARDIZATION VERSUS CUSTOMIZATION

A key issue in the development of a global strategy is the extent to which the strategy, particularly the marketing strategy, will be standardized across countries. The prime motivation for standardization is economies. The more standardization, the more potential there is for scale economies. The vision of a single global product sharing not only R&D and manufacturing but also a common name, position, package, and advertising drives some people's version of the ultimate global strategy. The assumption is that it will lead to decisive efficiencies and scale economies because the cost of developing product and marketing programs will be spread over a larger sales base.

A second motivation for globalization is to create impact for the marketing program outside the main country through media spillover and international customer travel. Brand awareness, and awareness of packaging and visual imagery in particular, can benefit from the exposure of a brand in a different country when customers travel between countries. When media coverage overlaps regions, a global brand can buy exposures much more efficiently. As the European common market matures, there is likely to be more and more media overlap and customer crossover and thus more payoff for a global brand strategy.

A third motivation for a standardized global marketing strategy is the associations that can result. The image of a global player such as that achieved by IBM, Ford, and Canon can provide prestige and reassurance to customers. In other contexts, a "home" country association can be the essence of a brand's positioning. For example, Levi's are U.S. jeans, Chanel is French perfume, Dewar's is Scotch whiskey, Kikkoman is Japanese soy sauce, and Bertolli is Italian olive oil. In each case, the brand is established

Parker Pen: A Global Strategy that Failed

In 1985, Parker Pen launched a global business strategy to combat Cross from above and the Japanese from below.[10] The centerpiece of the strategy was a rolled-ball pen called the Victor. Victor was to be priced throughout the world at a low (for Parker) $2.98 and made at a new automated production facility for $0.29. The common advertising campaign used the theme, "It's wrought from pure silver and writes like pure silk," and the slogan, "Make your mark with a Parker." The effort was a disaster. In many of Parker's 150 markets, local units resisted pressures to adopt the product. A Parker executive was quoted as shouting at a meeting of the London agency branch, "Yours is not to reason why; yours is to implement."

The common pricing was one problem, especially for the countries which had established a position either above or below the new price. The selected name did not have relevant associations in all countries. The advertising and resulting associations were judged by many to be bland and ineffective. Furthermore, there were manufacturing problems which affected Parker's ability to deliver its product.

Among the casualties of the global branding strategy were some effective local branding efforts. For example, an offbeat English advertising agency, one of 40 agencies used by Parker prior to globalization, had developed a particularly successful campaign. It associated the brand with people who had the élan to deliver a well-crafted insult written with a Parker. One such insult was a note to an airline reading, "You had delusions of adequacy?" The campaign's humor was very British and would not have worked elsewhere.

in its home country and the country itself is central to the image of the brand. In such a context, a standardized strategy may pay off. Figure 15.2 summarizes the advantages of standardization.

The reality is that a standardized global product and marketing effort is not always desirable or even possible. In general, each element of a marketing program needs to be analyzed to determine whether or not the advantages of standardization outweigh the effectiveness of tailoring the program to local markets. There are times when standardization is not the answer, and it makes sense to tailor the product and marketing program to a particular country.

The Customization Option

Achieving standardization in some aspects of a strategy can be difficult because of differences between countries and little potential for scale economies. For example, Kentucky Fried Chicken has been successful in Japan, but only after the firm realized that the U.S. model of free-standing units would not work in land-scarce Japanese cities. It also changed its

FIGURE 15.2 Marketing Strategy—Customization Versus Standardization

Standardization Provides	Customization Provides
• Scale economies in the development of advertising, packaging, promotion, etc.	• Names, associations, and advertising that can be • developed locally • tailored to local market • selected without the constraints of standardization
• Exploitation of • media overlap • exposure to customers who travel	
• Associations • of a global presence • of the "home" country	• Reduced risk from "buy local" sentiments

menu (fries replaced mashed potatoes, and slaw became less sweet), and adopted Japanese training methods. Insisting on a U.S. clone in Japan would have saved little money and guaranteed failure.

Distribution and personal selling are two elements that usually need to be adapted to the realities of a country. Hitotsubashi University's Hiro Takeuchi and Harvard's Michael Porter studied 7 major Japanese firms and 46 different product categories. Their research revealed that while brand name and advertising were often the same across countries, distribution and sales organizations tended not to be standardized—there were simply too few economies of scale involved, and there was often a substantial fit problem.[11]

Recognizing the need to customize distribution can be a key to success. Firms willing to make an investment and commitment to a different distribution/selling system in Japan, for example, have been able to attack or create competitive barriers. Coca-Cola developed an in-house delivery system that has become an important advantage, leading to its domination of the Japanese soft-drink market. Kodak in 1985 broke the Fuji lock on the Japanese market only when it built its own distribution network. The Kodak approach not only gave the firm access to markets but also direct contact with customers, providing better information on customer needs.

A product often needs to be adapted to the local market.[12] As Matsushita's marketing specialist for microwave ovens observed, "British people like crispy fat on top of meat, so you need a strong heating element in their ovens. Germans like their potatoes overcooked, but the British like them almost crunchy, so you have to design the cooking controls differently."

Even the use of a common brand name is not always desirable or even feasible. Some names with useful associations in one language will have a damaging meaning in other countries. For example, the Ford "Fiera" truck means "ugly old woman" in Spanish. Often a brand name will be unavailable in some countries. P&G's Pert Plus, the very successful combination shampoo and conditioner, is sold as Rejoy in Japan, Rejoice in much of the Far East, and Vidal Sassoon in the United Kingdom because the Pert Plus name (or something similar) has been preempted. The Budweiser name is not available to Anheuser-Busch in most of Europe because the name is owned by a small Czechoslovakian brewery.

A local association can be a useful point of differentiation and a basis for customer loyalty. A local brand—whether it is BellSouth telecommunications, Lone Star beer, a Catalan yogurt, a Japanese rice, a Malaysian appliance, or a French wine—can stimulate pride and a connection with local traditions or characteristics. Further, a global brand can have negative associations locally if it has an undesirable meaning in some countries or if it is tied to a country's politics and thus is subject to the ups and downs of international events.

A worldwide advertising theme may simply not be appropriate in some countries because of the competitive context. A British Airways globalization effort involved the centralization of advertising, which resulted in the "world's favorite airline" theme. It featured a 90-second commercial that showed the Manhattan skyline rotating slowly through the sky. Even in the United States, where the campaign originated, managers wondered if the replaced campaign (which emphasized traditional British values with the theme "we'll take good care of you") was not more effective. In countries where British Air was an also-ran, the claim

---

Indicators That Strategies Should Be Global

- Major competitors in important markets are not domestic and have a presence in several countries.
- Standardization of some elements of the product or marketing strategy provides opportunities for scale economies.
- Costs can be reduced and effectiveness increased by locating value-added activities in different countries.
- Competitors have the potential to use the volume and profits from one market to subsidize gaining a position in another.
- Trade barriers inhibit access to worthwhile markets.
- A global name can be an advantage and the name is available worldwide.
- A brand position and its supporting advertising will work across countries and has not been preempted.
- Local markets do not require products or service for which a local operation would have an advantage.

did not make much sense. Furthermore, there were operational problems. For example, 90-second ads could not be used in South Africa.

A decentralized approach to the development of marketing programs can generate a product or advertising campaign that can be used globally. Levi Strauss got its successful Dockers pants from a product development effort in its Brazilian operation. When Polaroid was repositioning from a "party camera" platform to a more serious, utilitarian one, a campaign that was developed in Switzerland was the most effective.[13] It promoted the functional use of instant photography as a way to communicate with family and friends—the "learn to speak Polaroid" campaign. If local units had not been free to generate their own campaigns, this superior campaign would not have surfaced.

The Costs of Creating a "Global Brand"

When a new product is developed, most firms will attempt to make it a global product with a common name and position. The pressure for standardization is particularly strong in Europe, where there is now considerable media overlap and fewer distinct distribution systems. However, a more difficult issue is whether or not to create a global brand when regional brands are in place.

When a brand is already established in a country, for example, it has an equity based on its awareness level and a set of associations that are often very valuable. Changing the name and/or position in order to simply conform to a standardized global brand may be extremely costly. The effort to change the Datsun name to the global brand Nissan in the United States in the early 1980s probably cost more than $1 billion.[14] As part of the effort, the effective "Datsun, we are driven" campaign was replaced with the expensive but punchless "the name is Nissan." Five years after the name change, the Datsun name was still as strong as the Nissan name.

A new name also kills any associations that the old name might have developed. The VW Rabbit attempted to recapture some of the funkiness and magic of the manufacturer's earlier Beetle by using imagery associated with the rabbit symbol. Although the Rabbit was a poor substitute for the Beetle for many reasons, it did develop some positive associations. It was later replaced with the global brand name, Golf, which was worse with respect to associations. Heinz does not put its name on the products it acquires outside the United States because it wants to retain their associations.

If an existing name has weak associations, of course, it has little to lose by changing. In the late 1980s in the U.S. market, Mars successfully changed the name of its Kal Kan dog food to "Pedigree" and its Kal Kan cat food to "Whiskas" to create worldwide names.[15] In contrast to Kal Kan, which was mainly associated with cans, the name Pedigree was associated with a quality, expensive pet that would only be served the best food, and the name Whiskas was feline-sounding and likable.

Some brands are positioned quite differently in different countries. For example, both Heinz baby food and Levi's jeans have a strong value position in the United States and a premium position in other markets. Clearly, it would be foolish to force a common position on such brands in order to achieve a standardized global brand.

The rush to standardized global branding is somewhat ironic as there is also a strong move to regional marketing in the United States. Firms like P&G, Campbell Soup, and others are giving local marketing units responsibility for sales promotions and advertising that have previously been centralized.

Creating a Standardized Offering—The Lead Country

Once the standardization route has been chosen, an implementation question arises. How should the standardization strategy be developed? One approach is to create a global product. Canon, for example, developed a copier that had a common design throughout the world in order to maximize production economies. Unfortunately, the copier could not use the standard paper size in Japan, creating substantial customer inconvenience. The problem with a truly global standardization objective is the risk that the result will be a compromise. A product and marketing program that almost fits most markets will not be exactly what is needed anywhere. Such a result is a recipe for failure or mediocrity.

Another strategy is to identify a lead country, a country with a market that is attractive because it is large or growing or because the brand has a natural advantage there. A product is tailored to that market so its chances of success in that country are maximized. It is then "exported" to other markets, perhaps with minor modifications or refinements. A firm may have several lead countries, each with its own product. The result is a stable of global brands, with each brand based in its own "home" country.

Nissan, for example, designs cars for the United States, Japan, or Europe, as opposed to designing world cars.[16] The firm has developed a corporate fleet car for the United Kingdom and a sporty "Z" model and four-wheel drive family vehicle for the United States. Once a lead-country model is developed, it can then be offered to managers in other countries. Thus, the Z model may be offered to Japan because it appeals to a small segment there. In fact, Nissan sells about 5000 Z models monthly in the United States and about 500 in Japan.

Implementing Global Strategies Involving Standardization

Implementing global strategies can be especially difficult when they focus on the standardization of some element of a product line or marketing program. Inevitably, foreign operations lose autonomy and two problems emerge. First, the ability of foreign managers to fine-tune strategies to their country is reduced. Second, a motivation problem arises. A talented and creative French advertising manager may not enjoy becoming simply the translator of a home-office advertising campaign, and a local business strategist may not readily accept a strategy developed elsewhere. A variety of approaches to deal with these problems have been tried.

Centralizing Decision Making. One approach is simply to centralize decision making and forcefully require standardization. A risk is the resulting temptation to avoid change or deviations in order to preserve scale economies. The case of Lego Toys illustrates this problem.[17] A Japanese competitor, Tyco, started successfully selling its toys in plastic buckets that could be used for storage after play. A suggestion by Lego's U.S. management that a similar package be sold by Lego was rejected, in part because the bucket did not seem compatible with the Lego image but also because it was a departure from the worldwide standardization policy that had been so successful. The Danish headquarters changed its mind two years later, but only after severe damage had occurred in the U.S. market.

The International Brand Company. IDV, a division of Grand Metropolitan, has developed its own international brand company (IBC) for its key international spirit brands, Smirnoff, Bailey's, and J&B. The IBC is charged with building and maintaining brand equity and encouraging standardization wherever possible. Strategic branding, positioning, and pricing decisions are controlled by the IBC. Each major country or region has a national marketing corporation (NMC) as a separate organization charged with implementing the strategies of the IBCs and the other IDV brands within that geographic area. The NMCs adapt the brand strategy to the country and coordinate the marketing of all the brands within the country, creating synergies wherever possible. There is a healthy tension between the IBCs and the NMCs.

Selective Standardization. Another approach is to centralize some elements of a strategy but leave others under the control of country managers—those who are most skillful at tailoring the strategy to local conditions. Timken believed that reinforcement of its technology position was going to be critical in the emerging global market.[18] Thus, it integrated its international research effort but decentralized manufacturing and other functions. Similarly, Corning centralized the pricing function for its TV tube but left other strategy elements to foreign managers.

Using Communication and Persuasion. The least disruptive way to create a change toward global thinking is by communication and persuasion.[19] Nestlé, a firm with a tradition of active autonomous subsidiaries, publishes a quarterly marketing newsletter that reports innovations in marketing programs and the results of new product introductions. Johnson's Wax holds meetings of all marketing directors twice a year to encourage global thinking and idea sharing. Systematically transferring people from line to staff positions can also help build a global thrust. Unilever employs high-caliber advertising and marketing staffs that become involved in subsidiaries' marketing programs by reviewing strategies, coaching managers, and making substantive suggestions. They frequently visit the field to discuss new concepts and deal with local problems.

Team Management. Procter & Gamble, in an attempt to move away from highly autonomous subsidiaries, launched the "Pampers experiment," in which a European manager developed a Pampers strategy for the whole continent.[20] The approach, designed to eliminate the diversity in brand strategy, failed because it ignored local knowledge, underutilized subsidiary strengths, and demotivated country managers to the point where they felt no sales responsibility. The replacement strategy was the creation of "Eurobrand" teams, management teams of product people from each country headed by a person from the "lead subsidiary" with the highest level of success and creativity with respect to the brand. The team approach, which successfully launched Vizir, a new liquid detergent, provided motivation, communication, and coordination.

STRATEGIC ALLIANCES

Strategic alliances play an important role in global strategies because it is common for a firm to lack a key success factor for some market. It may be distribution, a brand name, a sales organization, technology, R&D capability, or manufacturing capability. To remedy this deficiency internally might require excessive time and money. When the uncertainties of operating in other countries are considered, a strategic alliance is a natural alternative for reducing investment and the accompanying inflexibility and risk.

For example, IBM, which has relatively few alliances in the United States, has teamed up with just about everyone possible in Japan.[21] It has links with Ricoh in distribution of low-end computers, with Nippon Steel in systems integration, with Fuji Bank in financial systems marketing, with OMRON in CIM, and with NTT in value-added networks. There is even a book in Japanese entitled *IBM's Alliance Strategy in Japan*. As a result, IBM is considered a major insider in the Japanese market, and it competes across the board in all segments and applications.

Strategic alliance is thus becoming a key part of global competition. In fact, Kenichi Ohmae has said that

> Globalization mandates alliances, makes them absolutely essential to strategy. Uncomfortable, perhaps—but that's the way it is. Like it or not, the simultaneous developments that go under the name of globalization make alliances—entente—necessary.[22]

A strategic alliance is a collaboration leveraging the strengths of two or more organizations to achieve strategic goals. There is a long-term commitment involved. It is not simply a tactical device to provide a short-term fix for a problem—to outsource a component for which a temporary manufacturing problem has surfaced, for example. Furthermore, it implies that the participating organizations will contribute and adapt a needed asset or skill to the collaboration and that these assets or skills will be maintained over time. The results of the collaboration should have strategic value and contribute to a viable venture that can withstand competitive attack and environmental change.

A strategic alliance provides the potential for accomplishing a strategic objective or task—such as obtaining distribution in Italy—quickly, inexpensively, and with a relatively high prospect for success. This is possible because the involved firms can combine existing assets and skills instead of having to create new assets and skills internally.

Forms of Strategic Alliances

A strategic alliance can take many forms, from a loose informal agreement to a formal joint venture. The most informal arrangement might be simply trying to work together (selling our products through your channel, for example) and allowing systems and organization forms to emerge as the alliance develops. The more informal the arrangement, the faster it can be implemented and the more flexible it will be. As conditions and people change, the alliance can be adjusted. The problem is usually commitment. With low exit barriers and commitment, there may be a low level of strategic importance and a temptation to back away or to disengage when difficulties arise.

A formal joint venture involving equity and a comprehensive legal document, on the other hand, has very different risks. When equity sharing is involved, there is often worry about control, return on investment, and achieving a fair percentage of the venture. A major concern is whether or not such a permanent arrangement will be equitable in the face of uncertainty about the relative contributions of the partners and the eventual success of the endeavor. Also, a risk of the required commitment is that the firms involved may tend to drag their heels and the venture may lose a window of opportunity. Another concern is that equity positions and the accompanying limits on each partner's contribution can result in a lack of needed flexibility as conditions change. Furthermore, the parties involved may rely excessively on legal documents to preserve the health of the alliance.

Motivations for Strategic Alliances

Strategic alliances can be motivated by a desire to achieve some of the benefits of a global strategy, as outlined in Figure 15.1. For example, a strategic alliance can

- *Generate scale economies.* The fixed investment that Toyota made in designing a car and its production system is now spread over more units because of a joint venture with GM in California.
- *Gain access to strategic markets.* A Japanese firm such as JVC can provide VCR design and manufacturing capability but needs a relationship with Thompson to obtain help in accessing the fragmented European market.
- *Overcome trade barriers.* Inland Steel and Nippon Steel jointly built an advanced cold steel mill in Indiana. Nippon supplied the technology, capital, and access to Japanese auto plants in the United States. In return, it gained local knowledge and, more important, the ability to get around import quotas.

Perhaps more commonly, a strategic alliance may be needed to compensate for the absence of or weakness in a needed asset or skill. Thus, a strategic alliance can

- *Fill out a product line to serve market niches.* Ford, for example, has relied on alliances to provide key components of its product line.[23] Its long-time relationship with Mazda has resulted in many Ford models, as well as access to some Far East markets. More recently, when Mazda decided not to build a minivan, Ford turned to Nissan for help. One firm simply cannot provide the breadth of models needed in a major market such as the United States.
- *Gain access to a needed technology.* While JVC gained access to the European market, its European partner accessed a competitive VCR source.

- *Use excess capacity.* The GM/Toyota joint venture used an idle GM California plant.

- *Gain access to low-cost manufacturing capabilities.* GE sources its microwave ovens from Samsung in Korea.

- *Access a name or customer relationship.* NGK bought an interest in a GE subsidiary whose product line had become obsolete in order to access the GE name and reputation in the U.S. electrical equipment market. A U.S. injection molder joined with Mitsui in order to help access Japanese manufacturing operations in the United States that preferred to do business with Japanese suppliers.[24]

- *Reduce the investment required.* In some cases, a firm's contribution to a joint venture can be technology, with no financial resources required.

The Key—Maintaining Strategic Value for Collaborators

A major problem with strategic alliances occurs when the relative contribution of the partners becomes unbalanced over time and one partner no longer has any proprietary assets and skills to contribute. This has happened in many of the partnerships involving U.S. and Japanese firms in consumer electronics, heavy machinery, power generation equipment, factory equipment, and office equipment.[25]

The result, where the U.S. company becomes "deskilled" or "hollowed-out" and no longer participates fully in the venture, can be traced in part to the motivation of the partners. Japanese firms are motivated to learn skills; they are embarrassed when they lack a technology and they work to correct deficiencies. U.S. firms are motivated to make money by outsourcing elements of the value chain in order to reduce costs. They start by outsourcing assembly and move on to components, to value-added components, to product design, and finally to core technologies. The U.S. partner is then left with just the distribution function, whereas the Japanese firm retains the key business components such as product refinement, design, and production.

Hammel et al. studied 15 strategic alliances and offered suggestions as to how a firm might protect its assets and skills from its alliance partner.[26] One approach is to structure the situation so that learning takes place and access to missing skills and assets occurs. Compare, for example, the joint Toyota/GM manufacturing facility, where GM is involved in the manufacturing process and its refinements, to Chrysler's effort to sell a Mitsubishi car designed and manufactured in Japan. In the latter case, Mitsubishi eventually developed its own name and dealer network and now sells its car directly. When the motivation for an alliance is to avoid investment and achieve attractive short-term returns instead of developing assets and skills, the alliance will break down.

Another approach is to protect assets from a partner by controlling access. Many Japanese firms have a coordinated information transfer. Such a position avoids uncoordinated, inappropriate information flow. Other firms clearly limit access to a part of the product line or a part of the design. Motorola, for example, releases its microchip technology to its partner, Toshiba, only as Toshiba delivers on its promise to increase Motorola's penetration in the Japanese market. Still others keep improving the asset involved so that the partner's dependence continues. Of course, the problem of protecting assets is most difficult when the asset can be communicated by a drawing. It is somewhat easier when a complex system is involved—when, for example, the asset is manufacturing excellence.

The problem of protection is reduced substantially when the two partners bring complementary assets into the alliance that are core competencies of each and are the bases of other business areas. Thus, the danger that one will wither is low. Clintee International, formed in 1989 as a joint venture between Baxter, a healthcare giant, and Nestlé, the food and nutrition products firm, was realizing more than $400 million in sales just three years later. Baxter was strong in the parenterals business, which included products that delivered nutrition intravenously or through a catheter, and it had experience with medical markets, mainly in the United States. Nestlé had a strong background in basic nutrition, a growing interest in adult nutrition products, a strong R&D capability, and a presence in world markets. Neither firm was likely to see its core strengths dissipated in the context of the joint venture.

Making Strategic Alliances Work

Even if an alliance is strategically sound, a host of operational problems can arise. One study of 37 joint ventures uncovered a variety of management problems.[27] In one case, the partners differed in terms of priorities for short-term versus long-term objectives. In another, a British firm could not understand a U.S. partner's obsession with numbers and analysis. In still another, a sensitive decision about the location of a new plant became political.

With strategic alliances, at least two sets of business systems, people, cultures, and structures need to be reconciled. In addition, the culture and environment of each country must be considered. The Japanese, for example, tend to use a consensus-building decision process that relies on small group activity for much of its energy; this approach is very different from that of managers in the United States and Europe. Furthermore, the interests of each partner may not always seem to be in step. Many otherwise well-conceived alliances have failed because the partners simply had styles and objectives that were fundamentally incompatible.

There are several keys to making a collaboration work. Perhaps the most important is that it be well planned to provide ongoing mutual benefit. Partners should make sure they have real assets and skills that combine to provide strategic advantage. These assets and skills should continue to be relevant to the venture and to be maintained by the partners over time. If there is a significant ongoing strategic motivation reinforced by success, problems are more likely to be manageable.

When a joint venture is established as a separate organization, research has shown that the chances of success will be enhanced if

- The joint venture is allowed to evolve with its own culture and values— the existing cultures of the partners will probably not work even if they are compatible with each other.

- The management and power structure from the two partners is balanced.

- "Venture champions" are on board to carry the ball during difficult times. Without people committed to making the venture happen, it will not happen.

- Methods are developed to resolve problems and to allow change over time. It is unrealistic to expect any strategy, organization, or implementation to exist without evolving and changing. Partners and the organization thus need to be flexible enough to allow change to occur.

SUMMARY

A global strategy considers and exploits interdependencies between operations in different countries. One of the driving forces behind globalization is obtaining scale economies derived from standardization and made possible by commonalities in culture and demand across countries. Other motivations include the desire to access low-cost labor or materials, access national incentives, cross-subsidize, dodge trade barriers, access strategic markets, and create global associations.

A key issue is what elements of the strategy should be common across countries. In general, there will be a trade-off between the scale economies created by standardization and the impact of a customized strategy. A common brand name and position work well when a prestige brand is being marketed, the position is based on the country involved, and the technology drives the product. Significant management problems exist in attempting to impose a standardized policy in different countries, in part because of natural rebellion against a "headquarters knows best" attitude.

Enhancing the Chances of a Successful Alliance
1. Both sides must gain—now and in the future. Protect and enhance the assets and skills being contributed. Don't let a partner take over even if costs can be saved. Be a learner, particularly if the alliance is with a competitor or potential competitor. It is risky to be motivated solely by a desire to avoid investment. Make sure that your partner continues to benefit even when it means that you have to give up something.
2. Deal with the differences in organizations—people, cultures, structures, and systems—and in country cultures. If there is a separate organization involved, give it space to develop its own culture. If not, invest in working together as a team.
3. Build in some flexibility and capacity for change. Recognize that circumstances and markets can fluctuate. Be clear about expectations and contributions. When possible, have an agreement that covers eventual disagreements or disappointments that could be awkward. Don't rely on legal documents to handle all disagreements and conflicts.
4. If possible, live together before marriage. One study of 98 alliances found that a prior history of business relations was the best predictor of effectiveness.[28]
5. Have a balanced management team to avoid having one partner dominate the organization.

In global competition, competitors often lack a key success factor such as distribution or manufacturing expertise. A severe liability can sometimes be remedied quickly by a strategic alliance, a long-term collaboration leveraging the strengths of two or more organizations to achieve strategic goals. An alliance can be a formal joint venture or an informal agreement to work together to achieve a strategic end. Key to long-term success is that each partner contribute assets and skills over time and obtain strategic advantage. Toward that end, it is important that each partner make sure that its assets and skills are maintained and protected.

FOOTNOTES

[1] George S. Yip and Johny K. Johansson, "Global Market Strategies of U.S. and Japanese Businesses," Working Paper, Cambridge, Mass.: Marketing Science Institute, 1993.

[2] James Leontiades, "Market Share and Corporate Strategy in International Industries," *Journal of Business Strategy,* Summer 1984, pp. 30–37.

[3] John A. Quelch and Edward J. Hoff, "Customizing Global Marketing," *Harvard Business Review,* May–June 1986, pp. 59–68.

[4] Theodore Levitt, "The Globalization of Markets," *Harvard Business Review,* May–June 1983, pp. 92–102.

[5] Kenichi Ohmae, "The Triad World View," *The Journal of Business Strategy*, Spring 1987, pp. 8–16.

[6] Ohmae, "The Triad."

[7] Brenton R. Schlender, "Matsushita Shows How to Go Global," *Fortune*, July 11, 1994, pp. 159–166.

[8] Garz Hamel and C. K. Prahalad, "Do You Really Have a Global Strategy?" *Harvard Business Review*, July–August 1985, pp. 139–148.

[9] Hamel and Prahalad, "Do You Really."

[10] Joseph M. Winski and Laurel Wentz, "Parker Pen: What Went Wrong?" *Advertising Age*, June 2, 1986, pp. 1, 60, 61, 71.

[11] Hirotaka Takeuchi and Michael E. Porter, "Three Roles of International Marketing in Global Strategy," in Michael E. Porter, ed., *Competition in Global Industries*, Boston, Mass.: Harvard Business School Press, 1986.

[12] Op. cit. Schlender, "Matsushita Shows How to Go Global," *Fortune*, July 11, 1994, pp. 159–166.

[13] Kamran Kashani, "Beware the Pitfalls of Global Marketing," *Harvard Business Review*, September–October 1989, pp. 91–97.

[14] David A. Aaker, *Managing Brand Equity*, New York: The Free Press, 1991, Chapter 3.

[15] David Kalish, "Cat Fight," *Marketing & Media Decisions*, April 1989, pp. 42–48.

[16] Kenichi Ohmae, "Managing in a Borderless World," *Harvard Business Review*, May–June 1989, pp. 152–161.

[17] Kashani, "Beware the Pitfalls of Global Marketing."

[18] Christopher A. Bartlett, "MNCs: Get Off the Reorganization Merry-Go-Round," *Harvard Business Review*, March–April 1983, pp. 138–146.

[19] Quelch and Hoff, "Customizing Global Marketing."

[20] Christopher A. Bartlett and Summantra Ghoshal, "Tap Your Subsidiaries for Global Reach," *Harvard Business Review*, November–December 1986, pp. 87–94.

[21] Kenichi Ohmae, "The Global Logic of Strategic Alliances," *Harvard Business Review*, March–April, 1989, pp. 143–154.

[22] Ohmae, "The Global Logic of Strategic Alliances."

[23] Louis Kraar, "Your Rivals Can Be Your Allies," *Fortune*, March 27, 1989, pp. 66–76.

[24] Tyzoon T. Tyebjee, "A Topology of Joint Ventures: Japanese Strategies in the United States," *California Management Review*, Fall 1988, pp. 75–86.

[25] David Lei and John W. Slocum, Jr., "Global Strategy, Competence-Building and Strategic Alliances," *California Management Review*, Fall 1992, pp. 81–97.

[26] Gary Hamel, Yves L. Doz, and C. K. Prahalad, "Collaborate with Your Competitors— and Win," *Harvard Business Review*, January–February 1989, pp. 133–139.

[27] J. Peter Killing, "How to Make a Global Joint Venture Work," *Harvard Business Review*, March–April 1986, pp. 78–86.

[28] Louis P. Bucklin and Sanjit Sengupta, "Organizing Successful Co-Marketing Alliances," *Journal of Marketing*, April 1993, pp. 32–46.

PART FIVE

IMPLEMENTATION AND THE PLANNING PROCESS

16

IMPLEMENTING THE STRATEGY

The basic philosophy, spirit and drive of an organization have far more to do with its relative achievements than do technological or economic resources, organizational structure, innovation and timing.

Thomas Watson, JR, IBM

Structure follows strategy.

Alfred D. Chandler, Jr.

Never acquire a business you don't know how to run.

Robert Johnson,
Johnson & Johnson

Korvette's, which started as a luggage and appliance discounter selling from a second-floor loft in Manhattan, became by 1962 a profitable discount chain with a dozen stores.[1] Its initial success prompted an aggressive growth strategy, which turned out to be a disaster. The firm dramatically expanded both the number of stores and the number of cities served, expanded its product line by adding fashion goods, furniture, and grocery products, and added more store amenities.

This was a defensible growth strategy, similar to that of other successful discounters like Kmart. The problem was its implementation. The strategy was not supported by the right people, structure, systems, or culture. Korvette's personnel lacked the depth to staff the new stores and the expertise to handle the new product areas. The centralized structure did not adapt well to multiple cities and product lines. The management systems were not sophisticated enough to handle the added complexity. The culture of casual management with low prices as the driving force was not replaced with another strong culture that would be appropriate to the new business areas. As a result, by 1966 the firm was near death, and it never recovered.

The Korvette story graphically illustrates the importance of strategy implementation. The assessment of any strategy should include a careful analysis of organizational risks and a judgment about the nature of any required organizational changes and their associated costs and feasibility. Toward that end, this chapter first develops a conceptual framework that will help in analyzing an organization.

A CONCEPTUAL FRAMEWORK

The conceptual framework shown in Figure 16.1 can be used to identify and position organizational components and their interactions.[2] The heart of the framework is a set of four key constructs that describe the organization: structure, systems, people, and culture. The figure includes strategy, which must successfully interact with the four organizational components, and organizational performance. It also includes external analysis and self-analysis, which provide a link to Figure 2.1 and the strategy-development process. Recall that a strategy involves the product-market investment decision, the selection of functional area strategies, and the identification of bases for sustainable competitive advantage.

Consideration of organizational components can help a business identify actual and potential implementation problems, as well as determine how its organization would adapt to a new strategy. The first section of this chapter discusses each central component and its link to strategy. The need for achieving a fit or congruence among these four organizational components and strategy is then considered. Finally, ways by which an

FIGURE 16.1   A Framework for Analyzing
Organizations

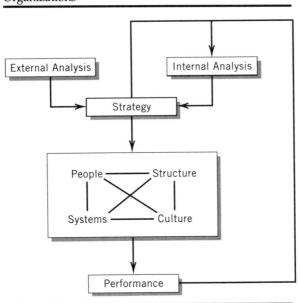

organization can become more innovative and responsive to change are
suggested.

STRUCTURE

Organizational structure defines lines of authority and communication
and specifies the mechanism by which organizational tasks and programs
are accomplished.

Centralization Versus Decentralization

One key structural dimension is the degree of centralization. At one
extreme is the centralized functional organization consisting of specialized
groups in marketing, sales, production, engineering, R&D, personnel,
and administration. Centralization will maximize economies of scale and
synergies across the organization. It is most appropriate when there are
a limited number of closely related product lines.

In contrast, the decentralized organization will have autonomous
business units based on product or market groupings with the ability to
develop strategies in response to the needs of the markets they serve.
Decentralization has been key to firms such as 3M and Hewlett Packard

because it provides focused performance assessment, places business strategists close to the market, allows innovation with a minimum of bureaucracy, and develops a subculture when the nature of the business warrants. The downside is that economies of scale and synergies across the organization are often difficult to achieve, and inefficiencies and duplications are created. Communication needs and efforts to coordinate branding strategies or market research, for example, can create strains and add costs which defeat the purpose of decentralization.

There are, of course, variants on these two models. Functional units such as advertising or production can be organized by product or market. A division might share a sales force with another division. A matrix organization is one in which a manager, such as a product advertising manager, might report both to a functional advertising manager and a division manager responsible for the product line.

An important strategic issue is determining whether a new business will fit into an existing organizational structure. GM, for example, correctly concluded that the Saturn automobile would have a chance only if it started with its own organization that did not have the burdens of the GM culture and union contracts. If a new business is placed in the existing organization, will it suffer from a lack of attention and interest? Will expected synergies emerge? What adjustments or major changes will have to be made?

The Borderless Organization

One of the challenges of the next decade is to find ways to break down boundaries within organizations. Robert Nardelli articulated the GE management philosophy:[3] "One clear message in our approach is the value of borderless culture which breaks down the horizontal barriers between functions and the vertical barriers between organizational layers. This means that employees are encouraged to collaborate with one another and given considerable freedom to turn their creativity into productivity. The 'what' is determined many times by the customer and the business environment. The 'how' is the involvement of our people. Read the market, determine what has to be done, and let the people do it."

One approach to cross-functional management is to organize around missions, such as new product development or total quality, that involve a variety of functions. Task forces can take the lead and provide role models. Informal communication can help. Thus, open-door norms, MBWA (management by walking around), the use of cross-company training programs to encourage networking, best practices conferences, video conferencing across countries, and e-mail systems all provide mechanisms to coordinate and communicate.

In addition to cross-functional integration, there is a need to communicate across organizational units such as divisions or country operating units. One approach is to have best practices conferences to share ideas. Another is to set up coordination committees to make sure potential synergies in brand management or manufacturing occur. If organizational communication is poor, a winning innovation may not get implemented. In the 1970s, Xerox's innovative computer group, PARC (Palo Alto Research Center), was a leader in the key microprocessor technology that was to be the heart of most machines in the 1980s. The failure of the copier group at Xerox to capitalize on this talent contributed to a dramatic loss of market dominance during that period.

Alliance Networks

In the global environment, markets and competitors can change significantly, and it is important to be able to respond quickly. There may not be time to develop needed assets and skills, and responses that require large commitments to new technologies or distribution channels may be risky, especially for a firm with little relevant background. One way to be able to go "on line" immediately with necessary business changes is to form a network of alliances and joint ventures with suppliers, customers, distributors, and even competitors. With such a network, needed assets can be made available instantly, the firm can focus on what it does best, the risk of failure is shared, and many more opportunities can be funded.

The use of strategic alliances, their motivations, and how to make them work are discussed in detail in Chapter 15. These alliances play an especially important role in global strategy development.

The Virtual Corporation

An extension of the alliance concept is the virtual corporation, a team of people and organizations specifically designed for a particular client or job. The organizations brought together may be suppliers, customers, and competitors. The people can be drawn from a variety of sources and might include contract workers who are hired only for the project at hand. The virtual corporation can sometimes be formed or modified in a matter of days, which means it is the ultimate response in a fast-moving environment.

Advertising agencies, for example, are now forming teams tailored to the needs of particular clients. Some members of the team will come from subsidiary firms specializing in corporate design, packaging, direct marketing, and promotions. Others may come from firms that specialize in brochures and the media. The core of the team is likely to be located in a single building, but some team members will be connected via computer workstations that share visual images and in-process advertising. Thus, clients do not have to wait for an agency with the optimal set of characteristics to evolve; it can be formed almost overnight.

SYSTEMS

Several management systems are strategically relevant. Among them are planning (which is discussed in the following chapter), and the budgeting, accounting, information, and measurement and reward systems.

Accounting and Budgeting System

Accounting and budgeting are key elements in any management system. The risk that these systems cannot be adapted to the needs of a new strategy can be very real. An accounting and budgeting system that is well conceived and contains valuable historical data may not fit the reorganized structure required by the new strategy. Or a system that worked well for an electronic instruments firm may not work when applied to a new service business. Another concern is the systems influence on investment decisions, especially when a new strategy is proposed that does not fit a familiar pattern.

Information System

The information system and the technology, databases, models, and expert systems on which it is based can fundamentally affect strategy. The link between manufacturers and retailers, for example, is increasingly being forged by information technology. New systems control inventory and handle ordering, pricing, and promotions. The ability to control the information generated by retail scanners can be key to strategies of manufacturers and retailers. The information bases that are emerging from interactive media forms are affecting strategies of advertisers and retailers. Thus, understanding the current capability and future direction of an organization's information system is a key dimension of strategy development.

Measurement and Reward System

Measurement can drive behavior and thus directly affect strategy implementation. The key to strategy is often the ability to introduce performance measures that are appropriate and linked to the reward structure.

A concern in designing measurement and reward systems is to balance the short-term and long-term perspectives. One approach is to have measures such as brand equity indicators that have long-term time horizons. A manager might be compensated if a loyalty measure or distribution goal is met three years in the future. In addition to putting the appropriate focus on the future, this policy implies that the manager would not earn the bonus if an early job change occurs. Another approach is to tailor the performance measurement to the nature of the business. A high-growth SBU (strategic business unit) for example, could be measured on the basis of market share and customer satisfaction, whereas a low-growth SBU might be exclusively evaluated on ROA and cash flow. Still another approach is to use stock options as a mechanism to introduce a long-term perspective.

PEOPLE

A strategy is generally based on an organizational skill that, in turn, is based on people. Thus, strategies require certain types of people. For each strategy, it is important to know how many people, with what experience, depth, and skills, are needed for

- Functional areas such as marketing, heavy manufacturing, assembly, and finance.
- Product or market areas.
- New product programs.
- Management of particular types of people.
- Management of a particular type of operation.
- Management of growth and change.

Make, Buy, or Convert

If a strategy requires capabilities not already available in the business, it will be necessary to obtain them. The "make" approach, developing a broad managerial or technical base by hiring and grooming workers, ensures that people will fit the organization, but it can take years.

The "convert" approach, converting the existing workforce to the new strategy, takes less time. AT&T is an example of a firm that attempted to change its orientation from that of service to marketing, largely by retraining existing staff. A host of strategies, particularly those precipitated by acquisitions, have failed because of the faulty assumption that an "old" staff could adapt to a new context. A supermarket buying team, for example, could not be adapted to the needs of a discount drugstore, mainly because a discount orientation and background was missing.

The "buy" approach, bringing in experienced people from the outside, is the immediate solution when a dramatic change in strategy needs to be implemented quickly, but it involves the risk of bringing in people who are accustomed to different systems and cultures.

Motivation

In addition to the type and quality of people, the motivation level can affect strategy implementation. There are, of course, a variety of ways to motivate people, including the fear of losing a job, financial incentives, self-fulfillment goals, and the development of goals for the organization or groups within the organization such as teams or quality circles.

Motivation usually is enhanced if employees are empowered to accomplish their goals even when a departure from the routine response is required. People who are inhibited from using their initiative will eventually lose interest and become cynical. Motivation also is enhanced when employees are linked to the corporate culture and objectives. Companies can accomplish these links in part by simply providing titles like "host" (Disney), "crew member" (McDonald's), and "associate" (J.C. Penney).

CULTURE

As suggested by Figure 16.2, an organizational culture involves three elements:

- A set of "shared values" or "dominant beliefs" that defines an organization's priorities.
- A set of norms of behavior.
- Symbols and symbolic activities used to develop and nurture those shared values and norms.

Shared Values

Shared values or dominant beliefs underlie a culture by specifying what is important. In a strong culture, the values will be widely accepted, and virtually everyone will be able to identify them and describe their rationale.

Shared values can have a variety of foci. They can involve, for example,

- A key asset or skill that is the essence of a firm's competitive advantage: We will be the most creative advertising agency.
- An operational focus: SAS focused on on-time performance.

- An organizational output: We will deliver zero defects or 100 percent customer satisfaction.

- An emphasis on a functional area: Black & Decker transformed itself from a firm with a manufacturing focus to one with a market-driven approach.

- A management style: This is an informal flat organization that fosters communication and encourages "oddballs" to do their thing.

- A belief in the importance of people as individuals.

- A general objective, such as a belief in being the "best" or comparable to the best: Komatsu set out to beat Caterpillar. Samsung strove to be a major player in microwave ovens. Sharp wants to be one of the most innovative in any area in which it competes.

Norms

To make a real difference, the culture must be strong enough to develop norms of behavior—informal rules that influence decisions and actions throughout an organization by suggesting what is appropriate and what is not. Charles O'Reilly of Stanford University talks of culture as a social control system with norms as behavior guides.[4] The fact is that strong norms can generate much more effective control over what is actually done or not done in an organization than a very specific set of objectives, measures, and sanctions. People can always get around rules. The concept of norms is that people will not attempt to avoid them because they will be accompanied by a commitment to shared values.

O'Reilly suggests that norms can vary on two dimensions: the intensity or amount of approval/disapproval attached to an expectation and

FIGURE 16.2   Organizational Culture

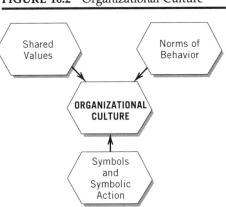

Values at Levi Strauss

Levi Strauss has a well-defined set of values that serves as the basis for a strong culture.[5] The values have two primary dimensions.

The first is a commitment to social ideals. The firm aspires to be a company that "our people are proud of and committed to," that values a diverse work force, and that epitomizes high standards of ethical behavior. This commitment is seen in the firm's approach to tough issues ranging from plant closings to AIDS in the workplace.

The second is a commitment to the people in its organization. Levi's explicitly sets out to provide employees with an opportunity to contribute, learn, grow, and advance on merit. It also wants its people to feel "respected, treated fairly, listened to, and involved" and to attain satisfaction from accomplishments, friendships, and balanced personal and professional lives. This commitment to its employees involves recognition of accomplishments, clear communication about individual goals and performance, and empowerment. Empowerment, which is a central concept, means that people have the authority and resources (including access to information) to act.

---

the degree of consensus or consistency with which a norm is shared.[6] It is only when both intensity and consensus exist that strong cultures emerge.

Norms encourage behavior consistent with shared values. Thus, in a "quality service" culture, an extraordinary effort by an employee, such as renting a helicopter to fix a communication component (a Federal Express legend), would not seem out of line and risky; instead it would be something that most in that culture would do under similar circumstances. Furthermore, sloppy work affecting quality would be informally policed by fellow workers, without reliance on a formal system. One production firm uses no quality-control inspectors or janitors. Each production-line person is responsible for the quality of his or her output and for keeping the work area clean. Such a policy would not work without support from a strong culture.

Symbols and Symbolic Action

Corporate cultures are largely developed and maintained by the use of consistent, visible symbols and symbolic action. In fact, the more obvious methods of affecting behavior, such as changing systems or structure, are often much less effective than seemingly trivial symbolic actions.

A host of symbols and symbolic actions are available. A few of the more useful are discussed below.

The Founder and Original Mission. A corporation's unique "roots," including the personal style and experience of its founder, can provide extremely potent symbols. The strong culture of the Shaklee Corporation is due largely to its founder's involvement in holistic medicine, his contributions to vitamin development and use, and his ability to arouse enthusiasm in groups. The concept of entertainment developed by Walt Disney, the customer-oriented philosophy of J. C. Penney, and the product and advertising traditions started by the founders of Procter & Gamble continue to influence the cultures of their firms generations later.

Modern Role Models.   Modern heroes and role models help communicate, personalize, and legitimize values and norms. Former IBM executive Archie McGill became a symbol of the new marketing-focused culture that he brought to AT&T. Other examples are the several managers at 3M who tenaciously pursued an idea despite setbacks until they succeeded in building a major division, and the Frito-Lay workers who maintained customer service in the face of natural disasters.

Activities.   An executive's use of time can be a symbolic action affecting the culture. An airline executive who spends two weeks a month obtaining a firsthand look at customer service sends a strong signal to the organization. Patterns of consistent reinforcement can represent another important symbolic activity. For example, a firm that regularly recognizes cost-saving accomplishments in a meaningful way with the visible support of top management can, over time, affect the culture.

Questions Asked.   A. W. Clausen of the Bank of America reportedly shifted concern from revenue to profit by continually asking about profit implications. When a type of question is continually asked by top executives and made a central part of meeting agendas and report formats, it will eventually influence the shared values of an organization.

Rituals.   Rituals of work life, from hiring to eating lunch to retirement dinners help define a culture. Tandem's extensive interview process for new employees, its requirement that a person must accept a job before salary is discussed, its orientation sessions involving senior executives, and its regular Friday afternoon beer bust are all rituals that contribute to the culture.

OBTAINING STRATEGIC CONGRUENCE

Figure 16.3 lists a set of questions that provide a basis for analyzing an organization and its relationship to a proposed strategy. As discussed above, a strategy must match the structure, systems, people, and culture

FIGURE 16.3 Obtaining Information About Organizational Components

---

STRUCTURE
- What is the organization's structure? How decentralized is it?
- What are the lines of authority and communication?
- What are the roles of task forces, committees, or similar mechanisms?

SYSTEMS
- How are budgets set?
- What is the nature of the planning system?
- What are the key measures used to evaluate performance?
- How does the accounting system work?
- How do product and information flow?

PEOPLE
- What are the skills, knowledge, and experience of the firm's employees?
- What is their depth and quality?
- What are the employees expectations?
- What are their attitudes toward the firm and their jobs?

CULTURE
- Are there shared values that are visible and accepted?
- What are these shared values and how are they communicated?
- What are the norms of behavior?
- What are the significant symbols and symbolic activities?
- What is the dominant management style?
- How is conflict resolved?

STRATEGY
- Where would the new strategy fit into the organization?
- Would the new strategy fit into the strategic plan and be adequately funded?
- Would the systems and culture support the new strategy?
- What organizational changes would be required for the new strategy to succeed?
- What impact would these changes have? Are they feasible?

---

of the organization. In addition, each organizational component needs to fit with the others. If an inconsistency exists, it is likely that implementation of the strategy will be affected.

The concept of organizational congruence suggests that interactions between organizational components should be considered, such as

- Do the systems fit the structure? Does the compensation system emphasize teamwork rather than individual performance when teamwork and cooperation are required?

- Do the people fit the structure? Can they operate within the organizational groups and integrate mechanisms to complete the task? For example, creative or entrepreneurial managers may be uncomfortable in a highly structured organization.

- Does the structure fit the culture? Does the structure complement the values or norms of the organization? For example, a top management group accustomed to controlling dedicated resources may be less effective in a matrix organization where persuasion and coordination are more important.

- Do the people fit the culture? Is there sufficient consensus in the organization about the "rules of the game" to enable the organization to achieve its goals? For example, can a rapidly growing organization be sure that new people will understand and accept a totally informal communications system?

Corporate Culture and Strategy

Organizational culture provides the key to strategy implementation because it is such a powerful force for providing focus, motivation, and norms. Many strategies concentrate on an organizational asset or skill such as the product quality level, service system, or customer support, or on a functional area like manufacturing or sales. A culture can provide support if it is congruent with the new structures, systems, and people required by a new strategy. If it is not congruent, however, the culture's motivations and norms could cripple the strategy.

A new strategy's fit with an organization's culture is of greater concern than the strategy's fit to the other organizational components because culture is so difficult to change. An oil company CEO developed elaborate diversification plans that failed because they were incompatible with the firm's oil business culture. The problems experienced by AT&T in its efforts to change from what was a service/production/internal focus to a marketing/external orientation illustrate how powerful and resistant to change a culture can be. AT&T very visibly changed its strategy and even the associated structure and systems (introducing product/market organizations and sales incentives), but was inhibited by the culture. When AT&T hired different types of personnel—MBAs and marketing people—it found inconsistencies between the new people and the change-resistant culture.

When a new strategy is proposed, it is important to understand the relationship of that strategy to the shared values and norms of the organization. Is it compatible? Will the culture have to be modified? If so, what impact will that have on the organization? Often the worst case develops when a strong positive culture is sacrificed to accommodate a new strategy, and the result is an absence of any positive culture. The Korvette case discussed at the beginning of this chapter illustrates this point.

Hit-Industry Toplogy[7]

The need for congruence between strategy and organizational components can be illustrated by the three very different types of firms that compete in "hit industries." A industry is one in which the goal is to obtain, produce, and exploit a product which will have a relatively short product life cycle. Examples of such industries include movies, records, fashion, publishing, video games, computer software, venture capital (especially in high-tech areas), and oil. Industries with short life cycles are interesting because many of their organizational problems are more intense and graphic.

The model in Figure 16.4 divides a hit industry into three functions. These functions are shown as being performed by different organizations,

FIGURE 16.4   A Model of Hit Industries

Strategy	Drillers	Pumpers	Distributors
Structure	• Flat, loose • Amorphous	• Centralized • Tight control	• Decentralized • Loose control
Bottom-line Performance Incentives	• High	• None	• Low
People	• Product development	• Production control	• Marketing and distribution
Culture	• Stay loose • Move fast • Take risks	• Disciplined • Cost-oriented • Avoid risks	• Promotion-oriented • Controlled risks
Key Success Factors	• Finding and keeping key people • Idea source • Get products to market quickly	• Exploit the experience curve • Operations • Production • Engineering	• Distribution channels • Inventory • Promotion • Positioning • Pricing

although often two or more will coexist within the same organization. An oil industry analogy provides the conceptual framework. The first organizational type is termed "drillers." They are the wildcatters who find oil fields and drill wells, the talent scouts and artists of the record industry, the producers and writers in the movie industry, and the editors and authors in the publishing industry. A key success factor is to locate or create the new wells, properties, or projects. An ultimate goal, in the record business, for example, would be to get a lock on performing talent and keep them so happy they would not consider leaving. Key people tend to be creative, high-energy, decisive risk-takers. They thrive in a flat organization with little structure and with high bottom-line incentives.

The second organizational type is termed "pumpers." They are the well operators and refiners of the oil business, the record pressers, the movie directors, and the printers in publishing. The key success factors in a pumping organization are operations, production engineering, and an ability to exploit the experience curve. The key people are disciplined, cost- and production-oriented, in production and control jobs, and risk-avoiders. A centralized organization with tight controls provides an appropriate context.

The third type specializes in distribution. These "distributors" are the pipeline operators and retailers in the oil industry and the distributors and retailers in the record, film, and publishing industries. The key success factors in a distribution business usually include inventory control, physical distribution, promotion, and access to or even control over distribution channels. The key people are in marketing and distribution. A decentralized structure with loose controls and some bottom-line incentives is often effective.

The hit-industry topology shows how the lack of fit between organizational components can develop. Typically, an organization starts as a drilling company. After establishing some products and experiencing rapid growth, the company finds that it desperately needs to control production costs, develop a secure, effective distribution channel, and professionalize the marketing effort. As a result, pumping and distribution people are brought in. The organization then takes the form of either a pumper or a distributor, depending on which function is most critical or which type of person becomes the CEO. In any case, the system, structure, and culture of the organization change and the drillers who started the business become uncomfortable and leave, perhaps to start a competing business. When the existing wells dry up or are damaged by competition, no one in the organization is available to create new ones.

It is a challenge in any business is to keep access to drillers. One approach is to keep the drillers satisfied by financial incentives and organizational mechanisms, such as ad hoc groups with extraordinary freedom and autonomy. However, these special incentives may create inequities and disincentives for others. If "entrepreneurial" engineers are becoming millionaires, whereas those charged with maintaining existing products are on a fixed salary, tensions are bound to mount. Furthermore, the entrepreneurial groups may need access to the facilities and expertise of the pumpers and distributors, and providing that access may compromise their "separateness."

Another way to approach a fit problem is to restrict a business to one function and allow other organizations to perform the other functions. Venture capital firms restrict themselves to being drillers and do not become involved in the other functions. Publishers are largely distribution companies; their production is farmed out and the drillers are actually the authors, who are not part of the organization. A business without in-house drillers may have limited access to new ventures, however, because other firms may successfully contract with the best independent drillers. Also, the price for the proven drillers may become so high that profits are limited.

Problems can also arise when pumpers and distributors share an organization. If one of the two clearly dominates, the problem is minimized. If each is equally significant, however, there could easily be a fit problem.

ORGANIZING FOR INNOVATION

Although the achievement of high congruence among an organization's components and strategy leads to organizational effectiveness in the short to medium term, it can also inhibit desirable and even necessary change. An organization can become so integrated and the culture so strong that only compatible changes are tolerated. For example, when faced with a technological threat, firms often respond with even greater reliance on the obsolete familiar technology.

The challenge is to create an organization that can successfully operate a congruent strategy and still have the ability to detect the need for fundamental change. If a significant change in strategy is needed, a major organizational change undoubtedly will be required as well. Also, even in the context of a congruent strategy, there needs to be a capacity for ongoing innovation—the ability to create new or improved products or processes and enter new markets. Several approaches, including task forces, alliances, joint ventures, the virtual corporation, and reengineering, are being used successfully to promote change and foster innovation.

Task Forces

Sometimes a firm will find that it must make a substantial change in operations because of a significant challenge such as a deterioration in competitive position or an opportunity such as a technological break- through. A cross-functional task force can look at the issues in depth and form a response that provides a meaningful change in direction.

Japanese companies couple task forces with a sense of urgency to create significant change agents. The sense of urgency will usually involve a competitor-oriented goal such as "Beat Cat" in the case of Komatsu, specific objectives such as reduction of costs by 20 percent, a tight time- table, and a process such as Total Quality Control or "just-in-time." The result is extreme pressure to work hard and perform and to break out of the mold and find creative new approaches.

Skunkworks

Major new business ventures may require separate entrepreneurial units because the slow decision-making process, the resource allocation biases against risky new businesses, and the overhead burden of the core organi- zation are too great a handicap. Small autonomous groups of people representing all the important functions join together to create a product or a business and nurse it through the early stages of life, often in an off- site garage operation called a skunkworks. Used by 3M, IBM, Xerox, and many others, such a group is usually autonomous enough that it can bypass the usual decision process and resist pressures to conform to existing formal and informal constraints. A key to entrepreneurial units is to have a business "champion" committed to the concept. Texas Instru- ments reviewed 50 new product introductions and found that every failure lacked a voluntary product champion.[8]

Kaizen

Kaizen, which means ongoing improvement involving everyone from top management on down, has been the basis of an increase in productivity for many Japanese firms.[9] Particularly Japanese, it does not easily fit into the U.S. managment style because it focuses on process rather than results, and because it depends on many small improvements rather than a quick fix based on a dramatic new product or technology. The bottom line is never the motivation. Rather, the idea is to continuously improve through- out the organization.

Reengineering

Reengineering, the antithesis of kaizen, is the search for and implementation of radical change in business operations to achieve breakthrough results.[10] The basic idea is to start with a clean sheet of paper and ask, If we were to start a new company, how would we operate? Rather than attempting to refine and improve, the effort is to create a revolution from within. The key to reengineering is to break down the old functional units and approach the problem from an interdisciplinary view using cross-functional teams. The starting point is usually considering how customers would like to deal with the firm, rather than how the firm would like to deal with them.

For example, GTE discovered that customers wanted a single phone number to call about any problem, rather than separate numbers for the repair, billing, and marketing departments. As a result it started a "customer care center" staffed by people who could field and deal with any inquiry. The goal was to have the people and systems in place so that 70 percent of all calls could be handled without being passed on to another department. This approach was indeed a radical departure which ended up not only improving service, but also reducing costs.

Reengineering, both risky and expensive, is most appropriate when there is a strong threat from a changing environment or competitor and marginal improvements in the old operation simply will not get the job done. Without a major change in operations, the business will be in jeopardy.

SUMMARY

An organizational analysis can help estimate the cost and feasibility of implementing particular strategies. The analysis is best structured by looking at organizational components such as structure, systems, people, and culture.

Organizational structure defines the lines of authority and communication and can vary in the degree of centralization and formality of communication channels. Management systems such as planning, budgeting and accounting, information, and measurement and reward can all influence strategy implementation. Types of people and their motivations provide the bases of skills needed to support SCAs. Because organizational culture, which involves shared values, norms of behavior, and symbols and symbolic activities, is so difficult to change, the fit of a new strategy to the culture is particularly important.

These organizational components must fit with each other as well as with the strategy. The "congruence" principle is illustrated by the hit-industry topology, which contrasts the functions of "drillers" who develop products, "pumpers" who focus on production, and "distributors" who specialize in marketing and distribution.

A final challenge is to create an organization that can change rapidly. Helpful approaches include the use of task forces, skunkworks, alliances, joint ventures, kaizen and reengineering.

FOOTNOTES

[1] Robert F. Hartley, *Marketing Mistakes,* 5th ed., New York: Wiley, 1992, Chapter 13.

[2] Many such frameworks have been advanced by behavioral scientists and management consulting firms. The McKinsey firm, for example, developed what it calls the 7-S framework, which includes strategy, structure, systems, skills, staff, style (of management), and shared values.

[3] Reinventing America: The 1993 Business Week Symposium of Chief Executie Officers, New York: *Business Week,* 1994.

[4] Robert Howard, "Values Make the Company: An Interview with Robert Haas," *Harvard Business Review,* September–October 1990, pp. 133–144.

[5] Charles O'Reilly, "Corporations, Culture, and Commitment: Motivation and Social Control in Organizations," *California Management Review,* Summer 1989, pp. 9–25.

[6] O'Reilly, "Corporations, Culture," p. 13.

[7] The hit-industry topology was developed in discussions with Dr. Norman Smothers.

[8] Peters and Waterman, *In Search of Excellence,* p. 203.

[9] Masaaki Imai, *Kaisen,* New York: McGraw-Hill, 1984.

[10] Thomas A. Stewart, "Re-engineering: The Hot New Managing Tool," *Fortune,* August 23, 1993, pp. 41–48

17

FORMAL PLANNING
SYSTEMS

Strategic planning isn't strategic thinking.
One is analysis and the other is synthesis.

Henry Mintzberg, McGill University

Those that implement the plans must make
the plans.

Patrick Hagerty, Texas Instruments

Strategy development requires systematic and structured information gathering, a willingness to consider new directions, managerial insight, and an ability to think strategically. Given that the effort, the will, and the talent all exist, the question addressed in this chapter still arises: How does one begin and sustain the process of developing, refining, and changing strategies? The reader may want to review the first two chapters, which provide an overview of the book and the concepts and methods that need to be captured in the strategy-development process.

THE FORMAL PLANNING SYSTEM

A structured planning process can help ensure that planning gets adequate time and intention. A calendar specifying what tasks need to be accomplished by what dates provides discipline. Planning forms and agendas for key meetings flesh out the structure, providing detail and clarifying the tasks to be accomplished.

The planning process can be a focused effort done in a one- to two-week period. The discussion agenda shown in Figure 17.1 can structure the effort (it includes a condensed version of the sets of questions that appeared in the external analysis chapters). However, spreading out the planning process over a longer period allows time to expand the information base, conduct analyses, and conceive and consider more strategic alternatives. Sometimes, for example, the identification of a key strategic question or issue cannot be anticipated but emerges during the process.

The following outline provides a four-step process that can be scheduled over a one- to four-month time period:

1. **External/self-analysis workshop**   1–2 days
   - Address the questions in Figure 17.1 that cover external and self-analysis.
   - Specify scenarios and identify strategic opportunities, threats, questions, strengths, weaknesses, and problems.

2. **Strategy development workshop**   1–2 days
   - Address the questions in Figure 17.1 that cover strategy development.
   - Reduce the strategy choices to a limited number of strategies and growth directions. Attempt to set priorities.

3. **Strategy presentation**   1–2 days
   - Present the selected strategy, or the two or three strategies from which one is to be selected.
   - Project key performance measures such as investment, sales, and profits through the planning horizon.

FIGURE 17.1   Strategy Development: A Discussion Agenda

CUSTOMER ANALYSIS

• What are the major segments?

• What are their motivations and unmet needs?

COMPETITOR ANALYSIS

• Who are the existing and potential competitors? What strategic groups can be identified?

• What are their sales, share, and profits? What are the growth trends?

• What are their strengths, weaknesses, and strategies?

MARKET ANALYSIS

• How attractive is the market or industry and its submarkets? What are the forces reducing profitability in the market, entry and exit barriers, growth projections, cost structures, and profitability prospects?

• What are the alternative distribution channels and their relative strengths?

• What industry trends are significant to strategy?

• What are the current and future key success factors?

ENVIRONMENTAL ANALYSIS

• What environmental threats, opportunities, and trends exist?

• What major environmental scenarios can be conceived?

• What are the major strategic questions and information-need areas?

(continued)

• Develop objectives, including one-year objectives to guide implementation.

4. **The annual plan**   1–2 days

• Present a refined, selected strategy.

• Present the programs that will support the strategy implementation.

• Present a detailed financial plan for the coming year.

Planning Forms

Standardized forms can help specify the content of presentations. When strategies are being tracked over time, the use of similar planning forms from year to year makes relevant comparisons much more feasible. In an organization containing multiple businesses, planning forms can encourage a common format and content so that cross-business comparisons will be easier.

FIGURE 17.1   *(Continued)*

SELF-ANALYSIS

• What are our strategy, performance, costs, point of differentiation, strengths, weaknesses, strategic problems, and culture?

• What is our existing business portfolio? What has been our level of investment in our various product markets?

STRATEGY DEVELOPMENT

• How can our offering be differentiated? How can we add customer value by doing something better than or different from competitors? How can perceived quality be enhanced?

• Can a cost advantage be gained by offering a no-frills product or by reducing product costs?

• Can synergy, focus, or a preemptive move be employed to gain advantage?

• What is the strategic vision? What are the key assets and skills to be maintained or developed?

• What alternative growth directions should be considered? How should they be pursued?

• What investment level is most appropriate for each market—withdrawal, milking, maintaining, or growing?

• What are the alternative functional area strategies?

• What strategies best fit our strengths, our objectives, and our organization?

The most useful and appropriate forms will depend on context. In general, they will vary for different industries and even for different firms within an industry. The appendix provides a set of illustrative forms that should be viewed as a starting point in form development.

Advantages of a Formal Planning System

Perhaps the most important benefit of a formal planning system with well-defined responsibilities is that it forces executives and managers to take time out to consider strategic questions. Without that impetus, artificial though it may be, routine tasks will generally absorb management's available time. A formal planning system can also aid in the tasks of responding to a dynamic environment and strategically managing a complex organization with limited resources. Formal plans will be most useful when a business is large or potentially large, when substantial changes are occurring either in the environment or in the organization, when uncertainty is high, and when complex tasks are involved.

Planning exercises also provide information and a structure that make strategy choices outside the system easier. Strategy research has shown that many strategic decisions are made opportunistically or incrementally.

Such decisions are easier to precipitate with the planning system as background. A study of nearly 1,100 strategic decisions made by 129 Fortune 500 firms during the mid-1980s found that in only one-third of the cases was the decision made in the context of a formal planning system.[1] The formal planning system tended to be more influential when the decisions were important, risky, global, or about a divestment.

There is modest evidence suggesting that those firms that employ formal planning systems perform somewhat better than others.[2] Scott Armstrong of Wharton reviewed 16 efforts to compare the performance of firms using formal planning systems with similar firms not using formal planning systems. Improved performance was found in 11 of the studies, in 3 there was no difference, and in 2 performance was inferior.

Role of the Planning Staff

Perhaps the most accepted fact about strategy development is that the function of a planning staff is not to create strategies. That function needs to be a line activity. Henry Mintzberg, the influential strategy researcher from McGill University, notes that planners should make their greatest contribution around the strategy-making process rather than inside it.[3] He suggests that, because they have the time and inclination to analyze, planners can provide a central and positive role in the process by being strategic programmers, strategy finders, analysts, and catalysts.

Planners as Strategic Programmers. Strategic programming is an implementation process that occurs after strategies are developed. As defined by Mintzberg, it includes clarification and elaboration of the strategies and adjustment of budgets and operations. Strategies need to be clarified and expressed in terms understood by all relevant parts of the organization if implementation is to succeed. Elaboration involves breaking down the strategies into sub-strategies, programs, and action plans. Budgets, objectives, policies, and procedures need to be adjusted to incorporate the new strategy. In essence, the CEO says to the planner, "The strategy is set; you package it and get things going."

Planners as Strategy Finders. Some of the most important strategies evolve without the awareness of top management. Fully exploiting a potential strategy requires that it be recognized early and elevated to the status of a formal strategy so that it can compete for resources and benefit from an implementation program. Planners can ferret out new applications or new technologies that could potentially be the bases for future strategies.

Planners as Analysts.   Planners can do much of the detailed information gathering that will support the external and self-analysis. They can also structure scenario analyses and pursue strategic questions, threats, and opportunities in some depth, and they can make sure that the managers do not miss some important element or perspective of the external and self-analysis.

Planners as Catalysts.   The challenge is to get managers out of their conceptual ruts and their tendency to think in terms of the past. To do so, planners need to ask provocative questions, suggest scenarios that break the mold, and question conventional assumptions. The planning process can be a vehicle to perform this role. External and self-analysis, if done correctly, should stimulate new ways of looking at the business and generate new strategic options. However, a planner may even need to attack the planning process itself. The final goal is strategic thinking rather than strategic planning.

Top-Down Versus Bottom-Up Systems

Planning systems can be top-down or bottom-up or some combination of the two. In a top-down system, top management creates the strategy, thus allowing easier resource allocation, synergy development, and strategy coordination across SBUs (strategic business units). Top management may be more comfortable with strategy development and long-range perspectives than operating managers.

In a bottom-up system, the process is driven by those at the lowest levels of business management responsibility. An SBU manager may be closer and more responsive to the immediate environment than top management and thus more capable of generating effective strategies. Furthermore, an SBU manager's authority to develop strategies may enhance his or her motivation to implement the strategy. The most appropriate system will depend, in part, on the level of decentralization that exists in a firm. A high level of decentralization is most compatible with a bottom-up planning system.

PITFALLS OF A FORMAL PLANNING SYSTEM

Several efforts have been made to systematically study the pitfalls and difficulties of operating an effective planning system.[4] Some of the recurring problems of planning systems, summarized in Figure 17.2, can be identified from these studies, numerous individual commentaries, and the experience of applying the ideas in this book.

FIGURE 17.2   Pitfalls of the Planning Process

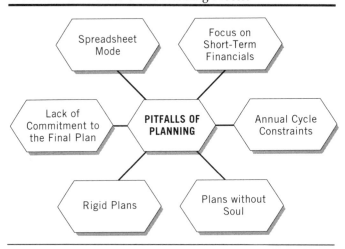

The Spreadsheet-Driven Process

One all-too-common version of planning is dominated by spreadsheet logic. The idea is to generate income statements and balance sheets for years into the future using nifty, powerful spreadsheet programs. The focus is on projecting past financial data into the future, featuring elegant accounting. There is a strong bias toward making next year's strategy an extension of last year's strategy. As a result, a firm's plan is internally oriented and there is little likelihood that any strategy change will be considered. To the extent that spreadsheets support such a process, they can be a real handicap.

In contrast, an effective process will be externally oriented, focusing on environmental threats and opportunities. The aim will be to develop new strategic options rather than to extrapolate last year's strategy. Thus, devices that are helpful for identifying new options, such as scenario analysis, portfolio analysis, and growth direction analysis, will be used. The identification of potential strategies, even if not pursued, can help an organization become more sensitive to change and more readily adaptable. The process can also stimulate the development of assets and skills so that options not now available to the firm might become feasible in the future.

Dominance of Short-Run Financial Objectives

Most businesses set goals that involve short-term financial measures such as sales, profit, ROI, or market share. If other goals exist, they are often vague and are dominated by these quantitative ones, which then influence strategy development and choice. A bias toward milking a business and underinvesting in the production process to improve the short-term financial performance is often introduced. Hayes observes that too many manufacturing companies have starved the production area in order to generate short-term cash.[5] He also suggests that financial goals may have encouraged firms to make unwise acquisitions in an effort to achieve growth.

The more appropriate focus would be on nurturing and developing assets and skills that will form the bases of SCAs (sustainable competitive advantages) in the future. What assets and skills will be needed to maintain an SCA or develop new strategic directions? What objectives and programs will be responsive? A key question to consider is which type of goal drives the planning system.

Planning Is Restricted to the Annual Cycle

The annual planning cycle ensures that at least once each year the day-to-day problems will be set aside and a strategic review will occur. The problem is that all too often managers finish a plan with a sigh of relief, feeling that their reward is being able to forget the difficult issues for yet another year. Because threats, opportunities, and strategic windows do not always coincide with a planning cycle, however, the system must allow time for information gathering, analysis, and decision making outside of the planning cycle.

Plans Without Soul

According to Mintzberg, a problem with planning is that it represents a calculating style of management, not a committing style: "Managers with a committing style engage people in a journey. They lead in such a way that everyone on the journey helps shape its course. As a result, enthusiasm inevitably builds along the way."[6] Mintzberg goes on to paraphrase the sociologist Philip Selznick, by saying that "strategies only take on value as committed people infuse them with energy."[7] The danger is that the formal planning process will generate an analytically sound strategy without soul. Thus, the emotional commitment needed to implement a strategy successfully would be missing.

Plans That Are Too Rigid and Detailed

A strategic plan with the blessings of top management can become a straitjacket to those implementing it, thereby inhibiting reactions by stimulating the "It's not in the plan" response to proposals for change. Jack Welch, the CEO at GE, noted that, "Once written, the strategic document can take on a life of its own, and it may not lend itself to flexibility. . . . An organization can begin to focus on form rather than substance."[8] William Bricker, CEO of Diamond Shamrock, has a similar concern: "Why has our vision been narrowed? To my mind there is one central reason our strategies have become too rigid. . . . A detailed strategy is like a road map . . . telling us every turn we must take to get to our goal. . . . The entrepreneur, on the other hand, views strategic planning not as a road map but as a compass . . . and is always looking for the new road."[9]

The planning process should help a business sense and adapt to change rather than inhibit it, in part by supporting the stimulation of strategic thinking and decisions outside of an annual planning cycle. Among the helpful devices are

- **An ongoing analysis of information-need areas.** The identification of strategic questions and associated information-need areas should lead to information gathering and analyses that will detect emerging threats and opportunities and stimulate a review of strategy.
- **Including flexibility in strategic decisions, especially those that involve substantial commitments or affect assets and skills.**
- **The use of contingency plans.** A contingency plan is an alternative strategy or set of actions that will be triggered by a particular event, such as a strike, the loss of a key raw material source, the loss of a major customer, or a technological shift.

Lack of Commitment to the Final Plan

The other extreme is the familiar story of a set of plans with gold-embossed covers lying on the shelf, unused. The plans may be too vague, with little relevance to actual operations, or, more likely, they may not be influential because they have not been integrated into the management system. Top management may not have been given objectives or interim decision points to monitor. The link to the operating plan may not be clear and effective. The operating plan and its associated short-term success measures may dominate the managerial system. This lack of commitment often reflects an overreliance on a planning staff to generate strategies and lack of time spent by top management on the process.

MODIFYING A PLANNING SYSTEM—A CASE STUDY

The Dutch multinational firm, SHV, provides an instructive example of a firm that modified its planning system when it was deemed to be ineffective for formulating strategy.[10] SHV is a $5-billion company, consisting of about 100 operating businesses organized into 14 industry-oriented groups covering a wide range of activities from shipping to retailing in 20 countries. Its planning system had deteriorated into rather sterile and repetitive annual rituals that rarely resulted in creative alternative strategies. Among the problems were excessive reporting requirements, undue emphasis on operating plans, and ineffective use of the time of both top management and the planning staff. In an effort to rejuvenate the planning activity, the firm has made the following changes in its system.

Streamlining Reports

Over the years, the quantity of information required by the system, especially financial data, had grown enormously. The need for much of this data was not obvious to those preparing it. New reporting requirements call for a small number of key financial measures to be supported by insightful analyses and explanations. For example, why was a measure below plan? In addition, a small number of nonfinancial parameters, carefully tailored to the individual businesses, are emphasized. These parameters tend to reflect

- "Early warnings" of changes in business performance.
- Progress toward the (not more than four) key, active programs that are supporting the strategy.
- Changes in key trends or events involving customer segments, competitors, or environmental factors that are deemed to affect the basic assumptions underlying each strategy.

The net effect of these changes has been to increase the proportion of nonfinancial data being reported and to tailor the information to the business involved.

Strategy Review Levels

Each SBU had generated a strategic plan that was reviewed by top management. One problem was that each SBU absorbed equal top management time, regardless of its strategic importance. The new system provides for three levels of analysis and review as portrayed by Figure 17.3.

The first, termed a maxi-review, applies to a business clearly in trouble financially and strategically or facing a major opportunity or threat that could transform the character of the business. A maxi-review represents a complete reappraisal of the business strategy and can take four or five months of planning effort. The second, a mini-review, applies to

FIGURE 17.3 Guidelines for Depth of Strategy Review

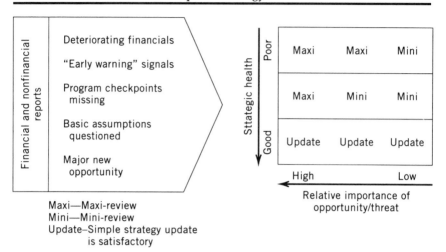

Maxi—Maxi-review
Mini—Mini-review
Update–Simple strategy update
is satisfactory

Relative importance of
opportunity/threat

SOURCE: Adapted from Arie J. Rijvhis and Graham J. Sharman, "New Life for Formal Planning Systems," *Journal of Business Strategy* 2, Spring 1982, p. 103.

businesses meeting their financial targets but facing one or more important opportunities or threats. The mini-review involves one or two months of planning effort, focusing on the validity of the existing strategy or a major decision. The third level is a simple strategy update in which progress is reported but no decisions are made.

Flexible Scheduling

The scheduling of the maxi- and mini-reviews under the new system is flexible rather than tied to a planning cycle. Reviews can start at any time of the year and can take whatever time is needed. In practice, strategy reviews have taken from two months to two years. Thus, the reviews can be pursued when they are timely. Even though they are not tied to a planning cycle, they are part of a planning system, so reviews do tend to be precipitated when they are needed. Furthermore, the SBU managers may choose whatever planning horizon is most appropriate—as few as three years for some SBUs and as many as seven years for others.

Top-Down Strategizing

The prior system of bottom-up planning tended to be constrained by the existing organizational units. In the new system, the executives heading the 14 business groups have primary responsibility for generating strategies, whereas operating-level managers provide input and develop the operating plans. The new system recognizes that major strategy changes can require the restructuring of an organization. Thus, SHV's strategic plans now consider implications for organizational structure and management resources, as well as financial implications.

Role of the Planning Staff

Under the old system, the planning staff had been inundated annually with a vast quantity of material, to the point where they only had time to detect shortcomings and inconsistencies and to organize the paper flow. Under the new system, the planning staff has a more constructive role. It consults with group management prior to the strategy reviews and also prior to the review presentations. Furthermore, line managers are cycled through the planning staff so that greater understanding exists between the staff and line people.

Results

These changes have had two major consequences. First, the enhanced flexibility of the planning process allows the process to be adapted to the needs of the individual businesses. Second, the new system reinforces the responsibility of group management for the development of strategy.

GETTING STARTED

A firm that is not already blessed (or burdened) with a formal planning system should not try to develop one, but instead should focus on developing strategies. The approach is to follow the structured process outlined in Chapter 2. An external analysis should aim to identify strategic threats, opportunities, and questions. The companion self-analysis should identify strategic strengths, weaknesses, problems, and constraints. Consideration of alternative missions and strategies should follow. The evaluation phase can then involve cycling back to strategic questions raised in the prior analyses and perhaps gathering more information.

The methods of generating information and conducting analyses can vary. However, it is usually helpful to bring participants to an off-site retreat for two to five days in order to guarantee uninterrupted time. The group, perhaps aided by prior research, can systematically review the elements of the external analysis, self-analysis, and strategy development. The Figure 17.1 agenda provides a series of questions that can help structure discussion. The use of a focused discussion at a retreat ensures that the strategy-development process at least gets started. It also provides a setting for developing objectives and policies, exchanging information, and testing strategic assumptions and alternatives.

SUMMARY

The planning process can be structured by four phases: an external self-analysis workshop, a strategy-development workshop, a strategy presentation, and presentation of the annual plan. The role of the planner includes being a strategic programmer, a strategy finder, an analyst, and a catalyst.

A formal planning system, which can be either top-down or bottom-up, forces attention on the process and provides mechanisms to handle the associated complexity. Among the pitfalls of a formal system are

- The spreadsheet orientation of projecting accounting measures.
- The dominance of short-run financial objectives.
- Plans that are too rigid and detailed.
- A lack of commitment to the final plan.

One effort to improve a formal planning process streamlined the reports, created levels of strategy reviews, provided flexibility in terms of scheduling, and moved to a more top-down planning system. When a strategy review is initiated for the first time, the emphasis should be on strategy formulation guided by external analysis and self-analysis rather than on the development of a planning system.

FOOTNOTES

[1] Deepak K. Sinha, "The Contribution of Formal Planning to Decisions," *Strategic Management Journal*, October 1990, pp. 479–492.

[2] Thomas C. Powell, "Strategic Planning as Competitive Advantage," *Strategic Management Journal* 13, 1992, pp. 551–558; J. Scott Armstrong, "The Value of Formal Planning for Strategic Decisions: Reply," *Strategic Management Journal* 7, 1986, pp. 183–185.

[3] Henry Mintzberg, "The Fall and Rise of Strategic Planning," *Harvard Business Review*, January–February 1994, pp. 107–114.

[4] Mintzberg, 1994, op. cit.; Daniel H. Gray, "Uses and Misuses of Strategic Planning," *Harvard Business Review*, January–February 1986, pp. 89–97; Benjamin B. Tregoe and Peter M. Tobia, "Strategy Versus Planning: Bridging the Gap, *The Journal of Business Strategy*, November/December, 1991, pp. 14–19.

[5] Robert H. Hayes, "Strategic Planning—Forward in Reverse?" *Harvard Business Review*, November–December 1985, pp. 111–119.

[6] Mintzberg, op. cit. p. 109.

[7] Mintzberg, op. cit., p. 109; Mintzberg cites Philip Selznick, *Leadership in Administration: A Sociological Interpretation*, New York: Harper & Row, 1957.

[8] Jack Welch, "Managing Change," keynote address, dedication convocation, Fuqua School of Business, Duke University, April 21, 1983.

[9] William Bricker, "Entrepreneurs Needed," *Oil and Gas Digest*, November 15, 1982. Arie J. Rijvnis and Graharn J. Sharman, "New Life for Formal Planning Systems," *Journal of Business Strategy* 2, Spring 1982, p. 103.

[10] Arie J. Rijvnis and Graham J. Sharman, "New Life for Formal Planning Systems," *Journal of Business Strategy* 2, Spring 1982, p. 103.

APPENDIX: PLANNING FORMS

A set of standard forms can be helpful in presenting strategy recommendations and supporting analyses. They can encourage the useful consistency of the presentation over time and across businesses within an organization. They can also provide a checklist of areas to consider in strategy development and make communication easier. The following sample forms are intended to provide a point of departure in designing forms for a specific context. The external analysis in the example is drawn from the pet food industry.[1] The forms are for illustration purposes only.

Planning forms need to be adapted to the context involved: the industry, the firm, and the planning context. They may well be different and shorter or longer given a particular context. Forms for use with other product types, an industrial product for example, could be modified to include information such as current and potential applications or key existing or potential customers.

The Pet Food Industry

Section 1. Customer Analysis

A. Segments

Segments	Market	Comments
Dog—dry	1.8B	Largest segment, no preservatives
Dog—wet	1.3B	Made from animal by-products, dairy products, etc.
Cat—dry	1.1B	No preservatives, low moisture content
Cat—wet	1.6B	Made from animal by-products, dairy products, etc.
Treats	.8B	Nabisco dominates with Milk-Bone
Pet Specialty	.1B	Large players—Science Diet and Iams, uses vets and pet stores, about 70% dog food, mostly dry, high growth (over 15%)

B. Customer Motivations

Segment	Motivations
Dog—dry	Nutrition, not messy, not smelly, healthy, easy to serve
Dog—canned	Quality, full line of products, for finicky dogs
Cat—dry	Nutrition, health, easy-to-serve, complement to meal, teeth cleaning

Segment	Motivations
Cat—canned	Quality, full line of products, cat will like, convenient sizes, easy to serve
Treats	Complement to meal, reward, animal likes it
Pet Specialty	Health concern, scientific nutrition, superior ingredients

C. Unmet Needs

Healthy food for pets distributed through supermarkets
Information on pets
Further subneeds of segments, like vegetarian cat food

Section 2. Competitor Analysis

A. Competitor Identification

Most directly competitive: Ralston Purina, Nestlé, Heinz, Mars, Doane, and Quaker Oats
Less directly competitive: Hill's Pet Products and the Iams Corporation
Substitute products: Human food, meat, fish and biscuits

B. Strategic Groups

Strategic Group	Major Competitors	Share (1990)
(1) Large, diversified, branded consumer and food products companies.	Ralston Purina	27%
	Nestlé USA/Friskies Petcare	11%
	Mars/Kal-Kan	11%
	H.J. Heinz	9%
	Quaker Oats	12%
	Grand Met PLC/Alpo	7%
		77%
(2) Small, highly focused, branded specialty niche pet-food producers	Colgate-Palmolive/Hill's Petfood	10%
	Iams Company	3%
		14%
(3) Private-label pet foods	Doane Products	6%

Strategic Group	Characteristics/ Strategies	Strengths	Weaknesses
(1) Large, diversified, branded consumer and food products companies	• Large portfolio of products. • Heavy use of advertising. • Recent push toward premium products by means of line extensions. Premium/niche products • Sell to multiple channels. • Emphasis on cost reduction.	• Production scale economies. • Huge presence in supermarkets, where 70% of industry volume is sold. • Deep financial resources.	• High fixed cost commitment to capacity, increases competitive pressure on all players to defend share through promotions, etc. • Consumers don't believe that supermarket brands can meet both taste and nutriton needs. • Supermarket channel is losing share to other channels.
(2) Small, highly focused, branded specialty niche pet-food producers	• Narrowly focused, premium priced product lines. • Sell primarily through nonsupermarket channels, such as in vet offices, pet breeders, or specialty stores.	• Product line focus on health, natural ingredients, and nutrition, resulting in very strong consumer demand. High margin business. • "First-in" advantage to high-end specialty segment, resulting in a perceptual edge that supermarket brands find difficult to overcome. • Sell through alternate channels, which are growing faster and are less competitive and offer limited access to other brands, a barrier to entry.	• Higher production costs. • Less financial resources than large brands, with exception of Hill's, which is owned by Colgate. • All major national competitors are going after the fast-growing specialty channels.

Strategic Group	Characteristics/ Strategies	Strengths	Weaknesses
(3) Private-label pet foods	• Sell through multiple supermarkets under house brand designation.	• Very high production, resulting in low unit costs. • Strong profit motive for stores to carry private-label product line.	• No brand differentiation. • Low margin business.

C. Major Competitors

Competitor	Characteristics/ Strategies	Strengths	Weaknesses
Ralston Purina	• Overall market leader, very broad product line. • Increasing emphasis on niche product lines and upgrade of products to premium status. • Competes in all segments, including vets (Clinical Nutrition Mgt. Brand), specialty stores, and private labels. • Proliferation of new products. • Massive promotional spending to protect share. • High commitment: Pet foods = 40% of profits.	• Economies of scale, low costs. • Efficient distribution system, particularly in larger package sizes. • Deep financial resources.	• Weaker in small-size package distribution than other large competitors. • Not well positioned to participate in the pet specialty segment.

Competitor	Characteristics/ Strategies	Strengths	Weaknesses
Nestlé	• Focus on cat segments only. • Grow share strategy, through aggressive promotion, consistent branding. • Increasing emphasis on niche product lines and upgrade of products to premium status.	• Strong distribution capacity in small package sizes. • Deep financial resources. • Company takes long term view on brand building efforts. High level of commitment to brands.	• Weak in nonsupermarket channels. • No private-label business.
H.J. Heinz	• Emphasis on canned cat and dog treats, but competes in all segments of cat market. • Targeting specialty and vet channels, while ugrading and niche marketing its supermarket lines. • Bought access to vet channel through acquisition of Vet Centers of America (VCA). • Growth by acquisition strategy.	• Economies of scale, low costs. • Efficient distribution system, particularly in larger package sizes. • Deep financial resources.	• Relatively weak in marketing • Are milking strong brands like "9-Lives."
Mars	• Internationally dominant, under same brand names as in the United States. • Focus on canned dog and cat. • Upgrading supermarket brands for premium appeal.	• Economies of scale, low costs. • Deep financial resources. • Private firm gives them freedom from short-term pressures.	• Gave up significant brand equity when Kal-Kan lines were renamed Whiska's in 1988. Slipping share in both dry and wet categories.
Doane Products	• Largest private-label producer in the United States	• Economies of scale, low costs.	• Low margin business.

Competitor	Characteristics/ Strategies	Strengths	Weaknesses
Hill's Petfood	• Leader in specialty and vet markets. • "Entry barriers" in effect in vet business for Science Diet brand.	• Leading recipient of veterinary recommendation. • Best niche market product positioning in the industry.	• No presence in supermarkets, where 70% of industry volume is sold.
Iams	• Also a specialty market leader, with emphasis on specialty store sales and referrals from pet breeders. • In growth mode, while seeking to defend position against incursion by other large national competitors.	• Strong position in growing channels. • Highly profitable.	• No presence in supermarkets, where 70% of industry volume is sold. • Limited financial resources compared with other industry competitors, remains privately held.
Alpo	• Focus on canned dog, good presence in canned cat. • Willing to spend heavily to promote new product entry, as did with Garfield-sponsored cat entry. • Seeking aggressive growth, with new line extensions and increasing emphasis on top-end of the market.	• Deep financial resources.	• Little presence outside supermarkets. • Slow to react to market shifts. • Image as cheap product
Quaker Oats	• Growth through acquisition. • Upgrading supermarket brands for premium appeal. • Leader in moist dog segment. • Candidate to sell out.	• Deep financial resources.	• Poor profitability. • Moist segment is weak. • Anderson-Clayton merger was disastrous for pet food division's profitability. • Little cat food.

D. Competitor Strength Grid

Pet Food Competitors in the U.S. Market

Assets and Skills	Ralston Purina	Carnation (Nestlé)	Quaker	Grand Met	Mars	Heinz	Hills	Iams	Doane
Name recognition									
Breadth of product line									
Breadth of channel coverage									
Specialty/veterinarian coverage									
Financial resources									
Cost structure									
Geographic coverage U.S.									
International									

Strong
Above average
Average
Less than average
Weak

Section 3. Market Analysis

A. Market Identification: The Pet Food Market: Dog and Cat in the United States

B. Actual and Potential Market Size and Growth

	1991	1992	Projected 1993
US domestic	*$6.4B*	*$6.4B*	*$6.53B*

Market Growth (Forecast/annually)

- Supermarket—declining.
- Specialty store—growing at 18%.

Factors Affecting Sales Levels

- Number of U.S. pets.

Segments with High Unrealized Potential

- As U.S. households spend less for pet food on average ($60/year) than the rest of the world ($90), there may be potential for growth.

C. Market Profitability Analysis

Barriers to Entry

- Brand awareness, budget for marketing programs, access to distribution channels.
- For pet specialty segment—loyalty to Iams and Pet (Scientific Diet).

Potential Entrants

- Other marketing giants like Unilever might enter this industry if they feel that this industry is attractive. However, the probability of new entrants is quite low, because pet food industry is already very competitive with lots of incumbents, and barriers to entry are moderately high.

Threats of Substitutes

- Human food leftovers.
- Food cooked especially for pets.

Bargaining Power of Suppliers

• Very weak. Raw material is vegetable, fish, meat, etc. These suppliers' industries are very competitive and cannot exercise much power over pet food industry.

Bargaining Power of Customers

• Grocery stores, warehouse clubs have strong bargaining power over pet food suppliers.
• Specialty stores, veterinarians might have moderate bargaining power.
• Pet superstores will have more and more power.

D. Cost Structure

• Diversified firms have lower cost because of economies in advertising and promotion.
• Specialized firms have higher cost.

E. Distribution System

Major Channels

• Supermarkets are dominant in terms of quantity they deal with (70%).
• Mass merchandisers handle about 9.6% of market.
• Pet foods are effective traffic builders in supermarkets and mass merchandisers.
• Farm supply stores are located in suburbs and local areas.
• Pet stores handle most premium brands and some national brands.
• Veterinarians handle only super-premium brands.

Observations/Major Trends

• Vets' sales have grown very rapidly, and their sales have very high margins both for producers and themselves.
• Specialty stores' sales have also increased very rapidly. Those two channels have significant implications.
• Above two channels have captured the customers' needs to take care of pets more and feed them healthier foods.
• Warehouses have gained footholds in lower end of market.
• Pet superstores had around 15% of sales and some are projected to have 50% within the next decade.

F. Market Trends and Developments

- Premium and super-premium brands have grown, and most producers are introducing new products in this area.
- Large manufacturers are introducing new products continuously.

G. Key Market Success Factors

Present

- Access to major channels.
- Gain market share in premium brands.
- Brand recognition.
- Introduction of new products.
- Marketing program.
- Cost reduction.
- Awareness or recommendation by specialists.
- Sounds tasty.
- Cleanness.
- Packaging.
- Understand need segmentation.

Future

- Packaging.
- Capture the trends of customers.
- Follow the trends of distributors.

Section 4. Environmental Analysis

A. Trends and Potential Events

Source	Description	Strategic Implication	Time Frame	Importance
Technological	*Very few issues.*	*Very limited.*		*Low*
Regulatory	*Minimal standards of content.*	*Very limited.*		*Low*

Source	Description	Strategic Implication	Time Frame	Importance
Economic	*Insensitive to economic changes.*	*Very limited.*		*Low*
Cultural	*Think of pets as members of families.*	*Growth of super-premium brands.*	*Since the middle of 1980s.*	*High*
	Demand for new healthy products.	*Introduction of healthy products.*		
	Users' needs have diversified	*Multiple specialized segments.*		
Demographic	*Household formation is slowing.*	*May have a negative impact on pet ownership.*	*Since 1980s.*	*Med-High*
	The numbers of cats are increasing more than dogs.			
	The baby boomer is aging.			
Threats	*Growth in the pet food industry depends on the popularity of pets.*	*Decline in pet ownership will have a negative impact.*	*Since 1980s.*	*Med-High*
Opportunities	*Growing market for premium brands.*	*There is still room for growth in specialized segments.*	*Since the middle of 1980s.*	*High*
	Expanding market for private labels.			
	Knowledge-intensive advertising.			

B. Scenario Analysis

Two most likely are

1. Little growth in specialty store, and increase in super-premium segments.
2. High growth in both specialty store and super-premium segment.

C. Key Strategic Questions

- Will growth in demand for super-premium specialty products continue?
- Will specialty stores share continue to grow at the expense of supermarkets?

Section 5. Self-Analysis

A. Peformance Analysis

Objective Area	Objective	Status and Comment
1. Sales		
2. Profits		
3. Quality/service		
4. Cost		
5. New products		
6. Customer satisfaction		
7. People		
8. Other		

B. Summary of Past Strategy

C. Strategic Problems

Problem	Possible Action

D. Characteristics of Internal Organization

Component[a]	Description—Fit with Current/Proposed Strategy

[a] Structure, systems, culture, and people.

E. Portfolio Analysis

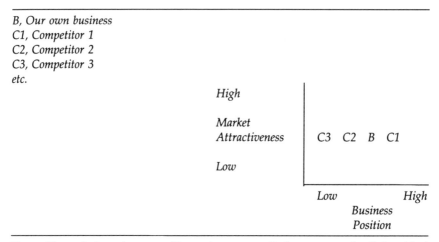

B, Our own business
C1, Competitor 1
C2, Competitor 2
C3, Competitor 3
etc.

NOTE: The analysis can be repeated by market segment. Each segment can be distinguished by dots, circles, squares, triangles, etc.

F. Analysis of Strengths and Weaknesses

| Reference Strategic Group | Skills/Skill Deficiencies, Assets/Liabilities, Strengths/Weaknesses with Respect to Strategic Groups |

G. Financial Projections Based on Existing Strategy

	Past	Present	Projected
Operating Statement			
Market share			
Sales			
Cost of goods sold			
Gross margin			
R&D			
Selling/advertising			
Product G&A			
Div. & corp. G&A			
Operating profit			
Balance Sheet			
Cash/AR/inventory			
AP			
Net current assets			
Fixed assets at cost			
Accumulated depreciation			
Net fixed assets			
Total assets—book value			
Estimated market value of assets			
ROA (base—book value)			
ROA (base—market value)			
Uses of Funds			
Net current assets			
Fixed asset			
Operating profit			
Depreciation			
Other			
Resources Required			
_____			
_____			
_____			
_____			

NOTE: Resources required could be workers with particular skills or backgrounds, or certain physical facilities. A negative use of funds (i.e., profit) is a source of funds. Projected numbers could be for several relevant years (i.e., 19___, 19___, 19___, and 19___).

Section 6. Summary of Proposed Strategy

A. Statement of Mission/Vision

B. Strategy Description

- Investment Objective
  Withdraw
  Milk
  Maintain
  Grow in market share
  Market expansion
  Product expansion
  Vertical integration

- Strategy Thrusts
  Differentiation
  Low cost
  Focus
  Synergy
  Preemptive move

C. Assets and Skills Providing SCAs

D. Key Strategy Initiatives

E. Financial Projections Based on Proposed Strategy

	Past	Present	Projected

Operating Statement
 Market share
 Sales
 Cost of goods sold
 Gross margin
 R&D
 Selling/advertising
 Product G&A
 Div. & corp. G&A
 Operating profit
Balance Sheet
 Cash/AR/inventory
 AP
 Net current assets
 Fixed assets at cost
 Accumulated depreciation
 Net fixed assets
 Total assets—book value
 Estimated market value of assets
 ROA (base–book value)
 ROA (base–market value)
Uses of Funds
 Net current assets
 Fixed assets
 Operating profit
 Depreciation
 Other
Resources Required

_____

_____

_____

_____

FOOTNOTE

[1] This example is drawn, in part, from a research paper by John Foraker, Daisuke Kawanami, Dan Norton, Hiroshi Ohkubo, and Vincent Weller, 1993

INDEX